PRECAUTIONARY RIGHTS AND DUTIES OF STATES

NOVA ET VETERA IURIS GENTIUM

PUBLICATIONS OF THE INSTITUTE OF PUBLIC INTERNATIONAL LAW OF THE UNIVERSITY OF UTRECHT

SERIES A: MODERN INTERNATIONAL LAW
NUMBER 25

PRECAUTIONARY RIGHTS AND DUTIES OF STATES

by
Arie Trouwborst

MARTINUS NIJHOFF PUBLISHERS
LEIDEN / BOSTON

A C.I.P. record for this book is available from the Library of Congress.

Printed on acid-free paper.

ISSN 1871-6725
ISBN 90 04 15212 1

Koninklijke Brill NV incorporates the imprints Brill Academic Publishers, Martinus Nijhoff Publishers and VSP.
http://www.brill.nl

Printed and bound in The Netherlands.

The outstanding scientific discovery of the twentieth century is not television, or radio, but rather the complexity of the land organism. Only those who know the most about it can appreciate how little is known about it. The last word in ignorance is the man who says of an animal or plant: 'What good is it?' If the land mechanism as a whole is good, then every part is good, whether we understand it or not. If the biota, in the course of aeons, has built something we like but do not understand, then who but a fool would discard seemingly useless parts? To keep every cog and wheel is the first precaution of intelligent tinkering.

– Aldo Leopold, "The Round River" (1953)

The precautionary principle may well be the most innovative, pervasive, and significant new concept in environmental policy over the past quarter century. It may also be the most reckless, arbitrary, and ill-advised.

– Gary Marchant & Kenneth Mossman, "Arbitrary and Capricious" (2005)

ACKNOWLEDGEMENTS

I am indebted to Fred Soons of Utrecht University and René Lefeber of the Dutch Ministry of Foreign Affairs for their willingness to supervise my dissertation and for their thorough and constructive commentary on the manuscript; to the members of the reading committee, Chris Backes of Utrecht University, Ellen Hey of Erasmus University Rotterdam and André Nollkaemper of the University of Amsterdam, for their helpful comments on the manuscript; to my colleagues at the Utrecht University Department of Public International Law and the Netherlands Institute for the Law of the Sea, for discussing aspects of this study with me and for being stimulating co-workers, particular reference being due in this regard to Kees Roelofsen who never tired of debating my views on a precautionary approach to alien species; to Marcel Vernooij and many others at the Dutch Ministry of Agriculture, Nature and Food Quality for sharing their experiences in implementing the precautionary principle with me; to Annebeth Rosenboom, Nienke van Schaverbeke and Joeri Coppejans of Martinus Nijhoff Publishers for their kind cooperation in the publication of this book; to Titia Kloos of the Wiarda Institute for her outstanding help in getting the manuscript ready for printing; to my cousin Robert Trouwborst – who has always tried to be one tiny step ahead of me and, accordingly, made a big deal of outpacing me to the Ph.D. title by a few months – for his patience in introducing me to the mechanism of bacterial manganese oxidation and its impact on the suboxic zone in the Black Sea and to plenty other intricate issues of biogeochemistry; to Wilmer Kloosterziel for commenting on the manuscript; to my mother, father, brothers and 'sisters' for their kind support and comments; to the in-laws in Spain, living examples of the good life; to my precious wife Elvira, who has listened to me explain the topic of my research to others an unpleasant number of times, for her frank and critical comments on the manuscript, her assistance with the indexes, helping me draw graphics on a computer, and endless other things; to Mark, our little future generation; and to all others who have made my work and free time into the rewarding combination that it is and thus contributed, directly or indirectly, to the pages that follow below. I dedicate this book to the memory of my friend and outdoor survival skills instructor Aart de Jong, who taught me the meaning of precaution. *Je moet niet nadenken. Je moet voordenken.*

Utrecht, April 2006

OUTLINE OF CONTENTS

PART ONE

INTRODUCTION

PART TWO

DEFINITION

PART THREE

IMPLEMENTATION

PART FOUR

CONCLUSIONS

TABLE OF CONTENTS

PART THREE

IMPLEMENTATION

PART FOUR

CONCLUSIONS

TABLE OF FIGURES

ABBREVIATIONS

AEPS	Arctic Environmental Protection Strategy
ASEAN	Association of South East Asian Nations
BAT	Best available technology
BEP	Best environmental practice
BSEP	*Baltic Sea Environment Proceedings*
CARICOM	Caribbean Commonwealth
CCAMLR	Convention on the Conservation of Antarctic Marine Living Resources
CE	Council of Europe
CEP	Caribbean Environment Programme
CEPA	Canadian Environmental Protection Act
CFCs	Chlorofluorocarbons
CIS	Commonwealth of Independent States
CISDL	Centre for International Sustainable Development Law
CITES	Convention on International Trade in Endangered Species of Wild Fauna and Flora
CO2	Carbon dioxide
COP	Conference of the Parties
CRAMRA	Convention on the Regulation of Antarctic Mineral Resource Activities
CSD	Commission on Sustainable Development
DDT	Dichlorodiphenyl trichloroethane
EC	European Community
ECJ	European Union Court of Justice
ECOSOC	Economic and Social Council of the United Nations
ECOSOC Doc.	*Economic and Social Council Documents*
EEA	European Economic Area
EEZ	Exclusive Economic Zone
EFTA	European Free Trade Association
EIA	Environmental impact assessment
EP	European Parliament
EPA	Environmental Protection Agency
EPL	*Environmental Policy and Law*
ESD	Ecologically Sustainable Development
ETS	*European Treaty Series*
EU	European Union
FAO	Food and Agriculture Organization of the United Nations
FIFRA	Federal Insecticide, Fungicide and Rodenticide Act
FRDO	Federale Raad voor Duurzame Ontwikkeling (Federal Council for Sustainable Development)
FRG	Federal Republic of Germany
GATT/WTO	General Agreement on Tariffs and Trade/World Trade Organization
GDP	Gross Domestic Product
GLOBE	Global Legislators Organization for a Balanced Environment
GMO	Genetically modified organism
HCFCs	Hydrochlorofluorocarbons
HELCOM	Baltic Marine Environment Protection Commission under (Helsinki) Convention on the Protection of the Marine Environment of the Baltic Sea Area

HR Rep.	*House of Representatives Reports*
IAEA	International Atomic Energy Agency
IATTC	Inter-American Tropical Tuna Commission
IBRD	International Bank for Reconstruction and Development
ICC	International Chamber of Commerce
ICJ	International Court of Justice
ICJ Rep.	*International Court of Justice Reports*
IDI	Institut de Droit International
IFF	Intergovernmental Forum on Forests
IGAE	Intergovernmental Agreement on the Environment
ILA	International Law Association
ILC	International Law Commission
ILM	*International Legal Materials*
ILO	International Labour Organization
ILR	*International Law Reports*
IMO	International Maritime Organization
IPF	Intergovernmental Panel on Forests
IPCC	Intergovernmental Panel on Climate Change
IPPC	Integrated Pollution Prevention and Control
IUSCT Rep.	*Iran-United States Claims Tribunal Reports*
ITLOS	International Tribunal on the Law of the Sea
IUCN	International Union for the Conservation of Nature
IWC	International Whaling Commission
LDC	London Dumping Convention
LNTS	*League of Nations Treaty Series*
LOS Convention	United Nations Convention on the Law of the Sea
MAP	Mediterranean Action Plan
MP	Member of Parliament
NAFO	Northwest Atlantic Fisheries Organization
NAFTA	North American Free Trade Agreement
NASA	National Aeronautics and Space Administration
NEAFC	North East Atlantic Fisheries Commission
NGO	Non-governmental organization
NMFS	National Marine Fisheries Service
NOOA	National Oceanic and Atmospheric Administration
NOx	Nitrogen oxides
NSW	New South Wales
OAS	Organization of American States
OAU	Organization of African Unity
OECD	Organization for Economic Cooperation and Development
OECS	Organization of Eastern Caribbean States
OJ	*Official Journal of the European Community*
OSCOM	Commission under (Oslo) Convention for the Prevention of Marine Pollution by Dumping from Ships and Aircraft
OSHA	Occupational Safety and Health Administration
OSPAR	Convention for the Protection of the Marine Environment of the North-East Atlantic
PARCOM	Commission under (Paris) Convention for the Prevention of Marine Pollution from Land-Based Sources
PCBs	Polychlorinated biphenyls
PCIJ	Permanent Court of International Justice

PCIJ Rep.	*Permanent Court of International Justice Reports*
PJP	Prior Justification Procedure
POPs	Persistent organic pollutants
RPM	Revised Management Procedure
SO2	Sulphur dioxide
SPA	Specially Protected Areas
TAC	Total allowable catch
TBT	Tributyltin
UK	United Kingdom
UN	United Nations
UNCED	United Nations Conference on Environment and Development
UNCHE	United Nations Conference on the Human Environment
UN Doc.	*United Nations Documents*
UNDP	United Nations Development Programme
UN-ECE	United Nations Economic Commission for Europe
UNEP	United Nations Environment Programme
UN-ESCAP	United Nations Economic and Social Commission for Asia and the Pacific
UNESCO	United Nations Educational, Scientific and Cultural Organisation
UNGA	United Nations General Assembly
UNGAOR	*United Nations General Assembly Official Records*
UNSC	United Nations Security Council
UNTS	*United Nations Treaty Series*
US(A)	United States of America
VOCs	Volatile organic compounds
WAF	Waste Assessment Framework
WCED	World Commission on Environment and Development
WCS	World Conservation Strategy
WHO	World Health Organization
WMO	World Meteorological Organization
WSSD	World Summit on Sustainable Development
WTO	World Trade Organization
WTO Doc.	*World Trade Organization Documents*
WWF	World Wildlife Fund
YIEL	*Yearbook of International Environmental Law*
YILC	*Yearbook of the International Law Commission*

PART ONE

INTRODUCTION

To know yet to think that one does not know is best;
Not to know yet to think that one knows leads to difficulty.
– Lao-Tzu (± 500 B.C.)

1. THE ORACLE OF DELPHI AND THE PRECAUTIONARY PRINCIPLE

1.1. Setting the Stage

Man is one of the apparently very few beings that are uncomfortable with uncertainty.[1] Most of his fellow creatures live from moment to moment, but *homo sapiens* is caught up in a continuous attempt to get a grip on the future, always anticipating the day of tomorrow. Others have submitted that human aversion of risk and uncertainty instead expresses a universal "natural fear".[2] Whether discomfort with the unpredictability of life is a relatively unique feature of mankind or not, throughout its existence humanity has had to live with the secrets of nature one way or another.[3] That challenge, the size and significance of which have not necessarily diminished in modern times – uncertainty can also arise where abundant knowledge is available[4] – is at the core of current discussions on risk, uncertainty and the precautionary principle.[5] Opinions tend to differ, however, on how the challenge is best met.

Societies must continually make decisions amidst a multitude of more or less grave and more or less likely threats to nature and the environment, the assessment of which is hampered more often than not by the labyrinthine complexity of the earth's ecosystems. The Ariadne's thread provided by international law to guide states through this maze of uncertain environmental hazards is the precautionary principle. That principle, according to which uncertainty is essentially not a valid excuse for failing to prevent environmental harm, is the subject of this study, the particular focus of which will be on the definition and implementation of the precautionary principle under general or customary international law. Before dwelling further on the research question and the purpose of the study lying ahead, it is thought useful to set the stage by sketching some of the wider context of the principle.

---

[1] Tennekes, 2001, p. 71.
[2] Philippopoulos-Mihalopoulos, 1999, p. 177 (footnote omitted).
[3] Also Tennekes, 2001, p. 45.
[4] See *infra* paragraph 4.1; Bouma *et al.*, 2002, p. 9.
[5] Martin, 1997, p. 278.

In ancient days, long before the precautionary principle came into being, when authorities needed to make difficult decisions in the face of an uncertain future it was not unusual for them, so the story goes, to consult an oracle. The most renowned of these was for a time the Delphic temple of the god Apollo, which played a crucial role in the tale of the labyrinth of Minos and the thread of Ariadne hinted at above.[6] All sorts of questions were taken to Delphi. The oracular responses were delivered by the Pythia, priestess of the temple, who pronounced them while seated on a three-legged chair. This tripod of Apollo, symbol of prophetic powers, stood over a fissure in the slope of Mount Parnassos from which hallucinatory vapours arose. The rather unintelligible utterances of the Pythia were interpreted by Apollo's priests, who transformed them into a more or less coherent answer. The resultant prognostications did tend to be multi-interpretable, however. The most famous example of this oracular ambiguity is no doubt the case of Croesus, the mighty ruler of Lydia, who was foretold that if he were to wage war on Persia he would destroy a great empire. Acting on this prediction, Croesus confidently went to war and a great empire was indeed destroyed, although it was not Persia...

Consulting the oracle of Delphi and applying the precautionary principle do not quite represent the same method of dealing with uncertain threats – although some of the principle's critics might have it otherwise. Nevertheless, all sorts of interesting comparisons can be drawn between the old Greek myths surrounding Delphi and the precautionary principle and the international law of the environment of which it is a part. Reportedly, before being passed on to Apollo the sanctuary at Delphi had been devoted consecutively to the Titanic deities Gaia, the earth goddess, and her daughter Themis, goddess of law and justice. Uniting several features of his predecessors and others besides, the solar god Apollo himself was a complex deity with seemingly contradictory characteristics and rather comprehensive competences. He was the god of morality, law and order; the patron of art and science. He held power over life by wielding the forces of nature, both for good and for bad. Above all else, he represented light and reason, wisdom and foresight. Three thousand years after the establishment of Apollo's reign in Delphi, earth, nature, science, law and foresight form the

---

[6] Although consideration of Greek mythology is hardly essential for attaining an understanding of the subject-matter at hand, some of the ancient myths are weaved through the legal analysis below to serve as a mental aid for illustrating or contrasting, as the case may be, the workings of the precautionary principle under international law, as well as simply to lighten up the content of this study. Klinke & Renn, 1999, have similarly drawn examples from Greek mythology to illustrate their study of risk classification and management. At p. 5 they opine that "[f]ar from providing recipes for managing technologies and risks, [myths] can help us to orient ourselves in the tension between courage and caution and to create powerful images that provide sources for understanding and handling risks in modern societies."

basic ingredients of the precautionary principle. Yet, just as the Delphic tripod was stolen and hotly contested by Heracles, who wished to employ it for his own private agenda, so may the precautionary principle, critics warn, be taken hostage by governments or non-governmental organizations to promote their particular interests, as a result of the principle's allegedly undefined and ambiguous nature.

The latter analogy calls for consideration of some of the pros and cons of the principle that have been emphasized by commentators. Obviously, advocates of the precautionary principle point to its potential to prevent human activities from inflicting undesirable environmental impacts. The principle is supposed to ensure that erring, which after all is human, is done on the side of caution and not to the detriment of the environment. As the Greek goddess of prudence, Metis, mothered the goddess of wisdom, Apollo's half-sister Athena, so the vulnerability of nature and the unpredictability of environmental effects are judged to warrant a prudent approach. Thus, when "wisdom and science combine to warn"[7] that actions may lead to environmental harm but uncertainty surrounds the threat in question, governments should take preventive action anyway, instead of letting a lack of conclusive proof paralyze them as if they were facing a Medusa. To illustrate the emphatic belief of some in the wholesomeness of this approach it suffices to quote the dedication at the outset of one book on the precautionary principle: "to all those beings that suffer from environmental damage, may the Precautionary Principle bring a better world."[8]

Conversely, opponents of the principle stress the disadvantages of excessive caution.[9] Applied consistently, so their argument goes, the precautionary principle would require prior evidence of environmental harmlessness before allowing human activities to proceed. In doing so, the principle is said to display a "profound ambiguity"[10] or, in somewhat friendlier terms, a "charming schizophrenia"[11] in respect of scientific knowledge. On the one hand, the scientific *uncertainty* that is so abundant in environmental affairs is one of the reasons for the principle's existence. On the other hand, permission of potentially harmful activities is made contingent on scientific *certainty* regarding their effects. As the complete safety of anything is impossible to guarantee up front the precautionary principle

[7] Boehmer-Christiansen, 1994, p. 39.
[8] Raffensperger & Tickner, 1999.
[9] E.g., Morris, 2000(b); Pieterman & Hanekamp, 2002; Marchant & Mossman, 2005; Sunstein, 2005(b).
[10] Pieterman & Hanekamp, *ibid.*, p. 6.
[11] Philippopoulos-Mihalopoulos, 1999, p. 193.

would thus amount to a duty to do the impossible.[12] Moreover, such a risk-averse approach would stifle innovation and lead to economic stagnation.[13] To cite one critic: "If someone had evaluated the risk of fire right after it was invented, they may well have decided to eat their food raw."[14] The same goes for steamships, trains or electric light.[15] The title of a 1990 contribution by Aaron Wildavsky sums it up: "No Risk is the Highest Risk of All."[16] To be brief, critics have drawn attention to a number of serious, even "fatal" flaws of the precautionary principle, which are allegedly not only of a legal kind, but also of a "logical, theoretical, moral, social, political and economic nature."[17] Perhaps the most frequently voiced criticism is that the principle is vague and undefined, and therefore unfit to guide the actions of governments.[18] As a legal principle, so it goes, the precautionary principle leaves all sorts of crucial questions unanswered. A recent study poses some of them:

> For example, is the principle triggered by the magnitude of a risk, the uncertainty associated with that risk, or some combination of both magnitude and uncertainty? How much of each is necessary to trigger the principle? If the principle applies only to 'serious' or 'irreversible' risks, how are such risks defined? If it applies to any risk, how can any product ever be approved? What types of 'precautionary measures' should be taken when a sufficient threat exists? If the precautionary principle requires postponing development of a product until sufficient safety data on that product are available, what type of evidence is required before the product is permitted to move forward? What factors can be considered in determining whether the product should or should not go forward? For example, can the economic benefits of the product be considered?[19]

In view of its many defects, it has been submitted that "it would be best to do away with this principle altogether."[20]

1.2. Purpose and Method

The Research Question

As it is, the precautionary principle is an important general principle of international environmental law. The origins, evolution and status of the

[12] Pieterman & Hanekamp, 2002, pp. v-vi.
[13] *Ibid.*, pp. ix and 2.
[14] Julian Morris, as cited in Appell, 2001.
[15] Blanchfield, 2000; Klinke & Renn, 1999, p. 6.
[16] Wildavsky, 1990; see Klinke & Renn, *ibid.*, p. 46.
[17] Pieterman & Hanekamp, 2002, p. 15; also McKinney & Hill, 2000, *passim*.
[18] See the beginning of *infra* paragraph 2.1.
[19] Marchant & Mossman, 2004, pp. 1-2.
[20] Pieterman & Hanekamp, 2002, p. 16; also Pieterman *et al.*, 2006, *passim*.

principle in public international law have been researched at length.[21] States have expressly endorsed the precautionary principle in (or under) at least 58 legally binding agreements[22] and in many dozens of declarations, resolutions and action programs with a bearing on the environment.[23] In line with developments at the international level, increasing numbers of states are implementing the principle within their domestic jurisdictions.[24] There is, moreover, copious evidence that the precautionary principle, at some point in the past two decades, has attained the status of customary international law.[25] Whichever way, the precautionary principle has apparently not been adopted by states "for the fun of it", as Ireland put it in the *MOX Plant OSPAR Arbitration*,[26] and its significance in international law is unlikely to diminish any time soon.[27] Whether this is cause for joy or concern – that is, whether the precautionary principle could bring a better world or had better be abolished – is not at issue in the present study. Rather than taking sides in this debate the purpose of this study, in one word, is *clarification*.

In the debate on the legal implications of the precautionary principle that is taking place at the international level as well as within many a nation state, varying interpretations give rise to recurrent misunderstandings. Amidst the multitude of subtly different formulations occurring in legal and policy instruments, much of the uncertainty appears to pertain to the parameters of the principle as part of *general* international law. Many questions, as in the above citation,[28] concern the definition and implementation of the principle in this general capacity. The need for answers to these questions is felt by proponents and opponents of the precautionary principle alike, and not in

---

[21] E.g., De Sadeleer, 2002, *passim*; Douma, 2003, *passim*; Marr, 2003, *passim*; Trouwborst, 2002, *passim*.

[22] Trouwborst, 2002, at pp. 63-112 and in Annex A, discussed and listed 53 treaties (all but one multilateral) with explicit precautionary references in either their own terms or in decisions taken within their contexts; to which can be added the 2002 *ASEAN Agreement on Transboundary Haze Pollution* (Article 3(3)), the 2002 *Convention for Cooperation in the Protection and Sustainable Development of the Marine and Coastal Environment of the Northeast Pacific* (2002 *Antigua Convention*, Articles 5(6)(a), 6(2)(e) and 10(1)(b)), the 2003 *Convention for the Strengthening of the Inter-American Tropical Tuna Commission* (2003 *Antigua Convention*, Article IV), the *African Convention on the Conservation of Nature and Natural Resources* as revised in 2003 (Article IV), and the 2004 *International Convention for the Control and Management of Ships' Ballast Water and Sediments* (*Ballast Water Convention*, fourth preambular paragraph).

[23] See Trouwborst, 2002, pp. 112-156 and Annex B, for an overview.

[24] Marr, 2003, *passim*; De Sadeleer, 2002, *passim*; Trouwborst, 2002, pp. 178-244.

[25] See below.

[26] *Verbatim Record* of the sitting on 24 October 2002 in the *Dispute Concerning Access to Information under Article 9 of the OSPAR Convention (Ireland v UK)*, p. 24 (Brady); see http://www.pca-cpa.org.

[27] Bodansky, 2004, p. 381 states it like this: "If international environmental law were to develop Ten Commandments, the precautionary principle would be near the top of the list."

[28] See the citation of Marchant & Mossman at the end of paragraph 1.1.

the least by the government bodies and public agencies whose job it is to apply and implement the principle.[29] The main research question of the present study, therefore, is this: *What are the rights and/or duties of states under the precautionary principle in general international law?*

This is much the same as asking to what degree of precision the principle has crystallized under general, or customary international law. As the customary law status of the precautionary principle is an important premise of this study it merits some contemplation at this point. The principle's legal status was assessed in a previous study by the present author.[30] (Inter)national law and policy instruments, domestic jurisprudence and other relevant statements and actions of states with implicit or explicit bearing on the precautionary principle were evaluated in light of the applicable standards concerning state practice, *opinio juris* and the formation of customary international law; taking account also of pertinent international case law and writers' opinions.[31] This evaluation prompted the conclusion that there is a core content of the precautionary principle on which there is apparent agreement amongst states;[32] which is concrete enough for national authorities and courts to base executive and judicial decisions on;[33] and which has attained the status of customary international law.[34] The trend since the performance of the former study seems, if anything, affirmative of this conclusion.[35]

Support for the precautionary principle is comparable to the support for the basic duty of states not to cause transboundary environmental harm,[36] and so is its legal status as a fully-fledged norm of customary law. The

---

[29] See *infra* paragraph 2.1.

[30] Trouwborst, 2002.

[31] *Ibid.*, pp. 33-286.

[32] *Ibid.*, pp. 51-53; see also *infra* Chapter 2.

[33] Trouwborst, *ibid.*, *passim*.

[34] *Ibid.*, p. 286, and the sources mentioned throughout the study.

[35] As De Sadeleer, 2003, submits at pp. 318-319: "In our view, the prevalence of the principle in recent State practice and in international law suggests that [..] it may indeed have attained this [customary law] status. Our own analysis of the evolution of the precautionary principle in international and EC law and a number of national legal orders provides firm evidence to substantiate that conclusion." Similarly, on the basis of an extensive analysis Van der Eynde, 2004 (see especially pp. 18-19 of the summary in English), concluded that in the examined period, 1990-2002, there is a positive trend in the relative amount of international legal instruments concluded each year which incorporate the precautionary principle (i.e., the share of instruments containing the principle as compared with the total number of environmental instruments concluded is on the increase). In addition, he found a clear positive trend in the 'strength', from an ecocentric point of view, of the principle as formulated in these instruments. Douma, 2002, p. 153, however, found it was "still too early to define the principle as a part of customary international law," although this "might change in the near future."

[36] See *infra* paragraphs 3.2 and 4.2.

differences that do exist, namely the shorter existence of the precautionary principle and the fact that the International Court of Justice (ICJ) has not yet affirmed its customary status, are not defining ones. Given that the criteria for the formation of customary international law have been amply fulfilled, it would seem that state practice which is ostensibly inconsistent with the precautionary principle should be viewed in the context of either persistent objection[37] or non-compliance. As it is, states have held each other accountable for alleged breaches of the customary precautionary principle on more than one occasion, the consequences attached to such non-compliance varying from diplomatic protests[38] to the instigation of judicial proceedings[39] and even Navy action.[40]

Concluding that the precautionary principle embodies a norm of customary international law is one thing. Determining what this *means* is quite another, and this is the challenge faced here. What precisely are the dimensions of the core content just mentioned? To what extent can and does the principle guide the decisions of governments in concrete instances? When is it triggered? What measures qualify for its implementation? What about the burden of proof, this crucial but thorny issue that keeps surfacing in any discussion of the precautionary principle? What about the role of socio-economic factors? These and other queries will have to be addressed in order to obtain an answer to the main research question posed above.

The advantages of obtaining such an answer are not limited to informing discussions in academic forums. It is the natural wish of states, and other interested parties besides, to know the precise extent of their rights and duties under international law. Although states often seem to prefer regulating their mutual relations, where feasible, by concluding treaties rather than by relying on the formation of customary law with its usually more amorphous and uncertain norms, for various reasons such customary norms keep playing their part, including in the international law of the environment. As their binding force is no less than that of treaty provisions the need for clarifying them is arguably no less urgent either. It may in this light therefore be useful, not only for the state(s) concerned but also for a

---

[37] The United States probably comes closest to being a persistent objector, although it is open to question whether it actually complies with all prerequisites for qualifying as such. Other (but less likely) candidates are Japan and Canada. See Trouwborst, 2002, pp. 50 and 278-282.
[38] E.g., 1996 United Kingdom v. Denmark, over industrial sand eel fishing in the North Sea; see McIntyre & Mosedale, 1997, p. 234; Trouwborst, 2002, pp. 203-204.
[39] E.g., Australia and New Zealand v. Japan, 1999 ITLOS *Southern Bluefin Tuna* cases; Ireland v. UK, 2001 ITLOS *Mox Plant* case; Malaysia v. Singapore, 2003 ITLOS *Land Reclamation* case. All will be discussed below.
[40] E.g., 1995 Chile v. Japan, over an ultrahazardous radioactive materials shipment through the Chilean EEZ; see Van Dyke, 1996, *passim*; Trouwborst, 2002, pp. 226-227.

judicial or arbitral tribunal resolving a dispute or for any other parties involved, to be able to identify in individual situations whether a state is acting in conformity with the precautionary principle or in violation of it.

Method and Use of Terms

The answer to the research question will be sought after chiefly by analyzing the practice of states with regard to the precautionary principle, in light of any expressions of *opinio juris sive necessitatis* accompanying it. Besides, it will often be indispensable for a proper understanding of the legal issues involved in this study to examine the wider contexts and backgrounds of concepts like uncertainty, complexity, irreversibility, scientific evidence and cost-benefit analysis. This accords with the submission by one author that writings in the field of international environmental law which are strictly limited to the plain analysis of the state of the law read much like novels from which the editor has deleted every second and third paragraph.[41]

The present writer's perception of the two main ingredients of customary international law has been expressed extensively on another occasion.[42] Suffice it to say that this perception is no revolutionary one and closely follows the relevant jurisprudence of the International Court of Justice (ICJ). The material sources of state practice as understood here, which at the same time constitute the primary materials in which evidence of *opinio juris* can be encountered,[43] are numerous and range from treaties, 'soft law' declarations and decisions of international organizations to national law and policy instruments.[44] The presence or absence, as the case may be, of patterns and common denominators in these material sources of custom will ultimately determine what can be specified and what cannot in respect of the dimensions and workings of the precautionary principle under customary international law. In the search for such patterns due attention will need to be paid to potentially treacherous categories such as treaties and national legislation. Treaty provisions may, for instance, (1) serve as practice contributing to the formation of custom; (2) lay down specific ways of applying existing custom; or (3) provide for the application of a legal regime between the parties to the agreement which deviates from customary law. Likewise, domestic acts, although they can be representative of customary international law, often provide for stricter environmental protection than that which is required by international obligations.

---

41 Hey, 2003, p. 155.

42 Trouwborst, 2002, pp. 55-63 and 249-260.

43 International Law Association, 2000(b), p. 718; Trouwborst, *ibid.*, p. 253.

44 See Trouwborst, *ibid.*, pp. 61-63 and the sources mentioned there.

As mentioned before, this study builds on previous research by the present author and should be viewed in association with it.[45] One of the main questions in that former research was whether the precautionary principle had attained the status of customary international law. The answer being yes, the logical next question, at issue presently, is what that means. Naturally, whereas their analysis will be different this time, many of the sources drawn from in that former research will be revisited here. The backgrounds and content of, and adherence to, the majority of the precautionary international instruments discussed in the present study have been described in the former.[46] To avoid overlap, such introductory information will mostly not be repeated below. With regard to the material sources considered in the current (and the previous) study completeness can, of course, not be utterly guaranteed.[47] As far as multilateral treaties and international case law incorporating the precautionary principle are concerned, completeness is probably approximated. The major non-binding intergovernmental instruments of relevance are covered quite comprehensively as well. As for law and policy instruments and jurisprudence at the national level, as much of these have been scrutinized as possible, including all national practice referred to in the secondary sources (literature) consulted for this study. A systematic enquiry of the legal systems of all nations of the world has not been performed, however. The same is true for bilateral treaties and non-binding international instruments of limited scope.

Continuity applies furthermore with regard to the use of the terms precautionary *principle* and precautionary *approach*. Without delving too much into the complexities of the possible reasons for preferring one term or the other, a few remarks are in place. Analysis of the practice of states has shown that the only real difference seems to be the terminological distinction itself.[48] The two terms stand for the same concept and have the same basic characteristics. No substantive differences can *prima facie* be detected between commitments to apply the "precautionary principle" and commitments to apply the "precautionary approach". To illustrate this, both terms are occasionally employed within one and the same legal instrument, with nothing to suggest that different concepts are meant.[49] By way of another example, the

---

[45] Trouwborst, 2002.

[46] See both the text and annexes of Trouwborst, *ibid.*

[47] See the tables of instruments and cases *infra.*

[48] *Ibid.*, pp. 3-5; Marr, 2003, pp. 17-21; also Hey, 1992, p. 304.

[49] Compare, e.g., paragraphs 23(i), 24 and 111(a) ("precautionary approach") and 104(b)(i), 118(b)(i) and 124(b)(i) ("precautionary principle") of the 1995 *Global Programme of Action for the Protection of the Marine Environment from Land-Based Activities.* The same is true for influential non-governmental instruments, one instance being the *Berlin Rules on Water Resources* adopted by the

Programme for the Further Implementation of Agenda 21 that was adopted by the UN General Assembly in 1997 refers to Principle 15 of the *Rio Declaration* as the "precautionary principle", while Principle 15 itself speaks of the "precautionary approach". Accordingly, as in the previous study, the two terms will be used interchangeably here.

The danger of monographs such as the present is that they are prone to causing the false impression that the world revolves around its topic. It is convenient to underline at this stage that the precautionary principle as it stands in customary law (and in treaty law for that matter) is one out of many legal norms and does not operate in a vacuum. Any rights or duties of states to take precautionary action may overlap or compete with other rules of public international law in the field of environment, development, trade, or any other subject matter. When this happens, such situations will have to be resolved by reference to the regular criteria governing the conflict of rules, such as the axioms of *lex specialis* and *lex posterior.*

The manuscript of this book was closed on 1 April 2006.

Scope: On Environment, Health and Security

Before moving on, some preliminary observations on the subject of scope are called for. The precautionary principle originated in (inter)national *environmental* law and policy and this is still where its influence is greatest.[50] As a norm of customary international law, it clearly applies to the natural environment.[51] Specifically, it may be asked whether the principle covers the field of *health* protection as well. Environment and health are evidently distinct issues, just as the United Nations Environment Programme (UNEP) and the World Health Organization (WHO) are distinct bodies. Rules concerning market access of medicines, safety measures for cars and measures to avoid Repetitive Strain Injury have as little to do with the natural environment as the legal protection of the last few giant pandas has to do with human health. The many provisions in legal instruments which mention health and the environment alongside each other affirm that two separate issue areas are involved.[52] All the same, the two are linked – linguistically 'environment' means: that which surrounds man – and it is not always possible to draw a

---

International Law Association in 2004, which refer in the text of Articles 23 and 38 to the precautionary "approach", while the Commentary points out that these two provisions lay down the precautionary "principle" (see Commentary to Articles 38 and 41).

[50] Trouwborst, 2002, *passim*.

[51] *Ibid.*, pp. 283-284; Backes *et al.*, 2001, p. 1761; see also *infra* paragraph 5.2.

[52] Paragraph 3 of the 2000 EU *Council Resolution on the Precautionary Principle* of the EU speaks, in the plural, of "the fields of environmental and health protection". Similarly, it is the stated purpose of the 2001 *Convention on Persistent Organic Pollutants* (*Stockholm Convention*) to "protect human health *and* the environment" from POPs; Article 1, emphasis added.

sharp dividing line between them. Human health improvement often constitutes one of the motives for environmental protection, for instance in the fields of air and water quality. Besides, given that a single protective measure may protect the environment proper and the health of a human population at the same time, humans may benefit healthwise from environmental action which was not as such undertaken for health purposes. The various reports that form the outcome of the 2001-2005 Millennium Ecosystem Assessment bear ample witness to the many ties that exist between environmental and human health.[53] For these reasons, health is sometimes encompassed in general definitions of the environment. According to the arbitral tribunal in the 2005 *Iron Rhine* case between Belgium and the Netherlands, for example, in international environmental law "environment" is broadly referred to as including "air, water, land, flora and fauna, natural ecosystems and sites, *human health and safety*, and climate."[54]

Now how does all this relate to the precautionary principle under customary international law? To be sure, application of the principle has not been confined exclusively to the natural environment. In several cases states have expressly adopted it in respect of health issues as well, for instance in the 1999 *Protocol on Water and Health*[55] to the *Helsinki Watercourses Convention.*[56] Some rules on the control of hazardous chemicals also place the precautionary principle in the context of the avoidance of adverse effects "on human health and the environment."[57] The precautionary principle as incorporated in the 2000 *Biosafety Protocol*[58] to the *Biodiversity Convention*[59] targets the potential adverse effects of live genetically modified organisms (GMOs) on "the conservation and sustainable use of biological diversity, taking also into account risks to human health."[60] The explicit application of the precautionary principle to human (and animal and plant) health is especially significant in the practice of the European Union (EU) and its member states.[61] Such application has besides been proposed frequently in

---

[53] See, especially, Corvalan *et al.*, 2005, *passim*.

[54] Paragraph 58; emphasis added.

[55] Article 5(a).

[56] 1992 *Convention on the Protection and Use of Transboundary Watercourses and International Lakes.*

[57] E.g., first preambular paragraph of the 2001 *Stockholm Convention on Persistent Organic Pollutants.*

[58] *Protocol on Biosafety* or *Cartagena Protocol.*

[59] 1992 *Convention on Biological Diversity.*

[60] Article 1; see also Articles 10(6) and 11(8).

[61] See, e.g., preambular paragraph B of the 2000 *Council Resolution on the Precautionary Principle*; pp. 8-9 of *Communication COM(2000)1 on the Precautionary Principle*; and paragraph 183 of the Judgment by the EU Court of First Instance of 26 November 2002 in the Joined Cases T-74/00, T-76/00, T-83/00 to T-85/00, T-132/00, T-137/00 and T-141/00.

legal and other doctrine.[62] One commentator has even argued that the precautionary principle "has much more to do today with human health protection than with nature protection."[63]

It is sometimes proposed to stretch the reach of the principle even more, to cover also issues which are not immediately related to the environment, such as social security and crime.[64] In the 1992 *Baltic Sea Convention* and the 1992 *OSPAR Convention* the reach of the principle has been defined particularly broadly, with preventive action called for when there is reason to believe marine pollution may "create hazards to human health, harm living resources and marine ecosystems, damage amenities or interfere with other legitimate uses of the [high] sea."[65] The purpose of precaution as formulated here is not only the protection of nature and health, but also of commercial shipping activity, to name one legitimate use of the sea. Lastly, in the course of 2002 the United States government built an elaborate case for what was in essence the application of the precautionary principle in the area of (inter)national security. In a televised speech to the American people, President George W. Bush expressly reserved the possibility of an anticipatory military strike against the Iraq of Saddam Hussein in the absence of conclusive evidence of harmfulness, in classic precautionary wording:

> Understanding the threats of our time, knowing the designs and deceptions of the Iraqi regime, we have every reason to assume the worst, and we have an urgent duty to prevent the worst from occurring. [..] There is no easy or risk-free course of action. Some have argued we should wait – and that is an option. In my view, it is the riskiest of all options – because the longer we wait, the stronger and bolder Saddam Hussein will become. [..W]e cannot wait for the final proof – the smoking gun – that could come in the form of a mushroom cloud.[66]

Notwithstanding such interesting developments, in the vast majority of cases where states have formally adopted the precautionary principle they have done so only in respect of "the environment", without a single mention

---

[62] E.g., paragraph 4.1 of the 2002 *Declaration on Principles of International Law in the Field of Sustainable Development* of the International Law Association (hereinafter *ILA Declaration on Sustainable Development*) defines the principle as applying to "human health, natural resources or ecosystems"; see also Faure & Vos, 2003; Corvalan *et al.*, 2005, p. 10; and the quotations of authors in *infra* paragraph 2.3.

[63] De Sadeleer, 2004, p. 117.

[64] E.g., by the Belgian Federal Council for Sustainable Development (FRDO); see Federale Raad voor Duurzame Ontwikkeling, 2001, p. 13.

[65] Article 3(2) of the *Convention on the Protection of the Marine Environment of the Baltic Sea Area*; Article 2(2)(a) of the *Convention for the Protection of the Marine Environment of the North-East Atlantic*. (The word "high" is employed only in the former.)

[66] Broadcast on 7 October 2002, see transcript at http://www.cnn.com.

of health – or, for that matter, any other of the less plausible candidates for inclusion within the scope of the precautionary principle. For instance, in the *Rio Declaration* the international community agreed that the precautionary approach should be applied widely by states "in order to protect the *environment*", by way of measures "to prevent *environmental* degradation."[67] It is hardly likely, to limit the discussion to health, that this commitment was intended to cover food safety or any other health issue proper. What is more, it is precisely in relation to such health issues proper that the express application of the precautionary principle has proved most controversial, as illustrated by various rulings by World Trade Organization (WTO) dispute settlement bodies on the interpretation of the 1994 *Agreement on the Application of Sanitary and Phytosanitary Measures*,[68] and by the difficulty of negotiations on the meaning of precaution in the context of the Codex Alimentarius Commission.[69] Similarly, a proposal by the EU to explicitly include human health within the ambit of the precautionary principle ran onto the rocks at the 2002 World Summit on Sustainable Development (WSSD or Johannesburg Summit).[70] In addition, some of the fiercest criticism of the precautionary principle by commentators has focussed not on its application to nature protection or environmental pollution, but on the principle's application to typical health issues such as pharmaceuticals, the use of antibiotics in animal feed, and bovine spongiform encephalopathy (BSE).[71] It is in such strictly human health areas that the precautionary principle has, as a matter of international law, gained a foothold only with difficulty and is continually struggling not to lose it. Even in the *EC Treaty* as amended in 1992 the precautionary principle can only be found in the *environment* title.[72] It seems the precautionary principle has "much more to do today with human health protection than with nature protection" only in terms of controversy, for instance with a view to the prominent effect awarded to the principle in the

---

[67] Principle 15 of the 1992 *Declaration of the UN Conference on Environment and Development*; emphasis added.

[68] See, e.g., the Appellate Body Report in *EC Measures Concerning Meat and Meat Products (Hormones) (Canada and United States v European Community)*, 16 January 1998, AB-1997-4, *WTO Doc.* WT/DS26/AB/R and WT/DS48/AB/R.

[69] See Trouwborst, 2002, pp. 136-139.

[70] See Schrijver, 2003, p. 73.

[71] E.g., Marchant & Mossman, 2005.

[72] See Article 174(2) of the 1957 *Treaty Establishing the European Community*. Preambular paragraph B of the 2000 EU *Council Resolution on the Precautionary Principle* illustrates the hierarchy involved here especially well: "Whereas the Treaty recognises, in Article 174(2), that the precautionary principle is one of the principles to be taken into account in Community policy on the environment; whereas this principle is also applicable to human health, as well as to the animal health and plant health sectors; [..]."

health area in recent jurisprudence of the EU Court of Justice (ECJ) and the critical commentaries that case law has provoked.[73]

As stated above, the field of environmental protection cannot be fully detached from the well-being of humans, in the sense that human health often benefits from the former. In this *indirect* sense, as part of the principle's rationale, health protection may probably be considered as encompassed within the scope of the precautionary principle under customary international law.[74] It seems, however, highly questionable whether health protection *in its own right* is currently included within the principle's scope as well.[75]

This is, at first sight, a striking outcome. Surely human health cannot be less protected than the environment? Clearly this is not the case. Public health has been and will in all likelihood remain more strictly protected than the natural environment, reflecting the priorities of states and their human citizens. A plausible surmise accounting for the current scope of the precautionary principle is that the *substance* of what is presently known as the precautionary principle (i.e., implicit precaution) has, with a view to these priorities, in effect been applied in respect of human health for a long time. No precautionary *principle* (explicit precaution) was needed to assure this. In respect of nature, where until recently foresight and caution had been lacking enormously, there *was* such a need, which is why the principle surfaced in this field. With health safeguards impressive as they are, the imposition of an *additional* safeguard in the form of an express 'precautionary principle' and the uncertainty as to the precise implications thereof for commerce and technological innovation, may well account for the resistance the principle has met in the health context – in contrast with its broad acceptance in the environmental field. Whatever the explanation, *strictly* human health issues are not likely to be covered by the precautionary principle under customary international law, which aims at the protection of the *environment*. Only a derivative role appears to be reserved for health protection in this context. It is important to bear this in mind throughout the present study.

---

[73] De Sadeleer, 2004, p. 117, quoted above, in fact refers to such case law to support the claim involved.

[74] See also Chapter 9 below.

[75] It is illustrative that the drafters of the *ILA Declaration on Sustainable Development* explicitly consider the inclusion of human health in the definition of the precautionary principle in paragraph 4.1 as an attempt to *broaden* the scope of the principle, and not as reflecting the current state of general international law; see Schrijver, 2003, p. 74.

1.3. A Brief Preview

"Elimination of all confusion surrounding this concept would be too great a task for one commentator," one author submitted in respect of the precautionary principle in 1992.[76] Since then few legal topics have generated as many scholarly publications as this principle. It is convenient, therefore, to look ahead and dwell for a moment on the presumed added value of the present study – to offer, in other words, some possible reasons why one might want to continue reading.

The first of these, obviously, takes the shape of the main research question and its relevance as elaborated above. As part of the answer, a right and a duty of states, each conditioned by a specific set of triggering thresholds, will be uncovered and defined below. The second possible reason is that, even though the research question acts as the guiding light, the study's utility is arguably greater than the answer to the question alone. Through the in-depth analysis of numerous treaties, declarations, resolutions, national laws and strategies and court proceedings, and through the meticulous treatment of issues like the burden of proof and socio-economic factors, equally numerous pictures are painted of *how* states, collectively and individually, practice precaution. This evidently goes beyond the customary law question. Besides, albeit that this study departs from the assumption that the precautionary principle constitutes customary international law, it is hoped that its results will be of equal use to those who, for the time being, consider the principle an *emerging* custom. From the latter perspective, the findings below can be regarded as describing the direction into which the principle is developing. The third facet of the presumed added value of this study is its interdisciplinary nature. It ventures across the boundaries of law into the realms of other branches of science, most notably ecology, economics and political science, alongside the odd bits of mathematics and philosophy. This does not mean that the following is a *lex ferenda* study. Rather, the focus is on *lex lata* in its wider context. Finally, all findings are abundantly illustrated by examples and graphics.

The study is structured as follows. Part Two deals with the *definition* of the precautionary principle under general international law. Part Three deals with its *implementation*. The main findings of these two parts are summarized and integrated in Part Four. To return to the stated purpose of the present work, despite (and perhaps partly because of) the multitude of recent publications on the precautionary principle the need for *clarification* is still great. It is not claimed, but merely hoped that the outcomes of this study will clear up some of the mist.

---

[76] Hey, 1992, p. 303.

PART TWO

DEFINITION

Knowledge is proud that he has learned so much;
Wisdom is humble that he knows no more.
William Cowper (1731-1800)

2. APOLLO'S TRIPOD: DEFINING RIGHTS AND DUTIES UNDER THE PRECAUTIONARY PRINCIPLE

2.1. Unity in Diversity?

It is often said that the precautionary principle has not yet received a uniformly applicable and imperative definition.[1] In a British judicial decision of 1994, for instance, it was stated that no single authoritative definition of the principle yet existed.[2] The same assertion can be found in a position paper of the European Chemical Industry Council (CEFIC)[3] and – although on several occasions its relativity has been highlighted as well[4] – persists in academic writings until today.[5] In the current and the following chapters the practice of states in respect of the precautionary principle will be scrutinized so as to verify whether this position actually exhausts the topic.

It is an undeniable fact that definitions vary, sometimes considerably, between the numerous legal and policy documents incorporating the principle, both at the national and international level.[6] Such variation is on several occasions the outcome of the intentional tailoring of the principle's formulation to a specific problem area or the result of a political compromise, and on other occasions was brought about for no directly apparent or verifiable reason.[7] Moreover, many instruments that name the precautionary principle do not define it at all.[8] For instance, at least sixteen global and regional environmental treaties and protocols, covering a wide range of topics and geographic regions, contain reference to the

---

[1] McIntyre & Mosedale, 1997, p. 223; Kaiser, 1997(a), p. 203; Lemons *et al.*, 1997, p. 210; Matthee & Vermersch, 2000, p. 61; Matthee, 2001, p. 184; Pieterman, 2001, p. 1024; Christensen, 2001, p. 6; Boisson de Chazournes, 2002, p. 10; Pieterman & Hanekamp, 2002, p. v; Marr, 2003, p. 5; Sands, 2003, p. 272; Bodansky, 2004, pp. 381-382; see also Trouwborst, 2002, p. 51.

[2] Smith J in *Duddridge*, 1994; see Cameron & Abouchar, 1996, p. 47.

[3] European Chemical Industry Council, 1995, paragraph 8.

[4] E.g., Tomme Young in the *IUCN Environmental Law Programme Newsletter*, No. 1, 2001, at p. 4.

[5] See *supra* note 1.

[6] A good look at Annexes A and B to this study will demonstrate this as regards international instruments. For national definitions and interpretations of the principle, compare Trouwborst, 2002, pp. 181-242. Also Lambers, 2000, p. 176.

[7] Backes *et al.*, 2002, p. 230.

[8] Lambers, 2000, p. 176.

"precautionary principle", "precautionary approach(es)", "precautionary measures" or "precaution" without actually defining these terms.[9] The same is true of many non-legally binding instruments.[10]

For the sake of clarity, this compilation of agreements and other intergovernmental documents does not include those explicitly precautionary instruments that, although lacking a definition of the precautionary principle in their own terms, refer directly to the provisions of other instruments that *do* define the principle. For instance, the 1998 *Agreement on the International Dolphin Conservation Program* sets out the duty to "apply the precautionary approach, consistent with the relevant provisions of the FAO Code of Conduct for Responsible Fisheries and the United Nations Agreement on

---

[9] Among them are the 1985 *Convention on the Protection of the Ozone Layer* (also known as the *Vienna Convention*, see preambular paragraph 5) and its 1987 *Protocol on Substances that Deplete the Ozone Layer* (*Montreal Protocol*, preambular paragraph 8), both as amended in 1990 (*London Amendments* of 1990); the 1990 *International Convention on Oil Pollution Preparedness, Response and Cooperation* (preamble, paragraph 3); the 1992 amendments to the *Treaty Establishing the European Community* (*EC Treaty*, Article 174(2)); the 1992 *Agreement on the European Economic Area* (*EEA Agreement*, see the sixth preambular paragraph); the 1994 *Convention on Cooperation for the Protection and Sustainable Use of the Danube River* (*Danube River Convention*, Articles 2(4) and 3(2)(e) and paragraph 2 of Part 2 of Annex I); the 1994 *Energy Charter Treaty* (Article 19(1)); the 1995 *Agreement on the Conservation of African-Eurasian Migratory Waterbirds* (*African-Eurasian Waterbirds Agreement*, see Article II(2) of this side agreement to the 1979 *Convention on the Conservation of Migratory Species of Wild Animals* (or *Bonn Convention*)); the 1980 *Protocol for the Protection of the Mediterranean Sea Against Pollution from Land-Based Sources* as amended in 1996 (*Mediterranean Land-Based Sources Protocol*, see paragraph 5 of its preamble; this is a protocol to the 1976 *Convention for the Protection of the Mediterranean Sea Against Pollution* or *Barcelona Convention*); the 1996 *Protocol (to the Barcelona Convention) on the Prevention of Pollution of the Mediterranean Sea by Transboundary Movements of Hazardous Wastes and their Disposal* (*Mediterranean Hazardous Wastes Protocol*, Article 8(3)); the Dutch-German 1996 *Protocol on Cooperation in the Area of Water and Nature Protection in the Ems River Mouth* (*Ems-Dollart Protocol*, to the 1960 *Treaty Between the Netherlands and Germany on Cooperation in the Ems River Mouth*, Article 1); the 1996 *Agreement on the Conservation of Cetaceans of the Black Sea, Mediterranean Sea and Contiguous Atlantic Area* (*ACCOBAMS*, another side agreement to the *Bonn Convention*; see Article II(4)); the *Agreement for the Establishment of a General Fisheries Commission for the Mediterranean* as amended in 1997 (*GFCM Agreement*, Article III(2)); the 1999 *Convention on the Protection of the Rhine* (*Rhine Convention*, Article 4(a)); the 1999 *Agreement Between the Government of Iceland, the Government of Norway and the Government of the Russian Federation Concerning Certain Aspects of Cooperation in the Area of Fisheries* (*Iceland-Norway-Russia Fisheries Agreement*, Article 1); the 1999 Arabic *Agreement for the Establishment of the Regional Commission for Fisheries* (*RECOFI Agreement*, Article III(2)); and the *African Convention on the Conservation of Nature and Natural Resources* as revised in 2003 (2003 *African Convention*, Article IV).

[10] A sample of non-legally binding instruments naming the precautionary principle but not defining it, contains the 1993 *Fifth Action Programme on the Environment of the European Community* (Chapter 2); the 1993 *Declaration on Environment and Development in the Arctic* (hereinafter also *Nuuk Declaration*, see paragraph 8); the 1995 *Environmental Programme for Europe* (third preambular paragraph); and the 2000 *Memorandum of Understanding on the Conservation and Management of the Middle-European Population of the Great Bustard* (hereinafter *Great Bustard Memorandum of Understanding*, see paragraph 4 of this side agreement to the *Bonn Convention*).

Straddling Fish Stocks and Highly Migratory Fish Stocks."[11] Comparable rules of reference, often to Principle 15 of the 1992 *Rio Declaration on Environment and Development*, can be found in scores of other instruments.[12] Furthermore, it may probably be assumed that even though this is not expressly stated, the two abovementioned Mediterranean protocols refer to the precautionary principle as defined in their parent instrument, the *Barcelona Convention* as revised in 1995, in line with the hierarchical relationship generally existing between treaties and their protocols.[13]

These considerations aside, the lack of definition of the precautionary principle in the remaining instruments listed *supra* may imply any of several things: (1) definition was thought too cumbersome or even impossible on account of the principle's perceived vagueness at the time; (2) the principle's contours were expressly meant to remain vague so as not to impair its future development; (3) there was essential disagreement on the definition; or (4) the principle's core elements and/or implications were thought to be so generally known as to render its definition superfluous. Combinations of these are also imaginable. Lack of definition in instruments that do mention it is not unique for the precautionary principle. The preventive principle, the polluter pays principle and the concept of sustainable development, to name a few, are often left unspecified as well. Again, any (combination) of the reasons sketched above may lie at the basis of this.

It would seem, nonetheless, that consciously or unconsciously the fourth option has been a factor of importance on all occasions, since the inclusion of any norm into an international agreement – particularly when it is a legally binding one – without there being at least some basic agreement as to its content, is hardly conceivable and must be deemed uncommon. *Ergo*, the substantial number of instruments containing unspecified reference to the precautionary principle appears to indicate the presence of at least some common understanding of the principle's constituent elements. Some support for this preliminary conclusion may be deduced from the dating of these instruments. In the early years of the precautionary principle in international law, from its first express appearance in the mid-1980s through to the early 1990s, nearly all relevant conventions and declarations set out the *content* of the principle. When, during the run-up to the 1992 United Nations Conference on Environment and Development (the Rio de Janeiro 'Earth Summit' or UNCED), the principle attained global recognition, the

[11] Article 4(1); see Principles 6.5 and 7.5 of the 1995 *FAO Code of Conduct* and Articles 5 and 6 and Annex II of the 1995 *Straddling Stocks Agreement*.
[12] See *infra* paragraph 2.3.
[13] See Article 4(3)(a) of the *Barcelona Convention* as amended in 1995.

incentive for doing so apparently diminished. This is reflected in the increased number of legal instruments concluded in this period and afterwards that merely affirm the precautionary principle as such without repeating the description of its content. This decreasing need for definition is, in fact, no more than a logical feature of the development of almost every norm or concept. Initially it has to be defined simply on account of its novelty. Later on, once it becomes firmly established and there is a common agreement on its meaning, it suffices for new instruments to confirm the concept as such without constantly reiterating its definition.

For a couple of reasons, among the various conventions that mention the precautionary principle while failing to secure a closer description of it, the *EC Treaty* merits a somewhat closer look. For one thing, it is the earliest binding agreement to have included the principle in one of its operative provisions without defining it. This was done in February 1992, as follows:

> Community policy on the environment shall [..] be based on the precautionary principle and on the principle that preventive action should be taken, that environmental damage should as a priority be rectified at source and that the polluter should pay.[14]

For another, comparison with the other three environmental principles employed in Article 174(2) – the preventive principle, the principle of rectification at source and the polluter pays principle – shows that these latter have at least received a minimum of definition, whereas the precautionary principle, as the ECJ has noted,[15] has not. The European Commission's 2000 *Communication COM(2000)1 on the Precautionary Principle* does not yield a cut and dried definition either,[16] nor does the related Council resolution.[17]

It has been suggested that the definitions of the precautionary principle used in other multilateral agreements to which the European Union is a party and in declarations signed by it, may be assumed to inform Article 174(2).[18] *Communication COM(2000)1* and the Council's *Resolution on the Precautionary Principle* indeed both mention several international legal

---

[14] This provision, which is presently Article 174(2) of the *EC Treaty*, was introduced by way of the *Treaty on European Union* (or *EU Treaty*) and entered into force in November 1993.

[15] Case T-70/99 (*Alpharma*), Judgment of the Third Chamber of the Court of First Instance of 11 September 2002, paragraph 138.

[16] Hereinafter *Communication COM(2000)1*; also Backes *et al.*, 2002, p. 63.

[17] *Council Resolution on the Precautionary Principle* of December 2000.

[18] Douma, 1997, p. 6, who names as one example the 1990 *Ministerial Declaration on Sustainable Development in the ECE Region* (or *Bergen Declaration*). According to Hancher, 1996, at p. 187, the inclusion of the precautionary principle in Article 174 "is generally assumed to be inspired by Principle 15 of the Rio Declaration." More likely the process leading up to the adoption of the *Rio Declaration* is meant, given that the *Treaty on European Union* was concluded several months before the UNCED.

instruments, but fail to directly link any or all of them to Article 174. Perhaps the key to understanding why the precautionary principle was left undefined in the *EC Treaty* relates rather to its capacity of *general* principle of international environmental law.[19] By the time of the drafting of the current Article 174 the precautionary principle was, after all, rapidly on its way to becoming one of the most significant such principles – a development that has been generously aided by the European Union and its member states from the outset.[20] It is likely, therefore, that the aim of introducing the provision under scrutiny into the *EC Treaty* was to bring to bear the application of the *general* precautionary principle in EU environmental policy making while guarding against any specific definition that could confine the potential reach of the principle too much. This second possible reason stated above for not defining the precautionary principle – i.e., the principle's contours were expressly meant to remain vague – may thus have played a part beside the fourth, already discussed reason.

After this brief excursion the main task of this chapter must be faced. In order to enable a determination of the customary rights and/or duties of states as generated by the precautionary principle, which is the chief purpose of this study, it is obviously essential to outline as precisely as possible the definition of the principle as it applies under customary international law. As precisely as possible, because there are likely to be limits in this respect given the nature of the precautionary principle as a *general principle* of international environmental law. According to one jurist, the principle "does indicate the direction of decision-making, but does not indicate the parameters of decision-making."[21] The merits of this statement will be reflected upon in the present chapter. The questions: "What are these parameters? What are they determined by?", asked by the same writer will be addressed to this end.[22]

Consequently, in this chapter and the ones that are to follow the identification will need to be attempted of the common ground apparently existing among the array of definitions occurring in the practice of states, mapping the various elements of the common understanding on the precautionary principle alluded to above. This requires a careful analysis of the numerous material sources of precautionary state practice and customary law – that is, *inter alia*, relevant treaties, declarations, resolutions, and national legislation, executive decisions and jurisprudence – as well as international judicial decisions and academic writings on the topic.[23] This analysis will

[19] On this capacity of the precautionary principle generally, see Trouwborst, 2002, pp. 34-35.
[20] *Ibid.*, pp. 142-148.
[21] Taylor, 1998, p. 25.
[22] *Ibid.*
[23] Generally on the material sources of state practice, see *supra* paragraph 1.2; Trouwborst, 2002, pp. 59-62; and Marr, 2003, pp. 203-210.

from time to time be viewed in light of the conceptual background of the principle and aided, where this is helpful, by the application of the rules of logic and the appropriate dose of common sense.

2.2. *Risk: A Framework for Understanding the Precautionary Principle*

As will soon become apparent, at the root of any meaningful discussion of the precautionary principle and its definition ought to lie a basic understanding of the notion of *risk*, warranting a concise *exposé* of the concept and its various meanings at this early stage. It is precisely on account of its various meanings that the term 'risk' is frequently used inconsistently, thus becoming a great source of confusion.[24] To begin with, the *Concise Oxford Dictionary* describes it as follows:

> Hazard, chance of or *of* bad consequences, loss, etc., exposure to mischance, (*there is the risk of his catching cold; at the risk of his life*); at risk, exposed to danger.[25]

"Risky", in turn, is defined as "Hazardous, full of risk."[26] So, roughly speaking, at the most general, everyday level 'risk' equals 'hazard' or 'threat'. These terms usually embody the two distinct elements of *chance* and *harm*, but their meaning is highly flexible in the sense that, depending on the context in which they are used, the emphasis may be placed more or less heavily on either element.

On the academic plane a vast literature on risk has developed, whereby the large variety of different disciplinary angles from which the concept is viewed is responsible for much of the confusion surrounding the theme.[27] Renn, for instance, has described distinct technical, economic, psychological, sociological and cultural approaches to risk.[28] The first, 'technical' approach is the one foremostly concerned with technological and environmental risks, and therefore also the one predominantly adopted in environmental policy and decision making. A brief discussion of the concept of risk from this technical perspective is necessary in order to better understand yet another approach to risk, not mentioned by Renn but intimately related to the technical approach, namely the legal perspective this study is concerned with.

---

[24] Bouma *et al.*, 2002, p. 13; Philippopoulos-Mihalopoulos, 1999, p. 175; Pieterman & Hanekamp, 2002, p. 36.

[25] Sykes, 1976, p. 972.

[26] *Ibid.*

[27] Bouma *et al.*, 2002, pp. 11-13, 20.

[28] Renn, O., "Three Decades of Risk Research: Accomplishments and New Challenges", in: *Journal of Risk Research*, No. 1, 1998, pp. 49-71, at pp. 52-64; summarized in Bouma *et al.*, 2002, pp. 11-13.

The technological/environmental discipline commonly views risk as the undesirable consequence of a particular event as related to the likelihood of its occurrence[29] or, in reverse, as "the magnitude of the hazard/error times the probability of occurrence."[30] The two respective meanings that the word risk may represent separately in ordinary speech, i.e. 'chance' and 'danger', are thus forged into a unity. Here, the magnitude of a given *risk* must be distinguished from the magnitude of the expected value of *harm*: the latter is an ingredient of the former. From a strictly environmental policy angle, risk may thus be defined as the product of (1) the likelihood that a given effect materializes and (2) the gravity of the ensuing environmental harm. This can be rendered in simplified fashion as follows:

Risk = Probability x Gravity[31]

This technical interpretation of risk is the one applied, for example, in the 1990 *Code of Conduct on Accidental Pollution of Transboundary Inland Waters* of the UN Economic Commission for Europe (UN-ECE).[32] The Code defines risk as "the combined effect of the probability of occurrence of an undesirable event and its magnitude."[33] Subsequently, the same approach was adopted by the International Law Commission (ILC) as part of its work on the prevention of transboundary harm from hazardous activities.[34]

Given that the dimension of a particular risk is a function of the dimensions of its two components, it will vary along with fluctuations in either one of them. The graver the expected environmental consequences and/or the chance of them occurring, the bigger the risk.[35] The two elements of risk may thus be pictured graphically as two interconnected axes with sliding scales.[36]

---

[29] See Pascual Trillo, 2000, p. 142, quoting from Soler, M. *et al.*, *Manual de Gestión del Medio Ambiente*, Barcelona 1997.

[30] Wildavsky, 2000, p. 25; *idem* Bouma, 2002, p. 11; Lefeber, 1996, p. 29; Klinke & Renn, 1999, p. 11.

[31] Variation on Pascual Trillo, 2000, p. 142.

[32] E/ECE/1125-ECE/ENVWA/16.

[33] As quoted in International Law Commission, 2001, p. 387.

[34] See the commentary on Article 2(a) of the 2001 *Draft Articles on Prevention of Transboundary Harm from Hazardous Activities* (hereinafter referred to as *Draft Articles on Harm Prevention*); International Law Commission, 2001. Drawing upon the UN-ECE Code, the ILC defines risk as "the combined effect of the probability of occurrence of an accident and the magnitude of its injurious impact."

[35] Bouma *et al.*, 2002, pp. 13-14.

[36] See, e.g., Backes *et al.*, 2002, p. 246. This understanding of risk is inherent, e.g., in the ILC *Draft Articles on Harm Prevention*, which take the term "risk of causing significant transboundary harm" to include "risks taking the form of a high probability of causing significant transboundary harm and a low probability of causing disastrous transboundary harm." Article 2(a), see International Law Commission, 2001.

When the values for both likelihood and gravity are huge, the result is maximum risk. Interesting are those situations in which the value of one of the composing factors is very high and the other very low.[37] For instance, in case the anticipated harm is of immense proportions but the chance it will ever come about almost *nihil*, this may still pass for a great risk, and *vice versa*.[38] An extreme example of the former situation is the risk of large asteroid impact.[39]

Originally, the technical approach to risk stems from a probabilistic tradition, and still attributes an important role to the calculus of probabilities.[40] When the respective values of probability and gravity can both be more or less reliably estimated, a risk can be computed as a certain amount of harm over a certain period of time and numerically ranked.[41] This category of quantifiable or calculable risks is sometimes also referred to as 'known' risks. The obvious advantage of quantification is that it enables comparison with other risks. Such comparison can yield interesting results. From a risk-neutral point of view there is no difference, for instance, between a fifty percent chance that two killer whales will die and a one-in-a-thousand chance that a thousand killer whales will die within the same time span. The expected *average* outcome in both cases is one killer whale death.[42] Below, the question will be addressed whether both outcomes would be rated equally under the precautionary principle as it stands in customary international law.

Before proceeding, the economic perspective on risk mentioned earlier deserves brief attention here. Instead of focussing on environmental or physical harm as one of the components of risk, the economic approach discusses and measures risks in terms of utility.[43] Consequently, unlike the technical approach just discussed, both negative *and* positive consequences are integrated into the analysis of individual risks, so as to make possible the balancing of expected pros

---

[37] Pascual Trillo, 2000, p. 142.

[38] Lefeber, 1996, pp. 29-30. The ILC perceives "ultra-hazardous activities" as activities "with a danger that is rarely expected to materialize but might assume, on that rare occasion grave [..] proportions." An example given is nuclear power generation. International Law Commission, 2001, Commentary to Article 1 of the *Draft Articles on Harm Prevention*, paragraphs 2 and 4.

[39] See Rubin, 2000, *passim*.

[40] Bouma *et al.*, 2002, p. 11.

[41] This is done by combining the probability of occurrence of the event concerned in a selected period of time with the expected value of harm. An exposition of exactly how the two values are arrived at mathematically would go too far for present purposes. See Lefeber, 1996, pp. 29-30.

[42] This example is adapted from Bodansky, 1991(a), p. 414.

[43] Bouma *et al.*, 2002, pp. 11-12, referring to pp. 55-57 of Renn, O., "Three Decades of Risk Research: Accomplishments and New Challenges", in: *Journal of Risk Research*, No. 1, 1998, pp. 49-71.

and cons of taking them.[44] This particular angle on risks will be revisited *infra* in the chapter on socio-economic interests.[45]

In this study the word 'risk' will mainly be used in the everyday general sense of 'threat'. However, when reference is made to the two components or axes of risk, or to the concept of risk, the more formalistic technical approach to risk is taken (Risk = Probability x Gravity). Finally, where calculable or quantifiable risks are meant this will be expressly indicated.

The most important thing for now is to take note of the significant overlap between the structure of the risk concept and the structure of the precautionary principle. The fundamental framework of the precautionary principle is composed of the very same axes of probability and gravity of harm. It is aimed at the prevention of environmental harm, the expected gravity of which may vary, in situations of varying (un)certainty or likelihood of the materialization of this harm.[46] Moreover, it will become increasingly clear below that the scope of application of the precautionary principle under customary international law is determined in large measure by these factors of probability and gravity of harm.[47]

2.3. Core Elements of the Precautionary Principle

The search for a definition of the precautionary principle that is representative of the present state of customary international law will start in earnest in the present paragraph. Beginning at the beginning, it is submitted that, at a very minimum, "[t]he precautionary principle does have a conceptual core."[48] The essence of applying the principle is often summarized as erring on the side of caution, in favour of the environment; giving the environment the benefit of the doubt; put another way: *in dubio pro natura.*[49]

---

[44] *Ibid.*

[45] Chapter 9.

[46] The obvious likeness of risk and precaution is illustrated by Boisson de Chazournes, 2002, at p. 11, where she describes risk as connoting "both uncertainty and damage." Risk, she states, is the "defining characteristic of precaution." *Ibid.*

[47] Also Backes *et al.*, 2002, p. 245.

[48] Cameron *et al.*, 1998, p. 98; also Backes *et al.*, 2001, p. 1761; Trouwborst, 2002, pp. 51-52.

[49] E.g., Hey, 1992, p. 305; Schmidt-Bleek, 1993, p. 83; Van Dyke, 1996, p. 380; Backes, 1997, p. 14; Backes *et al.*, 1997, pp. 49, 69 and 95; Van Wijmen, 1997, p. 14; Victor, 1997, p. 243; De Sadeleer, 2002, p. 203; Marr, 2003, p. 215; Molenaar, 1998, p. 45; Molenaar, 2005, p. 537; Borgers, 1999, *passim*; Santillo *et al.*, 1999, p. 39; Geiser, 1999(a), p. xxv; Jordan & O'Riordan, 1999, pp. 26-27; Barrett & Raffensperger, 1999, p. 117; Morris, 2000(b), p. 13; Tallacchini, 2000, p. 1097; see also Article 30(c) of the Canadian *Oceans Act 1996* ("the precautionary approach, that is, erring on the side of caution"); and the Canadian government's 1990 *Green Plan*, discussed in VanderZwaag, 1994.

International and national legal and policy instruments are usually a bit more detailed than that. Be this as it may, virtually all of the numerous articulations of the precautionary principle that can be encountered in state practice boil down to the basic understanding that when (more or less grave) environmental harm looms ahead, preventive or abatement action is appropriate even if the issues are surrounded by uncertainty.[50]

The Precautionary Tripod

In a nutshell, three common elements can be inferred, and this is where the Delphic tripod, announced in the title of the current chapter, comes into play. In essence anything triple, from the musical format of the trio sonata to the sides of the legendary Devil's Triangle could have served to illustrate the basic structure of the precautionary principle, but for the sake of consistence it is deemed more appropriate to pick up the thread of Greek mythology that was started to be unwound in the introductory chapter of this study. The most fundamental feature of the tripod of Apollo, namely that it rests on three legs, it has in common with the precautionary principle. The three legs of the precautionary tripod, then, are (1) a threat of harm, (2) uncertainty, and (3) action.[51]

There is broad concurrence on these quintessential elements among writers. Matthee and Vermersch, for example, affirm that the precautionary principle "is often divided into three components: (1) the lack of scientific certainty, (2) a risk of irreversible or serious damage, and (3) an obligation for states to take measures accordingly."[52] Epiney and Scheyli similarly distinguish three elements: when the first two of them, namely (1) uncertainty and (2) a potential threat, are present this has (3) legal consequence.[53] Yet another improvisation on the precautionary triple fugue has been performed by Cameron and Abouchar, as follows: "1) regulatory inaction threatens non-negligible harm; 2) there exists a lack of scientific certainty on the cause and effect relationships; and 3) under these circumstances, regulatory inaction is unjustified."[54]

Although differently phrased, the three basic components of the precautionary principle can easily be detected in each and every one of the following expressions by commentators and industry representatives of its core meaning:

---

[50] For an extensive treatment of the myriad sources of precautionary state practice, see Trouwborst, 2002, pp. 63-249.

[51] See also Trouwborst, 2002, pp. 51-52.

[52] Matthee & Vermersch, 2000, p. 61.

[53] Epiney and Scheyli, 1998, pp. 109-110.

[54] Cameron & Abouchar, 1996, p. 45; also Cameron *et al.*, 1998, p. 99. See also DeFur & Kaszuba, 2002, p. 157.

[T]he fundamental elements of the principle are: the existence of some indication of the threat of harm; the harm is serious or irreversible; scientific uncertainty as to the nature or severity of the outcome; and an obligation on decision-makers.[55]

The core is the understanding that precautionary measures must be taken – alternatively that certain conduct and projects must be avoided – when there is reason to assume that the substance/energy/project concerned may create adverse environmental interferences, *even if there is no conclusive evidence* of a causal relationship between cause and alleged effects.[56]

Where an activity raises threats of harm to the environment or human health, precautionary measures should be taken even if some cause and effect relationships are not fully established scientifically.[57]

The core of each statement of the precautionary principle is the idea that action should be taken to prevent harm to the environment and human health, even if scientific evidence is inconclusive.[58]

A precautionary approach is central to sustainable development in that it commits States [..] to avoid human activity which may cause significant harm to human health, natural resources or ecosystems, including in the light of scientific uncertainty.[59]

The precautionary principle [..] provides a tool for dealing with situations where there is a potential hazard, but scientific uncertainty as to the impact of the environmentally sensitive activity does not allow a clear prediction of the degree of the hazards to the environment. Thus, its core characteristic feature is environmental action in the face of scientific uncertainty.[60]

[T]he general idea [of the precautionary principle] could, indicatively, be expressed as follows: where there are sufficient grounds for believing that an activity or a product is likely to cause threat of serious and irreversible damage to health or the environment, measures must be taken for example to reduce or to prevent that activity or that product even if there is no fully conclusive evidence of a causal link between that activity or product and the feared consequences.[61]

The conceptual core of the precautionary principle seems to be that precautions should be taken, even if a cause-and-effect relationship between an activity and harm to the environment (or to human health) has yet to be established scientifically.[62]

---

[55] This was the opinion of most participants in a July 2000 Lauterpacht International Law Centre workshop on "The Precautionary Principle in Wildlife Conservation". See Cooney, 2000.

[56] Ebbesson, 1996, pp. 119-120; italics in original.

[57] *Wingspread Statement on the Precautionary Principle* (hereinafter also *Wingspread Statement*), Ashford *et al.*, 1998.

[58] Raffensperger, 2000.

[59] 2002 *ILA Declaration on Sustainable Development*, paragraph 4.1.

[60] Marr, 2003, p. 9.

[61] European Chemical Industry Council, 1995.

[62] Jones, 2000.

Principle 15 of the *Rio Declaration* – which, on account of its general scope and nearly universal endorsement at the 1992 UNCED represented a significant step in the coming of age of the precautionary principle in international law[63] – is often taken to approximate the essence of the principle as viewed by the international community of states particularly closely, when stating that "where there are threats of serious or irreversible damage, lack of full scientific certainty shall not be used as a reason for postponing cost-effective measures to prevent environmental degradation."[64] The elements of harm, uncertainty and action jump to the eye again. One indication of the weight the *Rio Declaration*'s definition of the precautionary principle is accorded by states is the frequent reference to Principle 15 in subsequently drafted instruments. These include the three most recent protocols to the 1979 *Convention on Long-Range Transboundary Air Pollution* (*LRTAP Convention*),[65] the 2000 *Biosafety Protocol*,[66] the 2000 *Malmö Declaration*,[67] the 2000 EC *Council Resolution on the Precautionary Principle*,[68] the 2001 *Agreement on the Conservation of Albatrosses and Petrels*,[69] the 2001 *Convention on Persistent Organic Pollutants*,[70] the 2001 *International Convention on the Control of Harmful Anti-Fouling Systems on Ships*[71] and

[63] See Trouwborst, 2002, pp. 117-120.

[64] Sands, 1995(a), p. 209, and Sands, 1995(b), pp. 65-66: "The core of the principle [..] is reflected in Principle 15 of the Rio Declaration." *Idem* Taylor, 1998, p. 330; Swanson & Johnston, 1999, p. 236. Van Dyke, 1996, p. 380: "perhaps the phrasing in Principle 15 of the 1992 Rio Declaration best reflects the international community's views on this principle." Kiss, 1996, p. 27: "One may consider that the formulation of Principle 15 of the Rio Declaration reflects the most generally accepted approach." Gullett, 1997, p. 55: "Arguably the Rio Declaration [..] is the most significant international recognition of the principle and the most accepted formulation." Kaiser, 1997(a), p. 203, and Kaiser, 1997(b), p. 311: "Probably the most influential statement of the Precautionary Principle we find in principle 15 of the *Rio Declaration* of 1992." See also Borgers, 1999, p. 435; Pieterman & Hanekamp, 2002, p. 6, referring to Graham, J.D., "Decision-Analytic Refinements of the Precautionary Principle", in: 4 *Journal of Risk Research*, 2001, pp. 127-141; Marr, 2003, pp. 7 and 215; and Trouwborst, 2002, pp. 118-120.

[65] See the eighth preambular paragraph of the 1998 *Protocol on Heavy Metals* (or *Heavy Metals Protocol*); the seventh preambular paragraph of the 1998 *Protocol on Persistent Organic Pollutants* (or *POPs Protocol*); and the eleventh preambular paragraph of the 1999 *Protocol to Abate Acidification, Eutrophication and Ground-Level Ozone* (or *Gothenburg Protocol*).

[66] *Protocol on Biosafety* to the 1992 *Convention on Biological Diversity*. See the Protocol's preamble, paragraph 4, and Article 1.

[67] *Declaration of the First Global Ministerial Environment Forum*, paragraph 3.

[68] Preambular paragraph E.

[69] Preamble, paragraph 16; the *Albatross Agreement* is yet another side agreement to the 1979 *Bonn Convention*.

[70] Hereinafter *POPs Convention*, Article 1. Principle 15 is also referred to in *Decisions 18/32* and *19/13C on Persistent Organic Pollutants* of the UNEP Governing Council, adopted respectively in 1995 and 1997.

[71] Hereinafter *Anti-Fouling Systems Convention*, see preambular paragraph 5.

the 2002 *Guiding Principles on Alien Species*.[72] In the *Plan of Implementation* that was the outcome of the 2002 Johannesburg Summit, Principle 15 of the *Rio Declaration* was reaffirmed and its text quoted integrally.[73] The British government has also founded its official interpretation of the precautionary principle explicitly on Principle 15.[74] The latter provision must thus be regarded as an important source when it comes to determining the precautionary principle's definition.[75] At the same time, however, it is also one of many, and non-legally binding besides.

In the core definitions of writers reproduced above the reader will have noted slight and not so slight variations in the formulations used. Some have incorporated particular qualifications for the application of the precautionary principle to be triggered, such as the presence of "sufficient grounds for believing" that harm may be caused, or the requirement for harm to be "non-negligible" or "serious". With respect to the latter, for instance, the *Rio Declaration* itself also employs a *de minimis* threshold of harm: there must be a threat of "serious or irreversible damage" for the principle to apply. The next three chapters will be devoted to the question of how these and other more detailed aspects of defining the precautionary principle relate to state practice at large. They will contain the separate in-depth discussion of all three core elements of the principle – the three legs of the tripod – in the following order: harm, uncertainty, action.

The Umbrella of Sustainable Development

Before moving on to this discussion, one more significant general characteristic of the precautionary principle must receive attention, namely its close relationship with the concept of sustainable development. The 2002 *ILA*

---

[72] *Guiding Principles for the Prevention, Introduction and Mitigation of Impacts of Alien Species that Threaten Ecosystems, Habitats or Species*, adopted at the 6th Conference of the Parties to the *Biodiversity Convention*. Reference to Principle 15 occurs in Guiding Principles 1 and 10(2). Reference is also made to the preamble of the *Biodiversity Convention*.

[73] Paragraph 103(f). Principle 15 is also recalled in paragraph 22 on chemicals management.

[74] UK Government, *A Better Quality of Life: A Strategy for Sustainable Development for the United Kingdom*, 1999, quotes Rio Principle 15 in paragraph 4.1. Based on this, Department of the Environment, Transport and the Regions, *Guidelines for Environmental Risk Assessment and Management: Revised Departmental Guidance*, 2000, paragraph 1.6.: states that "The UK Government's interpretation, which is set out in Chapter 4 of its sustainable development strategy, *A Better Quality of Life*, is based on the Rio definition." This is affirmed again in the UK government's *Response to the Royal Commission on Environmental Pollution's 21st Report*, dated November 2000, in paragraph 76 of which it is held that the British approach to application of the precautionary principle "takes as the starting point Principle 15 of the 1992 Rio Declaration."

[75] Other instruments containing reference to Principle 15 include the 1995 *Global Programme of Action for the Protection of the Marine Environment from Land-Based Activities* (hereinafter also *Land-Based Activities Action Programme*, see paragraph 88(a)); and the 1997 *Programme for the Further Implementation of Agenda 21* (paragraph 14).

Declaration on Sustainable Development notes that sustainable development is presently "widely accepted as a global objective" and has been "amply recognized in various international and national legal instruments, including treaty law and jurisprudence at international and national levels."[76] The Declaration presents a comprehensive definition of the concept, affirming that:

> the objective of sustainable development involves a comprehensive and integrated approach to economic, social and political processes, which aims at the sustainable use of natural resources of the Earth and the protection of the environment on which nature and human life as well as social and economic development depend and which seeks to realize the right of all human beings to an adequate living standard on the basis of their active, free and meaningful participation in development and in the fair distribution of benefits resulting therefrom, with due regard to the needs and interests of future generations.[77]

Two defining features of sustainable development are the goal of meeting the needs of present generations without compromising the ability of future generations to meet theirs and, to quote the International Court of Justice, the "need to reconcile economic development with protection of the environment."[78]

The application of the precautionary principle, with its aim of protecting the environment now and in the future, is widely regarded as a necessary condition for the attainment of sustainable development.[79] As the 1990 *Bergen* and *Bangkok Declarations* state, "in order to achieve sustainable development, policies must be based on the precautionary principle."[80] Or, in the words of Gro Harlem Brundtland: "If we err in our decisions affecting

---

[76] First preambular paragraph.

[77] Thirteenth preambular paragraph.

[78] *Case Concerning the Gabcikovo-Nagymaros Project (Hungary v Slovakia)*, Judgment of 25 September 1997, paragraph 140. On sustainable development generally see, *inter alia*, World Commission on Sustainable Development, 1987, *passim*; Birnie & Boyle, 2002, pp. 84-96; Epiney & Scheyli, 1998, pp. 35-86; Juste Ruiz, 1999, pp. 32-36; Verschuuren, 2003, pp. 13-25; Schrijver, 2003, *passim*; the *Rio Declaration*; and the *ILA Declaration on Sustainable Development*.

[79] See, e.g., the Separate Opinion appended by ICJ Judge Weeramantry to the 1997 *Gabcikovo-Nagymaros* judgment; Kiss, 1996, *passim*; Epiney & Scheyli, 1998; Schrijver, 2003, pp. 71-74; Douma, 2003, pp. 4-5; Marr, 2003, p. 41; Cooney, 2004, p. 2; Hey, 1992, p. 311; Vanderzwaag, 1994, p. 9; Ebbesson, 1996, p. 246; Trouwborst, 2002, pp. 12-13, 111 and 165; paragraph 4.1 of the *ILA Declaration on Sustainable Development*, which affirms that a "precautionary approach is central to sustainable development"; p. 19 of the *Verbatim Record* of the sitting on 25 September 2003 (Schrijver for Malaysia) in the ITLOS *Case Concerning Land Reclamation by Singapore in and around the Straits of Johor (Request for Provisional Measures) (Malaysia v Singapore)*; and paragraph 4 of the UK Government's *A Better Quality of Life: A Strategy for Sustainable Development for the United Kingdom* of May 1999.

[80] Paragraph 7 of the *Bergen Declaration* and paragraph 19 of the *Declaration on Environmentally Sound and Sustainable Development in Asia and the Pacific* (or *Bangkok Declaration*).

the future of our children, let us err on the side of caution."[81] During the negotiations for the 1997 *Watercourses Convention* several states even expressed the opinion that a mere reference to sustainable development automatically entailed the applicability of the precautionary principle within the framework of the agreement.[82] The close ties between the precautionary principle and the concept of sustainable development represent such an uncontentious issue that they need not be discussed in any more detail at this point. For present purposes it suffices to note the existence of this linkage and keep it in mind in the further course of this study.

---

[81] As cited in Gullett, 1997, p. 55.

[82] *Convention on the Law of the Non-Navigational Uses of International Watercourses*; see Canelas de Castro, 1997, p. 29.

Set the foot down with distrust on the crust of the world – it is thin.
– Edna Saint Vincent Millay (1892-1950)

3. FIRST LEG OF THE TRIPOD: THREAT OF ENVIRONMENTAL HARM

3.1. Threat of Environmental Harm

It is deemed appropriate to discuss the element of harm before the other two legs of the tripod, since environmental harm is the fundamental reason for the existence of the precautionary principle in the first place. Its anticipation and prevention has been the very purpose of the principle from the start. As Principle 15 of the *Rio Declaration* starts out: "*In order to protect the environment*, the precautionary approach shall be widely applied by States [..]."[1] Combined with the growing acknowledgment of the limits of scientific understanding and predictive capacity, the realization that much of human-induced damage to the natural environment is severe and can only be undone in the very long term, if at all, has been at the cradle of the precautionary principle and has boosted its subsequent proliferation in environmental policy and law.[2] The seeds for this proliferation were sown at the 1972 UN Conference on the Human Environment in Stockholm, where the host of participating states acknowledged that "[t]hrough ignorance or indifference we can do massive and irreversible harm to the earthly environment on which our life and well-being depend."[3] As regards more express precaution, according to the 1988 *Declaration on the Protection of the Marine Environment of the Baltic Sea Area*, the rationale for taking action in advance of the availability of full scientific proof of harmful effects was the conviction "that damage to the marine environment can be irreversible or remediable only in a long term perspective and at considerable

[1] Italics added.

[2] As Gullett, 1997, puts it at p. 64, the principle is "the foremost example of legal recognition of the aggregate nature of environmental harm and the potential for harm to be irreparable." See also Rose & Paleokrassis, 1996, p. 158, defining the awareness of the vulnerability of the environment and the scarcity of resources as part and parcel of the precautionary principle; and Hey, 1992, p. 308.

[3] Sixth preambular paragraph of the 1972 *Declaration of the UN Conference on the Human Environment* (*Stockholm Declaration*). Principle 6 of the Declaration calls for control of environmental pollution "in order to ensure that serious or irreversible damage is not inflicted upon ecosystems."

expense."[4] The following statement made by the government of Canada in 1990 says it all:

> Human actions can wreak serious, irreversible damage on the environment. Yet in deciding on an action, we rarely know all its environmental ramifications. Caution is therefore appropriate: we must be prepared to give nature the benefit of the doubt.[5]

A sheer endless amount of real-life examples can be produced of serious, persistent and irreversible environmental harm sprouting from a lack of foresight and precaution. In a 2001 report the European Environment Agency, for instance, has mapped the adverse results of a not sufficiently precautionary attitude in the previous century in respect of, *inter alia*, fisheries, radioactivity, acid rain, the ozone layer, and persistent organic pollutants such as dichlorodiphenyl trichloroethane (DDT), polychlorinated biphenyls (PCBs) and tributyltin (TBT).[6] Although in many cases it may be too late, even for time, to cure the damage done, it is never too late to learn. The rise of the precautionary principle in international law that took place during the last two decades is testimony of this. Better late than never.

At present, the *raison d'être* of the principle remains as valid as ever.[7] Two prominent instances of the continual need for precaution are the environmental risks associated with global climate change and genetic modification. Schellnhuber has expressed the potentially disastrous

---

[4] Preamble, paragraph 8; hereinafter also *Baltic Sea Declaration*. Similarly, paragraph 17.22 of *Agenda 21* advocates precaution to avoid degradation of the marine environment and "reduce the risk of long-term or irreversible effects upon it."

[5] Government of Canada, *Green Plan*, 1990, cited from the section headed "Respect for Nature". See VanderZwaag, 1994. Likewise, the *Massachusetts Precautionary Principle Act* prescribes the application of the precautionary principle "in order to prevent threats of serious or irreversible damage to the environment." Commonwealth of Massachusetts, House Bill No. 3140 of 1997; see Tickner *et al.*, 2000, p. 20.

[6] See European Environment Agency, 2001.

[7] As Claude Martin, Director General of the World Wildlife Fund (WWF) sums up just some of the most recent environmental threats: "The past decade has witnessed fires on an unprecedented scale in the tropical forests of Brazil and Indonesia, coral bleaching that has left vast areas of reef in the Caribbean, Indian and Pacific Oceans as ghosts of their former selves, the collapse of commercially valuable fish stocks in the Atlantic, the ecological devastation of the Black Sea, the Aral Sea, and Lake Chad, and the continual loss of precious wetland and freshwater ecosystems around the world." Foreword of World Wildlife Fund, 2002. The long-term nature of many environmental problems is illustrated with some examples by Bell, 2002, at p. 2: "Scientific evidence now confirms the decades-old prediction that increased levels of carbon dioxide and other greenhouse gases in the atmosphere have led to global warming. These effects will persist for years even if industrialized nations make dramatic reductions in the release of greenhouse gasses immediately. Toxic chemicals known as persistent organic pollutants (POPs) do not degrade after being released into the environment but instead persist and accumulate in the bodies of living creatures. The negative externalities associated with current and past industrial practices impact every human being alive today and will continue to impose costs for generations to come."

consequences for the future of irresponsible anthropogenic action today as follows: "Human interference with the ecosphere may provoke the perhaps irreversible transgression of critical thresholds, bringing about qualitatively different environmental conditions on a large scale."[8] Similar concerns were voiced by President Mbeki of South Africa when he opened the 2002 Johannesburg Summit: "All of us agree that unsustainable patterns of production and consumption are creating an environmental disaster that threatens both life in general, and human life in particular."[9] Many world leaders affirmed this assessment when addressing the conference.[10]

In this regard, one writer has asserted that "[e]nvironmental risks are uniquely more pervasive and dangerous than other risks because the damage flowing from taking them is irreparable, interminable, and not compensable."[11] Although environmental harm is indeed often irreversible, this is certainly and fortunately not always the case, in the sense that scientists and decision-makers distinguish between different types and levels of harm, as shall be illustrated below. Another statement by the quoted author, however, accurately summarizes the discussion of the current paragraph so far: "The assumption that there are certain risks relating to environmental quality, which are simply intolerable, is reflected in the precautionary principle."[12]

Types and Levels of Environmental Harm

At this point, a quick word on terminology is in place. First of all, it will be clear that 'harm' and 'damage' must be told apart from mere 'change'.[13] Like the

---

[8] Schellnhuber, 1999, p. C23. The ecosphere is the aggregate complex of geosphere and biosphere, which together represent the earth in its entirety. The geosphere is composed of those parts of the earth which do not contain life (i.e. part of the atmosphere, part of the hydrosphere and the larger part of the lithosphere); the biosphere is the layer of only a few kilometers of thickness, cutting through the atmosphere, hydrosphere and lithosphere, in which living organisms can be found. See Schellnhuber, p. C20; Kloeg, 1991, pp. 51, 130. See also Tennekes, 2001, p. 93.

[9] *Statement by Thabo Mbeki, President of the Republic of South Africa, at the Opening of the World Summit on Sustainable Development*, Johannesburg, 26 August 2002.

[10] "Notre maison brûle et nous regardons ailleurs," said President Chirac of France on 2 September 2002 in his WSSD statement, which was perhaps the most dramatic of them all. "La nature, mutilée, surexploitée, ne parvient plus à se reconstituer et nous refusons de l'admettre. [..] La terre et l'humanité sont en péril et nous en sommes tous responsables. Il est temps d'ouvrir les yeux. Sur tous les continents, les signaux d'allerte s'allument."

[11] Gray, 2000, p. 98.

[12] *Ibid.* As phrased alternatively by Bell, 2002, p. 4: "The shift to prevention embodied in the precautionary principle is a necessary and timely response to the increasingly severe environmental hazards that we collectively face. When the effects of industrial production were confined to a local area and a short time horizon, a 'wait and see' attitude towards externalities might have been justified." See also Rose & Paleokrassis, 1996, p. 158; Ponce Nava, 1993, p. 494.

[13] Morris, 2000(b), p. 14.

concept of 'risk' the former, which are dictionary synonyms, have a distinctly negative connotation and, in both common and legal speech, equal 'injury' or 'loss'.[14] Conversely, the word 'change' as such is value-neutral.[15] At a 2005 meeting of the *Biodiversity Convention*'s 'Group of Legal and Technical Experts on Liability and Redress' it was noted that "mere change in the state of biological diversity might not necessarily constitute damage."[16] To constitute damage, the change had to "result in an adverse or negative effect."[17] In short, harm is negative change. In environmental practice, however, the distinction between positive or neutral change and harmful change is not always as easy to make as in theory. Take, for instance, the many places where controlled hunting has been introduced as a tool for the management of wildlife populations in areas where natural predators have disappeared. That, on balance, such management brings about change in the ecosystems concerned cannot be disputed. The opinions of commentators tend to vary considerably, however, when it comes to the characterization of such impact as either positive, neutral or negative.[18] This classification problem will be dealt with to some greater extent below.[19] For now it suffices to stress the obvious fact that the precautionary principle is not intended to prevent environmental *change*, but only environmental *harm*.[20]

Although subtle differences could perhaps be made in the interpretation of the words 'harm', 'damage', 'injury' and 'loss', in international practice they are often used as synonyms.[21] Other variations that can be encountered in legal and policy instruments include "environmental

---

[14] According to the *Concise Oxford Dictionary*, "damage" is a "[l]oss of what is desirable [..]; injury impairing value or usefulness", with "harm" as its equivalent. Sykes, 1976, pp. 256 and 490. See also Klinke & Renn, 1999, p. 11.

[15] "Change" simply means "becoming different". *Ibid.*, p. 165.

[16] Paragraph 19 of *UN Doc.* UNEP/CBD/COP/8/27/Add.3 of 18 October 2005.

[17] *Ibid.*

[18] See, e.g., Gallacher, 1990, *passim.*

[19] See *infra* paragraph 5.3.

[20] This is expressly stated in, e.g., Article 23(2) of the 2004 *ILA Berlin Rules on Water Resources*; and Article 4(3) of 1997 *Lei no. 20/97* of Mozambique (reproduced at: http://faolex.fao.org/docs/texts/moz15370.doc). See also Freestone, 1999, p. 137.

[21] Lefeber, 1996, at p. 16 points out that "harm" may be used as a physical concept, "damage" as a financial concept and "injury" (or "loss") as a legal one. Some type of distinction would, at first sight, also seem to be suggested by the reference to "damage *or* harmful effects" that occurs in paragraph XVI of the 1987 *Declaration of the Second International Conference on the Protection of the North Sea* and is repeated in the 1989 *Declaration of the Nordic Council's International Conference on Pollution of the Seas* (italics added). This suggestion appears to be negated, however, by the sole use of "damaging effects" in the same precautionary context in the preamble of the former instrument, the similar use of "damaging impacts" in the preamble of the subsequent *Declaration of the Third International Conference on the Protection of the North Sea* of 1990 and the obvious coordinative employment of "damage" and "harmful effects" in preambular paragraph A.7 of the 1984 *Declaration of the First International Conference on the Protection of the North Sea.*

degradation",[22] "adverse impact",[23] and the like. In this study all these equivalents of harm are used interchangeably. A theoretical distinction can be maintained between adverse *effects*, or impacts, and the actual environmental *harm* these provoke. There is, however, not usually any practical difference between the *prevention* or abatement of harmful effects and the prevention or abatement of harm, which circumstance is deemed sufficient to justify their synonymous use in the present context. It ought to be borne in mind that in international environmental law the notion of harm is often taken to extend beyond the loss of resources or amenities of obvious worth – economic or otherwise – to humanity, so as to encompass damage to nature as such.[24] The 'intrinsic value'[25] of natural ecosystems is professed, *inter alia*, in the 1982 *World Charter for Nature* and the 1992 *Biodiversity Convention*.[26] The former, for example, states that "[e]very form of life is unique, warranting respect regardless of its worth to man." This feature is prominent in the precautionary principle itself, clearly stressing the need for environmental preservation in its own right.[27]

A useful, albeit somewhat arbitrary classification of threats of environmental harm is the one that focusses on their cause and distinguishes between (1) natural risks, (2) technological or cultural risks, and (3) mixed or induced risks.[28] This classification reflects the degree of causality corresponding to each of the two interacting systems involved: the natural and the human. Natural risks are those that are caused primarily by natural processes not influenced to any significant degree by human activities. Typical instances are the threats posed by volcano eruptions and earthquakes. Technological or cultural risks are found on the other side of the scale; they are the direct result of human action. Examples include air, water and soil pollution with toxic and radioactive substances, the excessive exploitation of wildlife, and the genetic modification of living organisms. This category of risk should not be confused with the technical *approach* to risk described above. Finally, when processes originally belonging to the category of natural risks, such as hurricanes, inundations, soil erosion, forest fires, and various biological processes, are

---

[22] See, e.g., paragraph 7 of the 1990 *Bergen Declaration*.

[23] E.g., paragraph 3 of section 2.4 of the 1995 *Pan-European Biological and Landscape Diversity Strategy*.

[24] See, e.g., Birnie & Boyle, 2002, p. 122.

[25] According to Reid *et al.*, 2005, p. v, intrinsic value is "the value of something in and for itself, irrespective of its utility for someone else." See also, e.g., Beeckman, 1996, pp. 460-461.

[26] Third preambular paragraph of the *World Charter for Nature*; first preambular paragraph of the *Biodiversity Convention*. Other instances are the third preambular paragraph of the 1979 *Berne Convention*; Article 3 of the 1991 *Protocol on Environmental Protection* to the 1959 *Antarctic Treaty*; and Article 2 of the 1995 *Draft International Covenant on Environment and Development* of the International Union for the Conservation of Nature.

[27] Trouwborst, 2002, p. 12; Canelas de Castro, 1999, p. 163.

[28] See Pascual Trillo, 2000, pp. 143-152.

induced or enhanced by human activities, they are called mixed or induced risks. The interaction between natural and human causes here is very close. Prominent examples are mudslides provoked by deforestation, plagues caused by introduced alien species or enhanced through increased uniformity of agricultural crops, and the numerous predicted effects of global climate change. As with all classifications executed on a sliding scale on which it is, moreover, difficult to simplify relevant factors, all kinds of intermediate situations can be imagined.[29]

Even though they may be the agent of serious and irreversible environmental harm, the precautionary principle will not always readily apply to risks of the first category, since natural risks frequently just cannot be prevented. For instance, the technological capacity to prevent environmental damage ensuing from asteroid impact, volcanic eruptions, earthquakes and naturally occurring wildfires, is very limited. Besides, from an ecological point of view, it is often not desirable to attempt such prevention in the first place. It is important to realize that, nevertheless, influential articulations of the precautionary principle such as Principle 15 of the *Rio Declaration* do not *prima facie* exclude this class of threats from their scope of application.

Anyhow, the relative importance of natural risks has greatly diminished over the centuries. Intensive human interaction with the natural environment has altered geo-ecological systems to such an extent that it is becoming increasingly difficult to find dangers of a purely natural origin.[30] These have to be looked for in outer space and in the most profound structure of the earth, that is, in the realm of seismic and volcanic activity, where the influence of mankind is (still?) negligible or nonexistent.[31] The same interaction causes the effects of technological risks to be augmented through the reaction they provoke in natural systems, thus giving rise to mixed risks. For instance, the overexploitation of natural ecosystems, itself a 'technological' risk, often causes the disappearance of the most specialized species such as top predators first, reducing biological diversity. The ecological niches thus vacated greatly benefit more opportunistic and former prey species – a recipe for plagues. Another example of an induced biological risk is the complicated theme of new biotechnology and genetically modified organisms (GMOs).[32] Mixed or

[29] *Ibid.*, pp. 143-145, 150.

[30] For instance, the human species is now considered the primary agent responsible for the modification of the world's terrestrial relief, more influential than the forces of wind, water, temperature and vegetation: "cuando se analizan los movimientos de tierras, el asfaltado y cementado de espacios, el dinamitado de relieves, el encauzamiento de ríos y las alteraciones de la cubierta vegetal originados por la tecnología humana, es posible entender esa afirmación." *Ibid.*, p. 150.

[31] *Ibid.*, p. 146.

[32] *Ibid.*, pp. 151-152.

induced risks have thus come to represent the host of current threats to the environment. In fact, the major environmental problems of today, the whole of which is ofttimes referred to as the global environmental crisis, are predominantly made up of this class of hazards. Global warming, chain extinctions of species, the worldwide alteration of biological and chemical cycles, they all concern natural patterns disrupted on account of disproportionate human interference.[33] The relevance of the precautionary principle is likely to be greatest with respect to technological and mixed risks, where the human factor can be tentatively discerned as (part of) the cause – although, as pointed out above, for the present there is no reason to assume that the principle cannot apply to natural risks as well.

The next question is whether, besides all *types* of environmental harm as regards its cause, the scope of the precautionary principle as it stands under customary international law also extends to cover all *levels* of environmental harm. One will remember the various minimum thresholds of damage included in several definitions discussed in the last paragraph of the previous chapter. These thresholds have apparently been introduced with a view to excluding from the reach of the principle those levels of harm that do not meet the appropriate standards of 'significant', 'serious' or 'irreversible'. The apparent reason for doing so lies in the fact that the taking of environmental risks by human society can never be banned completely given that, by definition, all human behaviour has some impact on the environment. As long as people walk the face of the earth, it will not be possible to prevent all levels of anthropogenic environmental damage, which makes it imperative to draw a line somewhere. Failure to recognize this "introduces a utopian element into the precautionary principle, which cannot be sustained."[34]

There are, however, also certain drawbacks inherent in the use of thresholds of harm. The numerous cases in the past wherein a lack of precautionary action in the face of uncertain threats resulted in serious and irreversible damage, point out that estimates of the gravity of expected environmental harm can hardly be conservative enough.[35] This casts some

---

[33] *Ibid.*, p. 149.

[34] Cameron *et al.*, 1998, p. 100. Similarly, Lyster, 1997, pp. 394-396; Holm & Harris, 1999; Rogers, 2001, p. 4; Pieterman & Hanekamp, 2002, p. viii. The fact that one cannot exclude every degree of danger can be illustrated with a parallel example from the sphere of human health risks: "Just as most accidents occur in or near home [..] and most foods contain carcinogens [..], as the axiom of connectedness suggests, so there is some degree of danger getting out of bed or taking a shower or eating a meal or walking across the street; or, need I say, in making love as well as war. Risking and living are inseparable (hospitals make people sick, exercise can hurt you, herb tea is laden with carcinogens); even breathing, according to a prominent theory in which cancer is caused by oxygen radicals created through the burning of fat, can kill." Wildavsky, 2000, p. 42, footnotes omitted.

[35] Lambers, 2000, p. 180.

doubt on the assumption that the application of the precautionary principle ought to be contingent upon any concrete condition of gravity. The European Environment Bureau, for instance, has challenged the utility of a threshold of 'serious or irreversible' harm precisely because regularly "the extent and seriousness of damage is uncertain, especially in a long-term perspective."[36] It has moreover been argued that on occasion such qualification could be viewed as offering a tempting escape clause from precautionary obligations, thus undermining the principle's very goal.[37] For present purposes it is not necessary, however, to choose sides in this debate on the advantages and disadvantages of threshold clauses, as this study is intended to figure out what the current state of the law is in this regard, and not so much to opine on whether that state of the law is desirable.

Hence, it must be asked whether indeed the application of the precautionary principle under customary international law is confined to hazards which transgress or are capable of transgressing a minimum threshold of environmental harm and, if so, what particular threshold(s) then trigger(s) the principle to have legal consequence.

3.2. Threshold of 'Significant' Harm

Clauses placing an emphasis on the required amount of environmental harm have quite a history in international law. One of the most fundamental rules of international environmental law is the customary duty of states to "ensure that activities within their jurisdiction or control do not cause damage to the environment of other States or of areas beyond the limits of national jurisdiction," laid down, *inter alia*, in Principle 21 of the 1972 *Stockholm Declaration*[38] and affirmed in numerous other instruments and judicial decisions, including Principle 2 of the *Rio Declaration*. Even though Principle 21 and Principle 2 themselves do not indicate it, this obligation is widely understood as not applying to risks of minor or insignificant transboundary harm.[39] In other words, there is some standard of gravity to be met for the duty to be triggered. Adjectives that have been proposed and used for qualification of the norm of Principle 21 are 'appreciable', 'significant', 'substantial' and 'serious', although it seems that 'significant' is the predominant

---

[36] European Environment Bureau, 1999, paragraph 3.2

[37] Lambers, 2000, p. 180.

[38] *Declaration of the UN Conference on the Human Environment.*

[39] For an overview and a discussion of pertinent sources, see Lefeber, 1996, pp. 24-25, 86-88; also Ebbesson, 1996, pp. 174-176. With an eye on the absence of threshold clauses in Principles 21 and 2, however, Birnie & Boyle, 2002, at p. 123, are more hesitant in respect of this proposition.

one.[40] In the words of the ILC, duties of transboundary harm prevention are thus "not only reasonable but also sufficiently limited so as not to impose such obligations in respect of virtually any activity."[41] The question now is how this compares with state practice on the precautionary principle.

Formulations Lacking a Threshold of Harm

Interestingly, there is a substantial number of international documents which, like Principle 21 and Principle 2, omit any threshold of harm whatsoever in their definitions of the precautionary principle. The text of the 1988 *Baltic Sea Declaration*, for instance, applies the principle widely to "harmful effects".[42] In this case, where the seriousness and irreversibility of environmental damage clearly served, as has just been discussed, as an important impetus for adopting the precautionary principle, it is not a *condition* for its application. Similarly, the Nordic Council's 1989 *Declaration on Pollution of the Seas* calls for precaution "where there is reason to believe that damage or harmful effects are likely to be caused." The precautionary principle as proclaimed in the *Second North Sea Declaration* of 1987[43], PARCOM's 1989 *Recommendation 89/1 on the Principle of Precautionary Action*[44] and the 1991 HELCOM *Recommendation 12/3*,[45] is aimed at the prevention of "certain damage or harmful effects on the living resources of the sea." According to the 1991 *Bamako Convention*, implementation of the precautionary principle entails preventing emissions of substances which "may cause harm to humans or the environment".[46] The *London Dumping Convention*'s[47] 1991 *Resolution LDC 44/14*[48] and its 1996 *Protocol*[49] both contain a formulation of the principle focussed on "substances or energy [..] likely to cause harm." Likewise, three instruments adopted in 1992, namely HELCOM *Recommendation 13/6*,[50] the new *Convention on the Protection of the Marine Environment of the Baltic Sea*

---

[40] Lefeber, 1996, pp. 16-17.

[41] International Law Commission, 2001, commentary on Article 2(a) of the *Draft Articles on Harm Prevention*, paragraph 2.

[42] See the eighth preambular paragraph.

[43] Paragraph XVI.

[44] PARCOM stands for the (Paris) Commission established under the late 1974 *Convention for the Prevention of Marine Pollution from Land-Based Sources.*

[45] Paragraph 1; HELCOM (Helsinki Commission) is the Baltic Marine Environment Protection Commission established under the 1974/1992 *Convention on the Protection of the Marine Environment of the Baltic Sea Area.*

[46] *Convention on the Ban of Import into Africa and the Control of Transboundary Movement and Management of Hazardous Wastes within Africa*, Article 3(f).

[47] 1972 *Convention for the Prevention of Marine Pollution by Dumping of Wastes and Other Matter.*

[48] *Resolution LDC 44/14 on the Application of the Precautionary Approach to Environmental Protection within the Framework of the London Dumping Convention* of 30 December 1991.

[49] See Article 3(1).

[50] See paragraph 1(3).

Area[51] and the *Convention for the Protection of the Marine Environment of the North-East Atlantic* (*OSPAR Convention*),[52] urge preventive action when there is reason to assume that substances or energy released into the environment may cause "hazards to human health, harm living resources and marine ecosystems, damage amenities" or interfere with other uses of the sea. The 1992 *Central American Hazardous Wastes Agreement* also applies the precautionary principle to "sustancias que podrían causar daño a los seres humanos o al medio ambiente."[53] The definition of the principle in the 1995 *Pan-European Biological and Landscape Diversity Strategy* contains unqualified reference to the "potentially adverse impact of activities on biological and landscape diversity."[54] As a final example, the precautionary principle as incorporated in the *Biosafety Protocol* is concerned with "potential adverse effects."[55]

Instances of definitions lacking a particular minimum standard of harm abound in European Union and national legal and policy instruments as well. E.g., a 1991 EU directive on urban waste water allows deviation from the stringent treatment procedure it prescribes only when there is evidence that discharges "will not adversely affect the environment."[56] According to the United States Gilchrest-Farr *Fisheries Recovery Act*, the precautionary approach applies "in *any case* in which information is absent [..] as to *the effects*" of fisheries on marine life.[57] The definition of the precautionary principle used by the Australian Commonwealth Environmental Protection Agency refers merely to "environmental damage".[58] Some of the core definitions of the principle expressed by commentators do not embody thresholds of harm either.[59]

None of the instruments just quoted – and many more could be named – *prima facie* require potential environmental damage to pass some kind of *de minimis* test for the precautionary principle to apply. This certainly implies that their drafters have meant for the precautionary principle's scope

---

51 Article 3(2).

52 Article 2(2)(a).

53 Translation: "substances that could cause harm to human beings or to the environment." *Regional Agreement on the Transboundary Movement of Hazardous Wastes*, Article 3(3).

54 Paragraph 3 of Section 2.4.

55 Articles 10(6) and 11(8). Marr, 2003, p. 106 has also noted this "low triggering threshold."

56 *Directive 91/271*, Article 6(2).

57 *HR Rep.*, No. 4046, as quoted in Thomas & Grader, 2000. Italics added.

58 See Christie, 1993, p. 482.

59 Already quoted *supra* were the 1998 *Wingspread Statement*, stating the application of the precautionary principle to "threats of harm to the environment or human health" (see Ashford *et al.*, 1998), and Ebbesson, 1996, at p. 119, speaking of "adverse environmental interferences." The interpretation of Lemons *et al.*, 1997, at p. 210, refers to "good reason to expect risk or harm to environmental or human health." Canelas de Castro, 1999, p. 199, in note 155 refers to the prevention of "environmental degradation".

of application to be as broad as possible, and not to be limited to instances of very serious harm only. What is more, a strict, literal reading of the above texts appears to allow for no other conclusion than that under the regimes concerned the precautionary principle requires *all* potential damage to the environment, however insignificant, to be forestalled or reduced.[60] At a minimum, this would seem to cast some doubt on the generally assumed existence of some absolute threshold(s) that must be crossed for the (customary) precautionary principle to come into play.

'Significant' Harm as a Threshold

All the same, no matter how enticing it may appear to some, this assumption, as has been stressed above, represents a utopian scheme. There can be no absolute prevention of environmental harm. Even in the extremely hypothetical case that we would all agree to stop breathing as of now, anthropogenic effects on the environment may well persist for much longer than one might think.[61] It is hardly tenable, therefore, to argue that it must have been the serious intention of the drafters of the above formulations to have the precautionary principle require action to counter each and every minor environmental impact. Instead, there is a need to distinguish between harm that embodies at least some degree of significance and harm that does not. The provisions involved thus show a strong parallel with Principle 21 of the *Stockholm Declaration*, and Principle 2 of the *Rio Declaration,* which, as pointed out *supra*, do not specify this need either.

The reality of the distinction just mentioned is reflected in a provision of the 1995 *Land-Based Activities Action Programme* applying the precautionary principle to radioactive waste storage by outlawing such storage near the coastal and marine environment unless the absence of any "unacceptable risk" is demonstrated, thus implying the existence also of risks that *are* acceptable.[62] Another germane paragraph of the same document, concerned with persistent organic pollutants, suggests that priority ought to be given to phasing out chemicals that pose "unreasonable and otherwise

---

[60] This may seem different in a case such as the *Second North Sea Declaration,* since its preamble states that the precautionary principle was adopted to protect the marine environment from the "most dangerous", as opposed to all, substances. However, according to the same Declaration the likelihood of merely "certain damage or harmful effects" brought about by these contaminants suffices to trigger the principle. Strictly speaking, it is not required that this harm be significant or serious. The same considerations apply to PARCOM *Recommendation 89/1.*

[61] For the sake of the exercise, merely consider the impact of this imaginary agreement itself, were it to be executed. Picture the short and long-term impacts of abandoned nuclear installations, oil tankers adrift at sea, ceased maintenance of toxic waste storage facilities, interrupted extermination programmes of harmful alien species, etcetera.

[62] Paragraph 111(a).

unmanageable risks."[63] It should be kept in mind, however, that the level of potential harm is most likely not the sole factor in the determination of the acceptability, reasonableness or manageability of the *risks* mentioned here, since the probability of the harm's materialization may also be expected to play a part.

Assumably, then, a minimum threshold of 'significance' may be read between the lines of those definitions that are silent in this respect. The application of the precautionary principle would thus be conditional on the crossing of this threshold. In an explicit manner, the term 'significant' itself makes up the required standard of harm in quite a few intergovernmental precautionary definitions. In 1991 the Council of the Organization for Economic Cooperation and Development (OECD) issued a recommendation stating that "the absence of complete information should not preclude precautionary action to mitigate the risk of *significant* harm to the environment."[64] In the framework of trilateral cooperation for the protection of the Wadden Sea, Denmark, Germany and the Netherlands have repeatedly agreed that the precautionary principle requires avoiding activities "which are assumed to have *significant* damaging impact on the environment."[65] The scope of the principle as embedded in the 1992 *Convention on the Protection and Use of Transboundary Watercourses and International Lakes* is restricted to the avoidance of emissions that may have a "*significant* adverse effect on the environment [..] within an area under the jurisdiction of another Party."[66] Similar thresholds can be encountered in the Convention's 1999 *Protocol on Water and Health*,[67] as well as in the 1994 twin agreements on the protection of the Meuse and Scheldt.[68]

Finally, the 1992 *Biodiversity Convention* recommends precautionary measures "where there is a threat of *significant* reduction or loss of biological diversity."[69] This definition is reiterated in the 1993 *General Guidelines for the*

---

[63] Paragraph 104(b)(i).

[64] *Council Recommendation C(90)164 on Integrated Pollution Prevention and Control*; author's emphasis.

[65] Paragraph 3 of the 1991 *Ministerial Declaration of the Sixth Trilateral Governmental Conference on the Protection of the Wadden Sea (Trilateral Wadden Sea Declaration)*; paragraph 8 of the 1997 *Trilateral Wadden Sea Plan*. Author's emphasis.

[66] Hereinafter also *Helsinki Watercourses Convention*, see Articles 2(5)(a) and 1(2); author's emphasis. Trouwborst, 2002, at pp. 94-95, apparently missed the link between these two provisions when (mistakingly) hinting at a possible discrepancy of thresholds between the 1994 agreements for the protection of the Meuse and Scheldt rivers (see below) and the *Helsinki Watercourses Convention*.

[67] Articles 2(1) and 2(7).

[68] See the respective Articles 3(2)(a) of the *Convention on the Protection of the Meuse* and the *Convention on the Protection of the Scheldt*.

[69] Preamble, paragraph 9. Emphasis added.

Conservation of the Biodiversity of European Forests[70] and the *Barcelona Convention*'s 1995 *Protocol Concerning Specially Protected Areas and Biological Diversity in the Mediterranean.*[71] That, at least in the case of the *Biodiversity Convention*, the qualification has been consciously included can be inferred from the fact that the fifth draft of the Convention did not yet feature it.[72] The draft provisions in question recognized the need to "anticipate, prevent and attack the causes of reduction or loss of biodiversity at source" and stipulated that uncertainty ought not to be used as a reason for postponing action to avoid or minimize "a threat to biodiversity", without any mention of significance.[73]

The qualification "significant" also forms part of the precautionary principle as laid down in the 1995 *Draft International Covenant on Environment and Development* of the International Union for the Conservation of Nature (IUCN) and the International Council of Environmental Law.[74] To offer some examples from the domestic level, Canadian provincial legislation obliges the Ontario Ministry of Environment to exercise a precautionary approach in decision-making that might *significantly* affect the environment,[75] whereas comparable duties can be encountered in the official Dutch planning guidelines for the Wadden Sea[76] and in the environmental laws of Mozambique[77] and Eritrea.[78] As for doctrine, according to the *Declaration on Principles of International Law in the Field of Sustainable Development* that was adopted by the International Law Association (ILA) at its 2002 Conference in New Delhi, a precautionary approach entails avoiding "human activity which may cause *significant* harm to human health, natural resources or ecosystems."[79] The scope of the precautionary principle as defined in the *Berlin Rules on Water Resources*, adopted by the ILA in 2004, is also limited to cases where there is a risk of "significant adverse effect" on the aquatic environment.[80] Freestone

---

[70] Preamble, paragraph F.

[71] Hereinafter also *Mediterranean SPA and Biodiversity Protocol*, see preambular paragraph 5.

[72] Boyle, 1996, p. 37.

[73] Draft Article 3(5)-(6), as quoted in Boyle, *ibid.*

[74] Hereinafter also *Draft Covenant*. Article 7 declares the principle's application to "potentially significant or irreversible harm to the environment."

[75] *An Act Respecting Environmental Rights in Ontario*, S.O. 1993, c-28, section 11 (as amended); as cited in Abouchar, 2002, p. 104.

[76] *Tweede Planologische Kernbeslissing (PKB) Waddenzee* of 1994, paragraph 2.3, which speaks of significant or important ("belangrijke") adverse consequences.

[77] Article 4(3) of 1997 *Lei no. 20/97*, reproduced at http://faolex.fao.org/docs/texts/moz15370.doc: "impactos ambientais negativos significativos ou irreversiveis".

[78] Article 17(b) of the *Environment Proclamation No. 1996*, as cited in Marr, 2003, p. 86: "potentially significant or irreversible harm".

[79] *ILA Declaration on Sustainable Development*, paragraph 4.1.

[80] Article 23(2).

likewise interprets the principle as covering "activities which are likely to have "significant negative impacts on the environment."[81]

Evidently, for present purposes 'significant' is significant. More specifically, in view of the above it appears safe to conclude that under customary international law the precautionary principle is of relevance only when feared harm is, at a minimum, significant. The other way round, it cannot be assumed that the principle comes into play when the projected harm is insignificant. (See Figure 1.)

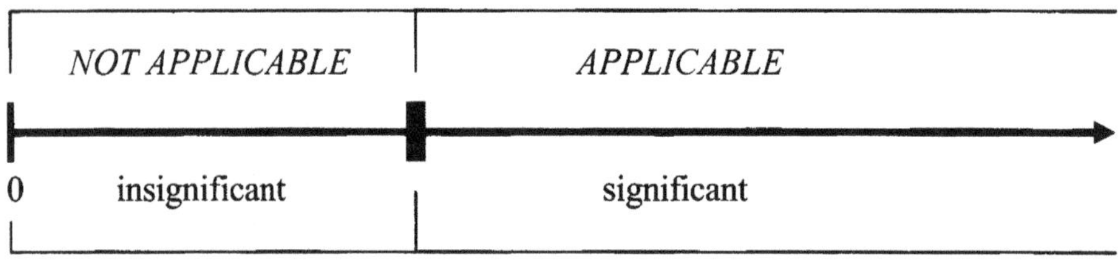

Figure 1. Scale of gravity of harm with the threshold of 'significant'. The arrowheaded axis represents the scale of gravity. The boldest printed bar is the minimum threshold of significance. Relevant qualifications of harm are indicated below the axis, and corresponding legal effects above it.

The Meaning of the Term 'Significant'

But what does 'significant' harm mean? By way of a general starting point, dictionary definition presents significant as "not insignificant or negligible."[82] Hence the threshold of "non-negligible harm" as used by Cameron *cum suis* in their summary definition of the precautionary principle.[83] Similarly, Lefeber explains that the standard of significance is met when harm is "not minor, i.e. if it is not trivial or insignificant."[84] Kiss and Shelton add that normally the term significant would rule out "minor incidents causing minimal damage."[85] Others locate it in between "serious" and "minor trouble to be tolerated."[86] In the text of the 1978 *Shared Resources Principles* of the United Nations Environment Programme (UNEP) the expression "significantly affect"

[81] Freestone, 1999, p. 137.
[82] *Concise Oxford Dictionary*, see Sykes, 1976, p. 1062.
[83] Cameron & Abouchar, 1996, p. 45; see also Cameron *et al.*, 1998, p. 99.
[84] Lefeber, 1996, p. 88.
[85] Kiss & Shelton, 2000, p. 269.
[86] See Beeckman, 1996, pp. 470-471, and the sources named there.

is defined as "any appreciable effects on a shared natural resource and excludes '*de minimis*' effects."[87]

The International Law Commission has provided some additional clues as to the meaning of 'significant' within the framework of international environmental law. The commentary to the 1994 ILC *Draft Articles on the Law of the Non-Navigational Uses of International Watercourses* notes that in order to pass for significant, harm must be "appreciable" and "tangible", as opposed to "trivial".[88] It need not, however, amount to the level of being "substantial".[89] As the ILC comments:

> A requirement that a State's use must be substantially affected before it would be entitled to participate in consultations and negotiations [as regards agreements that may affect its use of a watercourse] would impose too heavy a burden upon the third State. [..] That State should be required to establish only that its use may be affected to a significant extent.[90]

More in particular, according to the commentary the term significant is "intended to require that the effect is one that can be established by objective evidence (provided the evidence can be secured)."[91] An instance given by the ILC is pollution changing the chemical or thermical condition of river water.[92] Significant harm is also the standard used in the multilateral convention that was adopted on the basis of the ILC *Draft Articles* in the UN General Assembly in 1997.[93] In line with its predecessor, the commentary to this 1997 *Watercourses Convention* provides that harm need not be substantial but must be "more than trivial" for it to qualify as significant.[94]

The more recent work of the International Law Commission on the prevention of transboundary harm from hazardous activities is rather consistent with these previous comments. The 2001 *Draft Articles on Harm Prevention* employ a threshold of significant transboundary harm, which is described as "real" and measurable, but drawn lower than "substantial" or "serious" harm:

---

[87] *Principles on Conservation and Harmonious Utilization of Natural Resources Shared by Two or More States*, see the provision named "Definition" following the principles themselves.

[88] International Law Commission, 1994; see the commentary to Article 3, paragraphs 13-15.

[89] *Ibid.*, paragraph 15. See also the commentary to Article 4, paragraph 7.

[90] Commentary to Article 4, paragraph 7. This relatively lenient threshold of harm and the use of the word "may" give a distinctly precautionary ring to these remarks.

[91] Commentary to Article 3, paragraph 14. The bracketed phrase adds even more to the precautionary nature of the Commission's stance.

[92] *Ibid.*

[93] *Convention on the Law of the Non-Navigational Uses of International Watercourses*; also known as the 1997 *Watercourses Convention*.

[94] See Birnie & Boyle, 2002, p. 123.

> It is to be understood that *'significant' is something more than 'detectable' but need not be at the level of 'serious' or 'substantial'*. The harm must lead to a real detrimental effect on matters such as, for example, human health, industry, property, environment or agriculture in other States. Such detrimental effects must be susceptible of being measured by factual and objective standards.[95]

The various guidelines on the threshold of 'significant' that have passed in review here are foremostly concerned with duties of transboundary harm prevention. There is little to suggest, however, that this renders them meaningless for the interpretation of the same term as it is used to qualify the precautionary principle. Indeed, they clarify that in the context of precaution, what is sought to be avoided is environmental harm that, *if and when it comes about*, is not minor or trivial, but tangible, appreciable and measurable. Besides, although diverging opinions have occasionally been expressed, it seems to be generally understood that 'significant' embodies a lower threshold than 'substantial' or 'serious'.[96]

The extent to which this word juggle has actual consequences for the freedom of states in judging whether the expected environmental effects of a given project or activity are significant, and therefore the extent to which the applicability of the precautionary principle as a matter of international custom is a discretionary affair, remains to be discussed in another paragraph below, dealing with the determination of when thresholds are crossed.[97] One indicator, in any case, appears rather obvious, namely the breach of substantive norms of public international law, such as internationally agreed quality standards for river water or air purity, or commitments regarding the conservation of particular populations of wildlife. To maintain that environmental effects which transgress such norms can be dismissed as insignificant is evidently a mission impossible.

---

[95] International Law Commission, 2001; commentary to Article 2(a) of the *Draft Articles on Harm Prevention*, paragraph 4. Emphasis in original.

[96] See also Lefeber, 1996, pp. 16-17. As for an alternate point of view, Article 10 of the *Legal Principles for Environmental Protection and Sustainable Development* that were proposed by the legal expert group of the World Commission on Environment and Development (WCED) in 1986, may be mentioned. It equals significant and substantial harm by requiring states to "prevent or abate any transboundary environmental interference or a significant risk thereof which causes substantial harm - i.e. harm which is not minor or insignificant." See Lammers *et al.*, 1986.

[97] See *infra* paragraph 5.3.

3.3. Threshold of 'Serious or Irreversible' Harm

'Serious or Irreversible' Harm as a Threshold

It has already been recalled that the rise of the precautionary principle in international law and policy in the late eighties and early nineties of the previous century was, in large measure, spurred by the dawning recognition of the serious, long-lasting and irreversible character of much damage to the environment.[98] This recognition is reflected in formulations requiring precautionary action only or particularly when serious or irreparable harm is feared. Such formulations are now disseminated widely in state practice.

A prominent position in this respect is, of course, occupied by Principle 15 of the *Rio Declaration* – calling upon states to adopt a precautionary approach wherever there are threats of "serious or irreversible damage" – and by the great many posterior instruments, both international and national, which contain reference to this provision of the Declaration.[99] Identical thresholds are set out in the 1990 *Bergen Declaration*,[100] the 1990 *Ministerial Declaration of the Second World Climate Conference*,[101] the 1992 *Climate Change Convention*,[102] the 1994 *Second Sulphur Protocol* to the *LRTAP Convention*,[103] the 1995 *Barcelona Convention* amendments,[104] the 1995 *Waigani Convention*,[105] the 1995 *Land-Based Activities Action Programme*[106] and the 2002 *ASEAN Agreement on Transboundary Haze Pollution*.[107] In a comparable manner, the 2001 *Albatross Agreement* links the precautionary principle to "threats of serious or irreversible adverse impacts or damage."[108]

In its initial Application in the 1997 *Gabcikovo-Nagymaros* case before the International Court of Justice (ICJ), Hungary cited a version of the precautionary principle containing a similar qualifying standard of "serious or irreversible damage", while contending that the impending damage to the Hungarian environment on account of the disputed hydrological project was

---

[98] See *supra* paragraph 3.1. In the words of the European Environment Agency, 2001, at p. 13: "Forestalling disasters usually requires acting before there is strong proof of harm, *particularly if the harm may be delayed and irreversible*, an approach to scientific evidence and policy-making which is part of what is now called the precautionary principle." Emphasis added.

[99] See *supra* paragraph 2.3.

[100] *Ministerial Declaration on Sustainable Development in the ECE Region*, paragraph 7.

[101] Principle 7.

[102] *Framework Convention on Climate Change*, Article3(3).

[103] *Protocol on Further Reduction of Sulphur Emissions*, fourth preambular paragraph.

[104] Article 4(3)(a).

[105] *Convention to Ban the Importation into Forum Island Countries of Hazardous Wastes and Radioactive Wastes and to Control the Transboundary Movement and Management of Hazardous Wastes Within the South Pacific*, Article 1.

[106] See paragraph 24.

[107] Article 3(3); ASEAN stands for Association of South East Asian Nations.

[108] Article II(3).

"irreparable and enormous."[109] In the proceedings for provisional measures in the *Southern Bluefin Tuna* cases, ruled upon in 1999 by the International Tribunal for the Law of the Sea (ITLOS), Australia and New Zealand likewise alleged that the harm which the challenged Japanese experimental fishing program threatened to inflict upon the tuna stock in question, qualified as "serious or irreversible damage to the environment," and that this program therefore violated the customary precautionary principle.[110] Deciding that provisional measures were indeed appropriate, the Tribunal ordered the parties to the conflict to "act with prudence and caution to ensure that effective conservation measures are taken to prevent *serious harm* to the stock of southern bluefin tuna."[111] "Serious or irreversible damage" was also named as a threshold of the precautionary principle by Singapore in the 2003 *Land Reclamation* case before the ITLOS.[112]

Various countries out of the many that have implemented the precautionary principle in their domestic legal orders have made its application contingent on the requirement that potential harm be serious or irreversible as well. One example can be found in the *Canadian Environmental Protection Act (CEPA)*, as amended in 1999.[113] In fact, the tentative opinion of the Canadian government, set out in a 2001 discussion document, is quite rigorous in its rejection of any threshold for the application of the precautionary principle other than the one presently under scrutiny: "Situations where there is no threat of serious or irreversible harm to human health, safety, the environment or resource conservation should not be considered to be related to the precautionary approach."[114] In 1996, the US President's Council on Sustainable Development also restricted its recommendations for taking

---

[109] Paragraph 31 of the *Application of the Republic of Hungary v The Czech and Slovak Republic on the Diversion of the Danube River*, as quoted in Trouwborst, 2002, p. 163. Hungary actually also relied on the pertinent provisions of the 1992 *Helsinki Watercourses Convention* and the 1995 IUCN *Draft Covenant*, which, as related above, contain the more lenient thresholds of "significant" and "significant or irreversible", respectively. Apparently, however, Hungary wished to make clear that the expected harm satisfied even the strictest requirements for triggering the operation of the precautionary principle.

[110] See paragraphs 63-66 of the *Statements of Claim* of Australia and New Zealand, 15 July 1999, http://www.worldbank.org/icsid/bluefintuna/SBT-Statement-Claim.pdf.

[111] Paragraph 77 of the Order of 27 August 1999 in the *Southern Bluefin Tuna Cases (Requests for Provisional Measures)*. Italics added.

[112] Paragraph 139 of the *Response of Singapore* of 20 September 2003 in the *Case Concerning Land Reclamation by Singapore in and around the Straits of Johor (Request for Provisional Measures) (Malaysia v Singapore)*.

[113] Article 2(1)(a). See Friends of the Earth Canada, 2000.

[114] Government of Canada, 2001(b), p. 6. Although submitted by the Canadian executive, the proposed "Guiding Principles" on precaution contained in this source "should not be considered to be the official position of the Government of Canada or of federal departments and agencies. They are for discussion purposes only." *Ibid.*, cover page.

precautionary action to risks where possible harm "is thought to be serious or irreparable."[115] The stated aim of the 1997 *Massachusetts Precautionary Principle Act* is the prevention of "serious or irreversible damage to the environment," although it is less than clear whether this is actually intended as a limiting threshold.[116] This is more apparently the case in the environmental laws of the Czech and Slovak Republics, which stipulate that uncertainty shall not delay the adoption of preventive measures if it can be assumed that "irreversible or serious damage" could threaten the environment.[117] Similar thresholds can moreover be found in the definitions of the precautionary principle used, respectively, by the Federal Council for Sustainable Development (FRDO) of Belgium,[118] and in the Australian *Intergovernmental Agreement on the Environment (IGAE)* of 1992, a framework instrument intended to guide environmental policy at the federal, state and local levels.[119] Judge Stein of the New South Wales (Australia) Land and Environment Court applied comparable standards in the 1993 *Leatch* case, when commenting on the precautionary principle in relation to "the potential for serious or irreversible harm to an endangered fauna."[120]

An instance of a non-governmental entity mentioning the avoidance of "serious or irreversible environmental degradation" in relation to its own endorsement of the precautionary principle is the International Chamber of Commerce (ICC).[121] Besides, various academics emphasize the association between the principle and the criterion of seriousness or irreversibility that

---

115 US President's Council on Sustainable Development, *Sustainable America: A New Consensus*, 1996, as cited in Tickner *et al.*, 2000, see pp. 3 and 23.

116 To clarify this point, the text of the act is reproduced here: "The precautionary principle shall be applied to all policy and regulatory decisions of the administration in order to prevent threats of serious or irreversible damage to the environment. The precautionary principle shall be applied when there are reasonable grounds for concern that a procedure or development may contribute to the degradation of the air, land and water of the Commonwealth. Lack of full scientific certainty shall not be used as a reason for postponing cost-effective measures to prevent costly environmental degradation." Commonwealth of Massachusetts, House Bill No. 3140.

117 Article 13 of the *Federal Act on the Environment*, Law No. 17/1992, enacted by the former Czechoslovakia on 5 December 1991 and continued by both Republics after their separation in 1993.

118 Federale Raad voor Duurzame Ontwikkeling, 2001, p. 18: "ernstige of onherstelbare schade".

119 According to the Agreement, precaution is called for "[w]here there are threats of serious or irreversible environmental damage." See Harding & Fisher, 1994, pp. 253-254; Gullett, 1997, p. 61; Trouwborst, 2002, pp. 228-229.

120 *Leatch v Director-General, National Parks and Wildlife Service and Shoalhaven City Council*, 23 November 1993. See Trouwborst, 2002, pp. 232-234 and the sources mentioned there, especially note 1582.

121 International Chamber of Commerce, *Business Charter for Sustainable Development*, Principle 10, as quoted in Backes *et al.*, 2002, p. 79.

expected harm is supposed to meet.[122] Occasionally, a threshold of 'serious *and* irreversible' harm can be come across, as opposed to the habitual clause with *or*. It was used, for instance, by the Supreme Court of India in the 1996 *Vellore Citizens* case,[123] is incorporated in legislation of Slovenia,[124] France[125] and Cameroon,[126] and has also been adopted by European chemical industry interests.[127] This particularly strict formulation occurs so sporadically, however, that it must be regarded the exception rather than the rule.

'Serious' Harm

The qualifications of harm as 'serious' or 'irreversible' have also been stressed separately. As for the first, for instance, one interpretation by the British government of Principle 15 of the *Rio Declaration* reads as follows: "it is not acceptable just to say 'we can't be sure that *serious* damage will happen, so we'll do nothing to prevent it'."[128] The Supreme Court of Pakistan has singled out this element of the Rio definition threshold as well, holding in the 1994 *Shehla Zia v WAPDA* case that precautionary measures should be taken when there are "threats of serious danger."[129] Another case is the Czechoslovak national report to the 1992 UNCED, referring to "serious danger to the environment."[130] In accordance, Cameron and Abouchar have submitted that a minimum standard of "serious harm" is a key element of the precautionary principle.[131]

An apparent indicator of seriousness, besides geographic dispersion – widespread harm is more likely to qualify as serious than locally restricted

---

[122] See, e.g., the outcome of the 2000 Lauterpacht International Law Centre workshop on "The Precautionary Principle in Wildlife Conservation": see Cooney, 2000. Matthee & Vermersch, 2000, at pp. 60-61, speak of "irreversible or serious damage" in this respect; Raffensperger, 2000, of "serious, widespread, or irreparable harm"; DeFur & Kaszuba, 2002, p. 155, deem the principle applicable "especially when outcomes are irreversible and/or widespread."

[123] Paragraph 11 of the Judgment.

[124] Article 8(4) of the *Environmental Protection Act (No. 801-01/90-2/107)* of June 1993.

[125] Article 200(1) of the *Code Rural*; see *Loi Barnier* of 2 February 1995.

[126] Chapter III, Article 9(a) of Cameroon's 1996 *Law No. 96/12 Relating to Environmental Management.*

[127] European Chemical Industry Council, 1995.

[128] HM Government, *A Better Quality of Life: A Strategy for Sustainable Development for the United Kingdom*, May 1999, see http://www.sustainable-development.gov.uk/uk_strategy/quality/life/04.htm. Author's emphasis.

[129] *Shehla Zia v WAPDA*, PLD, 1994 Supreme Court 693, as quoted in Lyster, 1997, p. 396.

[130] Czechoslovak Academy of Sciences and Federal Committee for the Environment, *National Report of the Czech and Slovak Federal Republic*, March 1992, p. 117, as cited in Cameron & Abouchar, 1996, p. 39. Considering the word order in this phrase it can, however, not be ruled out that it is the aggregate risk, consisting of harm *and* likelihood, that is meant to be "serious" in this case.

[131] Cameron & Abouchar, 1996, p. 45.

harm – is the duration or persistence of environmental harm.[132] In other words, under the precautionary principle decisions must be avoided "which have a high risk of long-term adverse effects."[133] This notion has found explicit recognition in the proposed new Environment Code (*Umweltgesetzbuch*) of Germany, in which the principle is proclaimed to demand the prevention of, *inter alia*, "hinsichtlich ihrer langfristigen Folgen nicht absehbare Umweltbeeinträchtigungen."[134] A relevant concept here is that of so-called interim loss. After a harmful event, the extent and quality of the services normally provided by nature are often curtailed during the period of recovery.[135] Interim loss has been defined accordingly as the loss of value of an affected natural resource or environmental asset from the time when harm is inflicted upon it until its full recovery.[136] Take, for example, the decimation of a population of songbirds on account of pesticide intake or the effects of acid rain. Even if eventually the population recovers, in the meanwhile the birds have been severely hampered in performing their habitual roles in the ecosystem, people have hardly been able to enjoy their song, etcetera.

'Irreversible' Harm

Closely related to this discussion is the alternative component flanking the criterion of 'serious' in the threshold at hand, that is the potential irreversibility (or, synonymously, irreparability) of environmental impacts, which will now be examined closer. In a comment published at the outset of the 2002 World Summit on Sustainable Development, President Mbeki of South Africa, President Cardoso of Brazil and Prime Minister Persson of Sweden[137] expressed that "[t]he bounty of the earth is not inexhaustible. The oceans do not contain an infinite number of fish. Much of what is once

---

132 Klinke & Renn, 1999, p. 12. On indicators of seriousness, see also *infra* paragraph 5.2. To dwell on one example of long-term damage, the existing evidence regarding the persistence of organochlorine compounds in the Great Lakes of North America indicates that "it will probably be several more decades before the necessary remedial actions will have reduced concentrations sufficiently" in order to protect human health from chemically induced injury from consumption of contaminated fish. Gilbertson, 2001, p. 131.

133 Parkes, 2000, p. 84; also Canelas de Castro, 1999, p. 163.

134 Approximate translation: "environmental impacts which are not foreseeable on account of their long-term effects." Proposal for an Environment Code, paragraph 4, as quoted in Verschuuren, 1995, between notes 53 and 54.

135 See Brans, 2001.

136 *Ibid.*

137 These are the leaders of the nations that hosted the three respective major international conferences on the environment and sustainable development (i.e. Stockholm 1972, Rio de Janeiro 1992 and Johannesburg 2002).

destroyed by overexploitation or greed is gone forever."[138] In short, we live on a finite planet, where time is not always a healer. In the words of the Millennium Ecosystem Assessment, once an ecosystem is damaged "recovery to the original state may take decades or centuries and may sometimes be impossible."[139] The International Law Commission has likewise acknowledged that "compensation in case of harm often cannot restore the situation prevailing prior to the event or accident."[140] Whereas 'serious' is a typical direct indicator on the scale of gravity, it is evident that 'irreversible', like 'long-term', is in the first place associated with the scale of time. Its primarily temporal character has not prevented it, however, from coming to serve as an indicator of gravity at the same time in the present context.

The frequently stated purpose of preventing irreversible harm to nature and the environment has been translated into the formulation of the precautionary principle on many an occasion. The weighty report from the German government to the parliament on air pollution of 1984 indicated that the use of *Vorsorge* (precaution) implied that "irreversible types of damage [..] must be avoided."[141] It may well be that this position was inspired by the 1982 *World Charter for Nature*, which contains a provision of the same tenor.[142] In its 1990 *White Paper* on environmental strategy the government of the United Kingdom declared its conviction that the precautionary principle "applies particularly where there are good grounds for judging either that action taken promptly at comparatively low cost may avoid more costly damage later, or that irreversible effects may follow if damage is delayed."[143] Put differently, when irreversible damage is feared, precautionary action must be taken at all cost. The UK Department of the Environment published a less absolute interpretation in 1993, but still named "uncertainty combined with the possibility of the irreversible loss of valued resources" as an example of a situation in which, *prima facie*, precaution is called for.[144] In the IUCN *Draft Covenant* of 1995, "irreversible" has been inserted in a threshold clause alongside

---

[138] Mbeki, T., Cardoso, F.H. & Persson, G., "We Can Do This Good Work Together", in: *International Herald Tribune*, 28 August 2002.

[139] Reid *et al.*, 2005, p. 91.

[140] General commentary to the *Draft Articles on Harm Prevention*; see International Law Commission, 2001. Soria Jiménez, 1996, at p. 393 describes irreversible damage as "a catastrophic situation in which there is no possibility of restoring the previous environmental circumstances." See also Klinke & Renn, 1999, p. 1; Federale Raad voor Duurzame Ontwikkeling, 2001, p. 16.

[141] 1984 *Report from the German Government to the Federal Parliament on the Protection of Air Quality*, as cited in Boehmer-Christiansen, 1994, p. 36.

[142] Principle 11(a).

[143] *White Paper: "This Common Inheritance: Britain's Environmental Strategy"*, September 1990, as cited in Haigh, 1994, at pp. 249-250.

[144] Department of the Environment, *Consultation Paper on the UK Strategy for Sustainable Development*, July 1993, as cited in Haigh, 1994, p. 250.

"significant".[145] Indeed, it is commonly held that there is the least question about the existence of a duty to take precautionary measures in situations where the threatened environmental consequences are likely to be irreversible.[146]

Nevertheless, the use of the notion of irreversibility in thresholds of harm that must be met in order to bring about the application of the precautionary principle can be challenged from various perspectives, apart from any reservations that may exist in respect of the desirability of minimum standards of environmental harm in general.[147] On the one hand, as Morris submits:

> all change (and hence all damage) is irreversible in the strict sense that the precise structure of the world that pertained before cannot once again come into being. (This is a consequence of the second law of thermodynamics, wherein it is observed that the state of disorder (or entropy) of the universe is constantly increasing. Attempting to reverse some 'damage' will result in other changes occurring to the state of the world. Thus in recycling paper, energy and other resources are consumed and the fibres in the paper foreshortened, with the result that although what results may look very similar to the paper that existed previously, it will not be exactly alike and there will be fewer of whatever resources were consumed in its making.) This ultimately negates the utility of including 'irreversible' as a criterion as distinct from 'serious'.[148]

In other words, strictly speaking *everything* is irreversible.

To make matters worse, on a different level or, more specifically, on a larger and coarser scale, it may be held that, on the other hand, *nothing* can be proven absolutely irreversible. For instance, the vanishing of an entire island below the waters of the ocean on account of global warming is often presented as a typical scenario of damage that is not only extremely serious but also irreversible. Suffice it to call to mind the famous words of the Vanuatu delegate at the negotiations for the *Climate Change Convention*, pointing out that low-lying island states do not have the luxury of waiting for evidence of climatic change: "The proof, we fear, will kill us."[149] Still, it is not impossible – and, what is

---

[145] See Article 7.

[146] Backes *et al.*, 2002, p. 67; also Epiney & Scheyli, 1998, p. 121; DeFur & Kaszuba, 2003, p. 155. Goklany, 2000, p. 190, has noted the presence of an "irreversibility criterion" which gives "greater priority to outcomes that are irreversible."

[147] On general criticism of minimum thresholds, see the latter part of *supra* section 3.1.

[148] Morris, 2000(b), p. 14. See also Philippopoulos-Mihalopoulos, 1999, p. 183.

[149] Robert van Lierop (Permanent Representative of Vanuatu to the United Nations and co-chair of Working Group 1 of the Intergovernmental Negotiating Committee for a Framework Convention on Climate Change, ING/FCCC), *Statement to the Plenary Session of the INC/FCCC*, 5 February 1991, p. 3, as cited in Sands, 1995(a), pp. 208-209. The Statement of the President of the Maldives to UNCED in 1992, quoted in Cameron *et al.*, 1998, p. 102, was of much the same tenor: "I stand before you as a representative of an endangered people. We are told that [as] a result of global warming and sea level rise, my country, the Maldives, may, sometime during the next century, disappear from the face of the earth."

more, in a distant enough future not even unlikely – that after another alteration of the global climate it will resurface and become recolonized by plants, animals and people very much like the ones that perished when the island disappeared. Another classic example of irreversible harm is the extinction of species of flora and fauna. The slogan "Extinction is forever!" has frequently aided non-governmental organizations (NGOs) in rallying support for their conservationist efforts. It is not entirely unimaginable, however, that modern biotechnology will some day succeed in proving them wrong. In fact, as it is 'Jurassic Park'-like experiments are being attempted around the world in increasing number. One example is the intended resurrection of the Tasmanian tiger (*Thylacinus cynocephalus*), whereas another, less famous one concerns the Pyrenean ibex (*Capra pyrenaica*), a subspecies of ibex that went extinct in the year 2000.[150] Whether such experiments will ever actually succeed and conquer the huge practical and theoretical problems involved is not the issue;[151] the real point is that the possibility cannot be excluded. "The thing that hath been, it is that which shall be; [..] and there is no new thing under the sun."[152]

It would not fully do justice to either critique of the irreversibility standard to discard them as hair-splitting. At the end of the day, however, all of the above considerations fail to take away the plain fact that precautionary state practice is replete with references to the avoidance of 'irreversible' harm, alongside 'significant' or 'serious'. *Ergo*, there is evidently some kind of consensus on the meaning of the term, which is likely to be located somewhere in between the two extreme positions just discussed. In spite of the fast pace of biotechnological developments, for instance, the extinction of species is still widely regarded as irreversible harm.[153] Consequently, it is not necessary to enter here into a detailed study of the work of Ilya Prigogine and others on the nature of irreversibility.

What the second type of criticism *has* drawn attention to, however, is that the distinction between long-term and irreversible environmental harm is not a rigid, but a rather gradual one. As said before, both occur on the same temporal scale: what else is 'irreversible' but infinitely long-term? To a certain extent the difficulty of pinpointing an exact distinction between the two concepts is due to uncertainty. Frequently it is just not possible to predict whether damage will be irreparable or 'merely' long-lasting. This applies, e.g., to depleted fish stocks, which "can take a long time to recover from a crash, if ever."[154] Likewise, the effects of persistent and bioaccumulative

---

150 Delibes de Castro, 2001, p. 244.

151 See Cohen, 2004, pp. 83-86.

152 *Ecclesiastes* 1:9 (King James Version).

153 Cooney, 2001, p. 10; Backes *et al.*, 2002, p. 67.

154 European Environment Agency, 2001, p. 171.

contaminants such as DDT on eagles and falcons *may* be reversible, albeit slowly.[155]

Another important and related factor is the circumstance that damage may be considered irreparable not only for physical reasons, but also for technical or economic ones.[156] Moreover, a lot of long-term damage that is not *in stricto senso* irreversible, is nonetheless so enduring and/or unlikely to be undone that it is deemed "practically", "virtually", "apparently",[157] "essentially"[158] or "effectively"[159] irreversible. Thus, the 1982 *CCAMLR*[160] and the 1985 *ASEAN Agreement on the Conservation of Nature and Natural Resources*, both of which are among the first international legal instruments to introduce the concept of irreversibility into their operative terms, respectively require parties to prevent changes or minimize the risk of changes to ecosystems "which are not potentially reversible *over two or three decades*"[161] and "which are not reversible *over a reasonable time.*"[162] A telling instance of practical irreversibility is the process of desertification. Experience and scientific data indicate that once completely barren, an area is likely to remain so notwithstanding efforts to reverse the situation.[163] Other examples are offered by a number of decimated populations of marine living resources, such as the marbled rock cod (*Notothenia rossii*) and several whale species, that have not been exploited for quite some time since their collapse but nevertheless do not show signs of recovery;[164] by the sudden phase shifts from coral-dominated to algae-dominated reefs in Caribbean and Indo-Pacific waters;[165] and the release of radioactive materials.[166] In all these cases, the

---

[155] Goklany, 2000, pp. 191-192.

[156] See, e.g., Article 25 of the *Resolution on Responsibility and Liability under International Law for Environmental Damage* of the Institut de Droit International (IDI), adopted 4 September 1997; 37 *ILM*, 1998, p. 1473.

[157] E.g., Reid *et al.*, 2005, p. 90.

[158] E.g., Reid *et al.*, *ibid.*; Kumar Duralappah *et al.*, 2005, p. 22.

[159] E.g., Adeel *et al.*, 2005, p. 21.

[160] *Convention on the Conservation of Antarctic Marine Living Resources.*

[161] *CCAMLR*, Article II(3)(c); italics added.

[162] *ASEAN Agreement*, Article 4(1)(d); italics added. See also Sands, 1994, p. 21.

[163] "Once Land is Completely Barren, it Can't Bloom Again", in: *Daily University Science News*, 28 January 2002; see also Adeel *et al.*, 2005, pp. 5, 10 and 21.

[164] On the situation of marbled rock cod, see Parkes, 2000, 83. Generally on small populations of animals that fail to recover despite protective measures, see Delibes de Castro, 2001, pp. 231-254.

[165] Kumar Duralappah *et al.*, 2005, p. 22; Reid *et al.*, 2005, p. 90.

[166] As Philippe Sands, acting as counsel for Ireland in the ITLOS *Mox Plant* case, described the impact of radioactive discharges into the Irish Sea: "Many of these discharges will have a half life of thousands of years. They will be in the environment for generations. [..] Their effects are, to all intents and purposes, irreversible since they cannot be removed from the Irish Sea once they are in it." *Verbatim Record* of the sitting on 19 November 2001, p. 31.

label 'virtually irreversible' appears more than justified, and offers a meaningful clue as to how the second part of the *de minimis* clause of 'serious or irreversible harm' is to be understood.[167] Whichever way, the difficulty of discerning irreversible from long-term harm has evidently not kept the latter temporal notion from informing the interpretation of what consitutes serious damage. Irreversibility has even become a 'gravity trigger' for application of the precautionary principle in its own right.

Combining the Thresholds of 'Significant' and 'Serious or Irreversible' Harm

Wrapping up, for present purposes the threshold of 'serious or irreversible' is apparently at least as significant as 'significant' – forgive the repetition once more. Indeed, the weight of state practice on this count seems to be such that, by way of a tentative conclusion, in legal terms it does not seem correct nor tenable to speak of a general, customary *duty* to take precautionary action unless potential environmental harm is of a serious or irreversible nature. In other words, customary international law would appear to incorporate a threshold of serious or irreversible harm that needs to be crossed before precautionary measures may become compulsory.

Naturally, the former conclusion raises the question where this leaves the conclusion of the preceding paragraph of the current study on the threshold of *significant* harm. Careful recollection of the latter nevertheless reveals that there is nothing to suggest that both findings would be incompatible, quite the contrary. One will remember that a threat of significant environmental harm must be regarded as a prerequisite for bringing about the relevance or application of the precautionary principle under customary international law in the first place. Thus, in situations where the adverse effects of a given activity on the environment are feared to be *significant but not serious or irreversible*, the precautionary principle would be *applicable*, but there would be *no duty* to take precautionary action. By implication, it must necessarily be assumed that in this intermediate zone states would instead have a customary *right* to take such action, but no obligation. Despite the fact that few individual formulations expressly state this, it is difficult to see how any other conclusion could be coherent.

Suggestions to the contrary, such as the (unofficial) opinion of the Canadian government mentioned previously,[168] would seem to do nothing to negate this position. They are simply too few and far between to outweigh the considerable state practice – mainly the many definitions in instruments that

---

[167] Also Epiney & Scheyli, 1998, p. 118; De Sadeleer, 2002, p. 16; Bodansky, 2004, p. 387.

[168] Government of Canada, 2001(b), p. 6, where it is held that situations in which there is no threat of serious or irreversible harm should not be considered as related to the precautionary principle.

lack a threshold or set out a threshold of significant harm – supporting the existence of a threshold of significance as a trigger for the application of the precautionary principle. That existence, and therefore the reality of the graded system outlined here, is moreover supported by the fact that it would be rather more problematic to presume that in the numerous formulations *without* any threshold at all, the applicability of a *high* one like the 'serious or irreversible' clause may be implied. Building on the structure of Figure 1 above, the current findings can be visualized as follows:

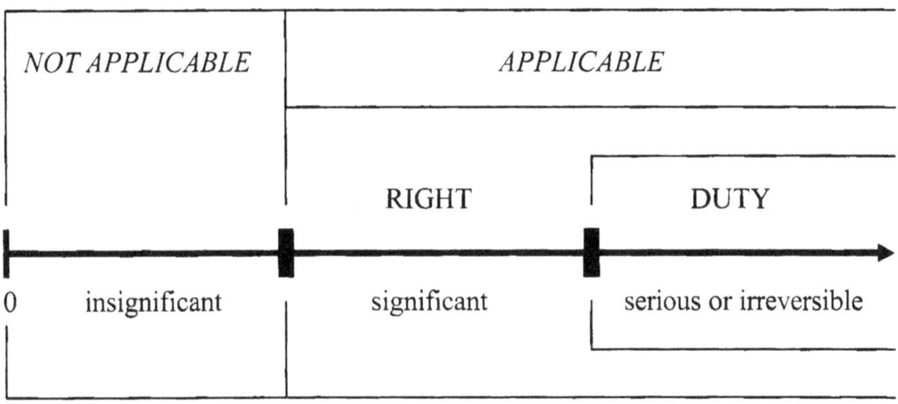

Figure 2. Scale of gravity of harm with two thresholds. The arrowheaded axis represents the scale of gravity. The two boldest printed bars are the thresholds of 'significant' and 'serious or irreversible' harm. Relevant qualifications of harm are indicated below the axis, and corresponding legal effects above it.

The axis of Figure 2 represents a scale of increasing gravity of environmental harm, which is intersected by two (boldly printed) threshold bars. On the stretch between zero and the first threshold, environmental damage is characterized as minor, trivial, insignificant. Under customary international law, the precautionary principle does not apply here. On the stretch above the first threshold bar, environmental effects are considered 'significant'. Here, given the fulfillment of any other requirements for application of the precautionary principle that may exist, international custom grants states the *right* to take precautionary measures. Finally, on the stretch above the second threshold bar, harm is not only significant but also deemed to be of a 'serious or irreversible' nature. Under these circumstances – again provided the absence of any other legal impediments, unrelated to the gravity of threatened damage –

states not only have a right, but a customary *duty* to undertake precautionary action as well.

At this point it is perhaps appropriate to elucidate some matters that may not be immediately obvious from observation of Figure 2 alone. Even though the diagram accurately reflects the reality of positive international law in that the various thresholds with their consequences have been placed in the correct order, it is for two good reasons that the scale of gravity has not been numbered. As regards the first, it is clear that the threshold of 'serious or irreversible' harm represents a relatively high standard.[169] Certainly 'serious' harm means worse damage than 'significant' harm.[170] But how much worse? In other words, where exactly is it located on the scale of gravity? The International Law Commission mentions the term "grave" itself as a standard of harm that is even higher than "serious".[171] Although the former term does not play a role of any significance in precautionary state practice, it does permit the conclusion that 'serious' is located in between 'significant' and 'grave', for what it is worth. As in the case of the 'significant' threshold, it is difficult to be much more exact, since in the determination of whether harm qualifies as serious a lot will depend, *inter alia*, on the particular circumstances of each case.[172] With an eye on this lack of precision, the spaces between threshold bars in Figure 2 are purposefully regular. For clarity's sake, in this study the terms 'grave' and 'gravity' have been and will continue to be used in a general sense, for instance to label one case of environmental damage as 'graver' or 'less grave' than another, and not as depicting a particular threshold value, unless stated otherwise.

The second reason for the absence of numbers on the axis of gravity in Figure 2 has to do with the fact that the right-hand bold bar represents a *single* threshold embodying two *distinct* standards. Whereas the former, 'serious', is a pure indication of gravity, the latter, 'irreversible', is primarily an indication of

---

[169] Also Epiney & Scheyli, 1998, p. 117; Beeckman, 1996, pp. 470-471; Birnie & Boyle, 2002, p. 123.

[170] For the sake of completeness, sometimes a comment may be encountered that does not clearly distinguish between the terms "significant" and "serious". E.g., the UK Department of the Environment, Transport and the Regions, in paragraph 1.6 of its 2000 *Guidelines for Environmental Risk Assessment and Management: Revised Departmental Guidance*, after confirming that the official UK interpretation is based on Principle 15 of the *Rio Declaration* and quoting it (i.e. "serious or irreversible"), later on speaks of "the possibility of *significant* environmental damage," adding that "it is in such cases that precautionary action is particularly valid." (Emphasis added.) Rare occasions such as this cannot, however, detract from the fact that the distinction between "significant" as relatively low and "serious" as relatively high is firmly based in state practice and doctrine. See also Beeckman, *ibid.*; Birnie & Boyle, *ibid.*

[171] International Law Commission, 2001, Commentary on Article 1 of the *Draft Articles on Harm Prevention*, paragraph 2.

[172] See further *infra* paragraph 5.1.

time, as noted previously. Despite having become a legally relevant qualification of gravity as well, the irreversibility criterion would not fit neatly onto any numerical scale on account of the simple fact that all levels of harm, from the most insignificant to the most serious, are liable to being irreparable. Had the dominant standard been 'serious *and* irreversible', things would have been rather more straightforward. The use of the word 'or' in the prevalent threshold, however, leaves all options open. To meet the test, harm may either be serious, irreversible or both at the same time.[173]

When the numbers of a given population of wild plants are rigorously cut back by excessive harvesting so as to become rare this is likely to be considered serious harm, even if subsequent protection measures may lead to full recovery. Regarding environmental damage that is irreversible, this will often simultaneously be qualified as serious. Few would disagree, for example, that species extinctions meet both standards.[174] Thus, the threshold clause under scrutiny will frequently be read as 'serious or *even* irreversible'. Such overlap does, nonetheless, not automatically occur at all times. Imagine the small-scale extraction of marble which disfigures only a miniscule proportion of the affected mountain range and, moreover, remains limited to a zone that is already degraded because of anthropogenic disturbance and erosion. No matter how irreversible the damage inflicted by this operation, it may well fall short of constituting serious harm.

Whether harm is either minor or significant is another issue. It is not entirely beyond doubt that irreversible damage must meet the same minimum standard of significance as harm that is reparable in order to have legal consequence. Even so, with an eye on what has been said above on the exclusion of insignificant harm from the reach of the precautionary principle, this is presumably the case. Otherwise the tiniest and most trivial damage could bring about an obligation to take precautionary action merely upon being irreversible.

Either way, above the second threshold bar, i.e., to the right of it in Figure 2, instances of harm may be found that are *not* serious but are present on account of their irreversible nature only. Although the boxes of the diagram

---

[173] Put alternatively, damage may either be serious *or* irreversible, or serious *and* irreversible. Soria Jiménez, 1996, p. 393. As far as the last option is concerned, a literal interpretation of the threshold text would not allow for this possibility, but it is plainly unthinkable that precaution would be called for when harm is serious and not when this harm is irreversible besides, and *vice versa*. Intuitively the need for precautionary action would precisely be greatest when serious and irreversible coincide – indeed, this is always so when comparing cases of equal "seriousness" (see *infra* section 3.4 on proportionality). An example is the argument advanced by Hungary in the *Gabcikovo-Nagymaros* case and already mentioned *supra*, that expected harm was "irreparable *and* enormous".

[174] Cooney, 2001, p. 10.

correctly depict this state of affairs, it will be evident that such a scheme cannot credibly be caught in numbers. In view of the above, then, the most complete and unambiguous description of the threshold at hand would be 'serious and/or significant irreversible' harm. Linguistically speaking this is somewhat less fortunate, which may well explain the widespread use of the simplified "serious or irreversible" in the practice of states. That use will be continued in the present study as well.

3.4. Conclusions

This chapter has centered on the first of the three core elements the precautionary principle is composed of, namely the prospect of environmental harm. Quite a few conclusions have been drawn along the way, which will be concisely lined up here.

Together with the recognition of the limitations of science, the awareness that human activities can bring about serious and sometimes irreversible damage to the environment accounts for the *raison d'être* of the precautionary principle. As for the scope of the principle under customary international law, it basically extends to include all *types* of environmental harm without regard to the agent responsible for it, whether natural, human or both, although it is bound to be of greatest relevance for the latter two categories. Whether or not environmental damage is likely to have directly discernible harmful consequence for human interests is not important either, since encroachment upon the intrinsic value of nature is clearly included within the principle's reach. Evidently, mere change is not within the bounds of the precautionary principle. Threatened effects need to be adverse in order to be eligible for precautionary action. Nevertheless, not all actually or potentially harmful activities are covered by the precautionary principle, and of those that are, not all entail an obligation to take preventive or abatement action. This is where the *gravity* or *level* of harm comes into play.

A considerable number of the formulations employed in state practice do not set out any minimum standard of gravity that anticipated harm must meet for the precautionary principle to become applicable, which would apparently shed some doubt on the general assumption that there are any such thresholds to be observed under customary international law. There are, however, various solid reasons – of which common sense is not the least – to presume that the precautionary principle cannot be held to apply in instances where threatened harm is not in any way considered to be *significant*, as opposed to minor or trivial. This hypothesis is further supported by the occurrence of another substantial portion of formulations that expressly set out such a threshold of significance. (See Figure 1 above.)

Of the higher, more restrictive thresholds that are used in precautionary state practice, *serious or irreversible* is the single most current one by far. For this and other reasons, there cannot be taken to exist any *obligation* to take precautionary measures unless threatened harm is expected to be serious or irreversible. By implication, when feared harm is significant but not serious and/or irreversible, customary law must be deemed to endow states with the *right* but not the duty to take precautionary action. (See Figure 2 above.)

Thus, when pondering any given threat of environmental impact a number of questions must be answered. Are the effects in question adverse, that is, would they constitute harm? If so, is this harm significant as opposed to minor, trivial, that is, insignificant? If so, is it also serious or irreversible? (See Figure 3 below.)

For instance, the fact that the expected or even intended death, as a result of human activities, of individual animals not forming part of vulnerable or protected populations, such as muskrats (*Ondatra zibethicus*) in the Netherlands, is likely to fall short of bringing about any legal effect under the precautionary principle, may thus be for two distinct reasons. Either the impact is not viewed as adverse and therefore not as harm or, if it is, it is not viewed as significant. Notably, this is regardless of whether or not the impact is qualified as irreversible – which it *is* in the strict sense that the specimens in question will never return to life – given that irreversibility does not exempt harm from the tests of adversity and significance.

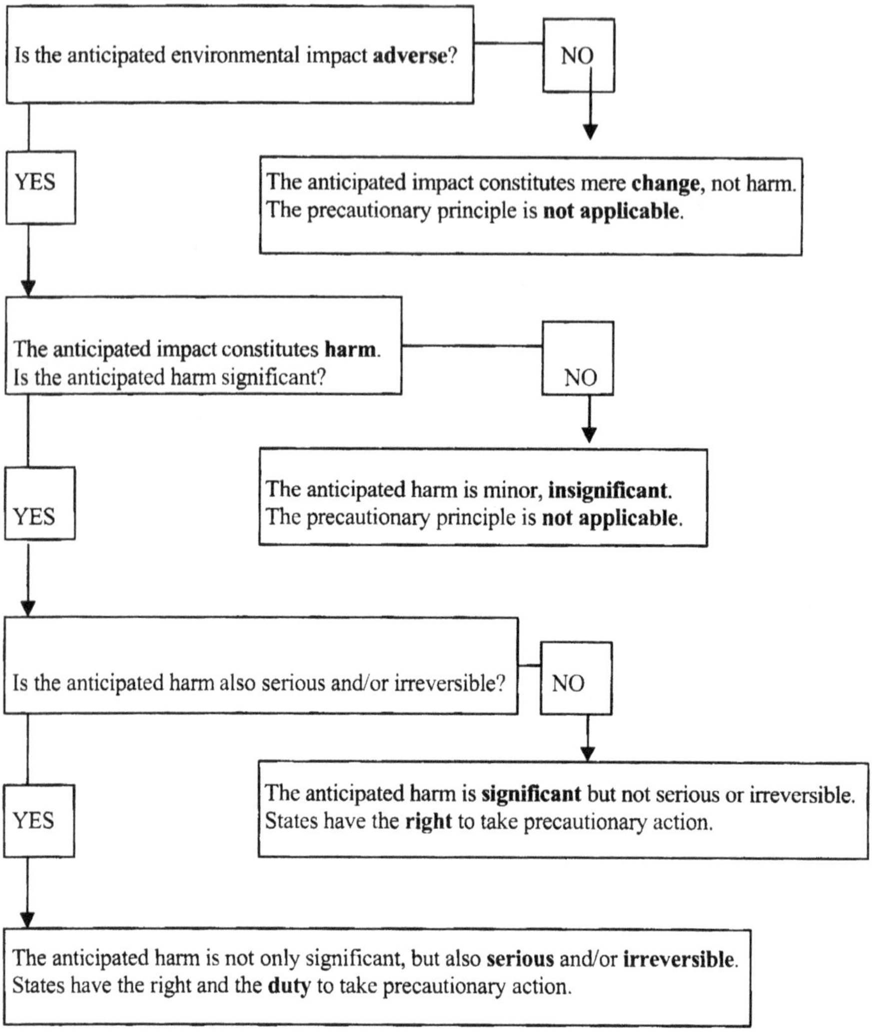

Figure 3. Schematic overview of legal effects related to nature and gravity of anticipated environmental impacts. The various qualifications of impact and the accompanying legal effects are printed boldly. For the purpose of this exercise, the fulfillment of potential other requirements for application of the precautionary principle, unrelated to nature and gravity of impact, is considered a given.

One will also recall the killer whale example discussed as part of the exposition on risk in the previous chapter, comparing a fifty percent chance that two killer whales will die with a one-in-a-thousand chance that one thousand killer whales will die.[175] The calculated result of both is an average risk of one killer whale death. It was asked whether under the precautionary principle both outcomes would accordingly be considered as equivalents. In other words, is the precautionary principle risk-neutral? Obviously, it is not.[176] Even though technically speaking the aggregate risks are identical, the loss of a thousand killer whales will likely cross the threshold of serious harm and may therefore entail a duty to take anticipatory action, whereas the risk of two deaths is unlikely to lead to any such obligation and may well fall short of generating even a right to the same effect.

Finally, it is important to bear in mind that thus far, considerations relating to the second major component of the precautionary principle, concerned with uncertainty and probability, have been largely left out of the analysis. The conclusions that have been reached up until now are only part of the picture and need to be complemented with an examination of this second element. This examination will be undertaken next.

---

[175] See *supra* paragraph 2.2.

[176] This affirms the position taken by Bodansky, 1991(a), p. 414, from whom the example was borrowed.

We live on an island surrounded by a sea of ignorance.
As our island of knowledge grows, so does the shore of our ignorance.
–John Archibald Wheeler (1911-)

4. SECOND LEG OF THE TRIPOD: UNCERTAINTY

4.1. Uncertainty

The Greek god Apollo knew how many grains of sand there were. He was omniscient. Mortals were not, and have not obtained this quality either since. Surely mankind's island of knowledge has increased tremendously, but so have the shores of its ignorance.[1] Uncertainty – that is, the absence of certainty – continues to mar planning and decision-making at every level, especially where the environment is in issue. It is, as discussed previously, a basic ingredient of the precautionary principle.[2] Any examination of international and national policy, legislation, jurisprudence or doctrine on the topic will confirm this. Uncertainty is a complicated element, however, probably more so than the element of harm. Meaningful discussion of the precautionary principle, as indeed of any matter, is difficult without a measure of understanding of its broader context. Some treatment of the nature, sources and types of scientific uncertainty is therefore indispensable as a prelude to the legal analysis proper of this element. Uncertainty comes in multiple forms. As the European Commission comments in its 2000 Communication on the precautionary principle:

> Scientific uncertainty results usually from five characteristics of the scientific method: the variable chosen, the measurements made, the samples drawn, the models used and the causal relationships employed. Scientific uncertainty may also arise from a controversy on existing data or lack of some relevant data. Uncertainty may relate to qualitative or quantitative elements of the analysis.[3]

Although the cutting edge between the two is not always razor sharp, a useful distinction is the one between epistemological and ontological uncertainty.[4]

---

[1] See the oft-quoted words of American physicist John Archibald Wheeler atop this chapter.
[2] See *supra* paragraph 2.3. See also Hey, 1992, p. 308; Rose & Paleokrassis, 1996, pp. 158-159; Gullett, 1997, p. 59; Kaiser, 1997(b), p. 314; Epiney & Scheyli, 1998, p. 110; *Communication COM(2000)1*, pp. 8 and 10; and Backes *et al.*, 2002, p. 245.
[3] *Communication COM(2000)1*, p. 14.
[4] Bouma *et al.*, 2002, pp. 9-14, who refer, *inter alia*, to Van Asselt, M.B.A., *Perspectives on Uncertainty and Risk; the PRIMA Approach to Decision Support*, Boston 2000, pp. 84-91.

Uncertainty Due to Lack of Information

Epistemological uncertainty corresponds to a lack of knowledge, and is sometimes referred to as parameter uncertainty.[5] It may result from lack of measurements, lack of precision, practical incommensurability, or hiatuses in scientific theory.[6] These may, in turn, be related to limitations of available tools and techniques for measurement and analysis, e.g. statistical models.[7] Doubtful validity of samples, data that are inter- or extrapolated from other sources, and historical records that are insufficiently complete, inaccessible or altogether absent all amount to epistemological uncertainty.[8]

The experts on liability and redress appointed under the *Biodiversity Convention* have stressed that information on environmental baseline conditions is absent in many cases.[9] And without knowledge of the 'normal' situation, environmental change can hardly be measured. To illustrate this, uncertainty over baseline conditions has been a very contentious issue in procedures concerning environmental harm before the UN Compensation Commission dealing with claims related to the Iraqi invasion of Kuwait.[10] Likewise, without the 'big picture' of reliable records an observer watching a particular system might see one kind of behaviour over a considerable length of time, yet an entirely different kind could be just as natural for the system.[11] This may give rise to deep questions such as this:

> *Does a climate exist?* That is, does the earth's weather have a long-term average? Most meteorologists, then as now, took the answer for granted. Surely any measurable behavior, no matter how it fluctuates, must have an average. Yet on reflection, it is far from obvious. As Lorenz pointed out, the average weather for the last 12,000 years has been notably different than the average for the previous 12,000, when most of North America was covered by ice. Was there one climate that changed to another for some physical reason? Or is there an even longer-term climate within which those periods were just fluctuations? Or is it possible that a system like the weather may *never* converge to an average?[12]

---

[5] *Ibid.*, p. 9; Tickner *et al.*, 2000, p. 12.

[6] Bouma *et al.*, *ibid.*; UK Department of the Environment, Transport and the Regions, *Guidelines for Environmental Risk Assessment and Management: Revised Departmental Guidance*, 2000, paragraph 1.6; Raffensperger, 2000; O'Riordan & Cameron, 1994(b), pp. 62-63; Tallacchini, 1999, p. 1095.

[7] Lemons *et al.*, 1997, p. 209; Tickner *et al.*, 2000, p. 12; UK Department of the Environment, Transport and the Regions, *ibid.*; Raffensperger, *ibid.*

[8] O'Riordan & Cameron, 1994(b), p. 62; UK Department of the Environment, Transport and the Regions, *ibid.*

[9] Paragraph 19 of *UN Doc.* UNEP/CBD/COP/8/27/Add.3 of 18 October 2005.

[10] E.g., paragraph 597 of *UN Doc.* S/AC.26/2005/10 of 30 June 2005.

[11] Gleick, 1998, p. 169.

[12] Gleick, 1998, p. 168, making reference to work by mathematician and meteorologist Edward N. Lorenz. See also the reflections on the complexity and variability of climate and weather below.

Neither is it known, for instance, whether plankton booms in the southern North Sea are episodic events tied to ocean currents, sea surface temperature and estuarine discharges, occurring with cyclic regularity, or must be attributed (also) to other causes. The study of organic detritus patterns in a sufficiently comprehensive sediment record could shed light on this issue, but such a record has never been obtained, mostly on account of the huge costs involved in any attempt to do so.[13] Similar epistemological uncertainty flows from the lack of a global system monitoring land degradation and desertification, the lack of a reasonably accurate global map of wetlands, and the scarcity of replicable data on global forest extent, to name a few.[14]

A particularly fascinating example of uncertainty on account of plain lack of data concerns the current amount of species of flora and fauna inhabiting the earth. Estimates range mostly from three to fifty million, whereas even hypotheses exceeding a hundred million have been submitted.[15] As one expert observed: "We do not know to within an order of magnitude how many species we share the globe with."[16] No more than an approximate 1.5 to 2 million species out of the elusive total have been described by scientists so far.[17] The fact that not even the number of *described* species can be stated with certainty is telling. It would seem that the only position that can be held with any certainty is that not nearly all existing biological diversity is known to science.[18] Nonetheless, the species diversity question is an eminent instance of uncertainty that could, in principle, be eliminated to a large extent if the proper scientific, *in casu* taxonomic, effort were enabled and made.[19] The amount of

[13] O'Riordan & Cameron, 1994(b), p. 63.

[14] Reid *et al.*, 2005, p. 101.

[15] See Delibes de Castro, 2001, pp. 38-43; Leakey & Lewin, 1996, pp. 112-123; Kumar Duralappah *et al.*, 2005, pp. 18-19; Tinker, 1995, p. 779.

[16] Robert M. May, as quoted in Leakey & Lewin, *ibid.*, p. 112.

[17] Delibes de Castro, 2001, p. 41; Leakey & Lewin, *ibid.*, p. 113; Kumar Duralappah *et al.*, 2005, p. 19.

[18] It should be noted that taxonomic or species diversity is in fact the "best" known component of biodiversity. Knowledge regarding genetic diversity, abundance and distribution of organisms over space and time, their functional traits and the interactions among them is much more incomplete. Kumar Duralappah *ibid.*, pp. 18-22.

[19] As Leakey & Lewin, 1996, p. 113 pointedly comment: "It is indeed a remarkable fact that we in this modern world, obsessed with measuring things, are so imprecise about the stuff of nature, to which we are intimately related and upon which we ultimately depend. We have a good estimate of how many stars there are in our galaxy, the Milky Way: some hundred billion. We know how many nucleotide bases constitute the human genetic blueprint: three billion. And we can calculate to within a few hours when a comet will collide with Jupiter, as it did at 4 p.m. (U.S. Eastern Daylight Time) on 16 July 1994. Yet we cannot put a secure number on current species diversity. It is not through lack of knowing how to obtain it, but through lack of commitment. Governments have spent hundreds of millions of dollars in the systematic study of the stars but only a tiny fraction of that sum on a systematic study of nature here on earth."

species, even though not presently known nor likely to become so in the very near future, belongs to a category of matters that are, at a minimum fundamentally, knowable, in other words deterministic. In effect, parameter uncertainty can often be diminished by gathering more information or improving techniques to analyze it.[20] Not all epistemological uncertainties can readily be reduced by an increase of research, however, if at all. Suffice it to call to mind the practical impossibility of counting all grains of sand in the world, alluded to at the beginning of this chapter. In short, some knowledge deficiency can be forestalled and some cannot, as the case may be. Consequently, epistemological uncertainty may or may not be surmountable.

Uncertainty Due to Complexity and Variability

Ontological uncertainty, on the contrary, is resilient by definition. It is the direct result of two intimately linked qualities of nature itself, namely its complexity and variability. As for the first, study of any given ecology handbook yields the same conclusion: in nature everything is interrelated.[21] In 1859 Charles Darwin already knew that "plants and animals, most remote in the scale of nature, are bound together by a web of complex relations," while stressing the profundity of mankind's ignorance in this regard.[22] The web of nature moreover extends beyond organic beings to include the abiotic world – air, water, soil, rocks, nutrients, etcetera – combining both worlds in sophisticated systems occurring at myriad levels, known as ecosystems. Cyclic and feedback constructions are everywhere. Ecosystems thus mirror the complexity of their component parts.[23] In the first half of the past century American conservationist Aldo Leopold branded the revelation of "the complexity of the land organism" as the outstanding scientific discovery of his time, adding that "[o]nly those who know the most about it can appreciate how little is known about it."[24] More recently the understanding has begun to crystallize that up until the level of the globe there is intimate, systematic interaction between the biological and physical realms.[25] The signatories of the *Rio Declaration* recognized this "integral and

---

[20] Tickner *et al.*, 2000, p. 12; Raffensperger, 2000.

[21] See, e.g., Smith & Smith, 2000. Also Pascual Trillo, 2000, pp. 15-33; Juste Ruiz, 1999, p. 9; Jiménez Beltrán, 2001, p. 4.

[22] Darwin, 1998, p. 58. As he observed furthermore in *The Origin of Species*: "Many cases are on record showing how complex and unexpected are the checks and relations between organic beings." *Ibid.*, p. 56. See generally pp. 56-62. Kumar Duralappah *et al.*, 2005, submit at p. 18 that "[n]o feature of Earth is more complex, dynamic, and varied than the layer of living organisms that occupy its surfaces and its seas."

[23] Tennekes, 2001, pp. 109-111.

[24] In essay "The Round River", see Leopold, 1970, p. 190. A fuller citation can be found at the very outset of this study.

[25] For illustrating the dynamic role of living organisms in determining the composition of chemicals in soil, water and atmosphere one need look no further than the tremendous impact

interdependent nature of the Earth"[26] and acknowledged the existence of a single "Earth's ecosystem."[27] Indeed, according to one influential theory the earth's organisms, atmosphere, hydrosphere and lithosphere together make up an intricate feedback system that maintains the optimal physical and chemical conditions for life.[28] This theory of global biogeochemical homeostasis aptly bears the name of the Greek earth goddess Gaia.

Logically, all this inextricable complexity seriously confounds human comprehension of natural processes and the ability of science to predict them.[29] A Spanish ecologist has observed that the ways of nature are much like the ways of God in that they are inscrutable, surprising and designed with enormous complexity.[30] His 13th century compatriot King Alfonso X, whose byname was The Wise, sighed one day: "If the Lord Almighty had consulted me before embarking on the Creation, I would have recommended something simpler."[31] The infamous climatic phenomenon El Niño, capable of transforming worldwide wind and precipitation patterns, may pose as an example here. It is known that the weather patterns associated with it are the consequence of a reversed flow of ocean currents between the Eastern and Western Pacific Ocean, and also that this reversal is caused in turn by small variations in water temperatures.[32] The factors that ultimately tip the balance of the system cannot be pinpointed nor predicted, however.[33]

Science, while excelling in the exploration and analysis of details, especially of the 'building blocks' of nature and of life, is often at a loss where it comes to comprehending the intricacies of ecological linkages.[34] In the multilayered planetary ecosystem with all its cycling and feedback, causes and effects are apparently inseparable, as effects become causes for new effects and so on.[35] Even the question where to begin scientific examination of such a system is difficult to approach.[36] The more is learnt about the dynamics of ecosystems, the more it is realized how extremely difficult it is to

---

humans have had on the physical aspects of the earth. Smith & Smith, 2000, p. 344. See also Lovelock, 2000, *passim*.

[26] Final preambular paragraph.

[27] Principle 7.

[28] Lovelock, 2000, *passim*; Smith & Smith, 2000, p. 344; Lewin, 1999, pp. 106-129; Kumar Duralappah *et al.*, 2005, p. 18.

[29] Bell, 2002, p. 3; Molenaar, 2002, pp. 33-34.

[30] Delibes de Castro, 2000, p. 68.

[31] As cited in Schellnhuber, 1999, at p. C23.

[32] Bell, 2002, p. 3.

[33] *Ibid.*

[34] Schmidt-Bleek, 1993, p. 67; Tennekes, 2001, p. 93.

[35] Tennekes, *ibid.*, p. 95; Lemons *et al.*, 1997, pp. 215-216.

[36] Tennekes, *ibid.*, p. 96.

comprehensively understand or even predict them.[37] In the words of the 2001 *Reykjavik Declaration on Responsible Fisheries in the Marine Ecosystem*, there is "incomplete scientific knowledge about the structure, functioning, components and properties of the ecosystem as well as about the ecological impact of fishing."[38] To illustrate this, repeated assessments of the Atlantic cod (*Gadus morhua*) living off Newfoundland, Canada, have done little more than demonstrate "just how little is understood about this most studied stock – why it collapsed, why it has failed to recover, what proportion are being taken by predators and other fishing activities – and of the poor status of capelin, small fish that are important prey for the northern cod. Even the linkage between inshore stocks and those offshore [..] is now open to question. There is also growing awareness that the 'stock' is made up of more or less discrete local populations."[39]

Again, Wheeler's expanding shores of ignorance come to mind, as well as statements of the same vein by Von Goethe,[40] Schweitzer[41] and J.F.K.[42] In truth, the uncertainties following directly from nature's complexity are of such magnitude and variety that they are highly unlikely to ever be significantly reduced, let alone resolved.[43] No environmental study can ever pretend to capture all checks and balances of an ecosystem; invariably there are conditions that escape observation or comprehension, or extend beyond the studied range. It is generally acknowledged, therefore, that scientific insight in the organization of nature is limited as a matter of principle.[44] This implies that there are cognitive deficits in human knowledge of the earth system which are irreducible regardless of the scientific study approach utilized.[45] This kind of uncertainty is denominated systemic indeterminacy.[46]

Such ontological uncertainty, as observed above, is not caused by complexity alone. The other, closely related agent is the capriciousness of

---

[37] Bell, 2000, p. 3; Kumar Duralappah *et al.*, 2005, p. 25.

[38] Hereinafter *Reykjavik Declaration*, see preambular paragraph 18.

[39] MacGarvin, 2001(b), p. 22; see also Rose & Paleokrassis, 1996, pp. 158-159.

[40] "The greater the knowledge, the greater the doubt." Johann Wolfgang von Goethe (1749-1832).

[41] "As we acquire more knowledge, things do not become more comprehensible, but more mysterious." Albert Schweitzer (1875-1965).

[42] "The greater our knowledge increases, the greater our ignorance unfolds." John Fitzgerald Kennedy (1917-1963).

[43] Tickner *et al.*, 2000, p. 12; Raffensperger, 2000.

[44] E.g., Lemons *et al.*, 1997, p. 215-216; Tickner *et al.*, *ibid.*; Schellnhuber, 1999, p. C23; Raffensperger, *ibid.*; Federale Raad voor Duurzame Ontwikkeling, 2001, p. 14; Tennekes, 2001, p. 89. The idea that mankind will ever know and comprehend all cycles and connections of the earth system, the latter author observes, must be dismissed as a logical error of the first magnitude.

[45] Schellnhuber, *ibid.*; Lemons *et al.*, *ibid.*

[46] Federale Raad voor Duurzame Ontwikkeling, 2001, p. 14.

nature. Many elements of the natural world are not linear, regular and periodical, but instead variable, non-linear and dynamic. Living organisms, for instance, vary a lot in that they do not behave according to mechanical laws and differences in susceptibility to external influences between them often seem random.[47] E.g., however equally fertilizer is spread out on a field, still not all plants will increase in size by the same amount.[48] Even ordinary outward appearance bears witness to the great variability of nature – not two zebras show the same pattern of stripes and not two human fingers make identical prints. It is important to stress that variation, in large measure, is an inherent quality of natural phenomena, i.e. not (solely) the result of adaptation, competition or other outward impulses. Even under carefully adjusted laboratory conditions, variable outcomes cannot fully be excluded. This is true particularly for the disciplines of biology and ecology; generally physical and chemical experiments are relatively more clear cut.[49] Linear systems are proportional: a doubled impulse always results in a doubled response. They are easily calculated and easily classified.[50] In the natural environment, however, linearity is not normally the rule.[51] Seemingly irregular change characterizes ecological processes as much as equilibrium, if not more.[52] Linked to their complex make-up, the variability and non-linearity of ecosystems make the challenge of understanding them even more daunting, not to mention foretelling future states.

Non-linearity and variability are the objects of the science of chaos, occupied with the uneven fluctuations of insect populations and the earth's magnetic field, heart rhythm disorders, oscillating exchange rates and all sorts of other phenomena that are irregular in essence.[53] It studies how even the simplest non-linear systems tend to possess complicated dynamical properties – chaos – causing them to become utterly unpredictable in the long run. A notion that is key to understanding the chaotic dynamics of non-

---

[47] Saunders, 2000; Tickner *et al.*, 2000, p. 12.
[48] Saunders, *ibid.*
[49] As Saunders, *ibid.*, explains: "If you want to know what will happen if you mix, say, copper and sulphuric acid, you really only have to try it once. If you want to be sure, you will repeat the experiment, but you expect to get the same result, even to the amount of hydrogen that is produced from a given amount of copper and acid. In biology, however, we are dealing with organisms which vary a lot and never behave in predictable, mechanical ways."
[50] Gleick, 1998, p. 153.
[51] Gleick, *ibid.*, p. 42; Tennekes, 2001, pp. 92-93.
[52] Lemons *et al.*, 1997, pp. 210-211. As Gleick, *ibid.*, puts it at p. 315, "ecology based on a sense of equilibrium seems doomed to fail. The traditional models are betrayed by their linear bias. Nature is more complicated."
[53] There is an extensive literature on this topic. See, e.g., Gleick, *ibid.*, *passim*; Lewin, 1999, *passim*.

linear systems is "sensitive dependence on initial conditions."[54] This term describes how tiny differences in input can quickly become overwhelming differences in output.[55] Every imprecision in the measurement of a system's initial conditions, even when arbitrarily tiny, makes itself felt after a long enough period. The more complex the system, therefore, the bigger the chance that mathematical methods will fail to adequately foretell its future behaviour.[56] Accurate long-term prediction in the 'real world' of nature outside the laboratory, composed of ecosystems that are inherently non-linear and far from simple, is thus impossible for the plain reason that there will always be some error, no matter how miniscule, in the measurement of the initial conditions.[57] Again, there is a "great gulf between knowledge of what one thing does – one water molecule, one cell of heart tissue, one neuron – and what millions of them do."[58] In sum, when non-linearity and complexity combine, the predictive capacity of mathematical models is fundamentally limited.[59] This is tightly related to what Bart Kosko has called the mismatch problem: "The world is grey but science is black and white."[60]

A typical example of a system uniting both features is the climate system and, by inference, the weather.[61] The climate system comprises the atmosphere, the oceans, solid earth and the life contained in the biosphere. The component systems each have their own dynamics, and interactions between them their own peculiarities. Endless linkages exist, much cycling and many feedback mechanisms – in brief, tremendous complexity.[62] In the atmosphere, for instance, at a large scale there are depressions and eddies that only satellites can detect, and at smaller scales cloud fronts, rain-showers, thunderstorms, minor clouds, dust devils, squalls, whirls around

---

[54] See Gleick, *ibid.*, especially pp. 8-31; Brilmont, 1996; Tennekes, 2001, pp. 31, 42, 70-71, 92-93; Paris & Paris, 1996.

[55] Sure enough not an altogether novel concept, given the following verse by George Herbert: "For want of a nail, the shoe was lost; For want of a shoe, the horse was lost; For want of a horse, the rider was lost; For want of a rider, the battle was lost; For want of a battle, the kingdom was lost!" As quoted in Gleick, *ibid.*, at p. 23.

[56] Tennekes, 2001, p. 92.

[57] Gleick, 1998, *passim*; Brilmont, 1996, Tennekes, *ibid.*, pp. 32, 70-71, 92-93; Paris & Paris, 1996; Lemons *et al.*, 1997, pp. 210-211. "Predictability is one thing in a cloud chamber where two particles collide at the end of a race around an accelerator. It is something else altogether in the simplest tub of roiling fluid, or in the earth's weather, or in the human brain." Gleick, *ibid.*, p. 7.

[58] Gleick, *ibid.*, p. 8.

[59] Tennekes, 2001, pp. 54, 92-93, 106; Bell, 2002, p. 4; as Bart Kosko has described the math modeler's dilemma: "linear math, nonlinear world. We know a great deal about linear math. In comparison we know almost nothing about non-linear math - except that almost all math is nonlinear."

[60] Kosko, 1994, p. 8.

[61] Tennekes, 2001, *passim*; Gleick, 1998, pp. 11-31 and 168-170; Jiménez Beltrán, 2001, p. 4.

[62] Tennekes, *ibid.*, pp. 67, 86-87.

trees, rocks and buildings: there is all manner of movement, up to the stirring of the air by the wings of a butterfly.[63] To view the intricacy of the atmosphere it is enough to look out the window. The atmosphere is, moreover, not periodical.[64] It does not repeat itself in neat cycles, displaying whimsical and chaotic behaviour instead.[65] "Lightning does not travel in a straight line."[66] According to one meteorologist the atmosphere offers no certainty other than that it is in permanent turmoil, constantly adapting to altering circumstances.[67] Cause and effect form an inextricable tangle, whereby one cause may have multiple effects and one effect multiple causes.[68] By definition its chaotic nature renders uncertain what will happen tomorrow.[69] Much the same goes for the other components of the planetary climate system. Conducting a quantitative analysis of a system this complex is a sheer impossibility.[70] Knowledge of the web of interactions and feedback linkages will never be sufficiently precise and complete so as to design a computer model capable of predicting exactly how the climate will respond to deforestation, pollution, and other kinds of impact. Any such predictions will always be approximate at best.[71]

The weather evidences a similar link between aperiodicity and unpredictability.[72] When the European Centre for Medium Range Weather Forecasts was founded in 1974, the official target was to attain reliable predictions of ten days ahead.[73] The super-computer of the institution soon delivered weather forecasts that were reportedly the best of the world and statistically better than nothing.[74] Up to the present, however, the best predictions are speculative beyond three days, and worthless beyond six or seven.[75] The current consensus is that through improvements of the computer model, the global observation system and diagnostical methodology, the reliability that has been achieved for three-day predictions could realistically be extended to cover five or perhaps, in case of virtually unlimited technical

---

[63] *Ibid.*, pp. 61 and 70; Gleick, 1998, pp. 8 and 20.
[64] In fact, its behaviour might never settle reliably into any long-term equilibrium. Gleick, *ibid.*, pp. 168-170.
[65] Tennekes, 2001, pp. 28 and 61.
[66] Gleick, 1998, p. 94.
[67] Tennekes, 2001, p. 62.
[68] *Ibid.*, p. 51.
[69] *Ibid.*, p. 62.
[70] *Ibid.*, p. 23.
[71] *Ibid.*, pp. 14-15, 23. Pottering is how Tennekes refers to it, at the latter page. Also Jiménez Beltrán, 2001, p. 4.
[72] Gleick, 1998, pp. 11-31; Tennekes, *ibid.*, *passim.*
[73] Tennekes, *ibid.*, p. 82.
[74] Gleick, 1998, pp. 19-20.
[75] *Ibid.*; Tennekes, 2001, pp. 12, 26-27.

possibilities, seven days. No more. Not with a million weather satellites.[76] Once more the main culprit is called sensitive dependence on initial conditions. The infinitely complicated microstructure of the atmosphere and its non-linearity amount to what is, only half jokingly, referred to as the 'butterfly effect', the idea that the dance of a butterfly in a Brazilian forest today may be related to the occurrence of a tornado in Texas next month.[77] Uncertainties and errors in the initial measurement of weather conditions are inevitable, and such deficiencies cascade rapidly upwards through the scales of the atmospheric system, ultimately derailing every forecast.[78] As James Gleick explains:

> The modern weather models work with a grid of points on the order of sixty miles apart, and even so, some starting data has to be guessed, since ground stations and satellites cannot see everywhere. But suppose the earth could be covered with sensors spaced one foot apart, rising at one-foot intervals all the way to the top of the atmosphere. Suppose every sensor gives perfectly accurate readings of temperature, pressure, humidity, and any other quantity a meteorologist would want. Precisely at noon an infinitely powerful computer takes all the data and calculates what will happen at each point at 12:01, then 12:02, then 12:03... The computer will still be unable to predict whether Princeton, New Jersey, will have sun or rain on a day one month away. At noon the spaces between the sensors will hide fluctuations that the computer will not know about, tiny deviations from the average. By 12:01, those fluctuations will already have created small errors one foot away. Soon the errors will have multiplied to the ten-foot scale, and so on up to the size of the globe.[79]

Ergo, it turns out that some of the restraints that must be faced when predicting the weather are of a very fundamental kind.[80] The weather thus poses as a perfect example of the imperfect predictability of the evolution of natural systems in general.[81] Put allegorically, the ball-shape of the planet does not fit the square logic of science.[82]

To avoid misunderstanding, in nature chaos and order are not mutually exclusive.[83] That ecosystems are non-linear and their future states highly dependent on slight perturbations of initial conditions does not imply a lack of organization. Quite the contrary, within the earth system, as stressed previously, everything is interrelated and points to a high level of organization. In that sense, no event is ever truly coincidental. That no event is ever completely predictable either is a separate issue. Frequently, within

---

[76] Tennekes, *ibid.*, pp. 12, 26-27, 51, 82; Gleick, 1998, pp. 20-21.
[77] Gleick, *ibid.*, pp. 8 and 20, referring again to the work of Lorenz.
[78] Tennekes, 2001, pp. 18, 26-28, 51; Gleick, *ibid.*, pp. 20-21.
[79] Gleick, *ibid.*, p. 21.
[80] *Ibid.*, pp. 20-21; Tennekes, 2001, pp. 18 and 26-27.
[81] Tennekes, *ibid.*, p. 8.
[82] Paraphrased after Tennekes, 2001, p. 95.
[83] Gleick, 1998, pp. 15, 44, 48, 152, 157, 300; Tennekes, *ibid.*, pp. 53-54.

well-marked timeframes one can discern patterns amidst complexity and chaos, suggestions of structure amidst seemingly random conduct.[84] It is not uncommon, for example, for animal populations to rise and fall almost regularly and for epidemics to come and go on tantalizingly near-regular schedules, whereas at the same time biological models of predator-prey interactions and the spread of epidemics provide some of the most classic demonstrations of chaotic behaviour.[85] They represent disorder channelled into patterns, or "orderly disorder".[86] On occasions like this, where precision and conclusiveness are out of the question, *trends* can nevertheless more or less reliably be indicated for the short, and sometimes even for the longer term. Imagine the chaotic dance of a fly around a lamp, whereby no trajectory is ever exactly repeated. Even though accurate prediction of the fly's whereabouts for even a few seconds onward is obviously problematic, it may still reasonably be expected to stay in the vicinity of the lamp – behaviour that is locally unpredictable but globally stable.[87] Returning to the weather, in certain regions depressions develop much more often than in others, one instance being the Newfoundland area; yet definite time and place can never be foretold.[88] However difficult it is to grasp this, nature is at once chaotic, complex and orderly.[89] Chaos, then, does not entail disorder. It *does* entail unpredictability.

The insights summed up here appear to have put a definitive end to the general idea of deterministic predictability, meaning that in principle, and in due time, everything is knowable and foreseeable, an idea often associated with the mechanical science of Newton, Leibnitz and, first and foremost, Laplace, who wrote:

> Given for one instant an intelligence which could comprehend all the forces by which nature is animated and the respective situation of the beings who compose it – an intelligence sufficiently vast to submit these data to analysis – it would embrace in the same formula the movements of the greatest bodies of the universe and those of the lightest atom; for it, nothing would be uncertain and the future, as the past, would be present before its eyes.[90]

---

[84] Gleick, *ibid.*, *passim*.

[85] *Ibid.*, pp. 22, 59-80; Bell, 2002, p. 3. One famous example is the fluctuating record of two hundred years of Canadian lynx (*Lynx canadensis*), as inferred from trapper data: see Gleick, *ibid.*, p. 79. It will be remembered that a tiny lack of linearity suffices to provoke chaotic and unpredictable behaviour.

[86] Gleick, *ibid.*, pp. 15, 152.

[87] Tennekes, 2001, p. 33, under reference to Lorenz; Gleick, *ibid.*, pp. 48-49.

[88] Tennekes, *ibid.*, p. 34.

[89] Gleick, 1998, p. 300; Tennekes, *ibid.*, pp. 53-54.

[90] Pierre-Simon Laplace (1749-1827), *A Philisophical Essay on Probabilities*, New York 1951; as quoted in Brilmont, 1996. See also Gleick, *ibid.*, p. 6; Pascual Trillo, 2000, pp. 161-162; Tennekes, 2001, p. 73.

After formulating this universal determinism Laplace himself, however, conceded that humanity would always remain "infinitely distant" from the intelligence just introduced, thus distancing himself from any belief in perfect predictability.[91] Indeed, in more recent times the surmise has been that given an *approximate* knowledge of a system's initial conditions and an understanding of natural law, the *approximate* future conditions can be calculated.[92] To be sure this notion often holds true.[93] A small error in fixing the position of Comet Halley in 1910 would only cause a small error in predicting its arrival in 1986, and would probably stay insignificant well into the future.[94] Excellent forecasting can also be done for eclipses, in spite of the rather complex dynamics of sun, moon and earth, as well as for oceanic tides, which can be predicted fairly well a few months ahead.[95] All the same, as explained before, in a good many cases an approximately accurate input can*not* be obtained and in a good many others where it *can*, the output is not nearly approximately accurate as a result of non-linear, chaotic features. Deterministic predictability has proven to be the exception rather than the rule.[96] According to Greek mythology Gaia, the earth goddess that symbolizes in the present context the complexity of nature, was fathered by the vacant, unfathomable space from which everything arose, the beginning of the genealogy of the gods: Chaos. As discussed above, the combined forces of Chaos and Gaia, variability and complexity, present science with frontiers that cannot be shifted[97] – although, of course, even on this count *absolutely* conclusive certainty cannot be guaranteed...

Other Sources of Uncertainty

Piling on all this uncertainty is the fact that the present-day ubiquity and intensity of human interaction with natural processes, i.e., the "complex feedbacks between socioeconomic and ecological systems,"[98] hampers the

---

[91] Brilmont, *ibid.*

[92] As theoretician Winfree phrased it once: "The basic idea of Western science is that you don't have to take into account the falling of a leaf on some planet in another galaxy when you're trying to account for the motion of a billiard ball on a pool table on earth. Very small influences can be neglected. There's a convergence in the way things work, and arbitrarily small influences don't blow up to have arbitrarily large effects." As cited by Gleick, 1998, p. 15.

[93] Gleick, *ibid.*

[94] *Ibid.*, p. 15.

[95] *Ibid.*, pp. 13-14, 18.

[96] Pascual Trillo, 2000, pp. 161-162; Tennekes, 2001, p. 73.

[97] The mythological analogy could actually be taken much further so as to include, for instance, the case of the atmosphere considered above – given that Uranus, the Father Sky, was held to be the common offspring of Gaia and Chaos.

[98] Kumar Duralappah *et al.*, 2005, p.

identification of observed developments as either genuinely natural, anthropogenic, or a combination of the two.[99] As related in the foregoing chapter, the latter is the case more often than not.[100] The sea otters of the Pacific coast of North America are a case in point. After intensive human harvesting severely reduced or even extinguished otter populations in many parts, numbers of sea urchins (one of the otters' prey species) soared, which led to marked reductions of kelp forests (the kelp being eaten by the urchins) and many dependent species. Otter reintroduction projects aimed at restoring former ecosystems, in turn, have failed on account of a diet shift of Alaskan killer whales, which switched to eating sea otters after seals and sea lions were overharvested by humans.[101] Two more familiar examples of environmental problems where the difficulty to distinguish between the three risk types is prominent are climate change and algal blooms. To continue, the geographical proportions of many anthropogenic impacts are vast.[102] Pollutants are carried across large distances by wind, water and in the tissue of organisms.[103] Another complicating circumstance is the common occurrence of, sometimes lengthy, delays between causal events and the moment environmental damage comes about or becomes apparent to science – a phenomenon known as inertia.[104] None of these features can, of course, be separated from the interrelatedness and complexity of nature. Inertia and complexity are conspicuous factors, for instance, with respect to ozone layer depletion, climate change and the 'extinction debt' incurred by habitat loss. Regarding the latter, even if the destruction and fragmentation of natural habitats were to end today, so the synthesis report of the Millennium Ecosystem Assessment affirms, "it would take hundreds of years for species numbers to reach a new and lower equilibrium due to the habitat changes that have taken place in the last centuries."[105] The process called bioaccumulation, whereby concentrations of

---

[99] See, e.g., the fourteenth preambular paragraph of the 2001 *Reykjavik Declaration*, stressing the "complex interrelationship" between fisheries and the components of marine ecosystems; or the preamble to the Eritrean *Environment Proclamation No. 1996* as quoted in Marr, 2003, p. 85, which takes note of the "dynamic interrelationships among terrestrial and marine ecosystems and the impacts of human activities on them."

[100] See paragraph 3.1.

[101] See Kumar Duralappah *et al.*, 2005, p. 27; Reid *et al.*, 2005, p. 90.

[102] See Trouwborst, 2002, pp. 8-10 and the sources mentioned there; also Bouma *et al.*, 2002, p. 18.

[103] *Ibid.*

[104] Trouwborst, *ibid.*, pp. 9-10 plus sources mentioned there; also Reid *et al.*, 2005, p. 88; Kumar Duralappah *et al.*, 2005, pp. 21-24; Bouma *et al.*, *ibid.*; Klinke & Renn, 1999, p. 18; Federale Raad voor Duurzame Ontwikkeling, 2001, p. 14; Bell, 2002, p. 2.

[105] Reid *et al.*, *ibid.*, who go on to explain: "Habitat loss can lead to rapid extinction of some species (such as those with extremely limited ranges); but for many species, extinction will only occur after many generations, and long-lived species such as some trees could persist for centuries before ultimately going extinct."

contaminants augment in each subsequent link of the food chain, from microscopic beings up to top predators, is also responsible for the occurrence of time lags between causes and effects.[106] Effects of a substance, for instance the insecticide DDT, may thus stay invisible until critical levels are exceeded in predator populations, offsetting harm that may not be easily undone.[107] Similar considerations apply to the buffering capacity of lakes, soils and other environmental recipients. As long as contamination with, e.g., phosphorus or cadmium remains within the bounds of this capacity no obvious changes in the dependent ecosystem occur. The one small increase that eventually pushes the level beyond the maximum, however, can provoke sudden and dramatic alterations.[108] Other examples of non-linear alterations caused in whole or in part by human pressures on ecosystems include explosive algal blooms due to nutrient loading,[109] the rapid shifts of some tropical reefs from a coral-dominated to an algae-dominated state,[110] sudden fish stock collapses due to overexploitation,[111] and the implosion of numerous African and Asian wildlife populations after sustained exploitation fuelled by a growing demand for bushmeat.[112] It goes without saying that for various reasons it is difficult to accurately gauge the ability of environmental media and ecosystems to accommodate or assimilate pollution and other disturbance, in other words, to pinpoint the location of the critical thresholds involved in non-linear changes,[113] although this has not always been acknowledged. Indeed, in its early days the precautionary principle was put forward largely as a response to the apparent failure of, as the *Bamako Convention* describes it, "a permissible emissions approach based on assimilative capacity assumptions,"[114] which had long been the leading approach.[115] As a final complicating factor, when various polluting substances meet in the environment the aggregate impact may be synergetic

---

[106] Ebbesson, 1996, pp. 8-9; Trouwborst, 2002, pp. 9-10.

[107] *Ibid.*

[108] Reid *et al.*, 2005, pp. 88-91; Ebbesson, *ibid.*; Trouwborst, *ibid.*; Bell, 2002, p. 3.

[109] Reid *et al, ibid.*, p. 89.

[110] *Ibid.*, p. 90; Kumar Duralappah *et al.*, 2005, p. 22.

[111] Reid *et al.*, *ibid.*

[112] *Ibid.*, p. 91.

[113] As Reid *et al.*, *ibid.*, p. 88, sketch the current state of affairs: "Capabilities for predicting some nonlinear changes are improving, but for most ecosystems and for most potential nonlinear changes, while science can often warn of increased risks of change, it cannot predict the thresholds where the change will be encountered." *Ibid.*, p. 102: "There is a lack of theories and models that anticipate thresholds that, once passed, yield fundamental system changes or even system collapse." Kumar Duralappah *et al.*, 2005, p. 22, explain that understanding the thresholds involved requires having long-term records, "but such records are usually lacking or monitoring has been too infrequent, of the wrong periodicity, or too localized to provide the necessary data to analyze and predict threshold behavior."

[114] Article 3(f).

[115] See Trouwborst, 2002, pp. 18-19.

(1+1=3).[116] Again, the prediction of such cumulative results is problematic. All in all, it will be evident that human-ecosystem interaction normally adds to the uncertainties already inherent in nature itself. As a result, it can take years, decades or indeed an eternity for the effects of anthropogenic activities to be known and understood.[117]

So as to attain at least some degree of understanding of intricate natural processes and to enable at least some degree of predictability of the consequences of human impacts scientists develop models, more or less detailed simulations of reality. By definition, however, models are simplifications, and only as reliable and precise as the information fed into them.[118] "Simulations break reality into chunks, as many as possible but always too few."[119] Frequently, scientific knowledge is adequate enough to describe and comprehend the functional relations of a system in general terms, but, and this is true especially when a complex non-linear system is concerned, not sufficiently refined to mathematically model its long-term behaviour with reasonable precision.[120] Even the most sophisticated models render *approximate* predictions at best.[121]

Rehearsing what has been outlined in this chapter so far, model uncertainties can have any of several causes. They could be due to lack of measurements, or accuracy thereof – epistemological uncertainty. They could also be due to systemic indeterminacy, the complexity and variability of natural systems – ontological uncertainty. When the uncertainty involved in a model is substantial and either ontological or of a practically irreducible epistemological nature, then genuine surprises are a constant possibility. The ecological impact of PCBs and the consequences of halocarbon degradation in the stratosphere were just two instances of "the unanticipated complexity of the real world."[122] Returning to the intensively studied Newfoundland cod mentioned above, the best management models currently available will legitimately support claims of stock status ranging from sustainable growth to dangerous decline.[123] Needless to say, beforehand it will not always be clear under which category a particular uncertainty resorts, that is, whether it is

---

[116] *Ibid.*, p. 9 and the sources named there.

[117] Also Bell, 2002, p. 2.

[118] Tickner *et al.*, 2000, p. 12; Molenaar, 2002, pp. 33-34; Von Moltke, 2000.

[119] Gleick, 1998, p. 210.

[120] Paris & Paris, 1996, under reference to Ehrlich, P.R & Ehrlich, A.H., *Healing the Planet*, New York 1991; also Reid *et al.*, 2005, p. 102.

[121] Lemons *et al.*, 1997, pp. 215-216. A French physicist, Albert Libchaber, liked to say he did not fancy flying in a simulated airplane, because he would not stop wondering what part had been missed (cited in Gleick, 1998, at p. 210).

[122] European Environment Agency, 2001, p. 175.

[123] Harris, L., *Independent Review of the State of the Northern Cod Stock*, Department of Fisheries and Oceans, Ontario 1990; quoted in MacGarvin, 2001(b), p. 21.

potentially resolvable or not. One way or the other, as Christine Todd Whitman, former Administrator of the US Environmental Protection Agency (EPA), put it: "We must acknowledge that uncertainty is inherent in managing natural resources."[124]

The justification of this relatively elaborate exposition of the various sources of uncertainty lies, *inter alia*, in the importance of driving home the notion that there is uncertainty that is surmountable and uncertainty that is not; things that are unknown and things that are unknowable.[125] Below, the question will be addressed whether the precautionary principle under customary international law covers both types. The distinction between deterministic and indeterminable matters also plays a crucial role in the discussion of the duration of precautionary measures that will be dealt with later on.[126]

Quantifiable Risk, Uncertainty Proper and Ignorance

There is a growing literature on uncertainty, wherein various detailed classifications of the concept have been proposed.[127] Thus far the discussion has primarily focused on its different *sources*. Several schemes that differentiate between types of uncertainty in reliance on the criterion of source go beyond the main divisions into epistemological and ontological, and reducible and irreducible uncertainty. It is not necessary to debate these at length in the current context.[128] Another way of looking at uncertainty turns not on the source but on the *angle*. That is to say, uncertainty may concern the hazard or the harm, or both. In the first instance there is uncertainty regarding the cause of established damage. In the second instance there is uncertainty regarding the

---

[124] October 2000 speech at the National Academy of Sciences, Washington, D.C., as cited in Appell, 2001. By then she was still governor of the state New Jersey. See also Lemons *et al.*, 1997, pp. 210-211; Beeckman, 1996, p. 474.

[125] Bouma *et al.*, 2002, p. 8, also emphasize the significance of this distinction.

[126] See *infra* paragraph 7.3.

[127] For an overview, see Bouma *et al.*, 2002, pp. 8-10.

[128] A number of authors with the kinds or sources of uncertainty they mention: Lemons *et al.*, 1997, p. 209 (informational uncertainty, limitations of available analytical tools, the complexity and indeterminacy of ecosystems, the need to make value judgments); O'Riordan & Cameron, 1994(b), pp. 62-68 (lack of data, variability of process, indeterminacy); Tallacchini, 1999, pp. 1095-1096 (*idem*); Raffensperger, 2000 (parameter, model and systemic uncertainty, indeterminacy); Tickner *et al.*, 1998/1999, p. 12 (parameter, model, systemic, smokescreen and politically induced uncertainty, indeterminacy, ignorance); Department of the Environment, Transport and the Regions, *Guidelines for Environmental Risk Assessment and Management: Revised Departmental Guidance*, 2000, paragraph 1.6 (model, sample, data, knowledge and environmental uncertainty).

effect of an established hazard.[129] In neither case can a cause and effect relationship be properly determined.[130]

It will be recalled that technically speaking, risk is a function of the expected adverse consequences of a particular event (gravity of harm) and the likelihood of these consequences actually coming about (probability of harm).[131] Uncertainty may relate to either or both of these elements.[132] Of the essence in this respect is the frequently applied approach that distinguishes between *quantifiable risk*, *uncertainty proper* and *ignorance*.[133] These analytically distinct concepts all resort under 'uncertainty' as commonly understood in every-day and legal speech. 'Uncertainty' may thus be used alternately to connote only technical uncertainty or as covering the other two types as well. Some elaboration of this classification is therefore obviously in place, if only to counter the confusion of tongues that sometimes blurs discussions on the definition and application of the precautionary principle as a result of this terminological overlap.

A risk is called quantifiable when both gravity and probability can be more or less reliably estimated and expressed in numbers. Possible outcomes and their relative likelihood are 'known' in advance.[134] Quantifiable risks can thus be measured against each other. Uncertainty in the limited sense corresponds to hazards where the array of possible effects can be adequately established, but the scientific basis, whether empirical or theoretical, for assigning probabilities to the various outcomes is insufficient.[135] Again, this may be due to lack of knowledge, the variability or complexity of nature, or simply the novelty of the activity or technology concerned. Finally, in cases of ignorance as formally defined, (some of) the possibilities themselves, and automatically also their likelihood of occurrence, remain unknown.[136] In other words, in those instances "we don't know what we don't know."[137] Thus in the

---

[129] Rogers, 2001, p. 2.

[130] Cameron & Abouchar, 1996, p. 45

[131] See *supra* paragraph 2.2.

[132] Backes *et al.*, 2002, p. 247.

[133] See, *inter alia*, European Environment Agency, 2001, pp. 169-170, 184, 192; Bouma *et al.*, 2002, pp. 9-10; Klinke & Renn, 1999, p. 11; Federale Raad voor Duurzame Ontwikkeling, 2001, pp. 12, 17-18.

[134] European Environment Agency, *ibid.*, p. 170.

[135] *Ibid.*

[136] *Ibid*; De Sadeleer, 2002, p. 153.

[137] Bouma *et al.*, 2002, pp. 9-10, referring to Wynne, B., "Uncertainty and Environmental Learning: Reconceiving Science and Policy in the Preventive Paradigm", in: *Global Environmental Change*, June 1992, pp. 111-127; and to Wynne, B., "Managing Scientific Uncertainty in Public Policy", Harvard GMOs background paper, Congress on Biotechnology and Global Governance, Cambridge, 26-28 April 2001; similarly, Tickner *et al.*, 2000, p. 12.

field of fisheries it is appropriate to distinguish between uncertainties attached to stock estimates and ignorance regarding ecology.[138] (See Figure 4.)[139]

	Gravity	*Probability*
Quantifiable risk	'known'	'known'
Uncertainty proper	'known'	unknown
Ignorance	unknown	unknown

Figure 4. Kinds of uncertainty: quantifiable risk, uncertainty proper and ignorance.[140] The word 'known' appears between quotes because it tends to represent approximations rather than genuine certainties.

Ignorance is the area of the unexpected. In the 1980s it was believed, for instance, that tributyltin (TBT), a substance used in antifoulants for ship hulls, would degrade rapidly in surface waters. As it turned out, their persistence had been greatly underestimated. The resulting accumulation of organotins in marine predators at the top of the food chain was just plainly not envisaged.[141] Other examples are the unpredictable combined effects of chemicals that separately enter the environment,[142] the potential, as yet little known impacts of genetically modified organisms on ecosystems,[143] the many unanticipated effects following introductions of species in and deletions of species from natural ecosystems,[144] and the entirely unforeseen deterioration of the ozone layer that was a side-effect of CFC emissions. The latter renders a particularly apt illustration of the potentially catastrophic consequences of human ignorance:

---

138 MacGarvin, 2001(b), p. 26.

139 In theory a fourth class can be distinguished, whereby gravity is unknown but probability is 'known'.

140 Adapted from European Environment Agency, *ibid.*, p. 192.

141 Santillo *et al.*, 2001, p. 141; European Environment Agency, *ibid.*, p. 170.

142 Philippopoulos-Mihalopoulos, 1999, pp. 188-189.

143 Pascual Trillo, 2000, p. 152.

144 For a selection of examples see Delibes de Castro, 2001, pp. 175-203; Kumar Duralappah *et al.*, 2005, pp. 25-27.

> There is overwhelming evidence that the stratospheric ozone shield against harmful UV-B radiation has been perforated accidentally by industrial by-products, in particular by chlorofluorocarbons (CFCs). The physicochemical processes causing this disturbing effect are intricate; they were deciphered only a few years ago and the elucidators awarded a Nobel prize. But 'things could be much worse', as one of the laureates, Paul Crutzen, puts it: 'Bromine is almost a hundred times more dangerous for ozone than chlorine. If the chemical industry had developed organobromine compounds instead of CFCs then... we would have been faced with a catastrophic ozone hole everywhere and all year-round during the 1970s – probably before atmospheric scientists had developed the knowledge necessary to identify the problem.'[145]

Indeed in the environmental field knowledge, no matter how sophisticated, will virtually always be subject to some degree of ignorance as to future effects. As the European Environment Agency put it: "Surprise is inevitable."[146]

Naturally, increased research can serve to convert aspects of ignorance into uncertainty proper, and uncertainties into quantifiable risks.[147] There are no guarantees that this will always be so, however.[148] In fact, sometimes the result is quite the opposite, when scientific research raises additional questions instead of supplying the answers sought after, uncovering new sources of ignorance in the process.[149] A clear instance is the intensive study of the Newfoundland cod already mentioned above. The more biological data were fed into a model designed to understand the dynamics between cod and other fish species, the more unpredictable these dynamics became.[150] Likewise, initially the extensive examinations into the contamination of the North-American Great Lakes progressively generated new questions regarding the potential causes of the bird population crashes that had been observed.[151]

Uncertainty and the Scope of the Precautionary Principle

In the practice of states, both internationally and nationally, the precautionary principle has been employed along the entire spectrum of uncertainty – from quantifiable risks through to cases where ignorance was the dominating feature, and equally to instances of epistemological and ontological uncertainty. The vast and diverse range of issue areas and environmental problems to which the principle has been applied bears

---

145 Schellnhuber, 1999, p. C22

146 European Environment Agency, 2001, p. 169; De Sadeleer, 2002, p. 153.

147 European Environment Agency, *ibid.*, p. 172.

148 Von Moltke, 1999.

149 European Environment Agency, 2001, pp. 172-173; Bouma *et al.*, 2002, pp. 9-10.

150 European Environment Agency, *ibid.*, p. 172.

151 *Ibid.*, pp. 172-173.

witness to this, from forests to fisheries, from the ozone layer to ocean dumping, and from migratory birds to climate change, to name a few.[152]

Furthermore, the texts of relevant provisions from legal and policy instruments yield no indications whatsoever that it was the intention of the drafters to exclude any particular class or classes of uncertainty from the principle's reach. Take, for instance, the unqualified reference to a "lack of full scientific certainty" in Principle 15 of the *Rio Declaration.* A similar statement of general scope can be found in the European Commission's *Communication COM(2000)1*, in which the precautionary principle is related to situations "where scientific information is insufficient, inconclusive, or uncertain."[153]

The following sample of provisions taken from international instruments with a more specific focus serves to reinforce this assumption, beginning with a passage from the 1991 *Action Plan for the Conservation of Cetaceans in the Mediterranean Sea*:

> Many important aspects of cetacean biology, behaviour, range and habitats in the Mediterranean are poorly known, but the actual degradation of the population is such that action can no longer be postponed, in line with the precautionary principle [..].[154]

For the parties to the *Bamako Convention* precaution means, among other things, "preventing the release into the environment of substances which may cause harm to humans or the environment without waiting for scientific proof regarding such harm."[155] The *OSPAR Convention* prescribes recourse to the precautionary principle when there is "no conclusive evidence of a causal relationship between inputs and the effects."[156] Such recourse is recommended "in cases of uncertainty" in a resolution agreed upon in 1994 by the states parties to the 1973 *Convention on International Trade in Endangered Species of Wild Fauna and Flora* (*CITES*).[157] The 1995 *Straddling Stocks Agreement* stipulates that "States shall be more cautious when information is uncertain, unreliable or inadequate."[158] The *Code of Conduct for Responsible Fisheries* that was adopted, also in 1995, within the framework of the UN Food and Agriculture Organization (FAO) urges action in the "absence of adequate scientific information."[159] The pertinent provisions of the *Biosafety Protocol*, meanwhile, speak of a "[l]ack of scientific certainty due to insufficient relevant scientific

---

152 See further *infra* paragraph 5.2 and Trouwborst, 2002, *passim*.

153 P. 8.

154 Paragraph 4.

155 Article 3(f).

156 Article 2(2)(a).

157 *Resolution Conf. 9.24 on Criteria for Amendment of Appendices I and II.*

158 Article 6(2) of the *Agreement for the Implementation of the Provisions of the 1982 LOS Convention Relating to the Conservation and Management of Straddling Fish Stocks and Highly Migratory Fish Stocks.*

159 Principles 6.5 and 7.5.1.

information and knowledge,"[160] whereas, finally, the wording of the provisions of the *POPs Convention* elaborating the precautionary principle contains "Lack of scientific certainty" and "any scientific uncertainty," respectively.[161] Again, seemingly all sorts of uncertainty are covered. The ECJ has drawn the scope of the principle equally broadly by observing that it applies where there is "scientific uncertainty as to the *existence* or *extent* of risks."[162]

Prima facie, then, not a single category of uncertainty can be considered as outside the reach of the precautionary principle under customary international law. This is hardly surprising, given that with most environmental risks it is often difficult, if not impossible, to know beforehand whether, and to what degree uncertainties will be reduced in the future.

4.2. Asking the Right Question

Is action under the precautionary principle taken *because* of uncertainty or *in spite* of uncertainty? The answer determines the angle from which the principle is to be approached. It determines which of the following two questions is the right one to ask:

(a) How much uncertainty *must* there be for the precautionary principle to apply?
(b) How much uncertainty *may* there be for the precautionary principle to apply?

Taking Action Because of Uncertainty...
It is quite common for environmental NGOs to oppose a novel activity or technology in reliance on the argument that its effects are not or insufficiently known. One obvious example is the introduction of GMOs into the natural environment. The scientific prospecting of Lake Vostok, a huge lake buried under almost four kilometres of ice in East Antarctica, is another. Uncertainty surrounding the lake's geochemical and biological composition and regarding the possible impact of mechanical drilling on this pristine environment is brandished as a key argument by NGOs, as well as many scientists and governments, to advocate a precautionary moratorium on such drilling.[163]

---

[160] Articles 10(6) and 11(8).
[161] See Article 8, paragraphs (7) and (9).
[162] *Alpharma Inc. v Council of the European Union*, Case T-70/99, Judgment by the Court of First Instance of 11 September 2002, paragraph 152; emphasis added.
[163] See *Resolution 2.54 on Antarctica and the Southern Ocean* that was adopted by consensus, albeit with the abstention of the United States, at the 2nd World Conservation Congress (General Assembly of the IUCN), held 4-11 October 2000 in Amman. See also the viewpoint of the

Neither is it unusual to come across academic lawyers suggesting that precautionary measures are measures taken *because of* a lack of knowledge as to potential harm.[164] Tickner *cum suis* submit with respect to the precautionary principle that "[h]igh uncertainty about possible harm is good reason not to go ahead with a project."[165] Moreover, Backes *cum suis* wonder what level of *un*certainty there must be for recourse to the principle to be enabled.[166]

Such statements ought to be carefully assessed. On the face of it, uncertainty appears to be presented in them as a *conditio sine qua non* for the application of the precautionary principle. In other words: action is taken because of uncertainty – no uncertainty, no action. There are, nevertheless, several good reasons to assume that this interpretation does not fully do justice to the opinions concerned, and perhaps even utterly misrepresents them, and reality besides.

...Or Taking Action in Spite of Uncertainty?

On a preliminary note, no matter how basic an ingredient of the precautionary principle it may be, uncertainty comes second, after the prevention of damage to the environment. As set out earlier, the recognition of the often serious and irreversible character of harm to nature constituted as important a reason for the evolution of the principle as the acknowledgment of the limitations of science when it comes to understanding and predicting the environmental consequences of human activities.[167]

Much more significantly, however, the position that the precautionary principle mandates action *because of* uncertainty does not adequately reflect the practice of states. In the first place, Principle 15 of the *Rio Declaration* and the many other provisions of international and national instruments that are either similarly phrased or directly refer to Principle 15, postulate that where environmental harm is threatened "lack of full scientific certainty shall not be used as a reason for postponing" preventive measures.[168] That is, action to ward off potential hazards may not be impeded by uncertainty. The trigger for any measures that may be required by the precautionary principle is obviously the concern that damage may be caused, and not the scientific uncertainty itself. Put another way, according

---

Antarctic and Southern Ocean Coalition, made up of 230 conservation NGOs, at http://www.asoc.org/Lake%20Vostok/LakeVostok.htm.

[164] Backes *et al.*, 1997, p. 63.

[165] Tickner *et al.*, 2000, p. 9.

[166] Backes *et al.*, 2002, p. 66.

[167] See *supra* paragraph 3.1.

[168] On these provisions see, *inter alia*, *supra* paragraph 2.3.

to these provisions the precautionary principle demands action *in spite of* uncertainty, not because of it.[169]

In the second place, another number of instruments state this premise even more explicitly. To name an instance, in the 1992 *Baltic Sea Convention* the precautionary principle has been specified to require preventive action when there is reason to assume that emissions of substances or energy into the marine environment may be harmful, "*even when* there is no conclusive evidence of a causal relationship between inputs and their alleged effects."[170] Clearly, action *despite* uncertainty.[171] Similarly, the 2002 *ASEAN Agreement on Transboundary Haze Pollution*[172] sets out that "where there are threats of serious or irreversible damage from transboundary haze pollution, *even without full scientific certainty*, precautionary measures shall be taken by Parties concerned." The 1992 *OSPAR Convention*,[173] the 1996 *LDC Protocol*,[174] the 1997 *Trilateral Wadden Sea Plan*,[175] the European Commission's *Communication COM (2000)1*,[176] and several intergovernmental declarations on the protection of the oceans contain like formulations.[177] Examples of such formulations at the domestic level include a 1984 judgment of the German *Bundesverwaltungsgericht* (Federal Administrative Court),[178] the 1996 report of the US advisory body, the President's Council on Sustainable Development,[179] a Belgian federal Act of 1999 on the protection of the marine environment,[180] and various UK policy documents.[181] The environmental law of Mozambique is especially categorical, stating that the precautionary principle calls for the avoidance of significant or irreversible adverse environmental impacts "*independently* from the existence of scientific certainty about the occurrence of such impacts."[182]

---

169 Also Trouwborst, 2002, p. 40.
170 Article 3(2), emphasis added.
171 Trouwborst, 2002, p. 40.
172 Article 3(3); emphasis added.
173 Article 2(2)(a).
174 Article 3(1).
175 Paragraph 8.
176 At p. 13.
177 1987 *London Declaration*, paragraph XVI(1); 1989 *Nordic Council Declaration on Pollution of the Seas*; 1990 *Declaration of the Third International Conference on the Protection of the North Sea* (*Hague Declaration*), preamble; 1991 *Trilateral Wadden Sea Declaration*, paragraph 3.
178 Judgment of 14 February 1984, 69 *BverGE*, 1985, p. 43; see De Sadeleer, 2000, p. 145.
179 President's Council on Sustainable Development, *Sustainable America: A New Consensus*, 1996.
180 Article 4(3) of the *Wet ter Bescherming van het Mariene Milieu in de Zeegebieden onder de Rechtsbevoegdheid van België*, Act of 20 January 1999, *MB* of 12 March 1999. See Larmuseau, 2000(b), pp. 41-42; Trouwborst, 2002, p. 212.
181 1990 *White Paper "This Common Inheritance"*; 2000 *Guidelines for Environmental Risk Assessment and Management*.
182 Author's translation of the original text in Portuguese, which speaks of "evitar a ocorrência de impactos ambientais negativos significativos ou irreversiveis, independentemente da

In the third place, what the above formulations appear to suggest is that the precautionary principle requires preventive action wherever there is a sufficiently substantial threat, *regardless the existence or not of uncertainty*. There is indeed substantial evidence that this suggestion represents the actual state of international law. Since this issue has already been extensively discussed in another contribution, a brief summary of this evidence will suffice here.[183] In theory, to avert 'certain' hazards is preventive and to avert 'uncertain' hazards is precautionary.[184] In the real world, as will be apparent at this stage, this distinction is a rather hazy one by any means. That the real world of state practice is no exception in this respect can be told from the blurred boundaries between the precautionary principle and the so-called preventive principle, or principle of prevention.[185] The latter is aimed at the prevention of environmental harm as such, that is *anywhere*, whether within or outside the borders of states. This preventive principle ought not to be confused with the customary obligation to refrain from causing *transboundary* environmental harm, also known as 'Principle 21' (of the *Stockholm Declaration*). As a separate general principle of international environmental law the preventive principle seems to be less firmly established than the precautionary principle, or Principle 21 for that matter.[186] Rather, states tend to rely on the precautionary principle as the flag that covers the entire cargo of preventive measures, whether taken under scientific uncertainty or not. In any case, it would be absurd to deny that precaution presupposes prevention. This is as true in international law as it is in ordinary life. The fact that many legal instruments prescribe the application of the precautionary principle while *not* separately mentioning the preventive principle, can impossibly be interpreted to mean that 'uncertain dangers' are to be prevented while 'certain dangers' may be allowed to materialize.[187] The precautionary principle can thus be considered alternatively as effectively comprising the preventive principle, as presupposing its application, or as constituting its most developed form. In legal terms, the outcome of either point of view is the same. As a matter of international law the precautionary principle calls for preventive action regardless of the presence or absence of scientific uncertainty – however strange this may initially appear.[188] More in particular, any customary rights or duties of states, deriving from the precautionary

existência de certeza científica sobre a ocorrência de tais impactos." Article 4(3) of 1997 *Lei no. 20/97*, reproduced at: http://faolex.fao.org/docs/texts/moz15370.doc. Emphasis added.

[183] See Trouwborst, 2002, pp. 35-44.

[184] E.g., De Sadeleer, 2002, p. 222.

[185] Trouwborst, 2002, pp. 37-39.

[186] *Ibid.*,pp. 35-36.

[187] *Ibid.*, pp. 40-42.

[188] *Ibid.*, pp. 39-44.

principle, to take preventive measures in the face of environmental risks apply *whether there is uncertainty or not.*

It would seem appropriate, if only in order to avoid misunderstandings on this count, to employ wording unequivocally reflecting this state of affairs when attempting the definition of the precautionary principle under customary international law. The principle as defined in the 1990 *Bergen Declaration* offers one useful option:

> In order to achieve sustainable development, policies must be based on the precautionary principle. Environmental measures must anticipate, prevent and attack the causes of environmental degradation. Where there are threats of serious or irreversible damage, lack of full scientific certainty should not be used as a reason for postponing measures to prevent environmental degradation.[189]

The period at the end of the second sentence says it all. Environmental degradation must be prevented. That scientific uncertainty may not hamper this prevention is a separate addition. Another option is a formulation in the vein of the 2002 *ILA Declaration on Sustainable Development*, which specifies that a precautionary approach commits states "to avoid human activity which may cause significant harm to human health, natural resources or ecosystems, *including* in the face of scientific uncertainty."[190] This bears close resemblance to the construction with "even when" of the *Baltic Sea Convention* and other instruments mentioned above. The 2004 *ILA Berlin Rules on Water Resources*,[191] the *Wingspread Statement on the Precautionary Principle*, the European Chemical Industry Council[192] and many scholars take the same approach.[193] It appears that both options have their merits, although the second represents the more frequently occurring type of formulation and may for that reason be preferable.

The arguments just presented reinforce the conclusion that under the precautionary principle action is not primarily, nor even normally, taken *because* of scientific uncertainty but rather *despite* it, and indeed even in its apparent absence. This is not to say, linking back to this paragraph's introduction, that the opponents of drilling into Lake Vostok are consequently mistaken in using uncertainty as part of their case for a precautionary moratorium. The wider context of their plea demonstrates this point. Lake Vostok is a literally untouched space and there are good grounds

---

189 Paragraph 7.

190 Paragraph 4.1, emphasis added.

191 Article 23(2).

192 European Chemical Industry Council, 1995, paragraph 8.

193 Ebbesson, 1996, pp. 119-120; Martin, 1997, p. 276; Lemons *et al.*, 1997, p. 210; Dzidzornu, 1998, p. 98; Freestone, 1999, p. 137; Borgers, 1999, p. 435; Canelas de Castro, 1999, p. 199, note 155; Jones, 2000; Perrez, 2000, p. 289; Raffensperger, 2000; Tallacchini, 2000, p. 1096; Bell, 2002, p. 3.

to assume that its characteristics are unique, that it may include life forms presently unknown to science, and that its more than 400,000 years of isolation have made it particularly vulnerable to outside interference.[194] In this light, if the possibility of environmental harm to the lake as a result of drilling cannot be ruled out to any sufficient extent, then this is a cause for great concern. Only in this *indirect* way a lack of certainty can and indeed does constitute a motive for precautionary action – the *direct* motive always being some threatening scenario of harm to the environment. No doubt this is how the assertion by Tickner *et alia*, that a high level of uncertainty about potential harm can justify precautionary restrictions, must be interpreted.[195] Naturally this indirect prompting of precautionary action by scientific uncertainty mostly occurs when, as is the case with Lake Vostok, the object or interest to be protected is valued very highly. The same logic was apparently applied, for instance, in 1999 by the Dutch government to inform its decision, based on the precautionary principle, not to permit natural gas exploration in the Wadden Sea.[196] In a way, in such cases precautionary measures are instituted at the same time in spite *and*, albeit indirectly, because of uncertainty. One way or another, as one commentator wraps up the essence of the whole discussion: "The problem lies, not in what we do not *know*, but in what we *expect* to know."[197]

In Search of the Maximum Tolerable Level of Uncertainty

This automatically leads to the next issue, which is closely related. From time to time it is claimed by the promoters of particular activities, projects or technologies that these entail no environmental risks whatsoever of any significant or irreversible nature. An instructive example is the following statement on a field trial of genetically modified oilseed plants, by the spokeswoman of a French research centre: "Given its location and small size, this trial parcel ran no risk of having any irreversible impact on the environment."[198] Evidently, however, the fundamental limitations of the ability of science to predict environmental effects examined in the previous

[194] See the position paper on this issue by the Antarctic and Southern Ocean Coalition at http://www.asoc.org/Lake%20Vostok/LakeVostok.htm.
[195] Quoted *supra* in the introduction to this paragraph.
[196] See Trouwborst, 2002, pp. 210-211; Pieterman & Hanekamp, 2002, pp. 20-21.
[197] Philippopoulos-Mihalopoulos, 1999, p. 195; emphasis in original.
[198] Catherine Bureau of the *Centre Technique Interprofessionel des Oléagineux Metropolitains* (CETIOM), as quoted in Reuters' *World Environment News*, "Bove Goes Back to Court for Trashing French Crops", 17 September 2002.

paragraph of this study render it impossible to credibly give off any such bold guarantees.[199]

What is more, strictly speaking, absolute scientific certainty of *anything* – let alone of the future – must be deemed intrinsically impossible.[200] It is the very nature of science that precludes its possibility. Not a single premise, for instance on a given causal link, can be positively proven with certainty; it can only be proven wrong. Only falsification counts, i.e. any scientific statement is provisionally valid so long as it is not dismissed by contrary evidence. All scientific knowledge is thus finite by definition. To take the classic example of the swans, the long-standing hypothesis that all swans are white could never be proven; it could only be *dis*proven by the observation of differently coloured swans – which happened with the discovery of black swans in Australia. The story goes that Ludwig Wittgenstein once asked fellow philosopher Bertrand Russell whether he could prove that there was *not* a hippopotamus in the room. Both were soon on their knees to check beneath the couch, but could not deliver the final evidence of the non-presence of the animal.[201]

Hence, for any given human activity a measure of uncertainty concerning the probability or gravity of its environmental impact will always prevail. Irresolvable uncertainty about the future is a basic fact of life.[202] No amount of empirical research can remedy this. This has been generally acknowledged, not only by scientists but also by governments,[203] courts,[204] industrials,[205] etcetera.

---

199 This concerns the words "no risk" and "any" in the statement. On potential difficulties associated with the word "irreversible", see *supra* paragraph 3.3.

200 Kaiser, 1997(b), p. 312; Hagenah, 1999, p. 14; Hattis & Anderson, 1999, p. 103; Philippopoulos-Mihalopoulos, 1999, p. 194; Morris, 2000(b), pp. 10, 14; Wildavsky, 2000, p. 26; Tennekes, 2001, p. 63; European Environment Agency, 2001, p. 183; Rogers, 2001, p. 4; Pieterman, 2001, p. 1025; Pieterman & Hanekamp, 2002, p. 7; Bouma *et al.*, 2002, p. 13; Marr, 2003, pp. 9-10; Van Kasteren, J., "Waar Voorzorg Nalatig Wordt," in Dutch newspaper *Trouw*, 24 August 2002.

201 Van Kasteren, *ibid.*

202 Wildavsky, 2000, p. 26.

203 Dutch Minister of Environment Jan Pronk in a 1999 parliamentary debate on the decision concerning natural gas drilling in the Wadden Sea, discussed above: "We have acknowledged that science will never be able to provide absolute certainty." Translated from a citation in Backes *et al.*, 2002, at p.73.

204 In the 1994 Australian *Nicholls* case, Justice Talbot of the New South Wales Land and Environment Court stressed that "[e]ven the applicant concedes that scientific certainty is essentially impossible. It is only 500 years ago since most scientists were convinced the world was flat." *Nicholls v Director General, National Parks and Wildlife Service, the Forestry Commission of New South Wales and the Minister for Planning*, 29 September 1994, matter no. 10151, 84 *LGERA*, 1994, p. 397. By the same token, the German *Bundesverwaltungsgericht* observed in the 1985 *Wyhl* case that "[s]cience in its present state is not capable of predicting with certainty the consequences of certain acts and can therefore not say whether or not these effects represent a

Consequently, an interpretation of the precautionary principle as exacting preventive action whenever there is the *possibility* of an activity having (serious or irreversible) adverse environmental effects – in other words, requiring one hundred percent certainty of harmlessness in order to forestall precautionary measures – would be entirely unworkable in practice.[206] As alluded to in the introduction to the present study, critics of the precautionary principle have drawn attention to this potential incongruity.[207] "It is not possible to prove something is harmless, any more than it is possible to prove that there are no fairies at the bottom of one's garden."[208] In truth, it may well be that at low enough, extremely unlikely probabilities, the majority of activities have total disasters associated with them.[209] As Aaron Wildavsky once commented: "Why, just imagine – if everything else is held constant, an increase in goat's milk projected to infinity could drown the earth and everyone on it!"[210] Accordingly, if systematically applied, such an interpretation of the precautionary principle would lead to the utter standstill of human societies around the world.[211]

This goes to explain the frequent occurrence in formulations of the precautionary principle of prerequisites like 'sufficient grounds for believing' or 'reason to assume' that there is a threat, which are to be complied with before action is taken. These qualifying thresholds are obviously intended to keep the effect of the principle within reasonable bounds.[212] "Quite possibly, advocates of risk aversion wish to be prudent, but not extreme."[213]

The query to be addressed in the remainder of this chapter is therefore rather similar to the question posed above when dealing with the gravity of harm.[214] Having ascertained in the preceding paragraph that as an international custom the precautionary principle ostensibly applies to all *types*

---

danger." Judgment of 19 December 1985, *NVwZ*, 1986, p. 208. Translation based on De Sadeleer, 2000, p. 146.

205 European Chemical Industry Council, 1995, paragraph 8: "'absolute certainty' of anything is impossible by definition."

206 Fukudu-Parr *et al.*, 2001, p. 70; Rogers, 2001, p. 4; Morris, 2000(b), p. 10; Christensen, 2001, p. 5; Van Kasteren, J., "Waar Voorzorg Nalatig Wordt," in Dutch newspaper *Trouw*, 24 August 2002. Also Foster *et al.*, 2000, p. 979.

207 See *supra* paragraph 1.1; Pieterman, 2001, p. 1025.

208 Morris, 2000(b), p. 10. Recorded in the evidence received by an Inquiry of the New Zealand Royal Commission on Genetic Modification, as cited in Christensen, 2001, at p. 5, was the following observation: "If we would only cross the street if we had a 100% certainty that nothing would go wrong during the crossing we would never leave the curb."

209 Elster, J., "Risk, Uncertainty, and Nuclear Power", in: 18 *Social Science Information*, 1979, pp. 371-400, as quoted in Wildavsky, 2000, pp. 28-29.

210 Wildavsky, 2000, pp. 28-29.

211 Pieterman & Hanekamp, 2002, pp. v-vi, ix, 2 and 6.

212 Larmuseau, 2000(b), p. 42; Pieterman, 2001, p. 1025.

213 Wildavsky, 2000, p. 34.

214 See the last part of *supra* paragraph 3.1.

of uncertainty, does it also apply to all *levels* of probability of harm? That is, what, if any, minimum standards of proof of likelihood must be met to trigger a customary right or obligation of states to take precautionary action? The debate on the pros and cons of using such *de minimis* thresholds that evidence of likelihood must cross, unfolds along much the same lines as the comparable debate on the pros and cons of thresholds of harm, sketched in the previous chapter of this study.[215] Here as much as there, however, the issue that actually matters is whether international law attaches any such thresholds to the application of the precautionary principle, and not whether that condition of the law is pleasing from whatever other point of view.

The present paragraph has all been about asking the right question. That question, in conclusion, is not as to how much uncertainty is *required*,[216] but as to how much uncertainty is *tolerable* for the precautionary principle to become applicable.

4.3. *A Threshold of Proof*

As before when dealing with thresholds of harm, the search for an answer to the question of how much uncertainty is tolerable for the precautionary principle to still be applicable ought to focus first and foremost on the international and internal practice of states. What thresholds of proof, if any, figure in articulations of the precautionary principle that have been accepted by states, and can any coherent pattern be discerned in this practice?

The Existence of a Threshold of Proof

Some formulations do not, at first sight at least, employ any threshold whatsoever. The 1990 *Third North Sea Declaration* and the 1995 *Pan-European Biological and Landscape Diversity Strategy* refer to the avoidance of, respectively, "*potentially* damaging"[217] and "*potentially* adverse"[218] impacts. The ministerial declaration issued at the Second World Climate Conference in 1990 asserts that precautionary measures must anticipate and prevent "environmental degradation that *might* result from climate change."[219] In 1995 the North Sea coastal states agreed that it was in accordance with the precautionary principle to dismantle obsolete offshore installations on land, given that even

[215] *Ibid.*

[216] See the reference to Backes *et alia* at the outset of this paragraph.

[217] *Third North Sea Declaration*, preamble. Emphasis added.

[218] *Pan-European Biological and Landscape Diversity Strategy*, Section 2.4, paragraph 3. Emphasis added.

[219] Principle 7; emphasis added.

when emptied of noxious and hazardous materials, "they *might* still if dumped or left at sea, pose a threat to the marine environment."[220]

Similarly, the 1991 *Bamako Convention* and the 1992 *Central American Hazardous Wastes Agreement* speak of impeding the release into the environment of substances that *may*,[221] or *could*,[222] cause harm. In the words of the former, precaution entails "preventing the release into the environment of substances which may cause harm to humans or the environment without waiting for scientific proof regarding such harm."[223] The precautionary principle in the Swiss *Federal Act on Environmental Protection* is phrased in broadly similar terms.[224] According to the *Galapagos Agreement* of 2000, "*scarcity or lack* of available information shall not be construed as a reason to prevent or delay the adoption of precautionary measures."[225] Equally generously, the *IUCN Draft Covenant* and the environmental law of Eritrea state that "*lack* of scientific certainty is no reason to postpone action to avoid *potentially* significant or irreversible harm to the environment."[226] These articulations, and others like them,[227] do not as such indicate any minimum level of proof as a condition for the institution of precautionary measures.

The Australian Commonwealth Environmental Protection Agency does not do so either when stating that it is committed to taking precautionary action "in cases where there is *possibility* of environmental damage."[228] The United States Gilchrest-Farr *Fisheries Recovery Act* of 2000,[229] moreover, seems to explicitly rule out the existence of a minimum threshold of

---

[220] *Fourth North Sea Declaration*, paragraph 54; emphasis added.

[221] *Bamako Convention*, Article 3(f).

[222] *Central American Hazardous Wastes Agreement*, Article 3(3).

[223] Article 3(f). See also Sands, 1995(a), pp. 210-211.

[224] Article 1(2) of the 1983 *Bundesgesetz über den Umweltschutz, SR* 814.01: "Im Sinne der Vorsorge sind Einwirkungen, die schädlich oder lästig werden *könnten*, frühzeitig zu begrenzen." Emphasis added.

[225] Article 5(1)(b) of the *Framework Agreement for the Conservation of Living Marine Resources on the High Seas of the South Pacific*. Italics added.

[226] Article 7 of the *IUCN Draft Covenant*; and Article 17(b) of the *Environment Proclamation No. 1996*, as quoted in Marr, 2003, p. 86. Emphasis added in both cases.

[227] For instance, Article 8(4) of the 1993 Slovenian *Environmental Protection Act (No. 801-01/90-2/107)*, as reproduced in Marr, 2003, p. 95 ("where there is a danger of serious and irreparable damage to the environment, lack of scientific certainty may not be used as a reason for postponing such actions as may be necessary"); preambular paragraph A.7 of the *First North Sea Declaration* of 1984 ("coastal states and the EEC must not wait for proof of harmful effects before taking action"); *UNEP Governing Council Decision 15/27*; and *Resolution Conf. 9.24* adopted in 1994 within the framework of the *Convention on International Trade in Endangered Species of Wild Fauna and Flora (CITES)*.

[228] See Christie, 1993, p. 482; italics added.

[229] *HR* 4046.

proof. Under the terms of this law, a precautionary approach is to be applied "in any case in which information [as to the effects of fisheries on marine life] is absent, uncertain, unreliable, or inadequate."[230] Arguing along the same line, the Irish government claimed in the 1996 *NIREX* affair concerning plans for a British radioactive wastes storage project, that the "mere possibility of adverse consequences to Ireland" triggered the application of the precautionary principle.[231] Likewise, in a 1985 judgment involving the Wyhl nuclear reactor, the Federal Administrative Court (*Bundesverwaltungsgericht*) of West Germany held that "security measures should also be considered according to 'purely theoretical' thinking and calculations, so as adequately to exclude risks arising from uncertainties and lacunae in scientific understanding."[232]

The question is whether such an interpretation is indicative of the way the precautionary principle stands as a general principle of international environmental law, or whether it should rather be regarded as an exception to the rule. In other words, can purely hypothetical threats constitute a sufficient basis for mandating precautionary action? As explained in the previous paragraph, a legal rule to that end would be unworkable. Pieterman and Hanekamp contend in this regard that a duty to do the impossible can never be legally binding.[233] Whether there is indeed, as a matter of principle, such an intimate relationship between the physical possibility of performing a duty and its potential legal status remains to be seen. Whichever way, for current purposes it quite suffices to verify whether or not the contention holds true for the precautionary principle under general international law.

On the one hand, taken literally, the *Honolulu Convention* of 2000 does not appear to present any minimum threshold of proof when it stipulates that "[t]he absence of adequate scientific information shall not be used as a reason for postponing or failing to take conservation and management measures."[234] In the end, the absence of *adequate* scientific information

---

[230] *Ibid.*

[231] See paragraphs 96-100 of the *Irish Statement*, short for the document *In the Matter of the Public Inquiry Concerning an Appeal by the United Kingdom NIREX Ltd Concerning the Construction of a Rock Characterisation Facility at Longlands Farm, Gosforth, Cumbria: Statement on Behalf of the Minister of State at the Department of Transport, Energy and Communications, Dublin, Ireland,* drawn up by Professor Elihu Lauterpacht, 12 January 1996. The *NIREX case* is discussed in McIntyre & Mosedale, 1997, at pp. 233-234. See also Trouwborst, 2002, pp. 202-203.

[232] Bundesverwaltungsgericht, Judgment of 19 December 1985, *NVwZ*, 1986, p. 208. See Rehbinder, 1991, p. 9; De Sadeleer, 2000, pp. 146-147. Translation based on De Sadeleer, *ibid.*; italics added.

[233] Pieterman & Hanekamp, 2002, p. vi.

[234] *Convention on the Conservation and Management of Highly Migratory Fish Stocks in the Western and Central Pacific Ocean*, Article 6(2). Like formulations can be found in Article 6(2) of the 1995 *Straddling Stocks Agreement*, in Principle 6.5 of the 1995 *FAO Code of Conduct for Responsible Fisheries* and in Article 7(2) of the 2001 *Convention on the Conservation and Management of Fishery Resources in the South-East Atlantic Ocean* (hereinafter *South-East Atlantic Fisheries Convention*).

includes the absence of *any* scientific information. When there is no information at all, there certainly is no adequate information. Neither does *OECD Council Resolution C(90)164 on Integrated Pollution Prevention and Control* seemingly employ an evidential threshold when it states that "the absence of *complete* information should not preclude precautionary action."[235] Strictly speaking, this again encompasses situations in which there is no information whatsoever. A plain matter of set theory. This argument can be extended to all comparable formulations, whether they speak of a lack of sufficient, adequate, complete, full, conclusive or undisputed scientific evidence. Viewed in this way, such formulations do not suggest the existence of a minimum threshold of proof conditioning the application of the precautionary principle.[236]

On the other hand, a second reading of the very same passages may well render precisely that suggestion. After all, may the statement from the OECD Resolution mentioned above, that the absence of *complete* information should not preclude precautionary action, not just as well be taken to mean that an absence of *all* information *is* allowed to preclude action? Does it not refer to situations where there is *some, albeit not complete* information? And when the *Rio Declaration* states that "lack of *full* scientific certainty" shall not be used as a reason for postponing action, does this not seem to imply that a total lack of *any* scientific data *would* constitute a valid reason for delay?[237] The same idea is implicit in the *Second North Sea Declaration* where it declares that the output of potentially harmful substances may have to be controlled "even before a causal link has been established by absolutely clear scientific evidence."[238] Again, does this not refer to situations where there is *some, albeit not absolutely clear* evidence? It appears not unlikely that the words 'complete', 'full' and 'absolutely clear' were inserted in these provisions for a reason and that they are expressions of the desire of the drafting states to define the precautionary principle within reasonable bounds. Identical considerations apply to instances where states have agreed not to wait for "full and undisputed scientific proof of harmful effects" before taking action;[239] not to postpone action on the ground that "scientific research has not fully proved"[240] causal links or when such links have "not yet been fully

---

235 See "Guidance". Emphasis added.
236 Also Bodansky, 2004, p. 388.
237 Principle 15; emphasis added.
238 Preambular paragraph VII.
239 *Baltic Sea Declaration*, eighth preambular paragraph.
240 See Article 2(5) of the *Helsinki Watercourses Convention* and Articles 3(2)(a) of the *Convention on the Protection of the Meuse* and the *Convention on the Protection of the Scheldt.*

confirmed";[241] or to take measures even in the absence of "conclusive",[242] "adequate"[243] or "sufficient"[244] evidence to confirm the threat in question.[245]

In sum, then, there are at least two ways of interpreting clauses disallowing states to wait for sufficient, adequate, absolutely clear, conclusive, complete, full or undisputed proof before taking precautionary action. According to the first, states are not permitted to wait for *any* scientific evidence. 'Complete lack of proof' is, after all, included in 'lack of complete proof'. According to the second, states are entitled to wait for *some*, as opposed to *full* proof. On the basis of purely textual interpretation, neither of the two explanations can be readily discarded. When taken to its logical conclusion, nonetheless, the former could lead to results which are unreasonably demanding, not to say absurd. As the European Commission has rightly remarked, zero risk is simply not a realistic option, and its achievement therefore not a goal of the precautionary principle.[246] It is submitted, therefore, that the latter is the more plausible interpretation.[247]

From this point of view, it is significant for present purposes that definitions of the precautionary principle in legal and policy instruments containing qualifications of the nature in issue here, greatly outnumber those lacking them. The 1990 *Bergen Declaration*,[248] the *Biodiversity Convention*,[249] the *Climate Change Convention*,[250] the revised *Barcelona Convention*,[251] the *Waigani Convention*[252] and the *Canadian Environmental Protection Act*[253] are just a handful

---

[241] Section 2.4, paragraph 3 of the *Pan-European Biological and Landscape Diversity Strategy*.

[242] 1991 *London Dumping Convention Resolution LDC 44/14*; 1996 *LDC Protocol*, Article 3(1); 1992 *Baltic Sea Convention*, Article 3(2); HELCOM *Recommendation 13/6*, paragraph 1(3); and 1992 *OSPAR Convention*, Article 2(2)(a).

[243] *Straddling Stocks Agreement*, Article 6(2); *FAO Code of Conduct for Responsible Fisheries*, Principle 6.5; 2000 *Honolulu Convention*, Article 6(2); and the 2001 *South-East Atlantic Fisheries Convention*, Article 7(2).

[244] 1991 *Trilateral Wadden Sea Declaration*, paragraph 3(iii); 1997 *trilateral Wadden Sea Plan*, paragraph 8. Articles 10(6) and 11(8) of the 2000 *Biosafety Protocol* refer to "[l]ack of scientific certainty due to insufficient relevant scientific information and knowledge."

[245] The 1989 *Nordic Council Declaration on Pollution of the Seas* speaks of "inadequate or inconclusive" scientific evidence. According to the *Declaration on the Environment* adopted by the 1990 Liberal International Congress, precautionary action "must not be further delayed with the argument that scientific data is incomplete." In *Communication COM(2000)1*, lastly, the European Commission stresses the relevance of the precautionary principle "where scientific information is insufficient, inconclusive or uncertain."

[246] *Communication COM(2000)1*, pp. 9 and 18.

[247] Legal commentators supporting this interpretation include Backes *et al.*, 1997, p. 72; González Campos *et al.*, 1998, pp. 798-799; and Molenaar, 1998, p. 45.

[248] Paragraph 7.

[249] Preambular paragraph 9.

[250] Article 3(3).

[251] Article 4(3)(a) of the Convention as amended in 1995.

[252] Article 1.

of the many instruments besides the *Rio Declaration* whose definitions of the precautionary principle incorporate the clause of "full scientific certainty".[254] Other variations on the theme abound as well, both internationally – as shown above[255] – and nationally.[256] As stated in an early German government report on the precautionary principle, *Vorsorge* means "acting when *conclusively ascertained understanding* by science is not yet available."[257] Belgian legislation on the protection of the marine environment calls for precautionary action "even in cases where there is no *conclusive evidence* of a causal connection" between emissions and effects.[258] In the British national program on greenhouse gases that was adopted as follow-up to the *Climate Change Convention* the appropriateness was declared of taking action "ahead of *unequivocal evidence* being established about the nature and possible effects of man-made climate change."[259] On other occasions, the UK government has committed itself to tackling environmental problems in a precautionary manner even if scientific knowledge is "not complete"[260] or "not conclusive"[261]. The 1998 *Wingspread Statement* proposes that precautionary measures should be taken "even if *some* cause-and-effect relationships are not *fully* established scientifically,"[262] whereas the CEFIC position on the precautionary principle reflects a similar understanding.[263]

Provisions calling for action to be taken on the basis of *(the best) scientific information (available)* apparently point in the same direction, in that they may be

---

253 Article 2(1)(a) of the *CEPA* as amended in 1999; see Friends of the Earth Canada, 2000.

254 Other instances include Principle 7 of the 1990 *Ministerial Declaration of the Second World Climate Conference*, referred to above; preambular paragraph 4 of the 1994 *Second Sulphur Protocol* to the *LRTAP Convention*; preambular paragraph 5 of the 1995 *Mediterranean SPA and Biodiversity Protocol*; paragraph 24 of the 1995 *Land-Based Activities Action Programme*; Article II(3) of the 2001 *Albatross Agreement*; Article 3(3) of the 2002 *ASEAN Agreement on Transboundary Haze Pollution*; as well as the myriad references to the *Rio Declaration* (see *supra* paragraph 2.3) and the *Biodiversity Convention* in other international and national instruments.

255 See the provisions listed in preceding footnotes.

256 This also includes rules of reference to relevant instruments, such as the *Straddling Stocks Agreement*.

257 1984 *Report from the Government to the Federal Parliament on the Protection of Air Quality*, *BMI* 1984, p. 53, as reproduced in Boehmer-Christiansen, 1994, at p. 37; also Trouwborst, 2002, p. 216. Emphasis added. *Vorsorge* is the German equivalent of precaution.

258 Article 4(3) of the *Wet ter Bescherming van het Mariene Milieu in de Zeegebieden onder de Rechtsbevoegdheid van België*, Act of 20 January 1999, *MB* of 12 March 1999; translation from Larmuseau, 2000(b), pp. 41-42.

259 See Cameron, 1994, p. 270.

260 Department of the Environment, *Environment in Trust*, March 1989; see Haigh,1994, pp. 248-249.

261 Paragraph 1.18 of the White Paper *This Common inheritance: Britain's Environmental Strategy*, September 1990, Cm 1200, reproduced partly in Haigh, *ibid.*, at pp. 249-250.

262 Emphasis added.

263 European Chemical Industry Council, 1995, paragraph 8.

seen to suggest the presence of at least some degree of evidence on which precautionary action is to be founded. The 1994 *WTO Agreement on Sanitary and Phytosanitary Measures*, *SPS Agreement* for short, does this especially clearly when stating that "[i]n cases where relevant scientific evidence is insufficient, a Member may provisionally adopt sanitary or phytosanitary measures on the basis of available scientific information."[264] Parties to the *Albatross Agreement* are to act in a precautionary manner when re-establishing albatrosses and petrels on traditional breeding grounds from which they have disappeared, whereby efforts to achieve such recolonization "shall be based on best scientific evidence."[265] The relationship between the precautionary principle and acting on the best scientific data available is not always set out this unambiguously. Various international agreements on fisheries, for instance, specify that *as part of* a precautionary approach conservation measures must be informed by "the best scientific information available,"[266] whereas under other fishery treaties states parties must "apply the precautionary approach [..] *and* take into account *also* the best scientific evidence available."[267] At any rate, whether the criterion is portrayed as part and parcel of the precautionary principle or as complementary to it, the result is no different. That is to say, the availability of some amount of information as the basis for action can, at first sight at least, be understood as implied in both cases.[268]

The provisions reviewed so far thus render several clues alluding to the existence of a minimum threshold of proof as a component of the precautionary principle. They do not, however, indicate the height of this threshold.

The Height of the Threshold of Proof

With respect to the dimensions of the apparently existing threshold of proof, a large number of definitions in legal instruments limit themselves to declaring the applicability of the precautionary principle in situations "where there are threats" or "where there is a threat" of – more or less significant,

---

[264] Article 5(7) of the *WTO Agreement on the Application of Sanitary and Phytosanitary Measures*.

[265] *Albatross Agreement*, Annex 2, paragraph 1.3.

[266] Articles 6(3)(b) and 6(7) of the *Straddling Stocks Agreement*; Articles 6(1)(a) and 6(6) of the *Honolulu Convention*; and paragraphs 6.5 and 7.5.5 of the *FAO Code of Conduct*, which speak of "evidence" instead of "information".

[267] Article III(2) of the 1949 *GFCM Agreement* as amended in 1997; Article III(2) of the 1999 *RECOFI Agreement*; emphasis added. The preamble to the *Honolulu Convention* also uses "and", although its operative provisions contain the "part of"-construction, as shown in the previous footnote. Article 4(1) of the 1998 *Agreement on the International Dolphin Conservation Program* requires parties to take conservation measures "based on the best scientific evidence available, and apply the precautionary approach." According to one of the predecessors of this instrument, the 1995 *Panama Declaration*, such measures "shall be based on the best scientific evidence, including that based on a precautionary methodology." First operative paragraph.

[268] That this is not the only possible interpretation will become clear in *infra* paragraph 5.3.

serious and/or irreversible[269] – environmental damage. This includes Principle 15 of the *Rio Declaration* and a host of similar provisions in other instruments.[270] It is not immediately obvious what the signification of the word 'threat' is in terms of evidentiary standards.[271] According to its dictionary meaning, a threat is an "indication of something undesirable coming," as in: "There is a threat of rain."[272] The word 'indication' is itself synonymous of sign, suggestion, hint, warning, or clue. Typically, it is said that there is a threat of rain when clouds are building or the wind is picking up. Three things are true of this situation:

(1) it is not raining yet;
(2) it is not certain that it will rain either; but
(3) there is some sign that rain is not unlikely.

Likewise, to be able to speak of a threat of harm to the environment there needs to be some indication, some hint, some concrete information suggesting that harm may occur. Hence, the choice of the word 'threat' in the definitions of the precautionary principle currently under scrutiny conveys that purely hypothetical scenarios were meant to be excluded from the principle's reach.

It is thus increasingly apparent that the plain theoretical possibility of environmental damage is not sufficient to trigger the application of the precautionary principle under general international law.[273] Once more, this is in utter conformity with common sense. Without at least a minimal requirement of proof the remotest possibilities would be eligible as a basis for precautionary action. After all, in theory everything is possible – even an invasion by aliens from outer space,[274] or Wildavsky's goat's milk deluge referred to previously.[275] To demand measures to prevent this kind of merely theoretical hazards would be bizarre as well as unfeasible. Assuming that indeed some concrete indication that a given threat may materialize, rather than sheer

---

[269] On thresholds of harm, see *supra* Chapter 3.

[270] Paragraph 7 of the *Bergen Declaration*; the ninth preambular paragraph of the *Biodiversity Convention*; Article 3(3) of the *Climate Change Convention*; the fourth preambular paragraph of the 1994 *Second Sulphur Protocol* to the *LRTAP Convention*; Article 4(3)(a) of the *Barcelona Convention* as revised in 1995; the fifth preambular paragraph of the *Mediterranean SPA and Biodiversity Protocol*; paragraph 24 of the 1995 *Land-Based Activities Action Programme*; Article 1 of the *Waigani Convention*; Article II(3) of the 2001 *Albatross Agreement*; Article 3(3) of the *ASEAN Agreement on Transboundary Haze Pollution*; and the great many provisions modelled on or making reference to any of these (see, *inter alia*, paragraph 3 of *supra* Chapter 2).

[271] Morris, 2000(a).

[272] Sykes, 1976, p. 1206.

[273] Also DeFur & Kaszuba, 2002, p. 157; Birnie & Boyle, 2002, p. 117.

[274] Morris, 2000(b), pp. 13-14.

[275] See *supra* paragraph 4.2; Wildavsky, 2000, pp. 28-29.

speculation, is required in order to activate any rights or duties under the precautionary principle, has as a result that the word 'possible' by itself can be disposed of as a candidate threshold of proof in any general definition.

A number of threshold formulations of a more distinct makeup than the sole reference to 'threat' can be encountered in international legal instruments relating to the protection of the oceans – in the cradle of the precautionary principle in international law, so to speak.[276] As stipulated in decisions adopted by the Paris and Helsinki Commissions (PARCOM and HELCOM) in 1989 and 1991, precautionary action to safeguard the marine ecosystem must be taken particularly "when there is reason to assume that certain damage or harmful effects on the living resources of the sea are likely to be caused" by discharged substances.[277] Under the *OSPAR Convention* and the *Baltic Sea Convention* of 1992 such action is to be taken, respectively, "when there are reasonable grounds for concern" and "when there is reason to assume" that discharges "may" bring about hazards.[278] Within the context of the *London Dumping Convention* the precautionary principle is defined as requiring action when there is "reason to believe" that wastes or other matter dumped into the ocean are "likely" to be harmful.[279] Lastly, the three coastal states of the Wadden Sea have pledged to heed the precautionary principle by avoiding activities "which are assumed to have significant damaging impact on the environment."[280]

The express application of thresholds is not uncommon either in the domestic practice of states. In a procedure before the *Bundesverwaltungsgericht* of the Federal Republic of Germany (FRG) in 1984, the court noted the relevance of the precautionary principle in respect of pollution when there are "sufficient grounds to believe that there is the danger that emissions might lead to environmental damage – even if a causal link has not been proven for the case under consideration."[281] Two years later it was the FRG Government's formal opinion that the principle demands action only when "general experience or scientific findings indicate with sufficient probability that damage will be caused," while adding that "any remote possibility that damage will be caused is

---

[276] See Trouwborst, 2002, pp. 24-27.

[277] PARCOM *Recommendation 89/1 on the Principle of Precautionary Action*; HELCOM *Recommendation 12/3*, first operative paragraph. Paragraph XVI of the *Second North Sea Declaration* is identically phrased.

[278] *OSPAR Convention*, Article 2(2)(a); *Baltic Sea Convention*, Article 3(2). The definition given in operative paragraph 1(3) of HELCOM *Recommendation 13/6* of 1992 is similar to the latter.

[279] See *Resolution LDC 44/14* and Article 3(1) of the *LDC Protocol*. A similar requirement is contained in the 1989 *Declaration on Pollution of the Seas* of the Nordic Council.

[280] Paragraph 3 of the 1991 *Trilateral Wadden Sea Declaration* and paragraph 8 of the *Trilateral Wadden Sea Plan*.

[281] Judgment of 14 February 1984, 69 *BverGE*, 1985, p. 43; translation based on De Sadeleer, 2000, p. 145.

not sufficient."[282] The Belgian Act on marine environmental protection cited earlier commands precautionary measures when there are "reasonable grounds for concern" about pollution of the sea.[283] In a 1999 case revolving around the potential health effects of magnetic fields generated by a high-voltage cable overhanging houses, the highest administrative court of Belgium, the Council of State, observed that "the Council can merely note that there are elements that lead it reasonably to suspect a health risk," but that this was enough to warrant a precautionary approach to the issue. [284] In the words of the Council, in this respect it sufficed for the risk of detriment to be "plausible".[285] Under Swedish law precautionary action shall be taken "as soon as there is cause to assume that an activity or measure may cause damage" to the environment or health.[286] Under legislation in Czechia and Slovakia the precautionary principle is triggered when "it can be assumed that irreversible or serious damage could threaten the environment."[287] In the United States, the President's Council on Sustainable Development has held that actions to avert risks should be taken "where the potential harm to human health or the environment is *thought* to be serious or irreparable,"[288] whereas the *Massachusetts Precautionary Principle Act* employs the standard of "reasonable grounds for concern that a procedure or development may contribute to the degradation of the air, land and water of the Commonwealth."[289] Where there are "significant risks of damage to the environment" preventive action may be expected of the British government, according to an early policy documents on the precautionary principle.[290] This is so "particularly where there are good grounds for judging" that costly or irreversible effects may follow if action is delayed.[291]

It is instructive, finally, to have a look at the way the principle is being implemented within the framework of the European Union. In the European Commission's 'Communication' on the topic, definitions of the threshold of proof that must be crossed for the precautionary principle to apply fluctuate

---

[282] Quoted in Gullett, 1997, p. 59.

[283] Article 4(3) of the 1999 *Wet ter Bescherming van het Mariene Milieu in de Zeegebieden onder de Rechtsbevoegdheid van België*; translation from Larmuseau, 2000(b), pp. 41-42.

[284] Judgment of 20 August 1999 by the French-speaking Chamber of the Council of State in the *Venter* case, as (partly) reproduced in English in Larmuseau, *ibid.*, at pp. 46-47. See also De Sadeleer, 2000, pp. 149-150.

[285] *Ibid.*

[286] See Article 3(2) of the 1998 *Environmental Code*; as quoted in De Sadeleer, 2002, p. 137.

[287] *Federal Act on the Environment*, Law No. 17/1992 of 5 December 1991, Article 13.

[288] From *Sustainable America: A New Consensus*, 1996; see Tickner *et al.*, 1997, pp. 3 and 23. Italics added.

[289] Commonwealth of Massachusetts, House Bill No. 3140.

[290] White Paper *This Common inheritance: Britain's Environmental Strategy*, September 1990, paragraph 1.18, as reproduced in Haigh, 1994, at pp. 249-250.

[291] *Ibid.*

somewhat throughout the document. According to the Commission, the principle comes into play both "where there are *indications* that the possible effects on the environment [..] may be potentially dangerous and inconsistent with the chosen level of protection,"[292] as well as "when there are *reasonable grounds for concern* that potential hazards may affect the environment."[293] In yet another formulation laid down in the same document these two alternatives are merged into one, where reference is made to "*indications*, through preliminary objective scientific evaluation that there are *reasonable grounds for concern* that the potentially dangerous effects [..] may be inconsistent with the chosen level of protection."[294] Many of the elements characterized thus far as suggesting or embodying a minimum standard of evidence are present in the following provision from the *Council Resolution on the Precautionary Principle* that was adopted by the fifteen EU member states in the year 2000. The Council, in this decision:

> Considers that use should be made of the precautionary principle where the *possibility* of harmful effects on health or the environment has been *identified* and preliminary scientific evaluation, based on the *available* data, proves *inconclusive* for assessing the level of risk.[295]

A large amount of instruments incorporating the precautionary principle have now passed in review, ranging from treaties, intergovernmental declarations and decisions of international organizations through to national legislation, policy documents and judgments of domestic courts. The majority of these material sources of state practice indicate, be it explicitly or implicitly, that under the precautionary principle action is only considered appropriate or mandatory when there are at least some indications, some (reasonable) grounds for concern that environmental harm, of whatever nature, may be brought about. In the instances where this condition is expressly laid down, its formulations diverge. So as not to lose sight of the forest for the trees, the explicitly stated thresholds of evidence that have been mentioned thus far are lined up here:

- there is a threat of (serious or irreversible) damage;
- there are significant risks of damage to the environment;
- there is a plausible risk of detriment;
- general experience or scientific findings indicate with sufficient probability that damage will be caused;

---

[292] *Communication COM(2000)1*, p. 8; italics added. Marr, 2003, p. 87 calls this a "low triggering threshold."

[293] *Communication COM(2000)1*, p. 9; italics added.

[294] *Ibid.*, p. 10; italics added.

[295] Paragraph 7. Italics added.

- the potential harm to human health or the environment is thought to be serious or irreparable;
- activities are assumed to have significant damaging impact on the environment;
- there are sufficient grounds to believe that there is the danger that emissions might lead to environmental damage;
- the possibility of harmful effects has been identified;
- there is reason to believe that damage or harmful effects are likely to be caused;
- there is reason to believe that substances, energy, wastes or other matter are likely to cause harm;
- there is reason to assume that certain damage or harmful effects on the living resources of the sea are likely to be caused;
- there is reason to assume that substances or energy may create hazards;
- there is cause to assume that an activity or measure may cause damage;
- there are indications that the possible effects on the environment may be potentially dangerous;
- there are good grounds for judging that costly or irreversible effects may follow;
- there is reasonable suspicion of a risk;
- there are reasonable grounds for concern that potential hazards may affect the environment;
- there are reasonable grounds for concern that substances or energy may bring about hazards;
- there are reasonable grounds for concern about pollution;
- there are reasonable grounds for concern that a procedure or development may contribute to the degradation of the environment.

Many states have subscribed to more than one of the various instruments that jointly portray this diversity of terms in which the evidential threshold is put, both at national and international levels. Two explanations may account for this. It may be that the differences between these formulations are to be considered negligible; that they are simply distinct ways of stating the same thing. Then again, it may also be that for different environmental problems slightly differently specified thresholds were held appropriate. A combination of the two interpretations is not unthinkable either. One way or the other, the various definitions have in common that at a minimum there must be reasonable grounds for concern that environmental harm may occur, before the precautionary principle is deemed to be applicable. As a lowest common denominator, 'reasonable grounds for concern' covers all of them by way of a threshold.

It is worthwhile to briefly return to the provisions that were mentioned at the outset of this paragraph as not, at first sight, incorporating any threshold of proof. *At first sight*, because a closer look at the entire provisions in their context reveals that quite a few of them do in fact also, be it directly or indirectly, contain certain elements by way of such a threshold. For example, the reach of the precautionary principle as formulated in the *Third North Sea Declaration* is confined to "substances that are persistent, toxic and liable to bioaccumulate," which implies the mapping of these qualities prior to the principle becoming applicable.[296] It will be remembered that the *Pan-European Biological and Landscape Diversity Strategy*, for another, advises against postponing preventive action on the ground that a causal link between an activity and an adverse impact has not yet been "fully" confirmed. This can be taken to suggest, as discussed above, that a *total* lack of evidence might well constitute a viable reason for doing so.[297] These considerations provide even more corroboration for the position that for the precautionary principle to take effect as a matter of general international law, there must be some kind of preliminary information constituting ground for concern. To be sure, there is much to be said for the assumption that in formulations truly lacking any textual hints in this respect, such as the relevant provision of the *Bamako Convention*,[298] some minimal standard of proof must nonetheless be read between the lines – in parallel to the duty not to cause transboundary harm laid down in Principle 21 of the *Stockholm Declaration* which, as related in the previous chapter, is widely understood to apply only to *significant* harm without itself stating this.[299] Refusing to do so could, in the end, easily lead to unreasonable outcomes.

Jurisprudence and Doctrine

Before rounding off the current paragraph it seems fitting to consult pertinent international jurisprudence and legal doctrine in their capacities of "subsidiary means for the determination of rules of law."[300] Judicial proceedings at the international level render a number of relevant pointers. Among the most notable are three cases before the International Tribunal for the Law of the Sea on the institution of provisional measures in order to prevent harm to the marine environment. The first of these concerns the *Southern Bluefin Tuna* Order of 1999.[301] After contemplating the acceptance by all parties to the dispute of the fact that the depleted state of the southern bluefin tuna stock was a "cause for serious biological concern" and taking note of the argument submitted by Australia and New Zealand that the scientific evidence *available* showed that Japan's additional fishing effort *could* endanger the survival of the stock, the Tribunal prescribed precautionary measures to avert further

---

[296] Preamble.

[297] See paragraph 3 of section 2.4.

[298] Article 3(f).

[299] See *supra* paragraph 3.2.

[300] Article 38(1)(d) of the 1945 *Statute of the International Court of Justice*. National case law also belongs to this category, but has been treated already in its capacity of source of state practice, *supra*.

[301] Order of 27 August 1999 in the *Southern Bluefin Tuna Cases (Requests for Provisional Measures) (New Zealand v Japan; Australia v Japan)*.

deterioration – despite the absence of scientific certainty regarding the effectiveness of past conservation measures and the inability of the ITLOS to "conclusively" assess the scientific evidence before it.[302]

The second is the case on the *MOX Plant*, in which Ireland contested the lawfulness of the authorization by the British Government of a new nuclear fuel reprocessing facility at the Sellafield site on the Irish Sea coast.[303] Ireland, among other things, expressed the view that the precautionary principle entailed that the United Kingdom must "apply caution, and take preventive measures even where there is no *conclusive* evidence" of a causal relationship between the operation of the MOX plant and related shipments of radioactive materials on the one hand, and marine environmental hazards on the other.[304] The UK, for its part, contended that it is "generally accepted that [the precautionary principle] can operate only where there are some reasonable grounds for concern."[305] The standard of proof to be met in circumstances such as the ones in issue, according to the British statement, is located somewhere between the sheer possibility and the probability of damage:

> [T]he risk of harm occurring must in some measure be a real risk. It cannot be simply the merest suggestion that harm might occur. While this is not to suggest that the threshold is one of the probability of harm occurring, it must be more than the hypothetical or remote possibility of such harm.[306]

It was argued that *in casu* the Irish allegations did not pass this test, and that in fact there were "no reasonable grounds for believing" that the MOX plant would cause unacceptable changes to the environment of the Irish Sea,[307] as the risks involved were "infinitesimally small".[308] The Tribunal, in its Order of December 2001, limited itself to declaring that "prudence and caution" require that both parties cooperate in exchanging information and in designing methods to cope with risks or effects associated with the plant.[309]

---

[302] *Ibid.*, paragraphs 71, 74, 77, 79, 80 and 85.

[303] See the Order of 3 December 2001 in the *MOX Plant Case (Request for Provisional Measures) (Ireland v United Kingdom)*.

[304] Paragraph 101 of the *Request for Provisional Measures and Statement of Case of Ireland* of 9 November 2001; emphasis added.

[305] Paragraph 184 of the *Written Response of the United Kingdom*, dated 15 November 2001. It was argued that Ireland had not demonstrated such grounds.

[306] *Ibid.*, paragraph 147.

[307] *Verbatim Record* of the public sitting held on 20 November 2001, p. 24 (Plender for the UK).

[308] "Nothing is adduced by way of evidence here. All we are told here is that there is some unspecified risk of pollution. [..] There are all sorts of possibilities that cannot be excluded. The point is that the United Kingdom has undertaken a protracted and detailed assessment of these risks and concluded that they are infinitesimally small." *Ibid.*, p. 17 (Bethlehem for UK).

[309] Paragraph 84 of the Order. The ITLOS did not deem it necessary to provisionally forbid the authorization of the MOX plant during the brief period before constitution of the arbitral

The third case, finally, involved a request for provisional measures filed by Malaysia in a dispute with Singapore in 2003.[310] This request was motivated, *inter alia*, by concern that impoldering projects carried out by neighbouring Singapore along its coast in the Straits of Johor were ecologically harmful in that they would produce considerable changes in flow regime, sedimentation and coastal erosion in nearby areas. Malaysia alleged that the execution of these reclamation projects thus infringed upon the precautionary principle.[311] Singapore, while stressing that it took the principle "very seriously" and had in fact complied with it by taking "the most rigorous preparatory arrangements to avoid dangers,"[312] responded that the precautionary principle was limited in that it did "not entitle Malaysia to require Singapore to suspend its reclamation works on the basis of *no evidence* of serious or irreversible damage."[313] The considerations of the ITLOS on this count were as follows:

> *Considering* that it *cannot be excluded* that, in the particular circumstances of this case, the land reclamation works *may* have adverse effects on the marine environment; [..]
> *Considering* that, given the *possible* implications of land reclamation on the marine environment, prudence and caution require that Malaysia and Singapore establish mechanisms for exchanging information and assessing the risks or effects of land reclamation works and devising ways to deal with them in the areas concerned; [..]
> *Directs* Singapore not to conduct its land reclamation in ways that *might* cause [..] serious harm to the marine environment.[314]

The case law of the European Union's judicial organs offers clues as well. For instance, the provisional restriction or prohibition by an EU member state of the use or sale within its territory of a product containing genetically modified organisms when it has "justifiable reasons" to believe that the product constitutes an environmental risk, in accordance with *Directive 90/220* on GMOs,[315] was judged by the ECJ to reflect observance of the precautionary principle.[316] Moreover, on several fairly recent occasions the Court has stressed

---

tribunal that would judge upon the merits of the case, in light, *inter alia*, of British assurances that until then no additional marine transports of nuclear material were to take place as a result of the commissioning of the plant.

310 Order of 8 October 2003 in the *Case Concerning Land Reclamation by Singapore in and around the Straits of Johor (Request for Provisional Measures) (Malaysia v Singapore)*.

311 See paragraphs 17 and 18 of the Malaysian *Request for Provisional Measures*.

312 *Verbatim Record* of the sitting on 27 September 2003, p. 32 (Reisman).

313 *Response of Singapore* of 20 September 2003, paragraph 141; emphasis added.

314 Paragraphs 96, 99 and 106(2) of the Order; emphasis added, apart from the first words of each paragraph.

315 Article 16 of *Council Directive 90/220/EEC on the Deliberate Release into the Environment of Genetically Modified Organisms* of 23 April 1990 (*OJ*, 1990, L 117, p. 15), as amended by *Commission Directive 97/35/EC* of 18 June 1997 (*OJ*, 1997, L 169, p. 72), to be precise.

316 *Association Greenpeace France and Others v Ministère de l'Agriculture et de la Pêche and Others*, Case C-6/99, Judgment of 21 March 2000; paragraph 44.

that precautionary measures cannot legitimately be founded on "purely hypothetical considerations," on "mere conjecture," or be taken "solely on the basis of rumours."[317]

Having said this, it is time to dwell for a moment on the opinions academic authors have voiced on the topic. Although some speak of "possible damage" as a threshold,[318] and one writer has submitted that the precautionary principle calls for action "at the least hint of environmental risk,"[319] most definitions proposed by scholars coincide with what has been found so far, namely that there must be some reasonable grounds for concern that harm may be caused for the precautionary principle to apply. As with the provisions of legal instruments, there is variation in the wording of the criterion, however. Many agree, for example, that "the existence of *some indication* of the threat of harm" is a fundamental element of the principle.[320] Others hold that there needs to be "reason to assume" that adverse environmental interferences may be created;[321] "good reason to expect" risk or harm to environmental health;[322] "a reasonable fear" for damage;[323] "reasonable scientific grounds" for believing that a new process or product may not be safe;[324] "a plausible threat" of harm;[325] "justified indications" of a link between a given act and possible adverse consequences;[326] a situation where certain effects are "suspected";[327] or, as one handbook puts it, "*some* scientific basis for predicting the possibility of harmful effects, some 'reason to believe' or 'reasonable grounds for concern'."[328] The *ILA Berlin Rules on Water Resources* alternatively speak of "a serious risk"[329] of adverse effects and "reason to believe"[330] harm will occur. Occasionally, it is submitted that negative impacts must be "likely" or

---

[317] See, among others, *Alpharma Inc. v Council of the European Union*, Case T-70/99, Judgment of 11 September 2002, paragraphs 156 and 165; *Monsanto Agricoltura Italia and Others*, Case C-236/01, Judgment of 2003, paragraph 106; *Commission of the European Communities v Kingdom of Denmark*, Case C-192/01, Judgment of 23 September 2003, paragraph 49; *Commission of the European Communities v French Republic*, Case C-24/00, Judgment of 5 February 2004, paragraph 56.

[318] E.g., Tallacchini, 2000, p. 1096.

[319] Dzidzornu, 1998, p. 101.

[320] See Cooney, 2000, on the outcome of the 2000 Lauterpacht International Law Centre workshop on "The Precautionary Principle in Wildlife Conservation"; emphasis added.

[321] Ebbesson, 1996, pp. 119-120.

[322] Lemons *et al.*, 1997, p. 210.

[323] Matthee & Vermersch, 2000, p. 60.

[324] Saunders, 2000.

[325] Raffensperger, 2000.

[326] Lambers, 2000, p. 179; author's translation.

[327] Klinke & Renn, 1999, p. 17.

[328] Birnie & Boyle, 2002, p. 117.

[329] Article 23(2).

[330] Commentary on Article 23.

"probable" for the precautionary principle to be triggered, although this appears to be the exception rather than the rule.[331] Several writers speak of "available knowledge" which is "not yet complete" and the like.[332]

Kaiser sketches a typical situation in which the precautionary principle would find application: "There exist scientific model scenarios with *reasonable plausibility* which indicate a development towards future [significant or irreversible] environmental harm," although uncertainties remain, whereas it is "*reasonable to assume* that these uncertainties will not vanish before the damage either has occurred or cannot be averted any longer."[333] A particularly broad scope appears to have been ascribed to the precautionary principle by the legal experts who drafted the *ILA Declaration on Sustainable Development* of 2002, according to which human activities must be avoided "which *may* cause significant harm to human health, natural resources or ecosystems, including in the face of scientific uncertainty."[334] That the assignment of such a wide scope of application to the principle was indeed the drafters' intention, is confirmed by the stipulation that states may have to instigate precautionary measures "even when the absence of risk seems scientifically assured."[335] This interpretation contrasts with the European chemical industry position paper on the principle[336] – reproduced here even though it is not, of course, a doctrinal publication in the sense of the *ICJ Statute*. It states that precautionary action is appropriate when there are "sufficient grounds for believing" that an activity or product is "likely" to cause a threat.[337] This requirement, which is described as a "significant threshold of plausibility", is to be fulfilled for the precautionary principle to apply.[338] The threshold is phrased alternatively as a "sufficient body of evidence which establishes that serious and irreversible damage to health or the environment could be caused by the challenged activity or product."[339]

The Threshold of 'Reasonable Grounds for Concern'

International case law and doctrine are thus, *grosso modo*, supportive of the conclusion that was already provisionally drawn above. Namely: in terms of preliminary evidence, there must be reasonable grounds for concern that

---

[331] See, e.g., Dzidzornu, 1998, p. 98; Freestone, 1999, p. 137.
[332] Among others, Lemons *et al.*, 1997, p. 210; Klinke & Renn, 1999, p. 17; Freestone, *ibid.*; Lambers, 2000, p. 179.
[333] Kaiser, 1997(b), p. 314; emphasis added.
[334] Paragraph 4.1 of the Declaration.
[335] Paragraph 4.3. Some limited form of demarcation of the principle's scope can, however, be found in paragraph 4.4, which states that such measures should be based on "up-to-date and independent scientific judgment."
[336] European Chemical Industry Council, 1995.
[337] *Ibid.*, p. 1.
[338] *Ibid.*, p. 2.
[339] *Ibid.*

environmental harm may occur for the application of the precautionary principle, as a general principle of international environmental law, to come about. The available evidence reflects the evident *communis opinio* of states that the principle simply does not take effect as long as there are no such 'reasonable grounds' to show.

It may be helpful to visualize this legal state of affairs schematically, recalling the technical concept of environmental risk. (See Figure 5.)

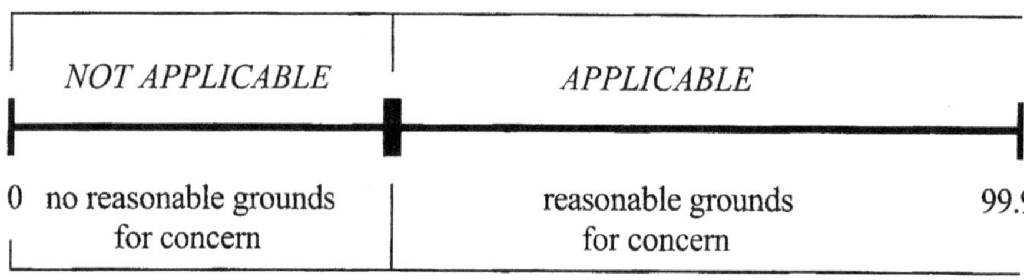

Figure 5. Scale of likelihood of harm with the threshold of 'reasonable grounds for concern'. The axis represents the scale of likelihood (%). The boldest printed bar is the minimum threshold of 'reasonable grounds for concern'. Relevant qualifications of evidence are indicated below the axis, and corresponding legal effects above it. No numerical value is assigned to the point where the threshold crosses the scale of likelihood, as the threshold of 'reasonable grounds for concern' does not correspond to a particular probability percentage.

'Reasonable grounds for concern' constitutes a threshold dividing the sliding scale of the *likelihood* of occurrence of harm in two, just like the other component of risk, i.e. the expected *gravity* of harm, was found to be marked by thresholds in the preceding chapter.[340] To be more precise, the threshold of reasonable grounds for concern is for the element of likelihood what the threshold of significance is for the element of gravity: below these minimum thresholds the precautionary principle is just not applicable.[341] In terms of general international law, then, this means that it is difficult to conclude that states have any customary right or duty to take precautionary action in the absence of reasonable grounds for concern that damage to the environment may be caused. Such rights and obligations are apparently conditioned by the minimum threshold in question. It thus puts a third check on the precautionary principle, in addition to the two thresholds of harm that were identified in the foregoing chapter.

---

[340] See the second and third paragraphs of *supra* Chapter 3, particularly Figures 1 and 2.
[341] Compare *supra* Figure 1.

With regard to the exact location of this threshold line on the scale of likelihood, it seems fair to say that it is positioned somewhere between the *possibility* and the *probability* of harm coming about.[342] The very least that can be warranted is that the sheer theoretical possibility of environmental damage being inflicted is situated below (that is, in Figure 5 to the left of) the threshold bar. It has, after all, become abundantly clear in the course of this paragraph that merely hypothetical scenarios do not put enough weight in the scale for triggering precautionary rights or duties.[343] In other words, Pieterman and Hanekamp can rest assured that as far as the precautionary principle is concerned, their contention that a duty to do the impossible can never be legally binding, does not conflict with the state of international law. As for the other submission, that the standard of reasonable grounds for concern does not equal proof of *probability* in the statistical sense,[344] it is striking that even when under 'precautionary fire' in the *MOX Plant* case just discussed, the United Kingdom conceded that probability of harm was not a prerequisite for the precautionary principle to be applicable.

4.4. Conclusions

The precautionary principle was designed in answer to the dual modern insight that the environment is more vulnerable to human interference than previously thought and that the capacity of science to predict the environmental effects of such interference is remarkably limited. The causes of this limited capacity and the resulting uncertainty, which form the topic of the present chapter, are various. Uncertainty can be due to lack of (accurate) measurements. Such epistemological uncertainty can sometimes, though not always, be reduced through additional research. Uncertainty can be due as well to systemic indeterminacy, to the variability and complexity of nature, which are as hallucinatory as the vapours rising from the fissure below Apollo's tripod in the heyday of the oracle of Delphi. Such ontological uncertainty is irresolvable by definition. There is thus uncertainty that can be overcome and uncertainty that cannot, although in individual instances it can be difficult beforehand to tell which kind one is looking at. In terms of risk, the general term 'uncertainty' encompasses situations of (1) quantifiable risk, whereby both gravity and likelihood of an anticipated environmental impact can be more or less reliably expressed in numbers; (2) uncertainty proper, whereby this can only be done with respect to gravity; and (3) ignorance, where neither gravity nor probability

---

342 Also Molenaar, 1998, p. 45.

343 See also González Campos *et al.*, 1998, pp. 798-799.

344 For a contrary opinion, see Dzidzornu, 1998, p. 98.

can be quantified. To cut a long story short: "Our power to predict the future may not be much better than the prognostications of the Oracle at Delphi. But at least we have stopped using chicken entrails."[345] The place of the chicken entrails has been taken by the precautionary principle.

The reach of the principle as formulated in legal and policy instruments is not limited to any particular class(es) of uncertainty. In conformity with this, the precautionary principle has been applied in state practice to uncertainty of all kinds, without discrimination between cases of epistemological and ontological uncertainty, or between quantifiable risk, uncertainty proper and ignorance. The conclusion is warranted, therefore, that the scope of the precautionary principle is all-inclusive as to the different *kinds* of uncertainty.

This is not to say that its scope is comprehensive as to all *levels* of uncertainty as well. The right question to ask in this respect is not, however, how much uncertainty there *must* be, but instead how much uncertainty there *may* be for the precautionary principle to apply. This relates to the at first sight perhaps peculiar circumstance that the precautionary principle does not only cover uncertain threats but *certain threats as well*. States do not take precautionary action *because* of uncertainty, but *in spite* of its presence, the direct motive for such action always being some environmental hazard – *not* scientific uncertainty. Clues abound that under the precautionary principle environmental harm must be prevented and abated whether there is uncertainty or not. There is, in other words, no minimum level of uncertainty which is to be reached for the principle to come into play.

There is, however, a maximum. The absence of such a maximum would give rise to the unworkable situation where every hypothetical threat, no matter how unlikely, would call for a precautionary response. The relevant practice of states contains many pointers, too numerous and diverse to reiterate individually in the present paragraph, which indicate that for precautionary action to be appropriate or required, a threshold of preliminary proof must be crossed. Specifically, there must be *reasonable grounds for concern* that environmental harm may be caused. Proof of probability of harm is not required, but at least there is to be some sort of warning, some concrete indication that harm may come about if precautionary action is not taken, something more than just the theoretical possibility of harm occurring. When such reasonable grounds for concern are lacking, the precautionary principle does not apply. (See Figure 5 above.)

---

[345] Speech called "Ten Signposts to Better Law Reform in Relation to Human Genetic Information" by Brian Opeskin of the Australian Law Reform Commission at a conference on "Juridical and Psychosocial Implications of Human Genetics", held in Rome on 21-22 March 2002; available at http://www.alrc.gov.au (accessed on 14 November 2002).

In sum, the threshold of reasonable grounds for concern occasions that mere possibility is insufficient to mandate precautionary action, although it requires something less than proof of probability of harm. But how precisely is one to determine in particular instances in between those two extremes, whether or not the threshold has in fact been crossed? This question, which to all intents and purposes is an essential one, will be addressed in the next chapter of this study.[346]

---

[346] See *infra* paragraph 5.3.

Blind fear, that seeing reason leads, finds safer footing
than blind reason stumbling without fear:
to fear the worst oft cures the worse.
– William Shakespeare (1564-1616)

5. THIRD LEG OF THE TRIPOD: ACTION

5.1. Action

In the previous two chapters the first and the second leg of the precautionary tripod have been examined. Just as Apollo's tripod would not have supported the Pythia with only two legs, the precautionary principle would be utterly meaningless without its third ingredient, the element of action. As discussed above, it is incorporated as a core element in virtually every definition of the principle, whether in legal instruments or literature.[1] To illustrate this point it suffices to call to mind that a generally accepted synonym of the precautionary principle is "the principle of precautionary *action*".[2]

Some Observations on the Right and the Duty to Take Precautionary Action

As for the normative quality of the precautionary principle in general international law, it has become clear in the previous two chapters that, where there are reasonable grounds for concern that significant environmental harm may ensue, states are deemed to have a customary *right* to do something about it. Where, however, the anticipated harm is not only significant but also serious or irreversible, states must be considered to also have an *obligation* to take action.[3] Hence, when the right conditions are met, precautionary action is not merely optional. In the words of the EU Court of Justice, under the precautionary principle "a public authority may be *required* to take action even before adverse effects have become apparent."[4] It is warranted to briefly contemplate this mandatory feature of precautionary action.

First and foremost, it is reflected in the majority of formulations of the precautionary principle that occur in international and national legal and

---

[1] See *supra* paragraph 2.3.

[2] See, e.g., the PARCOM *Recommendation 89/1 on the Principle of Precautionary Action*; Sands, 1994/1996, p. 22.

[3] See, especially, *supra* paragraphs 3.3 and 4.3.

[4] *Alpharma*, Case T-70/99, Judgment of 11 September 2002, paragraph 355; italics added. Also in the ITLOS *Land Reclamation* case, both Malaysia and Singapore agreed on this point; see the *Verbatim Records* of the sittings on 25 (p. 20, Schrijver for Malaysia) and 27 September 2003 (p. 32, Reisman for Singapore).

policy instruments and judicial proceedings. Almost invariably these are phrased in a compulsory fashion. When it comes to acting in a precautionary manner use is made of the words 'shall', 'will', 'must', 'should' and 'ought to', rather than 'may' and the like.[5] Second, the scholarly record mirrors this predominance. Representative of the academic majority viewpoint is, for instance, the observation by Matthee and Vermersch that the precautionary principle "allows and even obliges" governments to adopt measures if and when "a reasonable fear for irreversible or serious damage exists."[6]

Not always is it easy to strike a proper balance between the parallel goals of writing concisely and writing clearly. It is submitted in this respect that for present purposes at least, it is best to err on the side of clarity. At the risk of stating the obvious, therefore, a feature of Principle 15 of the *Rio Declaration* and similarly drafted provisions will be briefly dwelt upon here that might seem self-evident to many, but maybe not all readers. When it is stipulated that scientific uncertainty shall not be used as a reason for 'postponing' measures to protect the environment, this prohibition logically comprises the situation where measures are not merely delayed but just not taken at all. The French *Code Rural*, for example, sets out that the absence of certainty "ought not to delay"

---

[5] Out of all provisions of legal instruments reviewed in Trouwborst, 2002, only Article 5(7) of the *SPS Agreement* contains permissive instead of obligatory language. See also Matthee & Vermersch, 2000, p. 66.

[6] Matthee & Vermersch, *ibid.*, p. 60; see also at pp. 61 and 66. Other examples are the consensus among the participants to the 2000 Lauterpacht International Law Centre workshop on "The Precautionary Principle in Wildlife Conservation" (see Cooney, 2000), that "an obligation on decision-makers" is a "fundamental element" of the principle; DeFur & Kaszuba, 2002, p. 157, speaking of "the duty to act" as one of three basic elements of precaution; Borgers, 1999, p. 435, describing the duty to take protective measures as the core of the precautionary principle; Ebbesson, 1996, at pp. 119-120, similarly stating that "[t]he core is the understanding that precautionary measures *must* be taken" when there is reason to assume..., etc. (emphasis added); Canelas de Castro, 1999, p. 199, note 155, according to whom the principle "*demands* actions to prevent environmental degradation" (emphasis added); Cameron & Abouchar, 1996, p. 45, asserting that once relevant thresholds are crossed, there is "a positive obligation to terminate the harm" and that under these circumstances "regulatory inaction is unjustified"; Nollkaemper, 1996, p. 75, stating that, given fulfilment of conditions for the triggering of the precautionary principle, "prevention is mandatory"; the similar submission of Lemons *et al.*, 1997, p. 210, that the principle "requires" the adoption of preventive measures; Birnie & Boyle, 2002, p. 117, speaking of a "legal responsibility to act"; Hey, 1992, p. 305, stating that the principle "requires" that policy-makers adopt an approach ensuring that errors are made on the side of excess environmental protection; Marr, 2003, p. 79, speaking of an "obligation" to take the principle into account "as a legal principle"; Martin, 1997, p. 266, lining up various definitions all of which acknowledge the imperative nature of harm prevention; and Sands, 1995(a), p. 212. A permissively phrased version of the principle can be found in Federale Raad voor Duurzame Ontwikkeling, 2001, p. 18, where it is stated that in name of the precautionary principle measures *can* be taken.

the adoption of measures aimed at preventing environmental damage.[7] By outlawing the *delay* of preventive action, the suitability of taking such action in the first place is considered a given. Hence, what this provision and others like it amount to is simply an obligation to take action[8] – subject, of course, to any specified threshold conditions – while indicating the appropriate moment in time for taking it. Several instruments, evidently to avoid misunderstanding, even state this explicitly (thus suggesting that the balance struck in the present paragraph between conciseness and clarity is perhaps not such an outlandish one[9]). According to the 2001 *South-East Atlantic Fisheries Convention*, to name one, the absence of adequate scientific information shall not be used "as a reason for postponing *or failing to take* conservation and management measures."[10] The first of the 2002 *Guiding Principles on Invasive Alien Species*, to name another, is of similar purport:

> The precautionary approach should also be applied when considering eradication, containment and control measures in relation to alien species that have become established. Lack of scientific certainty about the various implications of an invasion should not be used as a reason for postponing *or failing to take* appropriate eradication, containment and control measures.[11]

Resuming, in accordance with Principle 15 of the *Rio Declaration* and similar provisions, action to protect the environment must be taken and uncertainty may not be used as an excuse for not doing so or delaying it. It may seem that, strictly speaking, the triple negative of Principle 15 and the such is without prejudice for the use of other reasons, not related to uncertainty, for postponing or failing to take precautionary action, such as social or economic motives.[12] This is an issue that will be addressed further on in this study.[13]

Not only the duty to take precautionary measures, but also the right of states to do so merits a closer look before moving on. This right applies in situations where there are reasonable grounds for concern that significant

---

[7] Article 200(1) of the *Loi Barnier* of 2 February 1995; translation from De Sadeleer, 2000, p. 148.

[8] Or, in the words of one writer, a prohibition on abstaining from action: Giraud, C., "Le Droit et le Principe de Précaution: Leçons d'Australie", in: *Revue Juridique de l'Environnement*, No. 1, 1997, as referred to in Matthee, 2001, at p. 184.

[9] Heukers, 1997, at p. 24, also found it worthwhile to expressly include this explanation.

[10] Article 7(2); author's emphasis.

[11] Second half of Guiding Principle 1; author's emphasis. For other provisions like this see Articles 10(6) and 11(8) of the *Biosafety Protocol*; Principles 6.5 and 7.5.1 of the *FAO Code of Conduct for Responsible Fisheries*; Article 6(2) of the *Straddling Stocks Agreement*; Article IV(2) of the 2003 *Antigua Convention*; and Section 10(d) of the 1996 New Zealand *Fisheries Act*; on the latter, see Mascher, 1997, pp. 77-78.

[12] Bodansky, 2004, p. 384.

[13] See *infra* Chapter 9.

environmental harm may come about. One may wonder whether this right is a novel phenomenon at all. Was precautionary action to avoid significant damage not always allowed?[14] As a matter pertaining to the sovereign entitlement of states to do within their territories what they please as long as they do not interfere with the rights of other states, it arguably was. Moreover, as documented elsewhere, implicit precaution has been a common element of state practice for a long time.[15] This is not the same, however, as saying that a fully-fledged international legal right to take precautionary action, of the kind that can compete with the legal privileges of other states – and the precautionary right will be especially relevant in cases of conflicting rules[16] – has always existed in public international law. That assertion is not made here. The present study has done no more and no less than to confirm the existence of such a fully-fledged right in *contemporary* international law and to partially define its extent. It is in any case submitted that the *obligation* to take precautionary action when particular, more stringent threshold conditions are fulfilled is a feature of comparatively recent origin. Only of late have states begun to exercise precaution out of a sense of duty.[17]

The following three paragraphs of this chapter will be concerned with the *where*, *when* and *how* of precautionary action. Where, i.e., in what areas of the world and to what environmental sectors does the precautionary principle find application? When precisely is action called for, i.e., when are thresholds crossed? And how, finally, is one to determine what action to take?

5.2. Where? – The Reach of the Precautionary Principle

Delphi, to stick with the Apollonian analogy, marked the navel of the world. When Zeus released two eagles, one from the west and one from the east, they met at Delphi. Apollo's gaze reached everywhere and his powers were very comprehensive. His lyre music charmed "the gods, the wild beasts, and even the stones." Whether the precautionary principle is to be considered the navel of international environmental law remains to be seen, although a thing or two

---

[14] Several scholars seem to suggest just this when asserting that "the concept of precaution can only present some specificity with respect to classical prevention if it consists in an obligation, and not solely a right to act in a situation of uncertainty." Hancher, 1996, p. 199, referring to Cameron, J. & Werksman, J.D., *The Precautionary Principle: A Policy for Action in the Face of Uncertainty*, 1991.

[15] See Trouwborst, 2002, pp. 20-24 and *passim*.

[16] On potential conflicts between the precautionary principle and the freedom of navigation see Marr, 2003, pp. 41-45 and 184-201; on the relationship between the principle and international trade law see, e.g., De Sadeleer, 2002, pp. 341-365; Cordonier-Segger & Gehring, 2003, *passim*; Matthee & Vermersch, 2000, *passim*.

[17] Trouwborst, 2002, pp. 276-278.

could be said in favour of this position.[18] In any case, with the powers of Apollo the principle has in common that its reach is apparently very wide indeed. How wide exactly is the subject matter of this paragraph.

It was already established above that the reach of the precautionary principle encompasses all types of uncertainty, regardless the classification used. To summarize, the principle covers cases of epistemological and ontological uncertainty alike, and applies equally to quantifiable risks, uncertainty proper and ignorance.[19] This paragraph concerns a different dimension of the principle's scope. For present purposes the enquiry 'where?' is made up of at least four component questions concerning the application of the precautionary principle, which will be treated consecutively:

(1) To what states;
(2) to what geographic areas;
(3) to what environmental issue areas; and
(4) to what plans, activities, products and technologies does the principle apply?

To divergent degrees some of these questions have been dealt with elsewhere.[20] Revisiting them in the present context is nevertheless befitting for the purpose of this study, namely to provide a picture of international legal rights and duties associated with the precautionary principle that is both as complete and as surveyable as possible.

The answer to the first question is threefold and relatively straightforward. As a general principle of international environmental law, the principle applies to all states.[21] As a treaty provision, it applies to the states that have expressed their consent to be bound by the treaties involved.[22] Finally, as part of the fabric of general customary international law, it applies to all states except those which have from the outset persistently objected to its application.[23]

The second, third and fourth questions have in common that the starting point for answering them is one and the same. That is to say, in all three cases significant clues can be encountered in the broadly accepted formulation of the precautionary principle that has been laid down, among other instruments, in the *Rio Declaration*, and in the fact that an important goal

---

[18] Pieterman & Hanekamp, 2002, p. 46, for instance, have dubbed the precautionary principle "the legal core of [international] environmental policy".
[19] See *supra* paragraph 4.1.
[20] Trouwborst, 2002, see relevant footnotes below.
[21] *Ibid.*, pp. 34-35.
[22] *Ibid.*, pp. 34, 63-112 and Annex A.
[23] See *supra* paragraph 1.2.

of the precautionary principle is the achievement of sustainable development through protection of the environment.

What Geographic Areas?

The first sentence of Principle 15 of the *Rio Declaration* states: "*In order to protect the environment*, the precautionary approach shall be *widely applied* by States [..]."[24] It does not read "the environment of other states or of areas beyond the limits of national jurisdiction", as do, for instance, Principle 2 of the same Declaration and Principle 21 of the *Stockholm Declaration*.[25] The latter provisions in a way represent the traditional approach of public international law with its predominant focus on the demarcation of the respective competences of states and the duty not to interfere in the affairs of other states. In the environmental, as in other fields such as human rights this approach is gradually giving way to a focus on global cooperation in order to safeguard collective interests. In international environmental agreements a growing awareness can be detected that states should assume responsibility "not only in relation to other states but also in relation to nature itself,"[26] a trend which is driven by the contemporary insight, discussed in the previous chapter, that everything in nature is interrelated and interdependent.[27] Accordingly, as Kiss and Shelton explain:

> The need to protect the entire biosphere implies that international rules should safeguard the environment within states, even when harmful activities produce no obvious detrimental effects outside the acting state. It also must guarantee protection to areas that are outside territorial control, including the high seas and deep sea bed, the atmosphere of the commons, Antarctica, outer space, the moon, and other celestial bodies.[28]

Just like the wider concept of sustainable development, the precautionary principle is a prominent representative of this modern approach by aiming for the protection of the environment as a whole.[29] It reflects the

---

[24] Emphasis added.

[25] See, e.g., Trouwborst, 2002, p. 35.

[26] Tinker, 1996, p. 58.

[27] See *supra* paragraph 4.1.

[28] Kiss & Shelton, 2000, p. 247. In the words of Lefeber, 1996, p. 126: "it is increasingly emphasized that the preservation of the environment, irrespective of whether it concerns the environment beyond or within the limits of national jurisdiction, is a collective interest, because all ecosystems are interrelated. Obviously, the legal protection of such a collective interest can only be achieved by an obligation pursuant to which all states must prevent and abate all environmental interference which is capable of causing significant harm irrespective of the fact whether such interference has a transboundary impact or not." Footnotes omitted.

[29] In the words of Birnie & Boyle, 2002, p. 104: "Like sustainable development, the precautionary approach is not limited to global environmental concerns, but encompasses in

understanding that it is not appropriate to speak of 'the environment of other states' since there is really only one, indivisible, global environment, which is all too fragile. In legal terms, therefore, the ambit of the precautionary principle is not confined to threats of transboundary harm.[30] Instead, the principle applies to threats of harm to *the environment*, wherever. If this were different, i.e., if states were to avoid transboundary harm only and would be permitted to pillage the environment within their borders at will, the preservation and sustainable development of the world's natural resources and acceptable environmental conditions for present and future generations of human beings could never be warranted.[31]

As it is, the precautionary principle *is* being applied by states to the environment within the limits of national jurisdiction as much as outside them. Examples abound of its application in domestic laws and policies for the sake of environmental protection within the national territory, whether or not the threats in question entail potential transboundary consequences.[32] Moreover, plenty instruments of general scope besides Principle 15 of the *Rio Declaration* affirm the precautionary principle's unconditional applicability to the environment as a whole.[33] Further testimony to this broad coverage are the extensive geographic ranges – some global, some regional – of the environmental agreements and 'soft law' instruments in which the precautionary principle has been incorporated.[34] Many of these instruments have express legal implications not only for interstate issues, but also for areas beyond territorial control and for the national territories of the states involved. Instances are, to mention just a few, the *Biodiversity Convention* and several side agreements to the *Bonn Convention*,[35] covering biodiversity and migratory species protection outside and within states; treaties concerned with the protection of the ecosystems of rivers such as the Danube,[36] Rhine,[37] Meuse and Scheldt,[38] equally combining the transboundary and the

---

addition both transboundary and domestic environmental harm." As Perrez, 2000, puts it at p. 249, "the acceptance of new environmental principles like the principle of sustainability or the precautionary principle is an illustration of the recognition of global common interests and the resulting transformation of the neighborly into a global approach."

[30] Handl, 1991, p. 78; Sands, 1995(a), pp. 194-195; Sands, 1995(b), p. 65; Birnie & Boyle, *ibid.*, p. 117; Trouwborst, 2002, p. 284.

[31] Trouwborst, *ibid.*

[32] *Ibid.*, pp. 178-244 and 283.

[33] See the enumeration in *ibid.*, p. 283.

[34] For one overview, see *ibid.*, pp. 109-110.

[35] E.g., the 1995 *African-Eurasian Waterbirds Agreement*, the 1996 *ACCOBAMS* and the 2000 *Great Bustard Memorandum of Understanding*

[36] 1994 *Danube River Convention.*

[37] 1999 *Rhine Convention.*

[38] 1994 *Meuse* and *Scheldt Conventions.*

domestic; the treaty regimes for the Baltic and Mediterranean Seas, which cover high seas, exclusive economic zones, territorial seas, internal waters and coastal land areas of states parties;[39] the *Climate Change Convention*; and a great number of fisheries treaties covering maritime zones around the globe. In one of the latter, the 1995 *Straddling Stocks Agreement*, the provisions on the precautionary principle are among the few provisions that are explicitly declared to apply also to areas under national jurisdiction.[40]

In summary, then, the precautionary principle must be 'widely applied'. This includes, to say it with Birnie and Boyle, "application to problems of global environmental risk, such as climate change and biological diversity, as well as domestically, in furtherance of the objective of sustainable development."[41] The 2004 *ILA Berlin Rules on Water Resources*, to provide an illustration of the latter, point out that the obligation under the precautionary principle to ensure that groundwater is used sustainably applies "even to an aquifer entirely within a Single state."[42]

The answer to the second question posed in this paragraph is that no geographic areas are excluded from the scope of the precautionary principle. This scope thus encompasses the national territory of states (land mass, air space, internal waters and territorial sea), shared natural resources (e.g., transboundary rivers and lakes), continental shelves, exclusive economic zones as well as areas beyond the boundaries of national jurisdiction (the high seas, the deep seabed, Antarctica,[43] the atmosphere outside national jurisdiction and outer space).[44]

What Issue Areas?

As stated before, the third and fourth questions have the starting points for addressing them in common with the second. Hence, addressing them involves partly similar reasoning. Regarding the third, the circumstance that the precautionary principle is to be *widely applied in order to protect the environment* and the principle's close association with the notion of sustainable development suggest that its reach comprises *all* environmental issue areas.[45] It simply applies *where there are threats* of environmental harm.[46] The only

---

[39] See the *Baltic Sea Convention* and *Barcelona Convention* regimes.
[40] See Article 3.
[41] Birnie & Boyle, 2002, p. 117. As Handl, 1991, p. 78, puts it, the application of the principle "is not limited to transboundary risks of harm, but instead reaches environmentally sensitive activities generally, i.e., irrespective of a direct transnational impact potential."
[42] See (Commentary to) Article 38.
[43] Notwithstanding the various 'frozen' territorial claims.
[44] Also Trouwborst, 2002, p. 284.
[45] *Ibid.*, pp. 283-284.
[46] See Principle 15 of the *Rio Declaration* and similar provisions.

restrictive qualifications in relevant formulations concern the *gravity* and *likelihood* of damage, a matter pertaining to the domain of thresholds of harm and likelihood.[47] The suggestion that the precautionary principle covers all environmental issue areas is in conformity with previous considerations regarding the *origins* and *types* of threats to the environment. In respect of the origins or causes, one will remember the discussion above on natural, technological and mixed risks.[48] It was concluded there that none of these categories was likely to fall outside the reach of the precautionary principle – even though in reality the principle's significance would probably remain modest with respect to threats with a purely natural cause. As to types of harm, it was confirmed above that the scope of the precautionary principle expressly encompasses threats of harm to the intrinsic value of the environment, that is, harm to nature as such, in addition to damage to resources and amenities of direct value to man.[49]

This wide ambit is reflected in the practice of states, in which the precautionary principle has been applied to a huge variety of environmental issue areas, ranging from offshore activities to trade in endangered species, from climate change to the protection of the Rhine, from the effects of road construction to high seas fisheries, from POPs to GMOs and from albatross protection to the ozone layer.[50] The reach of the precautionary principle, in answer to the third question, thus spans the natural environment in the broadest sense, i.e., all parts and processes that make up the interlinked whole of air, soil, water, flora and fauna.[51] Human health may be deemed as included within this reach as far as its protection from adverse environmental impacts is concerned. As set out before, however, it is doubtful whether as a matter of customary international law the precautionary principle also covers health issues *in stricto senso* such as food safety.[52]

What Activities?

The answer to the fourth question is now rather obvious. If the precautionary principle is to be widely applied in order to protect the environment as a whole and asks for preventive and abatement action to be taken wherever there is a sufficiently qualified threat of environmental harm, then *all* plans, activities, products and technologies that might pose such a threat are *prima facie* eligible for such action, in light also of sustainable development. A precautionary approach must accordingly be adopted

[47] See *supra* paragraphs 3.2, 3.3, 4.3 and *infra* paragraph 5.3.

[48] See *supra* paragraphs 3.1 and 3.4.

[49] *Ibid.*

[50] See, *inter alia*, Trouwborst, 2002, pp. 110 and 131.

[51] *Ibid.*, pp. 283-284; see also Backes *et al.*, 2002, p. 236.

[52] See *supra* paragraph 1.2.

consistently to "all human endeavors."[53] In order to protect fish stocks, precautionary action should be taken with respect to all factors adversely affecting stock development, not just one or two. Thomas and Grader have illustrated this by drawing an analogy with vessel safety: "if we use a precautionary approach and change the engine oil every time we come in to dock, but never paint the boat or take any measures to keep it from rotting we're still going to sink."[54]

A problem that is of relevance in this context relates to the dual task of administrations to regulate both existing, 'old' dangers like air pollution from automobiles as well as 'new' hazards, like the potential risks associated with modern biotechnology.[55] According to some researchers, governments are inclined to systematically treat existing risks more leniently than new ones, for the plain reason that politically speaking the vested interests surrounding settled activities and technologies tend to put more weight in the scale than the interests belonging to new ones that have not as yet become established in society.[56] The problem with this from an environmental point of view is that it can unintentionally delay or altogether prevent the substitution of existing hazardous technologies and products by potentially safer ones.[57] One example where this may just be the case is the meticulous screening of new pesticides that is common in many countries.[58] Some writers have contended that the precautionary principle does not contribute to solving this problem and indeed even aggravates it, arguing that only new technologies are 'prone' to application of the principle while relatively dangerous older technologies are not.[59] It is submitted here that this conception is erroneous insofar as public international law is concerned. There is nothing to insinuate that under the precautionary principle as agreed upon by the international community of states, precautionary action is to be applied only to new activities, technologies, plans and products as opposed to existing ones. None of the formulations of the principle expressly

---

[53] 1998 *Wingspread Statement*. According to Gullett, 1997, p. 65, the precautionary principle "is apposite for the entire spectrum of environmental decision-making, including individual development decisions." See also Pieterman & Hanekamp, 2002, pp. vii and 15.

[54] Thomas & Grader, 2000.

[55] Wildavsky, 2000, p. 39, quoting Huber, P., "The Old-New Division in Risk Regulation", in: 69 *The Virginia Law Review*, 1983, pp. 23-32.

[56] E.g., Wildavsky, *ibid.*, p. 40. "To wipe out tangible benefits people already enjoy – familiar products, traditional jobs [..] – is politically more difficult to do than to stop something new that is not yet surrounded with a self-protective belt of interest." *Ibid.*

[57] *Ibid.*, p. 39.

[58] Foster, D., "Letter to the Editor", in: *Regulation*, March/April 1984, p. 2; as cited in Wildavsky, *ibid.* On the regulation of existing and new pesticides see also *infra* paragraph 8.2.

[59] Pieterman, 2001, p. 1029; Pieterman & Hanekamp, 2002, p. 15.

takes this approach.[60] Instead, state practice confirms that the only criteria for triggering the application of the precautionary principle are the respective thresholds of harm and likelihood. When these are crossed precautionary action to prevent or abate the environmental hazard in question is considered appropriate, regardless whether this threat ensues from old or new factors.[61] By way of one illustration, the US *Fisheries Recovery Act* explicitly provides that the precautionary approach applies to "any existing or proposed action" affecting marine life.[62] It may be that uncertainties are generally, albeit not always, greatest where proposed activities are at stake.[63] This does not in any way imply, however, that in such cases there are more often reasonable grounds for concern that harm may be caused than in respect of existing activities. In conformity with this, the principle is being applied by states to risks emanating from long-standing activities such as established fisheries as much as to new risks such as those associated with genetic modification.

In accordance with the answer to the fourth question already given above, in legal terms the precautionary principle covers old and new risks alike. As phrased in one domestic legislative act, for governments this means that the principle "shall be applied to *all* policy and regulatory decisions of the administration," whether they concern permission for the continuation of existing activities, technologies and products or the introduction of new ones.[64] Where the principle *is* applied selectively to new risks only, this is apparently not in consonance with international law.

5.3. *When? – A Closer Look at Thresholds*

As it seems, the only factors delimiting the applicability of the precautionary principle in international law are the thresholds of gravity and likelihood that have been defined in the foregoing chapters. These embody objective tests.[65] The logical next query, and a crucial one for practical purposes, is how to

---

[60] Also Marr, 2003, p. 224; Bodansky, 2004, p. 389.

[61] Perhaps this is what is meant in the 1995 *Land-Based Activities Action Programme* where it states that the precautionary approach "should be applied through preventive *and corrective* measures" (paragraph 24, emphasis added) although the latter are arguably aimed at the prevention of environmental harm just as much as the former.

[62] US Gilchrest-Farr *Fisheries Recovery Act* (HR 4046), as quoted in Thomas & Grader, 2000.

[63] Bodansky, 2004, p. 389.

[64] 1997 *Massachusetts Precautionary Principle Act*; emphasis added. Judge Wolfrum in his Separate Opinion appended to the ITLOS *Mox Plant* Order of 3 December 2001, also stated explicitly that the principle applies to any state "interested in undertaking or continuing" potentially harmful activities.

[65] Compare, e.g., Foster, 2001, p. 597.

determine in concrete instances whether the thresholds in question are traversed or not. Knowing *what* the thresholds are, *when* are they crossed? In other words, when exactly are there 'reasonable grounds for concern', when does a given impact qualify as 'harm' and when is anticipated environmental harm 'significant', 'serious' or 'irreversible'? Who is to answer these questions and how?

The assessment of whether these thresholds are traversed may, at first glance, seem an utterly subjective exercise. In the end, what one person, or government, regards as serious harm another might regard as negligible.[66] Nevertheless, although there is undoubtedly such a subjective side to the matter, this is not the whole story. In the assessment in question there will often be room for subjectivity, but this room may be narrowed down in more than one way, depending on the particular threshold under consideration and the circumstances of each situation. A closer look at the various thresholds conditioning the precautionary principle will clarify this point. This look will be taken in the by now familiar order: first harm, then likelihood.

When taking this closer look it is useful to bear in mind the historical development of thresholds. The attitude of the international community towards the deterioration of the natural environment is rather different now from what it was a hundred years ago. "The question of determining what is significant harm in the modern world is not the same as determining what was significant harm in the *interbellum*."[67] By way of a first clue, therefore, it may be assumed that thresholds of harm have lowered over time. They have become easier to cross, so to speak. Cases of environmental degradation that failed the test of significance or were not even considered harmful in the first place in the days of the *Trail Smelter* case, may well pass the threshold of significance or even that of seriousness if they were to happen today.[68]

In respect of the first leg of the precautionary tripod, Chapter 3 rendered several distinct stages of legal relevance. These stages correspond to three consecutive questions that need to be addressed when endeavoring to establish the degree of applicability of the precautionary principle to a given anticipated environmental impact:

(1) Is the anticipated impact adverse?
(2) If so, is the anticipated harm also significant?

---

66 Morris, 2000(b), p. 14; Lambers, 2000, p. 180; Freestone, 1999, p. 137; Matthee, 2001, p. 184; Bouma *et al.*, 2002, p. 15.
67 Lefeber, 1996, p. 87.
68 Also International Law Commission, 2001, Commentary to Article 2(a) of the *Draft Articles on Harm Prevention*, paragraph 7.

(3) If so, is the anticipated significant harm also serious and/or irreversible?[69]

Is the Anticipated Impact Adverse?

Environmental change, to begin with the first question, qualifies as harm only when it is negative. In the context of the precautionary principle the impairment of values of nature to humans and the impairment of the intrinsic value of nature both count as adverse.[70] As has been shown above, distinguishing between beneficial, neutral and detrimental impacts, between welcome and unwelcome ones, is not always unproblematic.[71] The assessment of net effects will sometimes be a complicated affair.[72] And reference is not made here to the difficulty of predicting *what* the environmental effects of a certain activity will be. That problem pertains to the domain of uncertainty, the second leg of the tripod. At issue here is the difficulty of estimating how particular environmental effects, i.e. deviations from environmental baseline conditions, that can be envisaged – irrespective of their likelihood of occurrence – are to be *valued*. A given envisionable impact scenario may favour one species while hurting another. The overall assessment of the net effect here may depend on many factors, such as the global conservation status of the two species, the trends in the development of their respective numbers, the relative vulnerability of the populations involved, etcetera. Other scenarios may spell negative effects on a local scale but positive effects on a global scale. Windmills erected for the purpose of energy generation, for instance, kill birds and disfigure landscapes, but help fight climate change by reducing reliance on fossil fuels. Often, however, the matter will be more clear cut. The net environmental effects of clearcutting an old-growth forest, overexploiting a fish stock, draining a wetland or polluting a river, to name a few common activities, are evidently adverse. *Ergo*, in many cases room for subjectivity will be very limited or altogether absent. It quite suffices, to take one example, to imagine denying the adversity of the net impact on the environment of constructing a new highway through a rural or wilderness area.

Is the Anticipated Impact Significant?

Having ascertained the harmful nature of an anticipated environmental impact, the next question is whether the adverse effect would also qualify as significant. The precautionary principle, after all, does not apply to insignificant harm. When compared to the question of significance the issue of adversity as such

---

[69] See *supra* paragraph 3.4, especially Figure 3.

[70] See *supra* paragraph 3.1.

[71] *Ibid.*; also Klinke & Renn, 1999, p. 10.

[72] Generally, see Beeckman, 1996.

suddenly appears rather straightforward. What is required now is a more subtle exercise. To elucidate this point it might help to call to mind the scale of gravity of harm depicted earlier in Figure 1. The question here is no longer *whether* the impact at stake is represented on the axis, but *where* it is located on the axis. The answer, in other words, lies somewhere on a sliding scale. It will be remembered that harm qualifies as significant when it is tangible, appreciable and measurable, as opposed to minor or trivial.[73] (Again, the present discussion is not concerned with the probability of harm materializing: the precautionary principle is about the avoidance of tangible and measurable harm, not about effects that must be tangible and measurable before measures are taken!) The threshold of significance is thus a relatively low one.

But how exactly is one to draw the line between harm which is significant and harm which is not? There is no such thing as an authoritative manual on the threshold of significance.[74] Significance is a general notion and, as the International Law Commission put it, "not without ambiguity."[75] Value judgments by those responsible play a more frequent and more substantial role here than in respect of the first question just dealt with.[76] Naturally, this role is conditioned by the specific circumstances of each case.[77] Varying factual circumstances are bound to influence to a considerable extent the outcome of any assessment of expected gravity of harm. And there are as many cases as there are projects, activities, technologies and products potentially affecting the environment. Different regions, ecosystems and species have different sensitivities, carrying capacities and vulnerabilities to change. A single activity may have a significant impact in one place and a minor one in another.[78] Thus, as the EU Court explained in the *Cockle Fisheries Case*, when determining the severity of threatening environmental harm due regard must be had for the specific environmental characteristics and circumstances of the area concerned.[79] It may also be that a certain activity does not by itself give rise to significant harm, but does so in combination with others. Under EU nature protection law, to name an example, such cumulative effects are part and parcel of the assessment whether the expected impact of a particular activity

---

[73] See *supra* paragraph 3.2.

[74] Lefeber, 1996, p. 87.

[75] International Law Commission, 2001, Commentary to Article 2(a) of the *Draft Articles on Harm Prevention*, paragraph 4.

[76] Freestone, 1999, p. 137.

[77] International Law Commission, 2001, Commentary to Article 2(a) of the *Draft Articles on Harm Prevention*, paragraphs 4 and 7.

[78] E.g., Harding & Fisher, 1994, p. 252, contend in regard of Australia's natural assets that the "extraordinary diversity of ecosystems, which are unique on the world stage" imply that "impacts are likely to be perceived as significant."

[79] Case C-127/02, Judgment of 7 September 2004, paragraph 48.

qualifies as 'significant'.[80] Other beacons to steer by are embodied by factors such as the geographic dispersion and the longevity of harmful effects.

This is not all. Environmental law and policy instruments may provide indicators further defining the room eventually available for value determinations by decision makers when verifying whether anticipated harm is to be considered significant. A rather obvious one involves the breach of substantive norms of public international law, such as internationally agreed quality standards for river water or air purity, or commitments regarding the conservation of particular populations of wildlife. To hold that environmental effects which transgress such norms can be dismissed as insignificant is evidently a mission impossible. Once more, such norms may differ from place to place. Standards for the water of the Rhine will not necessarily coincide with those for Yangtzhe River water. Legal and policy documents and other formal expressions by one or more states may, in addition, contain explicit testimony as to what is deemed significant. The adverse environmental effects of converting a swamp into arable land are clearly not trivial to a state which has acknowledged "the fundamental ecological functions of wetlands as regulators of water regimes and as habitats supporting a characteristic flora and fauna."[81] Formal statements of this kind abound, at both international and national levels, and can offer important guidance in a lot of instances. Needless to say, like considerations apply to the adversity test. The following provision, for instance, evinces the adversity as well as the significance of various threats to European forests:

> Considering the adverse effects on forests in some parts of Europe of storms, inadequate management, pests, diseases, game, overgrazing and unregulated browsing, and of inadequately planned large industrial and infrastructure development, and being concerned over the destruction of large areas of forest by fires, [..].[82]

Some environmental instruments even contain elaborated checklists for assessing significance in relation to their subject matter. Specific guidance has been developed, for example, by the European Commission so as to facilitate the implementation of the *Habitats Directive* by EU member states.[83] All together

---

[80] See, e.g., the *Cockle Fisheries* judgment, *ibid.*, paragraphs 53 and 61.

[81] Second preambular paragraph of the 1971 *Convention on Wetlands of International Importance* (*Ramsar Convention*).

[82] Preambular paragraph K from *Resolution H1* of the 1993 Helsinki Ministerial Conference on the Protection of Forests in Europe.

[83] The guidance document in question sets out a non-exhaustive list of significance assessment factors, *inter alia*: the character and perceived value of the affected environment; the magnitude, spatial extent and duration of the anticipated change; the resilience of the environment to cope with change; the existence of policies, programmes, plans, etc. which can

the indicators discussed here compose a framework within which the pertinent authorities of states make determinations concerning the severity of potential harm, a framework which can take on varying shapes and sizes depending on the circumstances at hand.

Is the Anticipated Impact Serious?

The procedure is similar with respect to the first half of the third question listed above. That is, will the significant adverse effect that is anticipated also constitute serious harm? If so, as demonstrated earlier, precaution becomes mandatory.[84] Although the purpose this time is to find out whether threatening environmental harm would qualify as serious or not, the question that needs answering in order to achieve this purpose is essentially the same as in the significance test. Namely: *how* grave is the anticipated harm? After all, the threshold of serious (or irreversible) harm intersects the same sliding scale of gravity as the threshold of significant harm.[85]

Two typical indicators of gravity that were already mentioned are the duration and geographic extent of environmental harm.[86] The further on the scales of space and time, the more significant and/or serious an impact will be considered. This may be pictured as follows:

be used as criteria; and the existence of environmental standards against which a proposal can be assessed (e.g. air quality standards, water quality standards). European Commission, 2001, p. 62.

[84] See *supra* paragraphs 3.3 and 3.4.

[85] See *supra* Figure 2.

[86] Klinke & Renn, 1999, p. 12; DeFur & Kaszuba, 2003, p. 155; Bodansky, 2004, p. 387; see also *supra* paragraph 3.3. The extent and persistency of possible damage are also named as indicators of gravity by the European Commission in Communication COM (2000)1, p. 14.

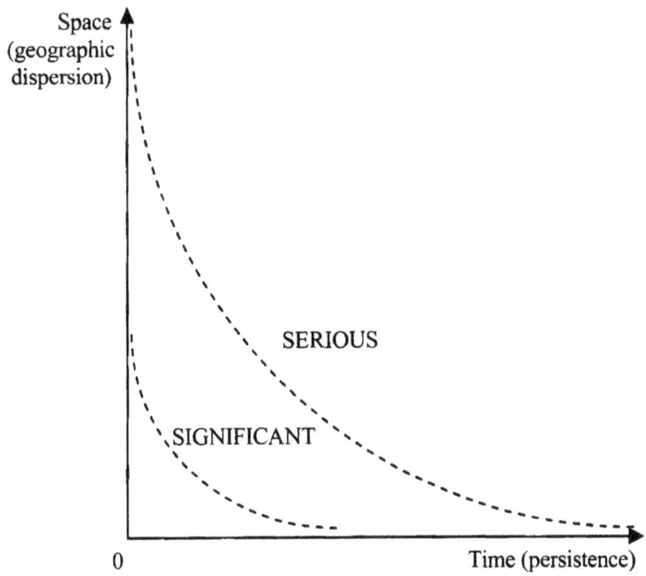

Figure 6. Time and space as indicators of gravity of harm. To a degree, the gravity of environmental harm is a function of temporal persistence and spatial distribution. The more enduring or widespread the harm - i.e., the further to the right or to the top of the diagram – the more significant and/or serious it will be qualified. The two curves reprcsent the respective thresholds of significant and serious harm.

Within the more or less triangular space at the bottom left of the diagram are plotted harmful effects that are so geographically confined and of such brevity that they are deemed insignificant. Conversely, away towards the top right of the diagram instances of virtually ubiquitous and highly persistent harm can be found. Such cases of extremely serious harm belong to a risk class that Klinke and Renn have dubbed Pandora's Box.[87] The evil powers released when the box was opened were so many and so dark that they obscured the very sun. The pinnacle of spatial extension is omnipresence. Hazards of this kind are of worldwide proportions, happening at a scale where there is, to put it with the European Environment Agency, only one experimental model.[88] The pinnacle of temporal extension, closely related, is the point at which damage becomes irreversible. Irreversibility, which forms a single threshold together with seriousness, will receive separate attention below.

[87] Klinke & Renn, *ibid.*

[88] European Environment Agency, 2001, p. 171.

As with significance, the question whether harm is serious is decided first and foremost, in the words of the ILC, by "factual and objective criteria", although value judgments may also be expected to play a part.[89] The room reserved for the latter is determined by the former. The actual division between objective and subjective elements will again vary from case to case, depending on the circumstances. As Lauterpacht put it when acting as counsel for Malaysia in the ITLOS *Land Reclamation* case, the "seriousness of damage increases as the scope for damage decreases."[90] The smaller the population of an endangered species, the sooner the removal of even a few specimens will be deemed 'serious'. The same is true for ecosystems and natural habitats. This reasoning was applied to Singapore's reclamation activities around Pulau Tekong: "The fact that so much reclamation has been carried out already only increases the seriousness of the harm that will be done to the remaining areas by reason of the reduction of the area remaining to be harmed."[91] Cumulative effects are as relevant here as in the 'significance' discussion. To return to Figure 6, the more towards the upper right of the diagram, the more evident the serious nature of environmental harm will be. When lion populations across the African continent are decimated as a result of habitat loss, uncontrolled hunting and disease, this undeniably constitutes serious harm. The other way around, the assessment of whether harm qualifies as serious or not will be more complicated for cases corresponding to dots in the close vicinity of the threshold line. What if, for instance, a twenty-five percent lion decline occurs due to similar causes in one National Park only? Cases of this type are the harder nuts to crack and it is here that the relative weight of subjective value determinations will be biggest.

Again as with significance, the room ultimately available for such discretionary judgments is shaped by multiple factors pertaining to the domain of international and national environmental law and policy. It is probably fair to say that the violation of substantive norms relating to nature and the environment gives rise to a presumption of seriousness, the rebuttal of which would demand sound argumentation on the part of authorities claiming that the harm in question is not serious. The characterization of an adverse impact as serious may also follow from formal statements made earlier by the state(s) concerned. One instance of such a recital manifesting the severity of harm can be taken from the 1999 *Southern Bluefin Tuna* cases, in which all three parties to the dispute agreed that the tuna stock at stake was "severely depleted" and "at its historically lowest levels" and that this was a "cause for serious biological

[89] International Law Commission, 2001, Commentary to Article 2(a) of the *Draft Articles on Harm Prevention*, paragraph 7.
[90] *Verbatim Record* of the sitting on 27 September 2003, p. 21.
[91] *Ibid.*

concern."[92] Returning to the lion example, to a signatory state of the *World Charter for Nature* – having acknowledged the "essential" functions of ecological processes, life support systems and the diversity of life forms, "which are jeopardized through excessive exploitation and habitat destruction by man," and aware of "the *urgency* of maintaining the stability and quality of nature and of conserving natural resources"[93] – the fate befalling a keystone predator such as the African lion will undoubtedly matter a great deal. This would be all the more evident if the state in question had also, as a party to the 1968 *African Convention on the Conservation of Nature and Natural Resources*, demonstrated its consciousness that "flora and fauna resources constitute a capital of *vital importance to mankind*."[94] These are just two of many instruments that could inform the gravity assessment in a case like the current example. The greater the worth accorded to an environmental asset, the graver the harm inflicted on the asset will be deemed. Consider, for example, the value bestowed on natural heritage as defined in the 1972 *World Heritage Convention*.[95] In the opinion of the parties to this agreement, the deterioration or disappearance of any item of natural heritage constitutes "a harmful impoverishment of the heritage of all the nations of the world."[96] It is hard to conceive how states could credibly go back on positions of this kind, whether portrayed in legally binding instruments, soft law documents or otherwise. It would take very solid arguments to convincingly maintain that impacts which were considered serious harm in the past are not viewed so any more. In light of the downward tendency of thresholds over time, discussed above, it is rather the opposite which is to be expected.

Yet another indicator relates to the concept of sustainable development. Given the close ties between this concept and the precautionary principle as discussed above, the assessment of gravity must evidently be informed by the extent to which future generations might be affected.[97] As discussed extensively in the previous chapter, it is not always foreseeable what impacts the behavior of the current generation will have on the (future) environment. Some have argued therefore, that harm is to be considered serious whenever there are grounds for concern that an activity may appreciably prejudice the interests of future generations.[98] It is submitted here that, at a minimum, such circumstances would generate a suspicion of

---

[92] Paragraph 71 of the ITLOS Order of 27 August 1999.

[93] 1982 *World Charter for Nature*, preambular paragraphs 4(a) and 3(b); italics added.

[94] Hereinafter 1968 *African Convention*, first preambular paragraph (emphasis added); see also the first preambular paragraph of the Convention as revised in 2003.

[95] *Convention for the Protection of the World Cultural and Natural Heritage*.

[96] Second preambular paragraph.

[97] See *supra* paragraph 2.3. See also Epiney & Scheyli, 1998, pp. 118-119; Soria Jiménez, 1996, p. 393.

[98] Epiney & Scheyli, *ibid.*, p. 119.

seriousness, similar to impacts transgressing substantive environmental standards.

Is the Anticipated Impact Irreversible?

Irreversibility, the other component of the threshold of 'serious or irreversible harm', is a singularly laden concept. It bears upon situations where harm may be definitive, where it is a matter of all or nothing. Irreversibility has no place in the diagram of Figure 6, even if *in stricto senso* it is an index of time. 'Serious' and 'irreversible', while forming part of the same threshold, represent different magnitudes. It is perfectly conceivable, as discussed in Chapter 3, for environmental damage to be irreversible but not serious.[99] As a threshold value irreversibility would seem less prone to subjective judgment than seriousness in that, in principle, damage is either reversible or it is not. It was explained earlier that in spite of this apparent simplicity it is possible, paradoxically, to argue both that everything is irreversible and that nothing is irreversible, depending on the angle. The bottom line was, nevertheless, that in the practice of states an apparent understanding has been formed of what the criterion implies, and that it is taken to include situations where harm is *virtually* or *practically* irreversible.[100]

As with the other threshold criteria the question arises how to determine in specific cases whether anticipated harm is of the irreparable kind? Once again the answer may be found in previous statements by states, in which explicit clues abound. Soil, water, flora and fauna are deemed by the states parties to the 1968 *African Convention* to be "irreplaceable assets".[101] Wetlands, in the words of the *Ramsar Convention*, constitute a resource of great value "the loss of which would be irreparable."[102] In the *World Heritage Convention* natural heritage is described as "unique and irreplaceable".[103] At its very outset *CITES* likewise states the recognition that "wild fauna and flora in their many beautiful and varied forms are an *irreplaceable* part of the natural system of the earth,"[104] whereas the 1979 *Bonn Convention* begins with a similar statement.[105] By way of a final example, the 1993 *European Forest Guidelines* speak of the *irreversible*

---

99 See *supra* paragraph 3.3.

100 *Ibid.* As Bodansky, 2004, puts it at p. 387, irreversible harm is characterized by "a very long time scale."

101 Fourth preambular paragraph. According to the first preambular paragraph of the Convention as revised in 2003, African natural resources are deemed an "irreplaceable part of the African heritage."

102 Third preambular paragraph.

103 Fifth preambular paragraph.

104 First preambular paragraph; emphasis added.

105 See the first preambular paragraph. Given that the focus of the *Bonn Convention* is on migratory animals, this provision concerns fauna only.

degradation of forest soils and sites, the flora and fauna they support and the ecological services they provide.[106]

These texts underline that the notion of irreversibility as conceived by the international community of states comprises both environmental harm which is factually irreparable, such as the extinction of species or the exhaustion of non-renewable resources, as well as harm which is practically irreversible, such as the severe depletion of fish stocks, the process of desertification or the diffusion of genetically modified crops into natural ecosystems.[107] It is thus not necessary –if this were at all possible – to draw a strict dividing line between the two. Arguably, the notion of sustainable development can help to determine when expected harm is to be considered irreversible. It has been submitted in this respect that in the context of the precautionary principle environmental harm is irreversible when the time required by the regenerative forces of nature to replenish what was taken away or to repair what was destroyed is likely to extend over several human generations.[108]

To summarize, together all the indicators dealt with here define the bounds within which states can exercise discretion. Their relevance and relative weight, however, will vary from one case to the other. Consequently, in some cases the determination of whether harm is to be deemed significant, serious and/or irreversible will be left largely to the discretion of state(s) involved, while in others there may be precious little room for subjective judgment.

Are There Reasonable Grounds for Concern?

Moving now from the gravity of harm to the other half of environmental risk, that is likelihood of occurrence, it is time to address the question as to when there are and when there are not 'reasonable grounds for concern'. As described above, this threshold implies that the mere theoretical *possibility* of a given level of environmental harm – "mere speculation", as Bodansky puts it[109] – is not enough to trigger precautionary action, although it does not require proof of *probability* of harm either.[110]

Part of any effort to further define the parameters of the requisite 'indications', of the necessary 'reasonable grounds for concern', is the contentious issue of whether these must take the shape of some amount of, albeit preliminary, *scientific* evidence – that is, knowledge which is the outcome of systematic study and method and not merely a product of general experience

106 First operational paragraph of *Resolution H1* of the 1993 Helsinki Ministerial Conference on the Protection of Forests in Europe.

107 See also *supra* paragraph 3.3; Epiney & Scheyli, 1998, p. 118.

108 Epiney & Scheyli, *ibid.*

109 Bodansky, 2004, p. 389.

110 See *supra* paragraph 4.3.

or common sense.[111] Obviously, under the precautionary principle states should not wait for scientifically documented *effects* before taking measures – precautionary action must precede effects in order to prevent them – but should they perhaps wait for scientifically documented *grounds for concern*? In other words, must there be at least some scientific gist to the indications in question or can other, non-scientific pointers amount to reasonable grounds for concern as well? Extensive discussions on this question continue to take place in academic discourse. The 2002 *ILA Declaration on Sustainable Development*, for example, maintains that precautionary measures "should be based on up-to-date and independent scientific judgment."[112] One writer even holds that there need be "a broad scientific consensus" that information is based on some "hard scientific evidence,"[113] while according to another the threshold of reasonable grounds imposes that harm must be indicated by "some level of scientific objectivity."[114] Others have expressed opinions to the contrary.[115]

As for pertinent state practice, the many clauses dealt with above that call for precautionary measures in advance of 'sufficient', 'adequate', 'absolutely clear', 'conclusive', 'complete', 'full' or 'undisputed' *scientific* evidence *could* be taken to presume the presence, nevertheless, of *some* level of scientific information, however small.[116] This understanding does in fact correspond to the course of things in abundant instances of precautionary action. Very often, grounds for concern *will* be based on some scientific data or other – however incomplete.[117] The tremendously important role that scientific research plays in the identification of (potential) threats to the environment cannot be stressed enough in this respect.

---

[111] This common description of scientific evidence squares, *inter alia*, with the views of the WTO Appellate Body and the US Supreme Court. According to the jurisprudence of these two bodies, the decisive criterion for evidence to qualify as "scientific" is that it be derived at through the scientific method. See Foster, 2001, pp. 588-590.

[112] Paragraph 4.4.

[113] Blanchfield, 2000.

[114] Dzidzornu, 1998, p. 98. This may be attributed to the dissentient viewpoint expressed by the same author that the concern for, or assumption of the detrimental effect in question, "supported by inconclusive scientific evidence, must point to the *probability* of harm or threats of serious or irreversible damage." Italics added.

[115] E.g., Pieterman & Hanekamp, 2002, p. vii. These authors have noted the absence of any legal criterion requiring "substantial empirical scientific evidence" before the precautionary principle can be invoked – while considering this a serious flaw of the principle.

[116] See *supra* paragraph 4.3. González Campos *et al.*, 1998, at pp. 798-799 even submit that the phrase "lack of *absolute* scientific certainty" necessarily implies that very precise knowledge has already been acquired in respect of the threat in issue although some uncertainties persist.

[117] Marr, 2003, p. 24, affirms that precautionary action is triggered by a possibility of environmental harm "based, in most cases, on scientific suspicion."

Much has been said and written on the relationship between the precautionary principle and science.[118] The two concepts meet in the area of environmental risks, which often "can only be identified by scientific research, but which scientific research is unable to characterize in an unambiguous fashion."[119] It is probably appropriate at this point to dwell for a moment on the remarkable allegation by critics of the precautionary principle that the principle would be 'unscientific', an allegation that recurs surprisingly often.[120] Surprisingly, because the relationship between precaution and science is really quite straightforward. It was scientific research that revealed the serious and irreversible nature of much environmental harm wrought by human action. It was scientific research that revealed the complex nature of ecology and the unpredictability of environmental effects. It is scientific research that is needed for the early detection of potential environmental hazards. It is scientific research that is needed for the reduction of existing uncertainties and the contribution of new data in the light of which precautionary measures taken can be evaluated and, if need be, modified or cancelled. Science has thus not only laid the very foundation of the precautionary principle, it also continues to be an indispensable and pre-eminent tool for the principle's implementation.[121] Undeniably, science and precaution are mutually reinforcing. The precautionary principle is evidently all but unscientific.

Having said this, it must be asked whether this entails that the precautionary principle can never find application in situations where there is no scientific evidence at all to back a particular environmental threat. The answer to this question, it is submitted here, must be in the negative, for the plain reason that it is not possible to distil any clear rule of this purport from the pertinent practice of states. The affirmation that science plays a predominant role in the early detection of potential threats means no more and no less than that. It does not play the *only* role. Sometimes reasonable grounds for concern leading to precautionary action consist of warnings, signals and clues of a not strictly scientific caliber.

Consideration of the criterion which requires decisions to be based on the 'best scientific information available', occurring in various instruments in various forms as discussed previously,[122] is exemplary. As stated above, this criterion can be understood, at first sight, to suggest the availability of at least

---

[118] See, e.g., De Sadeleer, 2002, pp. 174-201; Marr, 2003, pp. 24-34; Tanaka, 2005, pp. 954-956.

[119] Von Moltke, 1999.

[120] See *supra* paragraph 1.1.

[121] See *infra* paragraph 7.2.

[122] See *supra* paragraph 4.3.

some scientific information as the basis for decisions.[123] It is questionable, however, whether this is the only coherent interpretation. After all, as the case may be the best scientific evidence *available* may be constituted by precious little scientific evidence, or may even consist of no scientific evidence at all. Where there is no scientific information whatsoever, the 'best scientific information available' is zero. That this is not much to go by is not the point. The point is that logically the requirement of 'best scientific information available' captures this type of situation, however undesirable, just as much as it captures situations of exhaustive scientific evidence – and everything in between the two, for that matter. The following imaginary setting may clarify this point:

- State X has taken on a duty under public international law to take all decisions affecting the environment on the basis of the best scientific information available.
- A foreign ship loaded with several chemical substances has been severely damaged in a storm, its cargo beginning to leak out into the ocean, and requests permission from the authorities of State X to enter one of its ports.
- No scientific information is available regarding the effects of the chemicals in question on the environment.

Clearly, State X will have to respond to the request by choosing one of two alternatives. Either the ship is allowed into port or sent back out to sea. Not taking a decision is simply not an option. Moreover, the decision obviously is of the kind affecting the environment. Given the absence of scientific information, non-scientific information will have to inform the decision. Does this state of affairs nullify, modify or run counter to the obligation of State X to act on the best scientific information available? It is difficult to see why or how.

In short, what the criterion of the 'best scientific information available' entails is this: when scientific evidence *is* available, the best of it should be taken into account when making decisions. It does *not* mean that decisions cannot legitimately be taken without scientific evidence.[124] *Ergo*, even if this criterion were universally applied in combination with the precautionary principle – and it is not – it could hardly serve as proof that the threshold of reasonable grounds for concern requires a degree of *scientific* evidence for it to be crossed.

Yet this does not take away the fact that it is normal practice for governments, and in accordance with common sense, to base decisions on the best information that can be disposed of in order to produce decisions that are

---

[123] *Ibid.*

[124] Also Marr, 2003, p. 135.

as uncontentious as possible.[125] These best available data will frequently, though not always, happen to be the result of scientific research. It would appear that the practice referred to here ought to be looked on, however, as an expression of the generally applicable requirements of accountability and good governance, rather than as a specific feature of the precautionary principle.

With respect to the precautionary principle the inescapable bottom line of the matter is that both the availability of information, scientific and otherwise, and the ostensible urgency of precautionary action tend to fluctuate hugely from case to case. The relevance of this bottom line for the question at hand may again be set out by reference to a small example. Consider the following events:

- Large quantities of dead fish, mostly roaches, are suddenly turning up on the surface of a river in State Y.
- The mortality occurs only days after the setting in motion of a new factory located upstream which is dumping a number of residual substances into the river as part of its operation.
- The effects of the substances involved on roaches or any other of the affected species have never been scientifically investigated. According to scientific experts it will take several weeks to verify whether the fish mortality is indeed brought about by (any of) the substances.
- Under the circumstances, the competent authorities of State Y order the suspension of the factory's operation until more is found out about the suspected link between the emissions and the mortality.

What is this order if not a *prima facie* legitimate precautionary measure? Although nothing is known for sure and no *scientific* evidence whatsoever is available concerning the effects of the emitted substances on the implicated species there are arguably grounds for concern that are more than reasonable that the factory emissions are the cause of considerable harm to the fluvial ecosystem. The circumstances do not permit delay. Patently, it does not always take a team of scientists to corroborate that there are reasonable grounds for concern.

In surmise, it has become manifest that in the determination of whether there are reasonable grounds for concern that environmental harm may be produced by a given activity, project, plan, product or technology, it is fitting to have recourse to the *best information available*.[126] What the 'best' information is

---

[125] Also Foster, 2001, p. 587.

[126] "Decisions should be based on the best available information" is also how it is put, e.g., in Section 10(a) of the New Zealand *Fisheries Act* of 1996; in paragraph 2.3 of the *PKB Waddenzee*, i.e., the major Dutch policy instrument on the Wadden Sea; and in the report *Natuur Naderbij* by the

will vary from instance to instance, and may not in all cases be immediately apparent. What *is* apparent is that the information need not always be of a scientific quality for it to constitute reasonable grounds for concern.[127] The above findings are only little astounding in the sense that the threshold extracted from state practice in the course of the previous chapter of this study was 'reasonable grounds for concern' and not 'reasonable *scientific* grounds for concern'. And this is very fortunate, since the fundamental and, to be frank, rather hopeless discussion of what in fact is 'scientific' and what is not is thus kept at arm's length. On the other hand, if and when relevant results of scientific research *are* obtainable these will naturally be assigned priority as a basis for deciding whether precautionary action is called for. The European Commission's guidelines on how to apply the precautionary principle are illustrative in this respect:

> An assessment of risk should be considered where feasible when deciding whether or not to invoke the precautionary principle. This requires reliable scientific data and logical reasoning [..]. However, it is not possible in all cases to complete a comprehensive assessment of risk, but all effort should be made to evaluate the available scientific information.[128]

Speaking of risk, it is probably befitting in order to be complete and avoid confusion, to stress that the application of the precautionary principle is certainly not limited to calculable, or quantifiable risks, whereby gravity and likelihood of harm are both sufficiently 'known' for the risk concerned to be expressed in statistical numbers.[129] It is indisputable that the precautionary principle was designed to apply in situations of other classes of uncertainty as well.[130] Indeed, if the precautionary principle would not allow for anything less certain than calculable risk for it to sanction measures, then its added value in comparison with the principle of prevention – which, as described elsewhere, already mandated the prevention and countering of quantifiable risks – would

---

Dutch Council for Nature Management, as cited in Heukers, 1997, p. 32. Article 200(1) of the French *Code Rural* of 1995 and Chapter III, Article 9(a) of Cameroon's 1996 *Law No. 96/12 Relating to Environmental Management*, to take two more instrument from the domestic sphere, expressly do not limit the evidence that is to inform the application of the precautionary principle to scientific information either, by requiring that account be taken of "current scientific *and technical* knowledge" (emphasis added). Neither does the 1995 *Land-Based Activities Action Programme*, which states in paragraph 24 that precautionary measures should be "based on existing knowledge, impact assessments, resources and capacities at national level, drawing on pertinent information and analyses at the subregional, regional and global levels."

[127] See also Testart, 2000; Cooney, 2000.

[128] *Communication COM(2000)1*, p. 14.

[129] See paragraph 4.1. and Figure 4 above.

[130] Again, see *supra* paragraph 4.1.

be negligible.[131] Consequently, the threshold of 'reasonable grounds for concern' cannot be interpreted as conditioned by a criterion of calculability. It does not correspond to a particular probability or risk percentage.

As much as with the evaluation of the gravity of anticipated harm, at times it will just be plain obvious that there are 'reasonable grounds for concern'. However, if 'scientific' nor 'quantifiable' are rigid benchmarks in the determination of whether the threshold of reasonable grounds for concern is crossed, this makes one wonder how to act in individual instances where the best information available is despairingly puny? In the absence of these or other criteria the issue appears rather clear-cut. When it is clear that the indications involved comply with the minimum requirement of amounting to something more than a mere hypothesis, then by implication it really seems up to the government(s) in question to establish their further diagnosis of those indications as either 'reasonable grounds for concern' or not. In consequence, here perhaps more so than with the gravity assessment, a decisive role will be reserved for the circumstances of each case[132] and the discretion of the state(s) concerned.[133]

5.4. *How? – Effectiveness and Proportionality*

Retracing the steps that have been taken in the present study up to the current stage and adding them up yields the conclusion that under general international law precautionary action is appropriate when there are reasonable grounds for concern that significant, serious and/or irreversible adverse environmental effects may be caused. In the previous paragraph clues have been uncovered as to how to establish when this situation presents itself – that is, how to determine when the various thresholds involved are transgressed. Knowing at some point in time *that* precautionary action may or must be taken is, of course, not the end of the story. How to determine *what* precautionary action to take is, after all, still an open question. This question will be probed in the current paragraph and in Part Three of this study.

Effective Action

How to go about precautionary action? Effectiveness is likely to be the most fundamental prerequisite for any measure to be able to constitute a correct implementation of the precautionary principle. It is a *sine qua non*. Not heeding this requirement would render the principle meaningless and rob it of its very

[131] Trouwborst, 2002, pp. 37-38.

[132] Under Article 13 of the Czech and Slovak *Federal Act on the Environment*, Law No. 17/1992 of 5 December 1991, precautionary action is appropriate if, "considering all circumstances," it can be assumed that irreversible or serious damage could threaten the environment.

[133] See also Dzidzornu, 1998, p. 98; Matthee, 2001, p. 184; Nollkaemper, 1996, p. 82.

essence. Precautionary action must be effective action.[134] This is so logical that stating it equals accepting a certain risk of being pleonastic. On account of its cardinal importance the necessity of effectiveness may not go unnoticed in a study such as the present.

Anyhow, while on most occasions it is present only tacitly by way of a necessary implication, not infrequently the condition of effectiveness in the implementation of the precautionary principle is stated expressly. In its *Southern Bluefin Tuna* Order, the ITLOS directed parties to "act with prudence and caution to ensure that *effective* conservation measures are taken to prevent serious harm to the stock of southern bluefin tuna."[135] A comparable requirement can be found in the 2002 *Antigua Convention.*[136] Other examples occur at the domestic level, as a result of the translation of the precautionary principle into national law. For instance, according to the Supreme Court of Pakistan in its 1994 *Shehla Zia v WAPDA* judgment, the precautionary principle requires that "effective measures" should be taken to control environmental threats.[137] Under the 1997 *Massachusetts Precautionary Principle Act*, competent authorities "shall take all necessary steps to ensure the *effective* implementation of the precautionary principle to environmental protection."[138] The pertinent laws of Cameroon[139] and France[140] also explicitly call for "effective" precautionary measures.

A measure is effective if it is likely to produce the outcome desired.[141] The stated objective of the precautionary principle, to use the straightforward formulation from the *Rio Declaration*, is "to protect the environment".[142] Protection of the environment, in turn, is a vital condition for the achievement of sustainable development.[143] What are effective measures will depend on the specific circumstances of each instance, among other things on the kind of harm that is to be prevented or abated. The precautionary principle, to borrow the words of the Slovenian *Environmental Protection Act*, mandates "such actions as may be necessary."[144] Where there are, for example, reasonable grounds for

---

134 Epiney & Scheyli, 1998, p. 123.

135 Order of 27 August 1999, paragraph 77; italics added.

136 Article 5(6)(a): "effective measures to prevent environmental degradation".

137 *Shehla Zia v WAPDA*, PLD, 1994 Supreme Court 693.

138 Emphasis added.

139 *Law No. 96/12 Relating to Environmental Management* of 5 August 1996, Chapter III, Article 9(a).

140 1995 *Code Rural*, Article 200(1).

141 Lefeber, 1996, p. 61. At p. 18 of the European Commission's *Communication COM(2000)1* it is put as follows: "The measures envisaged must make it possible to achieve the appropriate level of protection."

142 Principle 15. See also *supra* paragraph 3.1 and *infra* Chapter 6.

143 See *supra* paragraph 2.3.

144 1993 *Act No. 801-01/90-2/107*, Article 8(4), as cited in Marr, 2003, p. 95.

concern that significant irreversible harm may be caused, then a course of precautionary action must be chosen that is likely to effectively prevent this significant irreversible harm.[145] In case of doubt as to whether particular measures are actually suitable for this purpose, it is in conformity with the precautionary principle to err on the side of caution. *In dubio pro natura.*

What it takes for the principle to be effectively implemented is, to quote from the argumentation of Australia and New Zealand in the *Southern Bluefin Tuna* cases, "caution and vigilance in decision-making",[146] that is, a stance on the part of governments that is not only careful but active as well.[147] As early as the year 1986 the government of the Federal Republic of Germany set out its belief that the *Vorsorgeprinzip* required the taking of "active measures".[148] Additional guidance in this respect can be drawn from the classical formulation of the precautionary principle in the 1990 *Bergen Declaration*, often repeated afterwards, stipulating that precautionary measures "must anticipate, prevent and attack the causes of environmental degradation."[149] The criterion of effectiveness will be treated in further detail below.[150]

Proportional Action

In public international law, proportionality is another concept of considerable importance besides effectiveness.[151] To bring this home one need only think of the rules governing the use of armed force in interstate relations, of international trade law, or of the rules on the legitimate use of countermeasures.[152] In a way proportionality can be seen as a counterweight to the criterion of effectiveness. Effectiveness ensures that the relevant purpose is served; proportionality ensures that this is *all* that happens and no more than that, by adjusting the means to the objective. It is not always easy to strike the right balance between the two, however. As for precautionary behaviour, it has been submitted that the balance between opportunity and risk is always a

---

145 In the words of Kaiser, 1997(b), p. 328, precautionary action must be "designed to effectively reduce the likelihood of the perceived environmental harm."

146 See the *Request for Provisional Measures* filed on 30 July 1999.

147 Epiney & Scheyli, 1998, p. 123.

148 See Gullett, 1997, p. 59.

149 Paragraph 7 of the *Bergen Declaration*. See also, *inter alia*, preambular paragraph 8 of the *Biodiversity Convention*; Principle 7 of the 1990 *Ministerial Declaration of the Second World Climate Conference*; paragraph 11 of the 1996 *Vellore Citizens* judgment by the Supreme Court of India; and the different version in Article 3(3) of the *ASEAN Agreement on Transboundary Haze Pollution* ("anticipate, prevent and monitor").

150 See *infra* Chapter 7.3.

151 Generally, see Cannizzaro, 2000, *passim*.

152 For the latter, see paragraphs 85 through 87 of the *Gabcikovo-Nagymaros* judgment.

precarious one.[153] There have always been those who warned against the disadvantages of an overabundance of prudence. Napoleon was one of them:

> The torment of precautions often exceeds the dangers to be avoided. It is sometimes better to abandon one's self to destiny.[154]

And Russian writer Aleksandr Solzhenytzin once sighed: "If one is forever cautious, can one remain a human being?"

From the start, proportionality has been a crucial feature in the application of the precautionary principle, in the sense that precautionary responses to environmental threats ought to correspond to the perceived dimensions of the risks involved. This notion is firmly anchored in pertinent state practice, in the first place through the widely disseminated use of thresholds of harm that was discussed in Chapter 3 above.[155] Threats of effects that are not adverse or of trivial harm do not call for precaution; threats of significant harm reserve the right of states to take action; and threats of serious or irreversible harm oblige states to do so – given the presence of reasonable grounds for concern, that is. This three-stage plan, which must be assumed to represent the current state of customary international law on the precautionary principle, is an expression *pur sang* of the idea of proportionality: the graver the anticipated harm, the more substantial the accompanying legal consequence.[156]

By no means does this exhaust the relevance of proportionality, however. It is also of the essence on the smaller scales *within* the stages of the scheme. The *more* significant or the *more* serious the expected environmental impact, the more rigorous preventive or abatement measures may, respectively must be. As put by the International Chamber of Commerce, precautionary action must be "proportionally responsive" to the environmental concerns in question.[157] It is not difficult to see the logic inherent in such an approach whereby, to paraphrase the 1986 propositions of the WCED legal experts group, requirements of alertness and precaution are connected to the gravity of possible damage.[158] Phrased in terms of the diagram of *supra* Figure 2: the higher the feared harm on the scale of gravity, the more radical the precautionary action to counter it, and the other way around – regardless of whether such action is taken pursuant to a right or to an obligation.

---

[153] Klinke & Renn, 1999, p. 9.

[154] Napoleon Bonaparte (1769-1821).

[155] Also Backes *et al.*, 1997, pp. 71-72; Backes, 1997, p. 4.

[156] As Rogers, 2001, at p. 8 remarked, "if the harm is neither serious nor irreversible, then 'doing nothing' is clearly a proportionate response to uncertainty." In legal terms, this certainly appears to be true.

[157] International Chamber of Commerce Commission on Environment, *A Precautionary Approach: An ICC Business Perspective*, 1997, as quoted in Backes *et al.*, 2002, p. 79.

[158] Lammers *et al.*, 1986, p. 80.

Accordingly, in the words of the commentary on the 1986 WCED *Legal Principles for Environmental Protection and Sustainable Development*, the nature and extent of the measures to be taken depends on the nature and extent of the harm which must be prevented or abated.[159] As far as the axis of gravity is concerned, it is thus often not sufficient to ask only *whether* threatened environmental harm is expected to be significant, or serious. That question should, whenever matched by an affirmative answer, be followed by the question as to *how* significant or serious that harm may turn out to be.

Of course, the frameworks of the concept of risk and the precautionary principle alike are not composed of a single axis. Gravity of harm is not the only variable in the formula of risk, nor is it the sole determinant of legal consequences under the precautionary principle. To complete the picture an axis of probability needs to be added to the axis of gravity. Similar considerations apply here. The threshold of reasonable grounds for concern intersects the axis of likelihood. Below it the precautionary principle does not apply, above the threshold it does – supposing for the moment that none of the thresholds of gravity prevent this. Again, this state of affairs by itself reflects the idea of proportionality but does not exhaust its relevance. The axis of likelihood, like the axis of gravity, represents a sliding scale. The more evidence there is relating to the suspected causality involved, i.e. the more likely the occurrence of the anticipated harm is – and thus the higher on the scale of likelihood it is found – the more rigorous the corresponding precautionary measures ought to be, and *vice versa*.[160]

What holds true for the scales of gravity and likelihood separately naturally holds true for the combination of the two: the aggregate risk. Being communicating vessels, the two sliding scales *together* determine the final proportions of the environmental risk in any given case, and therewith the final precautionary response required.[161] Thus, as will be remembered from the treatment of the risk concept earlier on, in cases of comparable likelihood of occurrence graver anticipated harm always results in greater risk. And the greater the risk, the more rigorous the precautionary action that is to match it.[162]

In keeping with its great logical appeal the validity of the proportionality criterion in respect of the precautionary principle has often been

---

[159] *Ibid.*, see Principles 10 and 15-17.

[160] Also Backes *et al.*, 2001, p. 1761.

[161] *Ibid.*

[162] As the commentary to Article 7 of the 1995 *IUCN Draft Covenant* puts it: "action will vary in accordance with the severity of the risk."

affirmed, both implicitly and explicitly,[163] and only rarely contested. Its application has been standard practice, e.g., in the birthplace of precaution as we know it, namely Germany: "the greater the threat, the greater the need for *Vorsorge*."[164] Belgium,[165] France,[166] the UK,[167] Cameroon[168] and New Zealand[169] are some of the countries providing further examples. The concept of proportionality can be aptly illustrated by reference to the following provision of the *World Charter for Nature*, in which both the gravity and the probability of harm are intimately linked to the strictness of measures:

> Activities which might have an impact on nature shall be controlled, and the best available technologies that minimize significant risks to nature or other adverse effects shall be used, in particular:
> (a) Activities which are likely to cause irreversible damage to nature shall be avoided;
> (b) Activities which are likely to pose a significant risk to nature shall be preceded by an exhaustive examination; their proponents shall demonstrate that expected benefits outweigh potential damage to nature, and where potential adverse effects are not fully understood, the activities should not proceed;
> (c) Activities which may disturb nature shall be preceded by assessment of their consequences, and environmental impact studies of development projects shall be conducted sufficiently in advance, and if they are to be undertaken, such activities shall be planned and carried out so as to minimize potential adverse effects; [..].[170]

In its jurisprudence the ECJ has also frequently stressed the importance of proportionality in the implementation of the precautionary principle, which is

---

[163] See, e.g., Van Dyke, 1996, p. 380; Gullett, 1997, p. 59; Freestone, 1999, p. 140; Lambers, 2000, p. 177; Rogers, 2001, pp. 4-5; Mohamed-Katerere, 2001, p. 9; Backes *et al.*, 2001, pp. 1760-1761; Birnie & Boyle, 2002, p. 120; Marr, 2003, pp. 35-37; Faure, 2003, p. 256.

[164] Boehmer-Christiansen, 1994, p. 36; also Marr, 2003, pp. 75 and 91.

[165] See the overview of Belgian and Flemish policy and law in Faure, 2003, and particularly p. 256.

[166] See Kourilsky, P.H. & Viney, G., *Rapport au Premier Ministre, le Principe de Précaution*, Paris 2000, as cited in Faure, *ibid.*, at p. 256.

[167] See Royal Commission on Environmental Pollution, *Twenty-first Report 'Setting Environmental Standards'*, London 1998, paragraph 4.44; UK Department of the Environment, *Consultation Paper on the UK Strategy for Sustainable Development*, July 1993, as cited in Haigh, 1994, p. 250; UK Government's *A Better Quality of Life: A Strategy for Sustainable Development for the United Kingdom*, May 1999, paragraph 4.2.

[168] 1996 *Law No. 96/12 Relating to Environmental Management*, Chapter III, Article 9(a).

[169] Both elements of proportionality are clearly present in the following pronouncement on the general precautionary principle by the New Zealand Environment Court: "Like all elements that contribute to the ultimate judgment, the weight to be given to the precautionary principle would depend on the circumstances. [..] The circumstances would include the extent of present scientific knowledge and the impact on otherwise permitted activities. However, we think that in an appropriate case they would also include the gravity of the effects if, despite present uncertainty, they do occur." *McIntyre v Christchurch City Council*, PA T 15/96, 5 March 1996, 1996 NZRMA (New Zealand Resource Management Act) 289, as quoted in Christensen, 2001, p. 6.

[170] Principle 11.

to ensure that of the available effective measures the least restrictive is chosen.[171] As the European Commission has commented: "In some cases a total ban may not be a proportional response to a potential risk. In other cases, it may be the sole possible response."[172] It appears open to little doubt that the latter would be the case in the relatively extreme situation where threatened harm is both probable, very serious and irreversible. All in all, that under customary international law the application of the principle ought to be informed by the doctrine of proportionality in the way set out in the current paragraph seems to make good sense.

The workings of this doctrine are set out graphically in simplified form in Figure 7, to illustrate what has just been said about aggregate risks and communicating vessels. To return to the three core elements of the precautionary principle, it is noteworthy that in the picture the element of action does not relate to any axis of its own in the way that the elements of harm and uncertainty relate, respectively, to the axes of gravity and probability. When combining the three basic features of the precautionary principle graphically, no third dimension appears. Graphically, no tripod appears. Instead, since the nature and extent of precautionary action depends on the degrees of harm and likelihood involved, the element of action is a function of the other two and can be depicted as such. Accordingly, in the diagram of Figure 7 it is represented by coordinates. The higher the combined value of the coordinates, that is, the further to the right and/or to the top of the diagram, the more rigorous the resultant precautionary action.

---

[171] For one example out of many, see paragraph 186 of Joined Cases T-74/00, T-76/00, T-83/00 to T-85/00, T-132/00, T-137/00 and T-141/00, Judgment of the EU Court of First Instance of 26 November 2002. See also Vos, 2003, pp. 152-153.

[172] *Communication COM(2000)1*, p. 18.

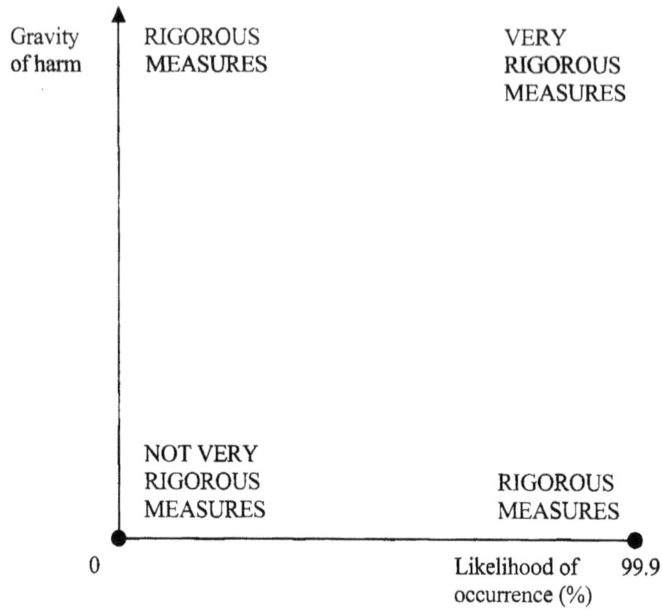

Figure 7. Proportionality (I). Each imaginary point in this diagram represents an aggregate risk, a combination of likelihood and gravity of environmental harm. The further on the scale of gravity and/or on the scale of likelihood, the greater the risk and the more rigorous the precautionary measures that may or must be taken. The various legally significant thresholds of gravity and proof have been left out of the picture for simplicity's sake.

In the next figure the three major threshold lines have been included in the same diagram to demonstrate a more complete picture of precautionary action under international law. (See Figure 8.) After all, account needs to be taken of the fact that some coordinates do not represent precautionary measures for the bare reason that the corresponding level of gravity and/or probability finds itself on the wrong side of one of the thresholds that have been found to condition the application of the precautionary principle. It will be apparent that what has been stated previously on the question as to how to determine when the various pertinent threshold lines are crossed, applies just as much to the question as to how to determine *how* significant, *how* serious and *how* probable anticipated environmental harm is to be deemed – the latter question being hardly less important for the purpose of making the right choice of precautionary measures than the former.[173]

[173] See *supra* paragraph 5.2.

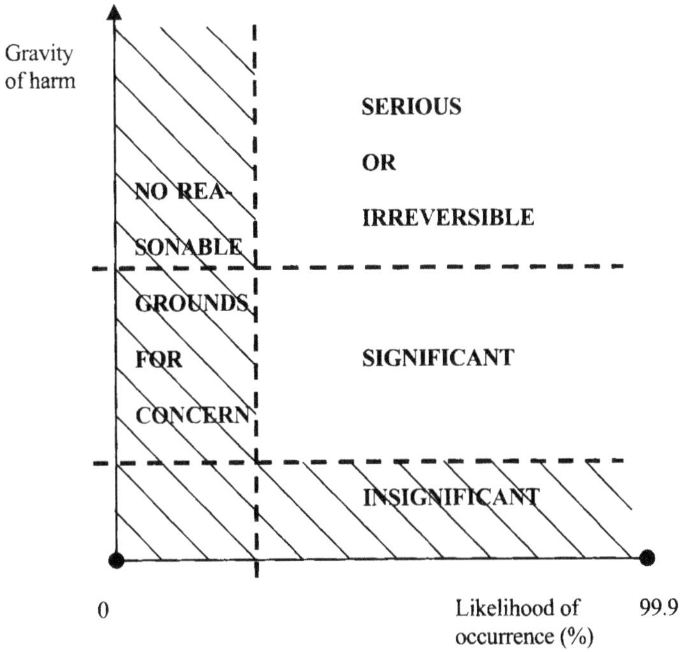

Figure 8. Proportionality (II). The same diagram as in Figure 7, but incorporating the legally relevant threshold lines of 'reasonable grounds for concern', 'significant harm' and 'serious or irreversible harm'. These are depicted by dotted lines. Coordinates located within the hatched parts of the diagram represent situations in which precautionary action is not called for.

A practical example is perhaps appropriate here to make it easier to catch on to the essence of all these abstract graphics. In 1990 the American space agency NASA was authorized by the US Congress to perform two costly studies concerning threats posed by near Earth objects (NEOs). The justification given by the Congress for the authorization was that whilst "the chances of the Earth being struck by a large asteroid are extremely small [..] the consequences of such a collision are extremely large [..so] it is only prudent to assess the nature of the threat and prepare to deal with it."[174] A step by step analysis of this case in terms of the three ingredients of the precautionary principle looks as follows. (1) The gravity of anticipated harm is evidently huge. If the scenario sketched in the above citation were to materialize the damage would be extremely serious and largely irreversible,

---

[174] Rubin, 2000, pp. 112-113, citing from Morrison, D. (ed.), *The Spaceguard Survey: Report of the NASA International Near-Earth-Object Detection Workshop*, Pasadena 1992, p. 2.

meaning the end for millions of species. (2) The likelihood of this scenario becoming reality, however small, still appears to pass the test of 'reasonable grounds for concern' by being more than purely hypothetical. "We know it will happen; we just don't know when."[175] Its probability thus exceeds the level of mere theoretical possibility and as such obviously incomparable to the goat's milk apocalypse described earlier on in this study. (3) These two values combined constitute, to say the least, a considerable risk, considerable enough to entail a duty of states to take effective and proportionate precautionary measures. Such measures have been taken, *inter alia*, in the form of the NASA studies mentioned above. The precautionary rationale of these measures has been strikingly expressed in a 1995 position paper by the American Institute of Aeronautics and Astronautics:

> If some day an asteroid does strike the Earth killing not only the human race but millions of other species as well, and we could have prevented it but did not because of indecision, unbalanced priorities, imprecise risk definition, and incomplete planning, then it will be the greatest abdication in all of human history not to use our gift of rational intellect and conscience to shepherd our own survival, and that of all life on Earth.[176]

5.5. *Conclusions*

This chapter on precautionary action, the third essential ingredient of the precautionary principle, has reflected on the *where*, *when* and *how* of such action. In this final paragraph the main findings concerning these three queries will be succinctly reproduced.

Where? In international law the reach of the precautionary principle is a wide one. Apart from its capacity of general principle of international environmental law, as a part of numerous treaties and general customary international law the precautionary principle has legal implications for the great majority of states. Its scope is all-encompassing in that it applies to the environment as a whole, in furtherance of the objective of sustainable development. This means that the principle's reach covers (a) the environment in all geographic areas, both within and beyond the limits of national jurisdiction; (b) all environmental issue areas, from wastes to wetlands and from acid rain to Antarctic krill; and (c) all human endeavors with environmental implications, all plans, activities, products and technologies, whether existing or new. In all these respects the precautionary principle, as the *Rio Declaration* puts it, is to be "widely applied by states".

---

[175] Rubin, *ibid.*, p. 111.

[176] Cited in Rubin, *ibid.*, at p. 110.

Precautionary action is appropriate *wherever* there are sufficiently qualified threats of environmental harm.

When? This is the same as asking when there *is* such a sufficiently qualified threat, as defined by the thresholds of gravity and likelihood identified in previous chapters. Concretely, when are there *reasonable grounds for concern* that *significant*, *serious* and/or *irreversible* environmental *harm* may be caused? Various guidelines exist for determining whether each of these conditions applies. For instance, on a general level, an anticipated environmental impact constitutes harm when the environmental change provoked by it is adverse and not positive or neutral. Likewise, harm is significant when it is tangible, appreciable and measurable, as opposed to minor or trivial – a relatively low threshold to cross. Prominent indicators of gravity are the duration and geographic dispersion of anticipated effects (see Figure 6 above). Frequently assessments will be uncomplicated in the sense that it is plain obvious that the impact at hand is adverse, significant, serious or irreversible. When anticipated harm would constitute a breach of substantive norms of international environmental law then it is surely significant and suspected to be serious as well. When circumstances are not so manifest, valuable clues can many a time be encountered in the shape of formal statements of states in, for example, legal and policy instruments, indicating expressly or implicitly that a certain environmental impact is considered as adverse, significant, serious or irreversible. Sometimes there will even be checklists available specifying what is regarded significant or serious in a particular context. Irreversibility is an apparently unambiguous criterion in that, in principle, harm is either reversible or not. Besides factually irreversible harm, in the context of the precautionary principle the notion includes damage that is practically irreversible in that it is unlikely to be undone in the course of several human generations. Together all these guidelines compose the framework that defines the room ultimately available for discretionary judgments by the authorities involved. The dimensions of this room reserved for subjective determinations and the difficulty of gravity assessments will depend heavily on factual circumstances and will therefore vary from case to case. This is true as much for likelihood as it is for gravity. Assessments of whether there are reasonable grounds for concern are to be informed by the best information available. There is, however, no minimum requirement that this information be scientific or that the risk in question be quantifiable, although it *does* need to amount to more than a mere theoretical hypothesis.

How? Precautionary measures need to "anticipate, prevent and attack the causes of environmental degradation," as the *Bergen Declaration* specifies. They must be tailor-made to fit the particular threat of environmental harm at hand. To that end they ought to be *effective* on the one hand and *proportional* on the other. The requisite of effectiveness demands that a course of action is chosen that suits the purpose of protecting that part of the environment which is at risk by effectively preventing or abating the threat in question. The requisite of proportionality demands that a course of action is chosen that corresponds to the size of the risk involved. The graver and/or more likely the anticipated environmental harm – that is, the greater the risk – the more rigorous the response, and the other way around. (See Figures 7 and 8 above.) Finally, when in doubt about what measure(s) to pick, it is in keeping with the precautionary principle to err on the side of environmental protection.

So far as the laws of mathematics refer to reality, they are not certain.
And so far they are certain, they do not refer to reality.
– Albert Einstein (1879-1955)

6. ASSEMBLING THE TRIPOD: SYNTHESIS

This study has taken up the task of defining as clearly as possible the legal implications for states of the precautionary principle as a part of general, customary international law. It has attempted to answer the question whether it is possible to discern any concrete rights or duties in this respect and, if so, how distinctive these are. The time has come to formulate the answer, by putting the three legs of the precautionary tripod together. To avoid filling paper for the sake of it, this chapter will not reproduce every separate conclusion that was drawn in preceding chapters, let alone the backgrounds and contexts of these conclusions or the steps leading up to them. The purpose of this study is better served by focussing directly on their aggregate result and the bare answer to the above question.

The Right and the Duty of States to Take Precautionary Action Defined

This answer is that, subject to particular conditions, the precautionary principle gives rise to both a customary right and a customary duty of states to take precautionary action, which can respectively be defined as follows:

> THE *RIGHT* OF STATES TO TAKE PRECAUTIONARY ACTION
>
> Wherever, on the basis of the best information available, there are reasonable grounds for concern that significant harm to the environment may occur, effective and proportional action to prevent and/or abate this harm may be taken, including in situations of scientific uncertainty regarding the cause, extent and/or probability of the potential harm.
>
> THE *DUTY* OF STATES TO TAKE PRECAUTIONARY ACTION
>
> Wherever, on the basis of the best information available, there are reasonable grounds for concern that serious and/or irreversible harm to the environment may occur, effective and proportional action to prevent and/or abate this harm must be taken, including in situations of scientific uncertainty regarding the cause, extent and/or probability of the potential harm.

These definitions clearly reflect that the precautionary principle applies to all types of environmental harm anywhere, but not to all levels; and that likewise the principle applies to all types of uncertainty, but not to all levels. The difference between the right and the duty concerns the gravity of the anticipated harm. There is an obligation to take precautionary action only when the anticipated harm is serious and/or irreversible.

The two definitions also reflect that there is quite a list of conditions that need to be met before a right or duty to take precautionary action arises in any given situation. Accordingly, when contemplating any particular threat of environmental impact a series of queries must be addressed. Are there reasonable grounds for concern that the impact may come about? Are the effects in question adverse, that is, would they constitute harm? If so, is this harm significant as opposed to minor, trivial, i.e., insignificant? If so, is it also serious and/or irreversible? And if significant or serious, how significant or serious is it? These several steps are rendered schematically in the overview of Figure 9 below, which builds on *supra* Figure 3.

As is characteristic of *general* principles with a wide scope of application, various elements of the precautionary principle as defined above are open to interpretation, as discussed previously.[1] The core of the principle is evidently agreed upon, however, as fleshed out in the course of this study. Already in 1997 it was noted by one commentator that "[t]he argument that the principle is incapable of being given clear definition is waning."[2] These chapters have been an attempt to rise above the tangled jungle of formulations, nuances en (seeming) contradictions concerning the definition of the precautionary principle as it stands under customary international law, so as to gain a view of the whole wood instead. It is hoped that the reader will be of the opinion that, seen from the altitude that has been reached, things turn out to be rather more straightforward than they may have appeared at first glance.

---

[1] See, *inter alia*, *supra* paragraph 5.3; also Cameron & Abouchar, 1996, p. 46.
[2] Gullett, 1997.

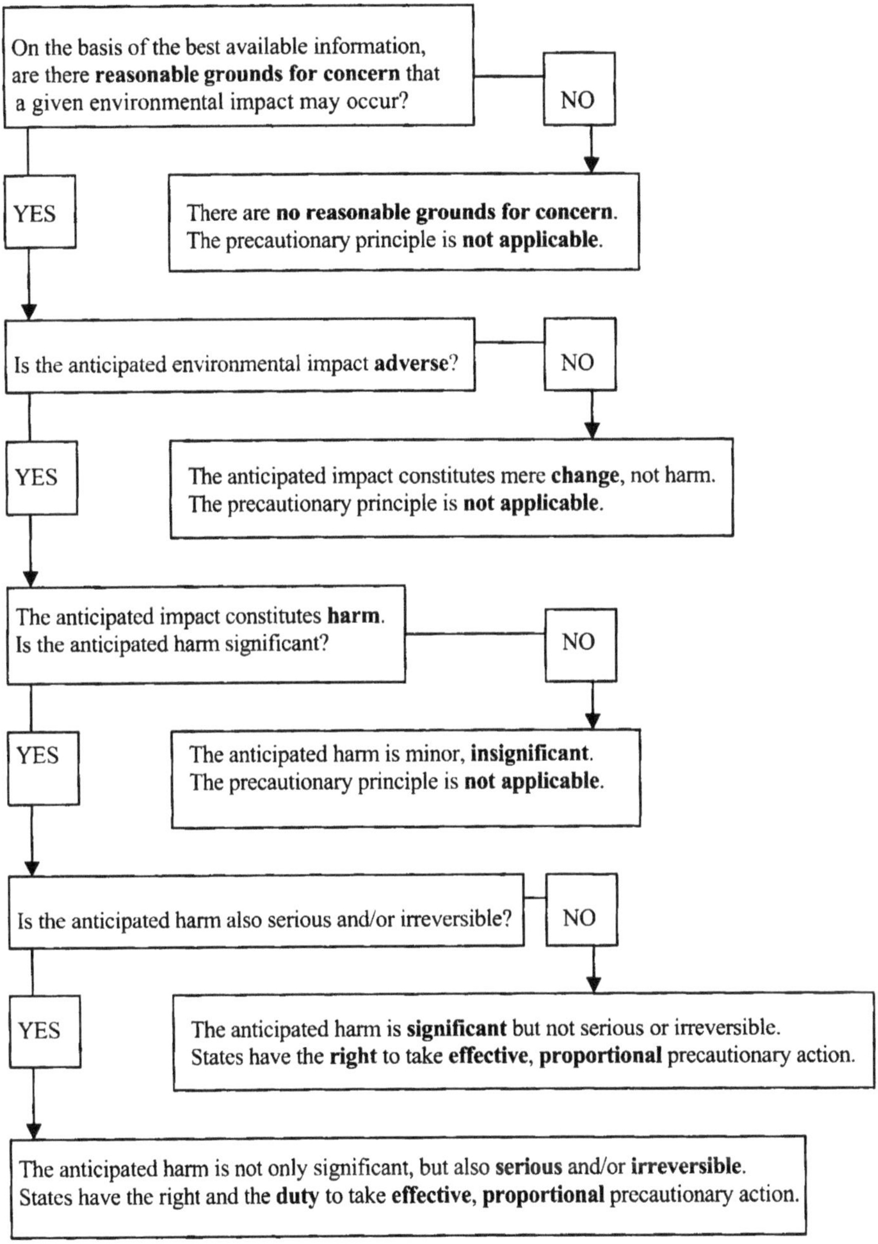

Figure 9. Schematic overview of legal effects related to anticipated environmental impacts. The various qualifications of impacts and the accompanying legal effects are printed boldly.

PART THREE

IMPLEMENTATION

It is impossible to begin to learn that which one thinks one already knows.
- Epictetus (± 55-135)

7. PRECAUTIONARY MEASURES

7.1. What Precautionary Measure(s)?

Although the *where*, *when* and *how* of precautionary action have been addressed in former chapters,[1] much remains to be said on the topic of the concrete measures that may or must be taken by states in observance of the precautionary principle. That precautionary action must be effective and proportional does not appear to be the final word. For instance, what types of precautionary measures are there to choose from? Should measures be contemplated at the international, the national, or both levels? What to do when precautionary action intended to prevent one environmental hazard itself entails another environmental risk? And once taken, how long should precautionary measures be left in force? These are among the questions still waiting to be answered. In search of the answers to them, the following paragraph of the current chapter will concentrate on examples of measures that have been agreed upon and taken by states in order to implement the precautionary principle, whereafter in the third paragraph an attempt will be made to discern whether there are any features those measures have in common. Supplementing the more general analysis that will take place in this chapter, Chapters 8 and 9 will successively be devoted to the specific issues of the burden of proof and the role of socio-economic considerations in the implementation of the precautionary principle.

7.2. Typical Precautionary Measures in Practice

There are a number of measures that have been typically associated with the precautionary principle. Some of the most prominent will be lined up here and considered in light of the practice of states.

Precautionary Bans

"Effective and proportional action to prevent and/or abate harm" may, to begin with, take the form of a ban, which can be total or partial, and

---

[1] See especially *supra* Chapter 5.

permanent or temporary.[2] Evidently, where an activity, technology or substance poses an unacceptable environmental risk, the most cautious approach is simply to abstain from performing or allowing them.[3] Most typically such abstention is applied provisionally, so that it can be reassessed as soon as the danger involved diminishes or as soon as more reliable information concerning the threat in question becomes available. Arguably, such provisional abstention, also known as the moratorium, constitutes the most pre-eminent *precautionary* measure.

Examples of precautionary bans abound in the practice of states. Notable ones are the moratorium on commercial whaling adopted by the International Whaling Commission (IWC) in 1982 and the moratorium on pelagic driftnet fishing agreed by the UN General Assembly in 1989.[4] Principle 11 of the *World Charter for Nature*, adopted by the same Assembly in 1982, contains the avoidance of potentially harmful activities as a prominent option as well.[5] Correspondingly, in the 1997 *Trilateral Wadden Sea Plan* the precautionary principle is understood as requiring "action to *avoid activities* which are assumed to have significant damaging impact on the environment."[6] Likewise, under *CITES* the principle has often been given effect by practically banning international trade in a potentially endangered species by placing it on Appendix I of the Convention.[7] Other instances include the prohibition under the 1980 *Convention on the Conservation of Antarctic Marine Living Resources* (*CCAMLR*) of the use for bait boxes of plastic packaging bands in which marine mammals might become entangled;[8] the near-complete phase-outs of supposedly hazardous chemicals as envisaged for, among other areas, the North Sea[9] and the Great Lakes;[10] the precautionary

---

[2] On the duration of precautionary measures, see *infra* paragraph 7.3.

[3] It is "the strongest precautionary action." Tickner *et al.*, 2000, p. 5. See also Dzidzornu, 1998, p. 100; Rogers, 2001, p. 1.

[4] Both will be discussed in more detail in *infra* paragraph 8.2.

[5] "(a) Activities which are likely to cause irreversible damage to nature shall be avoided; (b) [for a]ctivities which are likely to pose a significant risk to nature [..] their proponents shall demonstrate that expected benefits outweigh potential damage to nature, and where potential effects are not fully understood, the activities should not proceed."

[6] Paragraph 8, emphasis added. The same definition was laid down in paragraph 3(ii) of the 1991 *Ministerial Declaration of the Sixth Trilateral Governmental Conference on the Protection of the Wadden Sea*.

[7] See Cooney, 2001, p. 11.

[8] See Parkes, 2000, p. 88.

[9] As paragraph 17 of the 1995 *Fourth North Sea Declaration* states, the "precautionary principle [..] implies the prevention of the pollution of the North Sea by continuously reducing discharges, emissions and losses of hazardous substances, thereby moving toward the target of their cessation within one generation (25 years) with the ultimate aim of concentrations in the environment near background values for naturally occurring substances and close to zero concentrations for man-made synthetic substances."

restrictions imposed on emissions of chlorofluorocarbons under the *Montreal Protocol* in order to prevent further depletion of the ozone layer "with the ultimate objective of their elimination;"[11] the strict moratoriums on the dumping of industrial and radioactive wastes and incineration at sea as codified in the 1996 *LDC Protocol*;[12] and the European Union's *de facto* precautionary moratorium on the marketing of genetically modified food products that was instated in 1998, repeatedly adapted since, and only lifted when stringent food labelling rules which came into force in 2004 were deemed to warrant this.[13] Also in 2004 the UN General Assembly called upon states to take urgent action "including the application of the precautionary approach" and consider the "interim prohibition of destructive fishing practices, including bottom trawling," which latter is thought to have severe adverse impacts on vulnerable marine ecosystems such as seamounts and cold water corals located beyond national jurisdiction, "until such time as appropriate conservation and management measures have been adopted."[14] Shortly before this resolution was adopted, member-states of the North East Atlantic Fisheries Commission (NEAFC) decided, as an "interim measure", to close four seamounts and part of the Reykjanes Ridge to bottom trawling and static gear fishing for a period of two years.[15] At the domestic level as well myriad cases exist where application of the precautionary principle has led to the enactment of bans, e.g., the precautionary moratorium on drilling for natural gas in the Wadden Sea that was put in place by the Dutch government in 1999 and was discontinued under strict conditions recently.[16] Precautionary bans come in many guises, from protected areas to import restrictions and from fishing moratoriums to refusals to issue marketing permits for substances.

Clearly, under the precautionary principle banning or abstaining from whatever it is that causes a particular threat is a valid option. This is

---

[10] A strategy proposed by the Great Lakes International Joint Commission calls for the sunsetting of all persistent toxic substances in the Great Lakes ecosystem, reasoning that "all persistent toxic substances are dangerous to the environment [..] and can no longer be tolerated in the ecosystem, whether or not unassailable scientific proof of acute or chronic damage is universally accepted." 1992 *Sixth Biennial Report on Great Lakes Water Quality*; see Tickner *et al.*, 1998/1999, p. 6.

[11] Sixth preambular paragraph of the 1985 *Montreal Protocol*, as amended in London in 1990.

[12] See Trouwborst, 2002, p. 78.

[13] See *Regulation 1829/2003 on GM Food and Feed.*

[14] *Resolution 59/25* of 17 November 2004, paragraph 66; see also Molenaar, 2005, pp. 535-540.

[15] *Recommendation IV for the Protection of Vulnerable Deep-Water Habitats*, adopted with a reservation by the Russian Federation at the 23rd Annual Meeting of NEAFC in 2004. The moratorium is imposed from 1 January 2005 until 31 January 2007. See also Molenaar, *ibid.*

[16] Trouwborst, 2002, pp. 210-211.

affirmed by the commentary to the 1995 *IUCN Draft Covenant*,[17] the European Commission's *Communication on the Precautionary Principle*,[18] the 2002 *ILA Declaration on Sustainable Development*,[19] as well as by plenty publicists.[20] That the instrument of the ban represents a realistic – and perhaps even the most obvious[21] – option does not signify it is the only one, however. As will be detailed below, application of the precautionary principle does not automatically result in refraining from the potentially hazardous course of action involved. After all, although it is open to little doubt that for most environmental risks outlawing the potentially hazardous activity, technology or product in question would be the most *effective* precautionary strategy, it is not always at the same time the most *proportional* strategy. The *Straddling Stocks Agreement* is a case in point. During the deliberations leading up to its adoption, the European Union submitted that precautionary management "does not necessarily require moratoria or any other unnecessarily restrictive measures,"[22] a position that was echoed by the delegation of the United States[23] and is reflected in the terms of the *Straddling Stocks Agreement* as finally drafted. Under the Agreement, a moratorium on fishing is not the automatic or only outcome when a stock is under threat. Instead, what precautionary action to prevent depletion of fish stocks is appropriate depends on the circumstances and is to be determined on a case-by-case basis.[24] This is illustrative of the precautionary principle generally. As set out above, the criterion of proportionality occasions that out of the possible courses of precautionary action that are believed will be effective, the least restrictive be chosen. The less severe and/or the less probable the anticipated environmental harm, the less rigorous the precautionary response to counter it.[25] Whether avoidance is appropriate will thus depend on the dimensions of the aggregate environmental risk. To take an extreme example, when anticipated harm is probable, very serious and irreversible all at once – for instance, when an ancient woodland, unique wetland or other critical natural

---

[17] The commentary to Article 7 confirms that the precautionary principle "may require temporary or permanent restrictions."

[18] *Communication COM(2000)1*, p. 4.

[19] According to paragraphs 4.1 the precautionary principle commits states to "avoid" potentially harmful human activity. Paragraph 4.2 affirms that applying the principle may in certain instances entail "not proceeding with an envisaged activity."

[20] E.g., Tinker, 1995, p. 794; Borgers, 1999, p. 436; Saunders, 2000; Tickner *et al.*, 2000, p. 5; Dzidzornu, 1998, p. 100; Rogers, 2001, p. 1; Marr, 2003, pp. 15-16.

[21] Rogers, *ibid.*, refers to the ban as "the most obvious regulatory approach to uncertainty."

[22] Paragraph I.6 of the "Suggested Guidelines" put forth by the European Union during negotiations; see Orrega Vicuña, 1999, p. 160.

[23] United States "Position Statement", p. 4. See Orrega Vicuña, *ibid.*

[24] Birnie & Boyle, 2002, p. 676.

[25] See *supra* paragraph 5.4.

habitat is likely to be impaired[26] – imposing a ban would arguably be the only way to comply with the precautionary principle.[27] In the words of the European Commission, in certain cases this is "the sole possible response to a given risk."[28] In other cases avoidance may not be a proportional, and therefore not an appropriate precautionary measure.[29] The axiom *"When in doubt, don't!"* that has been coined by some as a rule of thumb to capture the meaning of the precautionary principle,[30] is thus evidently an oversimplification and, as far as general international law is concerned, beside the truth in that it suggests that the principle compulsorily calls for abstention from any potentially injurious activities.[31]

Safety Margins

Another typical precautionary measure is the employment of safety margins, ecological buffers, as practical manifestations of the general idea enshrined in the precautionary principle that errors in decision-making ought to be in favour of the environment – the greater the uncertainty, the wider the margin of error.[32] Handl counts the setting of reasonable margins of safety among the "basic ingredients" of precautionary environmental action.[33] As Wildavsky phrased the rationale of using healthy buffers: "Why be half safe? When in doubt, add margins of safety."[34] The use of safety margins in the implementation of the precautionary principle is probably most pre-eminent with regard to the exploitation of living natural resources. The stringent criteria governing the downlisting of species under *CITES* form one instance of an attempt to provide for a sufficiently wide natural cushion.[35] Abundant examples of such safeguarding of "environmental room for manoeuvre"[36]

---

[26] Jordan & O'Riordan, 1999, p. 24.

[27] See *supra* paragraph 5.4; Tinker, 1995, p. 794; Borgers, 1999, p. 436.

[28] *Communication COM(2000)1*, p. 4.

[29] This is attested to by paragraph 4.2 of the *ILA Declaration on Sustainable Development*; the commentary to Article 7 of the 1995 *IUCN Draft Covenant*; Cooney, 2000; Mohamed-Katerere, 2001, p. 9; and by Rogers, 2001, pp. 1 and 9. As Raffensperger *et al.*, 1999, explain: "application of the principle may result in saying 'yes' as well as 'no'. 'No' does not always mean a prohibition, but can mean any of an array of measures to prevent harm."

[30] E.g., Bodansky, 1996.

[31] Similarly critical of such an understanding are Godard, 2000; Pieterman & Hanekamp, 2002, p. vi.

[32] O'Riordan & Cameron, 1994, pp. 17-18; Brunnée, 1996, pp. 73-74; Victor, 1997, p. 243; Jordan & O'Riordan, 1999, p. 26; Cooney, 2000; Birnie & Boyle, 2002, p. 117; Marr, 2003, p. 15.

[33] Handl, 1991, p. 79.

[34] Wildavsky, 2000, p. 33.

[35] See 1994 *Resolution Conf. 9.24 on Criteria for Amendment of Appendices I and II*; Jordan & O'Riordan, 1999, p. 26.

[36] O'Riordan & Cameron, 1994, p. 17.

can furthermore be found in the area of fisheries management. One of the measures forming part of the regime of *Conservation Measure 65/XII on Exploratory Fisheries*, adopted under the *CCAMLR* in 1993, is the application of ample safety buffers in the setting of catch levels and fishing effort limitations where uncertainty is great.[37] The system of stock-specific precautionary reference points not to be exceeded as elaborated in the *Straddling Stocks Agreement*[38] and the *FAO Code of Conduct for Responsible Fisheries*[39] builds on the same premises, whereas the US *Gilchrest-Farr Fisheries Recovery Act* defines the precautionary approach as "exercising additional caution in favor of conservation in any case in which information is absent, uncertain, unreliable, or inadequate."[40] A particularly detailed elaboration of safety margins and buffer zones forms the core of the *Precautionary Approach Framework* adopted by the NAFO Fisheries Commission in 2004.[41] As the Commission acknowledges: "The more uncertain the stock assessment, the greater the buffer zone should be."[42] The Framework distinguishes between five different states in which fish stocks may find themselves – the safe zone, the overfishing zone, the cautionary zone, the danger zone and the collapse zone – and sets out the appropriate precautionary management action for each.[43]

Precautionary Measures in the Context of Pollution

In the context of the prevention and abatement of environmental contamination the precautionary principle has been associated with the control of pollution at the source.[44] In 1984 the *First North Sea Declaration* set out the intention of the signatories to take precautionary measures for air quality control by the reduction of emissions at source,[45] whereas five years later PARCOM *Recommendation 89/1* called for the reduction at source of polluting emissions of persistent, toxic and bioaccumulative substances as part of the "principle of precautionary action."[46] The EU Court of Justice (ECJ) has also stressed the link between the precautionary principle and

---

37 See Parkes, 2000, pp. 86-87.

38 Article 6 and Annex II.

39 Principle 7.5.

40 *HR* 4046, as quoted in Thomas & Grader, 2000.

41 *NAFO/FC Doc. 4/18*, adopted at the 26th Annual Meeting of the Commission in September 2004. NAFO stands for Northwest Atlantic Fisheries Organization.

42 *Ibid.*, p. 3.

43 *Ibid.*, pp. 2-5.

44 According to Handl, 1991, p. 79, this is another of the "basic ingredients" of precautionary action; also Brunnée, 1996, pp. 73-74; Gullett, 1997, p. 58.

45 Operative paragraph D.3, see also paragraph C9 of the 1987 *Second North Sea Declaration*.

46 1989 *Recommendation 89/1 on the Principle of Precautionary Action*.

preventing pollution by hazardous wastes at the source.[47] One common way to realize prevention at source, to borrow the words of one domestic law on the precautionary principle, is through the application of "clean production methods, including raw materials selection, product substitution and clean product technologies and processes and waste minimization throughout society."[48] There appears to be a rather tight linkage between the precautionary principle and the requirement of utilizing such alternative non-polluting technologies.[49] Clean production methods have, e.g., been propagated as "a means of implementing a precautionary approach" in a 1990 UNEP Governing Council decision on hazardous waste.[50] Several regional agreements concerning hazardous wastes concluded afterwards contain stipulations of similar purport, obliging states parties to apply clean production methods as an appropriate measure for the implementation of the precautionary principle.[51] A quite comprehensive provision in this respect is the one incorporated in the 1991 *Bamako Convention*:

> The Parties shall cooperate with each other in taking the appropriate measures to implement the precautionary principle to pollution prevention through the application of clean production methods [..] applicable to entire product life cycles including:
>
> - raw materials selection, extraction and processing;
> - product conceptualization, design, manufacture and assemblage;
> - materials transport during all phases;
> - industrial and household usage;
> - reintroduction of the product into industrial systems or nature when it no longer serves a useful function; Clean production shall not include 'end-of-pipe' pollution controls such as filters and scrubbers, or chemical, physical or biological treatment. Measures which reduce the volume of waste incineration or concentration, mask the hazard by dilution, or transfer the

---

[47] Case C-318/98, Judgment of the Sixth Chamber of the Court of 22 June 2000, paragraph 37.

[48] 1991 *Resolution LDC 44/14 on the Application of the Precautionary Approach to Environmental Protection within the Framework of the London Dumping Convention*; 1997 *Massachusetts Precautionary Principle Act*.

[49] Stairs & Taylor, 1992, pp. 137-139; Hey, 1992, p. 309; Boehmer-Christiansen, 1994, p. 37; Van Dyke, 1996, pp. 380 and 382; Molenaar, 1998, p. 45; Tickner *et al.*, 2000, p. 5; see generally Epiney & Scheyli, 1998, pp. 236-238.

[50] *Decision SS II/4 on a Comprehensive Approach to Hazardous Waste.*

[51] Article 8(3) of the 1996 *Mediterranean Hazardous Wastes Protocol* to the *Barcelona Convention* states that "to implement the precautionary approach [..] the Parties shall ensure that clean production methods are applied to production processes." Article 3(3) of the 1992 *Central American Hazardous Wastes Agreement* is much the same in that it requires "aplicar el enfoque precautorio a la prevención de la contaminación mediante la aplicación de producción limpia".

> pollutants from one environmental medium to another, are also excluded.[52]

In addition, the *Malmö Declaration*, issued by the First Global Ministerial Environment Forum that was held in the year 2000, proclaims that a precautionary approach in investment and technology decisions "must be linked to the development of cleaner and more resource efficient technologies."[53] Finally, in Germany it is reportedly part of implementing *Vorsorge* for the state to contribute to the introduction of cleaner processes and technologies into the private sector.[54]

Requiring the application of the best environmental practices (BEP) or of the best available technologies (BAT) is generally considered a suitable tool for the achievement of clean production.[55] Not surprisingly, BEP and BAT are measures closely affiliated with the precautionary principle, both in state practice and in academic writings.[56] To cite a couple of examples from the intergovernmental level, in 1990 the ministers participating in the Third International Conference on the Protection of the North Sea agreed that "the application of the precautionary principle requires the application of the Best Available Technology in order to minimize discharges of wastes and residues,"[57] while Principle 11 of the *World Charter for Nature* demands the use of "best available technologies that minimize significant risks to nature or other effects."[58] BAT has besides been set out as a requirement of the precautionary principle in Swedish legislation,[59] German case law[60] and the jurisprudence of the Dutch Council of State.[61] The bond between the precautionary principle and the application of BEP or BAT can be a mutual one. Quite a number of environmental treaties set forth that when

---

[52] Article 3(f)-(g).
[53] Paragraph 11.
[54] Boehmer-Christiansen, 1994, p. 37.
[55] E.g., Stairs & Taylor, 1992, pp. 137-139; Gullett, 1997, p. 58.
[56] As for the latter, see Gullett, *ibid.*; Hey, 1992, pp. 305-306, 309 and 311; Boehmer-Christiansen, 1994, p. 50; Tinker, 1995, p. 793; Brunnée, 1996, pp. 73-74; Epiney & Scheyli, 1998, pp. 141-147; Molenaar, 1998, p. 45; Borgers, 1999, p. 435; and Marr, 2003, p. 15. BAT is yet another of the "basic ingredients" of precaution mentioned by Handl, 1991, at p. 79.
[57] Paragraph 25 of the *Third North Sea Declaration*. Paragraph D.3 of one of its predecessors, the 1984 *First North Sea Declaration*, states: "Precautionary measures for air quality control by reduction of emissions at source should also be determined for the protection of the North Sea, based on the best available technology."
[58] See the *chapeau* of Principle 11.
[59] Article 3(2) of the 1998 *Environmental Code*; as quoted in De Sadeleer, 2002, p. 137.
[60] See De Sadeleer, 2000, p. 145.
[61] Afdeling Bestuursrechtspraak van de Raad van State, Judgment of 19 April 1996, No. G05.93.2238, as quoted in Backes *et al.*, 1997, p. 99.

determining in a given situation what combination of measures exactly *is* the best environmental practice or what set of processes, facilities and methods constitute the best available technology, "particular consideration should be given to [..] the precautionary principle."[62] A clear example is the 1996 EU *Directive on Integrated Pollution Prevention and Control (IPPC)*.[63] The duty of employing BAT when information on environmental impacts is inadequate is, as acknowledged by the European Commission, a "direct application" of the precautionary principle.[64] At the same time, in defining what are the best available techniques in concrete instances that same principle is to be borne in mind.[65]

Bodansky has argued that it is, nevertheless, not self-evident that the precautionary principle implies adoption of a BAT standard.[66] Indeed the emphasis on technological solutions that seems to characterize, e.g., German environmental law need not by definition be a universal phenomenon.[67] Besides, a few international legal instruments mention BAT – and BEP, for that matter – not as part of, but as parallel to the precautionary principle.[68] Even on the assumption that BEP and BAT *are* compulsory measures under the precautionary principle, it cannot be concluded that giving effect to these standards would in all cases be sufficient for a state to comply with the precautionary principle. This can be inferred if only from the wording of, *inter alia*, the *1987 Second North Sea Declaration*[69] and PARCOM *Recommendation 89/1*,[70] both of which speak of "best available technology *and other appropriate measures*" to be adopted within the framework of the precautionary principle.[71] Likewise, in proceedings concerning the Kalkar nuclear fast breeder the Federal Constitutional Court of the Federal Republic of Germany judged that precaution is "not limited by what is technically

---

62 1992 *Baltic Sea Convention*, Annex II, Regulations 2(2) and 3(2). Similar provisions are Annex I, Part 2 of the 1994 *Danube River Convention*, with regard to BEP; and with regard to BAT, Annex III of the 1998 *Heavy Metals Protocol* and Annex V of the 1998 *POPs Protocol* to the *LRTAP Convention*; and Annex C, Part V(B) of the 2001 *POPs Convention*.

63 *Directive 96/61* of 24 September 1996, *OJ*, 1996, L 257, p. 26.

64 Article 8. See *OJ*, 1996, C 9; McIntyre & Mosedale, 1997, p. 230; Chalmers, 1996, pp. 572-582.

65 Annex 4.

66 Bodansky, 1991(a), p. 416.

67 Kaiser, 1997(b), p. 309.

68 Paragraphs 118(b)(i) and 124(b)(i) of the 1995 *Land-Based Activities Action Programme* set out BEP and BAT *alongside* the precautionary principle. The same is true of Article 1 of the 1996 *Protocol on Cooperation in the Area of Water and Nature Protection in the Ems River Mouth* (*Ems-Dollart Environment Protocol*) to the 1960 *Treaty Between the Netherlands and Germany on Cooperation in the Ems River Mouth*, in respect of BAT.

69 Paragraph XVI(1).

70 *Recommendation 89/1 on the Principle of Precautionary Action*.

71 Emphasis added in both cases.

achievable," implying that BAT will not always be enough for the *Vorsorgeprinzip* to be fully implemented.[72] According to the Court, if the necessary level of safety cannot be attained by technological solutions, authorization for risky activities must altogether be withheld.[73]

It would in any case seem fair to say, wrapping up what has been discussed here with respect to precautionary measures to combat pollution, that implementation of the precautionary principle can be achieved, *inter alia*, by control of pollution at source; that implementation of pollution control at source can be achieved, *inter alia*, by clean production methods; and that implementation of clean production methods can be achieved, *inter alia*, by the application of BAT and BEP. One measure fits the other, in the way of Russian dolls.

Research

The last of the measures typically associated with the precautionary principle to be considered here in some detail is research, a related theme which was already touched upon to some degree above.[74] For an effective implementation of the precautionary principle research is of the essence along the entire trajectory.[75] It is, in particular, an indispensable tool to (1) detect dangers in an early stage; (2) assess environmental impacts; (3) overcome or reduce uncertainties; (4) develop and examine alternatives to potential hazards; and to (5) monitor the effects of precautionary action taken.[76]

The second function referred to relates to the performance of an environmental impact assessment (EIA) prior to carrying out or permitting a potentially harmful activity, in order to get an understanding of that activity's environmental impact that is as complete as possible.[77] In the ITLOS *Land Reclamation* case Malaysia submitted that an independent EIA is a "central tool of the international law of the precautionary principle."[78] One may envisage at least two viable ways in which an EIA may function in regard of the right and

---

[72] Bundesverfassungsgericht, Judgment of 8 August 1978, *BverGE*, 49, 89 (143) and 53, 30 (58/58); see De Sadeleer, 2000, pp. 145-146.

[73] *Ibid.*

[74] See *supra* paragraph 5.3.

[75] Hey, 1992, p. 311; Boehmer-Christiansen, 1994, pp. 37 and 53; Van Dyke, 1996, pp. 380 and 382; McIntyre & Mosedale, 1997, pp. 239-240; Backes *et al.*, 1997, p. 68; Tickner, 1999, p. 174; Tickner *et al.*, 2000, p. 10; Raffensperger & Tickner, 2000; Saunders, 2000; Pollan, 2001; Reid *et al.*, 2005, pp. 101-102.

[76] *Ibid.*; as regards monitoring see also *infra* paragraph 7.3 on the duration of precautionary measures.

[77] Generally, see Epiney & Scheyli, 1998, pp. 126-141; Gray, 2000, *passim*.

[78] *Verbatim Record* of the sitting on 25 September 2003, p. 20 (Schrijver).

the duty of states to take precautionary action as defined previously.[79] The outcome of such an assessment may, on the one hand, constitute the 'best information available' that gives rise to reasonable grounds for concern that significant, serious and/or irreversible harm to the environment may be caused, thus warranting precautionary action. The 1995 *Land-Based Activities Action Programme*, for instance, speaks of precautionary measures based on, *inter alia*, impact assessments.[80] An EIA may also, on the other hand, be carried out as a first precautionary measure in cases where reasonable grounds for concern have arisen by other means, in order to learn more about the prospective adverse effects of a certain activity before giving it the green light. Relevant provisions of *Agenda 21*[81] and the 1993 *Declaration on Environment and Development in the Arctic*[82] – calling for prior assessment as part of the application of "precautionary approaches" to projects with environmental implications – and the 2002 *Antigua Convention* – calling for "environmental assessment and systemic observation as preventive and precautionary measures in the planning and implementation of projects"[83] – as well as the *World Charter for Nature*[84] and some domestic legislation[85] would seem to have been drafted in this vein. EIA, in other words, can either provide the basis for precautionary action or constitute a precautionary measure in itself. Many authors have accordingly stressed the link between the precautionary principle and impact assessment.[86]

Also with respect to the other functions of research in the present context, numerous legal and policy statements bear witness to an apparent consensus in the international community on the fact that precaution and science must and do in truth go hand in hand. As the 2001 *Reykjavik Declaration* goes:

---

[79] See especially *supra* Chapter 6.

[80] Paragraph 24.

[81] Paragraph 17.5(d).

[82] Paragraph 8.

[83] Article 10(1)(b).

[84] As Principle 11 of the Charter states: "(b) Activities which are likely to pose a significant risk to nature shall be preceded by an exhaustive examination [..]; (c) Activities which may disturb nature shall be preceded by assessment of their consequences, and environmental impact studies of development projects shall be conducted sufficiently in advance [..]."

[85] E.g., the 1997 *Massachusetts Precautionary Principle Act*, which calls for evaluation of environmental consequences of alternative methods, including long term consequences as a "necessary step" in implementing the precautionary principle; see also Section 3.5.1 of the 1992 Australian *Intergovernmental Agreement on the Environment*.

[86] E.g., Hey, 1992, pp. 305-306, 309, 311; Freestone & Hey, 1996(a), pp. 12-13; Van Dyke, 1996, p. 380; Cameron & Abouchar, 1996, p. 51; McIntyre & Mosedale, 1997, pp. 238-239; Epiney & Scheyli, 1998, p. 126; Molenaar, 1998, p. 45; De Sadeleer, 2002, pp. 207-209; Trouwborst, 2002, p. 43; Schrijver, 2003, pp. 71-74; Marr, 2003, p. 15; 2004 *ILA Berlin Rules on Water Resources*, Commentary to Article 23.

> While it is necessary to take immediate action to address particularly urgent problems on the basis of the precautionary approach, it is important to advance the scientific basis for incorporating ecosystem considerations, building on existing and future available scientific knowledge.[87]

The *Montreal Protocol* as amended in 1990 tells of protecting the ozone layer by taking "precautionary measures to control equitably total global emissions of substances that deplete it, with the ultimate objective of their elimination *on the basis of developments in scientific knowledge*,"[88] a proposition which has in point of fact been matched by a series of subsequent adjustments of emission reductions based on the results of scientific research.[89] UNEP Governing Council *Decision 18/32 on Persistent Organic Pollutants* of 1995 notes the "urgent need to improve scientific understanding of persistent organic pollutants, their sources, transport, and pathways as well as their effects."[90] By the same token, in its 2000 *Resolution on the Precautionary Principle* the European Council called on EU member states and the European Commission to "attach particular importance to the development of scientific expertise."[91] After adopting precautionary measures under the *SPS Agreement*, WTO member states must "seek to obtain the additional information necessary for a more objective assessment of risk."[92] The European Commission agrees that "scientific research should be carried out with a view to obtaining a more advanced or more complete scientific assessment," so that precautionary measures can be reevaluated "in the light of new scientific information."[93] Likewise, according to the UK Government, precautionary decisions should be reviewed "to reflect better understanding of risk as more evidence becomes available."[94] In Germany in the 1970s, precautionary measures in answer to the prospect of massive deterioration of forests (*Waldsterben*), supposedly on account of air pollution, not only included changes in energy policy but also huge investments in forest research.[95] An authoritative definition of the precautionary principle issued by the FRG Government in 1984 postulates that *Vorsorge* stands for, among other things, "the early detection of dangers to health and environment by comprehensive, synchronized (harmonized) research, in

---

[87] See paragraph 5, which goes on to enumerate the many sorts and fields of necessary research.
[88] Sixth preambular paragraph; emphasis added.
[89] Backes *et al.*, 1997, p. 68.
[90] Sixth preambular paragraph.
[91] Paragraph 25.
[92] Article 5(7).
[93] *Communication COM(2000)1*, p. 20.
[94] UK Government, *A Better Quality of Life: A Strategy for Sustainable Development for the United Kingdom*, May 1999, paragraph 4.2.
[95] Boehmer-Christiansen, 1994, p. 49.

particular about cause and effect relationships."[96] Parties to the 2002 *ASEAN Agreement on Transboundary Haze Pollution* have taken on the obligation to "take precautionary measures to *anticipate*, prevent and *monitor* transboundary haze pollution" resulting from forest fires.[97] The *Declaration on the Environment* adopted by the 1990 Liberal International Congress proclaims that while it is "essential that research facilities are strengthened," action to protect the environment must not be put off with the argument that scientific knowledge is incomplete.[98] Similarly, a 1997 *Biodiversity Convention* working document on forest biodiversity stresses that the "obvious limitations of our current knowledge should not restrain us from acting upon it, but do emphasise the importance of directing resources to the development of better measures for identification and monitoring of forest biological diversity."[99] To complete this short list of examples, the *Massachusetts Precautionary Principle Act* includes the obligation to "encourage and use as fully as possible scientific and socioeconomic research in order to achieve an improved understanding on which to base long-term policy options." In brief, there is good news for the academic world: the precautionary principle calls for more, not less, scientists.[100]

Other Precautionary Measures

This inventory is far from complete.[101] A salient measure which will be analyzed at length in the next chapter is that which requires proponents of a potentially harmful activity to prove that the execution of their plans will not produce unacceptable environmental impacts before permitting the activity. This measure, which is popularly referred to as the 'reversal of the burden of proof' is closely linked to the moratorium discussed above. Other examples of precautionary action include the substitution of products such as pesticides by less hazardous alternatives,[102] prior information and consultation,[103]

---

[96] *Report from the Government to the Federal Parliament on the Protection of Air Quality*, *BMI* 1984, p. 53, as reproduced in approximate translation in Boehmer-christiansen, 1994, at p. 37.

[97] Article 3(3); emphasis added.

[98] Section III, paragraph 5.

[99] Secretariat, *Forests and Biodiversity*, UNEP/CBD/SBSTTA/3/Inf.22, 11 August 1997, paragraph 59.

[100] Tickner, 1999, p. 174.

[101] For numerous additional illustrations of precautionary measures in the context of the law of the sea, see Marr, 2003, Chapters 4 through 8. On the wide range of measures adopted under the precautionary principle in Sweden, see Wahlström, 1999, p. 66; for Germany, see Boehmer-Christiansen, 1994, p. 48.

[102] *Communication COM(2000)1*, p. 18; see, e.g., Wahlström, *ibid.*, pp. 54-55 on the substitution of the insecticides aldrin, dieldrin, endrin and others by less risky substances in Sweden. Product substitution is often viewed as a component of clean production methods.

[103] Brunnée, 1996, p. 73.

liability and compensation rules,[104] the use of economic instruments like subsidies or taxes,[105] and participatory decision-making procedures.[106]

Furthermore, precautionary action frequently comprises a combination of various measures. For instance, within the 2001 *POPs Convention* banning[107] and restricting[108] the use and production of listed chemicals, reducing and eliminating the unintentional release of certain substances,[109] trade restrictions,[110] the use of BAT and BEP,[111] and research and monitoring[112] have all been agreed under the umbrella of the precautionary principle.[113] The preamble of the 1980 *Land-Based Sources Protocol* to the *Barcelona Convention*, as amended in 1996, mentions EIA, BAT, BEP and clean production in one breath with the precautionary principle.[114] It is instructive to run over the package of measures the cumulative performance of which has been agreed on by the states parties to the *London Dumping Convention*:

> Contracting Parties shall take all necessary steps to ensure the effective implementation of the precautionary approach to environmental protection and to this end they shall:
> (a) encourage prevention of pollution at the source, by the application of clean production methods, including raw materials selection, product substitution and clean production technologies and processes and waste minimization throughout society;
> (b) evaluate the environmental and economic consequences of alternative methods of waste management, including long-term consequences;
> (c) encourage and use as fully as possible scientific and socio-economic research in order to achieve an improved understanding on which to base long-range policy options;
> (d) endeavor to reduce risk and scientific uncertainty relating to proposed disposal operations; and

---

[104] Boehmer-Christiansen, 1994, p. 48; Tickner, 1999, p. 173.
[105] Boehmer-Christiansen, *ibid.*
[106] Tickner, 1999, pp. 175-176, who names the example of a consensus conference on genetic engineering in Norway.
[107] Article 3(1)(a).
[108] Article 3(1)(b).
[109] Article 5.
[110] Article 3(2).
[111] Article 5(d)-(g).
[112] Article 11.
[113] See the eight preambular paragraph and Article 1. For a similar range of measures relating to POPs, see paragraph 104(b)(i) of the 1995 *Land-Based Activities Action Programme*.
[114] Fifth preambular paragraph (which also mentions the polluter pays principle).

(c) continue to take measures to ensure that potential adverse impacts of any dumping are minimized, and that adequate monitoring is provided for early detection and mitigation of these impacts.[115]

Other examples are the long lists of measures enumerated in pertinent provisions of *Agenda 21*[116] and the 1994 *Energy Charter Treaty*.[117]

7.3. General Features of Precautionary Measures

Any Measure can be a Precautionary Measure

Clearly, the range of different measures that are and have been taken by states to implement the precautionary principle is very wide, both in the international and the national sphere. Nevertheless, none of the actual measures described in the previous paragraph are novelties. The use of "Safe Minimum Standards" in the field of nature conservation, for instance, was already proposed by Ciriacy-Wantrup as early as 1952.[118] Neither were EIA, bans, clean production methods, or BAT or BEP standards singularly created for the implementation of the precautionary principle. All of these have been applied in international environmental law long before the principle made its entry in the field.[119] What is new and unique for the precautionary principle is the purpose of these measures and, related to this, the moment and the circumstances in which they are to be taken.[120] The measures themselves are not. Nor is the precautionary principle their exclusive patentee.[121]

What is more, it has become noticeably clear from the above review that not a single one of the measures treated is so inextricably linked to the precautionary principle that its application is called for every single time there are reasonable grounds for concern that serious and/or irreversible harm to the environment may be caused. Quite the contrary, it would seem that essentially every type of environmental measure can be a precautionary measure in the scheme of the precautionary principle.[122] A considerable number of formulations of the principle actually do no more than call for "action", "measures" or the like when the right conditions are met, without

---

115 1991 *Resolution LDC 44/14 on the Application of the Precautionary Approach to Environmental Protection within the Framework of the London Dumping Convention.*

116 E.g., paragraph 17.21.

117 Article 19(1).

118 Ciriacy-Wantrup, S.V., *Resource Conservation, Economics and Policies*, Berkely 1952; see Castells & Ravetz, 2001, p. 410.

119 Also Dzidzornu, 1998, p. 101.

120 See also Freestone, 1999, p. 141.

121 Dzidzornu, 1998, pp. 91 and 104.

122 Also Borgers, 1999, pp. 435-436.

indicating any specific measures. One example of such a definition containing little or no guidance as to the course of precautionary action to be chosen is the one from the 1992 *Baltic Sea Convention*, urging parties to take "preventive measures";[123] another is Principle 15 of the *Rio Declaration*, requiring "cost-effective measures". These provisions and others like them apparently leave options open as to the appropriate measures.[124] As a matter of linguistic definition a measure, any measure, is called precautionary as soon as it is taken out of precaution. It would seem that in the present context linguistics match state practice, as apparently action to implement the precautionary principle can take any form as long as it is effective and proportional. The list of candidate precautionary measures, in consequence, is sheer endless.[125] As the *ILA Berlin Rules on Water Resources* simply state, the precautionary principle entails the obligation to "take *all appropriate measures* to prevent, eliminate, reduce, or control harm to the aquatic environment."[126]

How, then, is the precautionary principle to be applied in individual cases? That is, how can governments know in concrete instances which of the virtually limitless amount of candidate measures to choose? As it turns out, in the practical implementation of the precautionary principle states have tended to simply select the effective and proportional measure, or

---

[123] Article 3(2). The same is true of several other instruments from the Baltic regime, e.g., the eighth preambular paragraph of the 1988 *Baltic Sea Declaration* ("action to prevent and abate pollution"); paragraph 1 of 1991 HELCOM *Recommendation 12/3* ("action"); paragraph 1(3) of 1992 HELCOM *Recommendation 13/6* ("preventive measures").

[124] Other instances include the 1989 *Declaration of Nordic Parliamentary Conference* and the 1989 *Declaration of the Nordic Council's International Conference on Pollution of the Seas* ("eliminating and preventing pollution emissions"); 1991 OECD Council *Recommendation C(90)164 on Integrated Pollution Prevention and Control* ("precautionary action to mitigate the risk of significant harm to the environment"); Article 2(2)(a) of the 1992 *OSPAR Convention* ("preventive measures"); Article 19(1) of the 1994 *Energy Charter Treaty* ("precautionary measures to prevent or minimize environmental degradation"); ninth preambular paragraph of the *Biodiversity Convention* and fifth preambular paragraph of the 1995 *SPA and Biodiversity Protocol* to the *Barcelona Convention* ("measures to avoid or minimize such a threat"); Article 7 of the 1995 *IUCN Draft Covenant* ("action to avoid potentially significant or irreversible harm to the environment"); section 2.4, paragraph 3 of the *Pan-European Biological and Landscape Diversity Strategy* ("action to introduce appropriate procedures to avoid or minimize potentially adverse impact of activities on biological and landscape diversity"); paragraph 24 of the 1995 *Land-Based Activities Action Programme* ("preventive and corrective measures"); Article 3(1) of the 1996 *LDC Protocol*: ("appropriate preventative measures"); Article II(3) of the 2001 *Albatross Agreement* ("measures to enhance the conservation status of albatrosses and petrels"); and Article 13 of the Czech and Slovak *Federal Act on the Environment* of 5 December 1991 ("measures intended to prevent such [irreversible or serious] damage").

[125] Boehmer-Christiansen, 1994, p. 48; Lefeber, 1996, p. 35; Gullett, 1997, p. 60; Klinke & Renn, 1999, pp. 23-36; Freestone, 1999, pp. 140-141; Raffensperger *et al.*, 1999; Borgers, 1999, pp. 435-436; Tickner *et al.*, 2000, p. 5; McNelis, 2000, p. 547; De Sadeleer, 2002, pp. 221-222; Marr, 2003, pp. 215-216. See also *Communication COM(2000)1*, pp. 16 and 18.

[126] Article 23(2); emphasis added.

combination of measures, that suits the circumstances of the case best. Thinking it over this could hardly be different, bearing in mind the huge variety of natural conditions and human actions, i.e., the huge variety of environmental risks to which the precautionary principle is potentially applicable.[127] Returning to the familiar example of the precautionary conservation and management standards of the *Straddling Stocks Agreement* and similar instruments,[128] precautionary reference points and the action to be taken by the parties to the Agreement when these points are approached or exceeded are to be designed specifically for each fish stock. What precise precautionary response is befitting will depend on the circumstances.[129] Other cases illustrating the tailor-made nature of measures adopted under the precautionary principle encompass the detailed conservation and management measures that have been elaborated under the *CCAMLR*;[130] the precautionary decision-making procedures of the 2001 *POPs Convention*;[131] the 1994 criteria for the amendment of the Appendices of *CITES*;[132] the 2004 *Precautionary Approach Framework* of NAFO;[133] and the procedure for decisions concerning individual plans and projects potentially affecting designated protected areas laid down in the 1992 EU *Habitats Directive*.[134] Obviously, measures of a legislative, administrative and juridical make-up can all serve to implement the precautionary principle.[135] It is equally clear that some threats call for a local or national response, others for international cooperation and yet others for a combination of the two.[136] An instance of the latter is provided by the protection of the ozone layer.[137] Time and again, what constitutes the appropriate effective and proportional precautionary action depends on the particularities of each environmental hazard.[138]

It can thus be concluded that the precautionary principle does not as a rule dictate any regulatory measures in particular.[139] When thresholds are

---

[127] See *supra* paragraph 5.2.

[128] Article 6 of the *Straddling Stocks Agreement*; Article 6 of the 2000 *Honolulu Convention*; and Principle 7.5 of the 1995 *FAO Code of Conduct for Responsible Fisheries*.

[129] Birnie & Boyle, 2002, p. 676.

[130] Parkes, 2000, *passim*; Kimball, 2001, p. 29; Trouwborst, 2002, pp. 91-92.

[131] See Articles 8(7) and 8(9).

[132] See especially Annex 4 of *Resolution Conf. 9.24 on Criteria for Amendment of Appendices I and II.*

[133] *NAFO/FC Doc. 4/18.*

[134] Article 6(3)-(4) of the Directive; Heukers, 1997, p. 24.

[135] Lefeber, 1996, p. 61.

[136] See *supra* paragraph 7.2.

[137] E.g., the eighth preambular paragraph of the multilateral 1985 *Montreal Protocol*, as amended in London in 1990, notes "the precautionary measures [..] that have already been taken at national and regional levels."

[138] See also Lefeber, 1996, p. 35.

[139] Freestone, 1999, p. 141; Dzidzornu, 1998, p. 101; Jordan & O'Riordan, 1999, p. 16; Birnie & Boyle, 2002, pp. 119-120.

crossed it dictates the adoption of tailor-made measures, conditioned by the criteria of effectiveness and proportionality and fashioned to fit the concrete circumstances of each case. No more, no less.

Guidelines for Choosing the Right Precautionary Action

For all that, a number of general guidelines do exist that may help determine what constitutes effective and proportional action in a given instance. It was noted before that *effective* precautionary action presupposes a dynamic and vigilant stance on the part of governments, resulting in measures that anticipate, prevent and attack the causes of environmental degradation.[140] As Singapore conceded in the *Land Reclamation* case, the precautionary principle "requires a State undertaking activities within its territory not to use scientific uncertainty as a reason for not undertaking *the most rigorous preparatory arrangements* to avoid dangers."[141] Furthermore, on the risk of stating the obvious, for action to be effective – i.e., to truly prevent significant, serious and/or irreversible harm to the environment from happening – it is crucial that measures are taken as early as practicable. As recognized in the *First North Sea Declaration*, "the environment is best protected against pollution through *timely* preventive measures."[142] Swiss federal environmental legislation requires that "with a view to precaution" potentially harmful effects must be "curtailed at an early stage."[143] This is evidently a guideline touching upon the core of the precautionary principle. Applied, for instance, to the risk of environmental harm inflicted by invasive alien species, the guidelines of vigorous and timely action mean that:

> Mitigation measures should take place in the earliest possible stage of invasion, on the basis of the precautionary approach. [..] Hence, early detection of new introductions of potentially or known invasive alien species is important, and needs to be combined with the capacity to take rapid follow-up action.[144]

Just as importantly, the criterion of effectiveness implies the adoption by governments of a comprehensive, integrated approach in matters concerning the environment; an approach that is comprehensive both in

---

[140] See *supra* paragraph 5.4; Jordan & O'Riordan, 1999, p. 29.

[141] *Verbatim Record* of the ITLOS sitting on 27 September 2003, p. 32 (Reisman); emphasis added.

[142] Preambular paragraph A.6; emphasis added.

[143] 1983 *Bundesgesetz über den Umweltschutz*, Article 1(2): "Im Sinne der Vorsorge sind Einwirkungen, die schädlich oder lästig werden könnten, frühzeitig zu begrenzen." English translation from Marr, 2003, p. 96.

[144] 2002 *Guiding Principles on Invasive Alien Species*, Guiding Principle 12; see also Guiding Principle 13.

terms of space and time.[145] In terms of space, in the sense that it encompasses the environment in its totality and all human activities, as discussed above when dealing with the scope of the precautionary principle,[146] and is holistic in that it takes account of the fact that everything in nature is interdependent. The close ties between the precautionary principle and the so-called ecosystem approach have been stressed recurrently in this connection.[147] An approach that is comprehensive also in terms of time, in the sense that the dimensions of the precautionary principle go, in the words of the European Commission, "beyond the problems associated with a short or medium-term approach to risks" and plainly concern "the longer run and the well-being of future generations,"[148] thus illustrating the inseparability of the precautionary principle and the concept of sustainable development. As the special envoy of Papua New Guinea put it in his address to the 2002 Johannesburg Summit, the earth's resources must be used in a way that is responsible and sustainable "for as far as we can see into the future."[149] Only by looking far enough ahead can environmental problems be anticipated.[150] Potential long-term effects should thus be taken fully into account in evaluating the effectiveness and proportionality of candidate precautionary measures.[151] The criteria of timeliness and comprehensiveness can be found side by side in the 2004 *ILA Berlin Rules on Water Resources*, which set out that states, "in accordance with the precautionary approach, shall take early action and develop long-term plans" to ensure the sustainable use of groundwater aquifers.[152]

A final and critical aid in the selection of effective and proportional measures in concrete cases is the general guideline prescribing prudence in decision-making and a bias towards environmental protection, briefly touched

---

[145] Handl, 1991, p. 78; Hey, 1992, p. 308. According to paragraph 4.2 of the 2002 *ILA Declaration on Sustainable Development*, a precautionary approach should include "planning based on clear criteria and well-defined goals."

[146] See *supra* paragraph 5.2. To take the example of global climatic change, Article 3(3) of the *Climate Change Convention* points out that policies and measures to deal with this problem should "be comprehensive, cover all relevant sources, sinks and reservoirs of greenhouse gases and adaptation, and comprise all economic sectors."

[147] Hayashi, 1999, p. 49; Tickner *et al.*, 2000, p. 6; Robinson, 2000; Tanaka, 2004, pp. 500-504; Parsons, 2005, *passim*. A case in point is the *CCAMLR* regime; see Parkes, 2000, *passim*; Redgwell, 1999, p. 219; Parsons, *ibid.*, pp. 408-411.

[148] *Communication COM(2000)1*, p. 8.

[149] Statement by the Right Honourable Sir Rabbie L. Namliu KCMG, MP Special Envoy of the Prime Minister and Minister for Foreign Affairs and Immigration of Papua New Guinea, at the World Summit on Sustainable Development, Johannesburg, 3 September 2002.

[150] Jordan & O'Riordan, 1999, p. 29. That is, arguably, at least further than the next elections.

[151] *Communication COM(2000)1*, p. 18; Hey, 1992, pp. 308-309.

[152] Article 38 ("Precautionary Management of Aquifers").

upon above.[153] He is the best general who makes the fewest mistakes, as the saying goes. Materially, this guideline means that governments should play it safe when choosing a course of precautionary action, making sure that natural systems are altered as little and as slowly as feasible.[154] Just as US authorities are to give "the benefit of doubt to the species" under the *Endangered Species Act* when taking decisions possibly affecting a threatened species in cases of inadequate knowledge,[155] so states should in general err on the side of environmental protection when determining appropriate action. When in doubt as to what measure(s) to pick, governments ought to ensure that "any errors of judgment made will lead to excess, rather than inadequate, protection."[156] Under the precautionary principle the requirement of effectiveness thus implies, to cite from the US *Gilchrest-Farr Fisheries Recovery Act*, "selecting and implementing any action that will be significantly more likely than not to satisfy the conservation objectives."[157] This adagium of *in dubio pro natura* is so fundamental that not applying it practically equals not applying the precautionary principle.[158]

Choosing Between One Risk and Another

In some situations there may be a problem, however, in finding out what *is* the most cautious course of action.[159] What to do, for instance, in the following situation?

> A lake seems to be dying for reasons that we do not fully understand. The proposal has been made to save it by adding substantial amounts of iron acetate to the lake. According to opinion (1), the lake will be saved if iron acetate is added, otherwise not. According to opinion (2), the lake will self-repair anyhow, and the addition of iron acetate makes no difference. According to opinion (3), the lake will die whether iron acetate is added or not. Proponents of all three scientific opinions agreed that

---

[153] See *supra* paragraph 5.4. This is closely related also to the use of ample margins of safety as discussed in *supra* paragraph 7.2.

[154] Schmidt-Bleek, 1993, p. 83.

[155] *Roosevelt Campobello International Park v Environmental Protection Agency*, 648 F.2d 1041, DC Cir. 1982; Bodansky, 1994, p. 210.

[156] Santillo *et al.*, 1999, p. 39; also Birnie & Boyle, 2002, p. 117.

[157] *HR* 4046, as quoted in Thomas & Grader, 2000.

[158] Schmidt-Bleek, 1993, p. 83; Van Dyke, 1996, p. 380; Backes, 1997, p. 14; Backes *et al.*, 1997, pp. 49, 69 and 95; Van Wijmen, 1997, p. 14; Victor, 1997, p. 243; Molenaar, 1998, p. 45; Molenaar, 2005, p. 537; Borgers, 1999, *passim*; Santillo *et al.*, 1999, p. 39; Geiser, 1999(a), p. xxv; Jordan & O'Riordan, 1999, pp. 26-27; Barrett & Raffensperger, 1999, p. 117; Morris, 2000(b), p. 13; Tallacchini, 2000, p. 1097. As the Canadian government put it in its 1990 *Green Plan*: "we must be prepared to give nature the benefit of the doubt. We should err on the side of protecting the environment;" see VanderZwaag, 1994.

[159] Bodansky, 1991(a), p. 417; Cooney, 2004, pp. 27-28.

> the addition of iron acetate will have certain negative effects on land living animals that drink water from the lake.[160]

In cases like this one, as critics of the precautionary principle have propounded time and again, the matter is not simply one of erring on the side of caution.[161] It must be decided *which* is the cautious side.[162] Similar dilemmas are the choice between the adverse impacts of acid rain on forests and the potential adverse impacts of the use of lime to counter the acid rain effects; between the dumping of wastes at sea and their discharge on land;[163] between the use of the relatively little toxic but highly persistent DDT and alternative pesticides that are less persistent but more acutely toxic;[164] between the negative and the positive environmental effects of energy generation by wind mills;[165] between encouraging the use of antifoulants on ship hulls to prevent transport of potentially harmful alien species and preventing the use of those same antifoulants because of the noxious effects of some ingredients on the marine environment;[166] or the choice between the risk of an asteroid colliding with the earth and the risks involved in setting up a global system involving nuclear missiles to prevent such collisions.[167] Precautionary action to counter one threat may itself generate a new, unintended threat, transferring risk from one medium to another.[168] Apparently, the choice is not always between risk and caution. Sometimes governments must choose between one risk and another.[169]

Several possible solutions have been contrived for dealing with this predicament; a predicament which, to some degree, is similar to the difficulties that can be encountered when determining whether a given multiple impact

---

160 Hansson, 1997, p. 297.

161 Bodansky, 1991(a), p. 417; Tickner, 1999, pp. 173-174; Pieterman & Hanekamp, 2002, pp. 12-13.

162 Bodansky, *ibid.*

163 As Gullett, 1997, at p. 58 illustrates, "in Norway there has been considerable debate over the discharge of ilmenite (a black mineral composed of iron titanium oxide), which is insoluble and accumulates in water, but is non-toxic. Environmental groups insisted that it is a pollutant because not all its effects on marine biota are known. They argued that it should be stored in a specially constructed dam on land. On the other hand, local residents and a number of marine biologists have been opposed to the construction of the dam, arguing that it would be too costly and would have its own environmental impacts and further, that the dumping of ilmenite at sea is not risky."

164 Bodansky, 1991(a), p. 417.

165 See *supra* paragraph 5.3.

166 See *supra* paragraph 4.1.

167 See Rubin, 2000, *passim*.

168 Bodansky, 1991(a), p. 417; Gullett, 1997, p. 58; Rubin, *ibid.*, p. 107.

169 Bodansky, *ibid.*; Hansson, 1997, p. 305; Gullett, *ibid.*; Rubin, *ibid.*; Pieterman & Hanekamp, 2002, pp. 12-13.

qualifies as harm or not.[170] Often problems can be anticipated by applying the guidelines of a cautious and comprehensive approach that were just discussed. Important parts of such an approach are, first, the very awareness that precautionary measures may have implications that extend beyond the specific risk of their primary focus and, second, the ultimate aim of reducing the overall impact on ecosystems to a minimum.[171] As one commentator has put it, an "adequate implementation of the precautionary principle does not require that the first risk that meets the eye is erased, but that risks are considered comprehensively."[172] In this regard it is formal policy of the UK Department of the Environment, Transport and the Regions to give careful thought to the possibility of unintended consequences elsewhere whenever precautionary action is contemplated.[173] Under the *Bamako Convention*, measures which transfer pollutants from one part of the environmental to another are expressly prohibited in the implementation of the precautionary principle.[174] In like manner, according to the *IUCN Draft Covenant* states must "not transfer, directly or indirectly, harm or hazards from one area to another or transform one type of environmental harm into another."[175] In a way, this comes down to applying the precautionary principle to itself. When the envisaged implementation of a precautionary measure to prevent or abate environmental harm gives rise to reasonable grounds for concern that harm to another part of the environment may be caused as a result of that measure, there are good grounds for considering alternative courses of action. A crystalline example of such application of precaution *to* precaution can be found in the 2001 *Albatross Agreement*, where the treaty obliges its parties to "take a precautionary approach when re-establishing albatrosses and petrels into parts of their traditional breeding range," requiring a detailed scheme based on the best scientific evidence and prior notification of the Agreement

---

[170] See *supra* paragraph 5.3.

[171] Santillo et al., 1999, pp. 47-48: "In this regard, it is essential to recognize that the Precautionary Principle is not intended to be applied in a simple one-sided approach to decision-making, without consideration of the potential hazards of alternatives. For action to be truly precautionary, it must also ensure that the fundamental objective of the reduction of overall environmental burden is strictly observed. [..] In order to meet this objective, it must be recognized that a decision, for example, to prevent the use or discharge of a certain chemical may require a fundamental reevaluation of societal need for that product and may not always imply simple substitution with an alternative." Also Tickner, 1999, pp. 173-174.

[172] Nollkaemper, 1996, p. 92.

[173] *Guidelines for Environmental Risk Assessment and Management: Revised Departmental Guidance*, 2 August 2000, paragraph 1.6.

[174] Article 3(g).

[175] Article 14.

Secretariat as part of this approach[176] – re-establishment itself being a precautionary measure to protect the species.

In any decision much will, of course, depend on the comparative sizes of the risks involved. Evidently, of two (or more) evils governments should choose the lesser in order to comply with the precautionary principle. It will usually become clear, sooner or later, which risk is the more weighty, which danger the most substantial. One instance is the agreement reached among the North Sea Ministers at the 1995 Esbjerg Conference, that with respect to decommissioned offshore installations not dumping at sea but "more environmentally acceptable and controllable land-based solutions are preferable."[177] But what if it is not at all apparent which evil is the lesser and which outcome is the worst; what if the exclusive choice is between two equally grave, equally plausible, but diametrically opposed worst case scenarios?[178] To this particular question the precautionary principle does not appear to provide an answer.[179]

What constitutes appropriate action for the purpose of implementing the precautionary principle is thus the result of the interplay of various guidelines, some of which may in concrete instances be at daggers drawn. *Exempli gratia*, the need to take measures as early as possible has the potential to conflict with the need to make sure precautionary measures do not give rise themselves to outcomes that are worse than the ills they are intended to remedy. In the end, as in the determination of whether thresholds are crossed,[180] there may be room for interpretation in deciding what precautionary measures to take. By way of an illustration, at their tenth Conference of the Parties (COP) in Harare in 1997 states parties to *CITES* disagreed on whether application of the precautionary principle entailed either (a) the continued inclusion of elephant populations in Botswana, Namibia and Zimbabwe in Appendix I or (b) their downlisting to Appendix II under stringent conditions. Both options were deemed, by their respective advocates, to represent the most cautious course of action and serve the interest of the species best.[181] Deciding on precautionary action has been compared to criminal procedural law as it applies in the US: "We cannot expect the precautionary principle by itself to tell us what to do about GM crops or any other new technology. Like a jury, we have to weigh up the evidence, and like a jury we have to come to a decision."[182]

---

176 Annex 2.
177 Paragraph 54 of the *Fourth North Sea Declaration*.
178 Rubin, 2000, p. 120.
179 Hansson, 1997, p. 305.
180 See *supra* paragraph 5.3.
181 See Mohamed-Katerere, 2001, p. 8.
182 Wan Ho & Saunders, 2000.

The Duration of Precautionary Measures

One more query remains to be addressed in the current chapter. Once taken, how long should precautionary measures stay in force? The provision of the *SPS Agreement* dealing with this matter indicates that in cases of insufficient data concerning a potential hazard a WTO member state may "provisionally adopt sanitary or phytosanitary measures on the basis of available scientific information" on the condition that they shall "seek to obtain the additional information necessary for a more objective assessment of risk and review the sanitary or phytosanitary measure accordingly within a reasonable period of time."[183] Although it does not state this in so many words, this formulation has been taken to suggest that precautionary measures are temporary measures and even that their duration might be subject to a specific maximum.[184] The ideally temporary character of precautionary management was underlined as well in proposals submitted by several countries during preparatory work for the *Straddling Stocks Agreement*,[185] and is reflected in the Agreement's requirement that provisional precautionary reference points established in data-poor situations are to be "subject to enhanced monitoring in order to enable revision [..] as improved information becomes available."[186] Similarly, the affirmation by the ECJ that the precautionary principle entitles states to take "provisional" protective measures "on the basis of *as yet* incomplete scientific knowledge"[187] appears to involve an expectation that such knowledge will sooner or later become 'complete'.

As it happens, no matter what precautionary measures are finally adopted, it is cardinal to monitor them over time to identify their results, both expected and unexpected, and to modify or even cancel them if any new insights gathered so warrant in order to ensure observance of the proportionality criterion.[188] The *Action Plan for the Conservation of Cetaceans in the Mediterranean Sea* that was adopted on a precautionary basis by the states parties to the *Barcelona Convention* in 1991 "will be adjusted, as necessary, when more information becomes available," as the Plan itself states.[189] Similar considerations apply to precautionary import restrictions under the *Biosafety*

---

[183] Article 5(7).

[184] See Von Moltke, 1999; Matthee & Vermersch, 2000, p. 69.

[185] Argentina, Canada, Chile, Iceland and New Zealand, *Draft Convention*, Article 5. See Orrega Vicuña, 1999, p. 160.

[186] Paragraph 6 of Annex II.

[187] *Alpharma Inc. v Council of the European Union*, Case T-70/99, Judgment of 11 September 2002, paragraphs 181 and 318; italics added.

[188] Tickner *et al.*, 2000, p. 10; Matthee & Vermersch, 2000, p. 69; Kourilsky, P.H. & Viney, G., *Rapport au Premier Ministre, le Principe de Précaution*, Paris 2000, as cited in Faure, 2003, at p. 256; Marr, 2003, p. 37; see also *supra* paragraph 7.2.

[189] Paragraph 4.

Protocol[190] and precautionary conservation and management measures taken by the Inter-American Tropical Tuna Commission (IATTC) under the 2003 *Antigua Convention*.[191] To add another example, in the opinion of the UK Government that was already cited earlier, precautionary action must from time to time be reviewed "to reflect better understanding of risk as more evidence becomes available."[192] It is the view of the European Commission, finally, that measures based on the precautionary principle "shall be reexamined and if necessary modified depending on the results of scientific research and the follow up of their impact."[193] Thus, not only forethought is needed but also afterthought – both Prometheus *and* Epimetheus.[194]

That monitoring and regular review are called for does not automatically entail that each and every precautionary measure will sooner or later be revoked, nor even that the majority of precautionary measures will be short-lived. Everything depends on the headway made by (scientific) knowledge.[195] In the context of Article 5 of the *SPS Agreement* that was just quoted from, Von Moltke has detected an underlying assumption that science will ultimately provide answers and that therefore uncertainty customarily is a fleeting phenomenon.[196] As discussed above, however, reality tends to be rather more grim than that.[197] Even though uncertainty may indeed be momentary, it is in many cases remarkably persistent and unlikely to disappear in the foreseeable future. The idea of a generally applicable maximum duration for precautionary measures is therefore clearly out of step with reality.[198] Hence the assertion by the European Commission that the provisional nature of precautionary action, including under the *SPS Agreement*, is "not bound up with a time limit but with the development of scientific knowledge."[199] When it is of the ontological or the practically irreducible epistemological kind, uncertainty is irresolvable.[200] Consequently, as the

---

190 See Article 12(2); also Marr, 2003, p. 38.

191 *Convention for the Strengthening of the Inter-American Tropical Tuna Commission*; under Article IV(3) such measures shall be revised "regularly in the light of new scientific information available."

192 UK Government, *A Better Quality of Life: A Strategy for Sustainable Development for the United Kingdom*, May 1999, paragraph 4.2.

193 *Communication COM(2000)1*, p. 21.

194 See Klinke & Renn, 1999, pp. 3-6.

195 *Ibid.*

196 Von Moltke, 1999.

197 See *supra* paragraph 4.1.

198 Also Von Moltke, 1999.

199 *Communication COM(2000)1*, p. 12; also p. 20.

200 See *supra* paragraph 4.1.

commentary to the *IUCN Draft Covenant* rightly affirms, the precautionary principle "may require temporary *or permanent* restrictions."[201]

7.4. Conclusions

Incontestably, the precautionary principle is not an exhaustive algorithm for decision-making in the field of environmental risks.[202] Although a throng of measures, including EIA, moratoriums, safety margins, clean production methods, and research, is closely associated with its implementation, in the majority of cases the principle does not prescribe any specific measures. In fact, the list of international and national measures that may serve to implement it is nearly interminable. The precautionary principle does define leeway, however. When its thresholds of gravity and likelihood are crossed, states are entitled or obliged, as the case may be, to take precautionary action that is effective and proportional and conforms to the given circumstances. For measures to qualify as effective action they must be timely and reflect a dynamic, cautious and comprehensive approach to environmental protection. They should not replace one risk with another risk of equal or greater dimensions. Measures taken under the precautionary principle must be subject to regular review and stay in place as long as the environmental risk in question so requires. The application of these guidelines may in some cases result in the correctness of only one specific course of action, whereas in others it may leave ample room for discretion. On a general note, *'When in doubt, don't!'* turns out not to be a fitting motto to describe what it takes to implement the precautionary principle. *'In dubio pro natura'* does.

In sum – while keeping in mind that the issues of proof and socio-economic factors remain to be discussed in the following chapters – the outcomes of the present chapter concerning the action to be taken by states in the implementation of the precautionary principle confirm what was already concluded in Chapter 5 above and, as a matter of fact, add to it only modestly.[203] Apparently, as far as the precautionary principle in general international law is concerned, things do not get much more specific than what

---

[201] Commentary to Article 7; emphasis added. Tinker, 1995, p. 794 agrees that under the precautionary principle a moratorium, for instance, could "continue indefinitely, until sufficient scientific knowledge developed about the effects of proposed activities or uses."
[202] Wan Ho & Saunders, 2000.
[203] See *supra* paragraphs 5.4 and 5.5.

has just been set out. Fortunately, to know there is no more to know is knowledge too.

There is no such uncertainty as a sure thing.
- Robert Burns (1759-1796)

8. THE PRECAUTIONARY PRINCIPLE AND THE BURDEN OF PROOF

8.1. Precaution and Proof

In situations of uncertainty mistakes are inevitable.[1] In the field of environmental decision-making, it is possible that some time after protective action is taken by public authorities this action turns out to have been unnecessary. It is also possible that in hindsight a decision *not* to take protective action turns out to have been wrong, when environmental effects that were not anticipated do occur. Seldom are both kinds of mistake valued equally. The closely related question of the burden of proof is inevitable in matters of environmental regulation, and certainly in any discussion of the precautionary principle.[2] Who carries the evidentiary burden? Is it either the proponent or the opponent of potentially harmful projects or products? Or, to change the perspective, is it either the proponent or the opponent of environmentally protective action?

The Traditional Model Versus the Precautionary Model

Traditionally, in international law 'clear and convincing evidence' has been required from the state(s) complaining of or wishing to prevent environmental harm supposedly caused by others. In the 1938/1941 *Trail Smelter* case the Arbitral Tribunal placed the burden to meet this high evidential standard on Canada, the victim of air pollution from a US smelter.[3] The burden of proof in this traditional model lies, in principle, with those aiming for environmental protection by opposing possibly harmful activities.[4] It has frequently been suggested that the precautionary principle implies a reversal of this situation, to the effect that the burden is placed on the proponents of development to demonstrate that the activities envisaged

---

[1] Saunders, 2000.

[2] E.g., Bryde, 1993, p. 11; Bosselmann, 1995, p. 431; Cooney, 2000.

[3] *Trail Smelter Arbitral Tribunal Decision (United States v Canada)*, 35 *AJIL*, 1941, pp. 648-736, at p. 716; also Birnie & Boyle, 2002, pp. 115-116; Trouwborst, 2002, p. 19.

[4] Sands, 1995(b), p. 212: "According to traditional approaches the burden of proof currently lies with the person opposing an activity to prove that it does or is likely to cause environmental damage."

by them will (most likely) *not* entail unacceptable environmental consequences.[5]

It may be expedient to compare these two contrary positions regarding the burden of proof in environmental law and policy to the field of scientific research. In principle, two types of erroneous outcome are possible when conducting scientific experiments. For instance, when testing in a laboratory whether chemical substance X has an effect on the reproduction of alga Y, a researcher may conclude there is such an effect when actually there is none. This sort of false positive is generally referred to as a 'Type I error'.[6] Alternatively, the researcher may conclude there is no effect when actually there is one. Such a false negative is called a 'Type II error'. The two error types are not rated equally, however. A long-established principle governing scientific methodology dictates that committing a Type I error is worse than committing a Type II error.[7] It is regarded 'better science' to incorrectly claim there is no effect than to incorrectly claim there is an effect.[8] Scientific experiments incorporate this bias. Stringent standards of experimentation and replication are implemented to minimize the possibility of false positives.[9] The burden of proof, so to speak, is assigned accordingly to the scientist deviating from the null hypothesis. In the above example, that is the hypothesis that there is no effect of substance X on the reproduction of alga Y. A researcher would typically reject such a null hypothesis only when a confidence level of around 95 percent has been reached, clearly reflecting the bias towards avoiding false positives just mentioned – in an unbiased situation a 51 percent confidence level would suffice.[10]

The researcher in this example is looking for 'clear and convincing evidence' before concluding that there is an effect, whereby the link has been made to traditional international environmental law as sketched earlier, with its predominant preference for 'environmental false negatives' over 'false

---

[5] E.g., Christie, 1993, pp. 481-482; O'Riordan & Cameron, 1994, p. 17; Rose & Paleokrassis, 1996, p. 159; Van Dyke, 1996, p. 380; Van Wijmen, 1997, p. 14; Martin, 1997, p. 277; 1998 *Wingspread Statement on the Precautionary Principle*; Molenaar, 1998, p. 34; Jordan & O'Riordan, 1999, p. 24; Barrett & Raffensperger, 1999, p. 109; Geiser, 1999(a), pp. xxiii & 326; Wahlström, 1999, p. 54; Ashford, 1999, p. 203-205; Leroy & Ciliento, 1999, p. 3; Tickner, 1999, pp. 163-164 and 168; Tickner et al., 2000, p. 4; Raffensperger & Tickner, 2000; Miller & Conko, 2000, p. 95; Matthee & Vermersch, 2000, pp. 60 & 66; Jones, 2000; Cooney, 2000; Wan Ho & Saunders, 2000; Saunders, 2000; Pollan, 2001; Hanekamp, 2002, pp. 6 and 9-10; Bell, 2002, p. 3; Marr, 2003, pp. 16-17.

[6] Lemons *et al.*, 1997, p. 227; Raffensperger & Tickner, 1999, p. 3; Barrett & Raffensperger, *ibid.*, p. 112.

[7] Lemons *et al.*, *ibid.*; Raffensperger & Tickner, *ibid.*; Barrett & Raffensperger, *ibid.*; European Environment Agency, 2001, p. 184.

[8] O'Riordan, 2001, p. 102, citing Kirsten Schrader-Frechette.

[9] Barrett & Raffensperger, 1999, p. 112.

[10] Lemons *et al.*, 1997, p. 227.

positives'. This preference and the associated allocation of the onus of proof to the critics of development with possible environmental implications has not only been emblematic in the international arena, but also in domestic public policy and in the business community. One instance is the position that was taken by the US Department of Energy in the debate on a high-level nuclear waste repository in Yucca Mountain, Nevada. While recognizing that significant uncertainties regarding geohydrological conditions at the site persisted, the Department nevertheless maintained that the location should be considered suitable if available information did not indicate its *un*suitability.[11] In a similar vein, four years after a massive die-off of fish in the lower Mississippi that was eventually traced to a factory producing the pesticide endrin, the Shell Chemical Company maintained that "[t]he implication of endrin in the 1963 Mississippi River fish kill has not been verified by recent studies."[12] In 1975 the firm DuPont, first and biggest industrial producer of CFCs, publicly declared its willingness to stop manufacturing certain fluorocarbons if and when "reputable evidence" would show that any such compounds were posing a hazard through depletion of the ozone layer.[13] For ten more years the firm denied the existence of such evidence.[14] By the same token, at the intergovernmental level serious negotiations to deal with the problem did not begin until strong evidence linked ozone layer damage with CFCs and severe depletion had already occurred.[15] Likewise, multilateral action to prevent environmental harm caused by sulphur dioxide emissions has long been taken only on the basis of proof beyond reasonable doubt.[16] A primary rationale of those in favour of such a wait-and-see approach, requiring proof of harmfulness before taking environmentally protective action, is obviously fear of the costs of unnecessary measures.

During the last decades of the previous century the increasing awareness of the unpredictability, severity and potential irreversibility of the environmental effects caused by human activities shed doubt on the soundness of this approach and, as related earlier in this study, gave rise to the ascent of the precautionary principle in (inter)national law and policy.[17] It was realized that what may be sensible practice for scientific experimentation, may not necessarily be sensible practice for public policy in

---

[11] *Ibid.*, p. 223.

[12] Shell Chemical Company, *Aldrin, Dieldrin, Endrin: A Status Report*, 1967; reproduced in Gilbertson, 2001, at p. 128.

[13] *New York Times* of 30 June 1975; cited in Farman, 2001, p. 80.

[14] Farman, *ibid.*

[15] *Ibid.*, p. 82.

[16] Semb, 2001, p. 106.

[17] See *supra* paragraphs 3.1 and 4.1.

the field of environmental protection. Quite the contrary.[18] The need for a precautionary approach to environmental protection was recognized, entailing minimization of Type II, not Type I errors.[19] From this perspective, the vulnerability and unpredictability of natural ecosystems indicate that it is preferable for governments to wrongly act on the premise that a certain activity *will* cause unacceptable harm and accordingly restrict or outlaw the activity, instead of wrongly acting on the premise that the activity will *not* cause such harm and permit it. *In dubio pro natura* implies a bias towards avoiding environmental false negatives, in the sense that it is better to err by taking excessively protective action than to err by taking too little action.[20] Hence the common claim, referred to above, that under the precautionary principle the burden of proof rests with the initiators of potentially harmful activities. It is for them to demonstrate the (relative) harmlessness of their projects in order to get them authorized and not, as in the traditional model, for the opponents of projects to demonstrate harmfulness to get the activities restricted.[21] Put simply, in the traditional model of environmental decision-making there is a green light for activities with a possible environmental impact, which is only switched to red when there is convincing evidence of harm*ful*ness. Conversely, in a purely precautionary model there is a red light which is only switched to green when there is convincing evidence of harm*less*ness. The reasons behind both models are evident. Whereas proponents of the traditional approach stress the (mainly economic) costs of erroneously taken environmental measures, proponents of a precautionary approach stress the (mainly ecological) costs of erroneous *lack* of environmental measures.

The story of the Californian sardine fishery in the previous century clearly illustrates the different possible approaches and the respective philosophies behind them. In the mid-1920s, at a time when no catch limitations were in force, Californian state scientists involved in overseeing the ever intensifying sardine fishery argued that any additional fishing effort "should be avoided until research has shown that it is possible to detect

---

[18] European Environment Agency, 2001, p. 184; Raffensperger & Tickner, 1999, p. 3; Barrett & Raffensperger, 1999, p. 112.

[19] European Environment Agency, *ibid.*; Barrett & Raffensperger, *ibid.*, p. 109.

[20] Barrett & Raffensperger, *ibid.*, p. 117; Beeckman, 1996, p. 491.

[21] Botanist Hugh Iltis has defended this position strongly: "I have no patience with the phony requests of developers, economists, and humanitarians who want us biologists to 'prove' with hard evidence, right here and now, the 'value' of biodiversity and the 'harm' of tropical deforestation. Rather, it should be for them, the sponsors of reckless destruction, to prove to the world that a plant or animal species, or an exotic ecosystem, is *not* useful and *not* ecologically significant before being permitted by society to destroy it." Iltis, 1988, pp. 102-103.

overfishing in time."[22] In other words, in their view expansion of the fisheries ought to be made contingent on the availability of evidence demonstrating that overexploitation can be prevented.[23] A precautionary allocation of the burden of proof. Meanwhile, catches no longer increased in proportion to increases in fishing activity. Fishermen had to sail further and fish longer every time for the same harvest; and the average age of caught sardines was dropping. Under the circumstances the State Fisheries Laboratory recommended that catch restrictions be put in place until it would be known what level of fisheries would be sustainable.[24] The federal United States Bureau of Fisheries, however, had a different interpretation of the available information and a different perspective on how to allocate the onus of proof. As MacGarvin describes this federal view and the rest of the story:

> While acknowledging that the evidence of depletion was strong, there was 'no clear-cut or convincing evidence that will satisfy everyone' that the sardines were overexploited. Its view was 'to us conservation means wise use. We do not believe in hoarding our fisheries resources'. Rather, 'We believe very firmly that restrictions that are unnecessary hamper or restrict legitimate business enterprise' [..]. The fishers were divided. [..] The dispute rumbled on unresolved until, in 1939, the new Californian Governor replaced the state experts with 'emergency' appointees, and the tone of the reports changed from 'unmistakable' signs of depletion and an 'imperative' need to reduce the catches (1938) to 'no reason to be concerned' (1942). It was then agreed to increase the catch (to 'assist the war effort'), but in that year the sardine stock collapsed. It only began to show signs of a recovery in the mid-1980s.[25]

The approach leading to the sardine stock collapse contrasts starkly with the position currently taken by, among others, Greenpeace and Unilever, who broadly agree that the precautionary principle "shifts the burden of proof onto those that seek to exploit marine ecosystems and onto those institutions responsible for fisheries management, to demonstrate that there will be minimal risk of serious or irreversible harm."[26]

The way the burden of proof is allocated under a precautionary approach to environmental protection can, apart from science, be usefully

---

[22] Quoted in MacGarvin, 2001(b), p. 19.
[23] MacGarvin, *ibid.*
[24] *Ibid.*, pp. 19-20.
[25] *Ibid.*, p. 20 (notes omitted).
[26] Unilever, 1996, p. 5, paragraph 20. They furthermore agree, among other things, that "[n]o fisheries shall be established or expanded in the absence of reliable estimates of the minimum size of the target species biomass. Where scientific data or other reliable forms of information are inadequate to determine the likely impact of fishing on the populations and ecosystem of which they are a part, fishing effort should be restricted to an extremely low percentage of the lowest estimate of the unfished biomass, pending proper analysis." *Ibid.*, paragraph 23.

compared to the burden of proof in criminal law.[27] Just as in environmental decision-making there may be discrepancies between the effects an activity is *assumed* to have and the effects an activity actually *has*, in criminal procedures there is an important difference between a suspect *being* guilty or innocent on the one hand and being *found* guilty or innocent in trial on the other. False negatives and false positives can and do occur in criminal procedures as much as in environmental decision-making. In case a suspect has in fact committed the crime he or she is charged with but is judged not guilty, a crime is left unpunished and a criminal goes free. In case the suspect is innocent but is nonetheless convicted, an innocent person's life is wrecked or, in the worst scenario, taken. In neither of both cases justice is done, but most societies consider the second outcome so much worse than the first that the majority of legal systems incorporate the fundamental rule that every defendant is assumed innocent until proven guilty. The idea behind this rule is captured in the saying that it is better that a hundred guilty men should go free than that one innocent man be convicted.[28] A heavy burden of proof is accordingly assigned to the prosecutor, not to the defendant. As movie watchers around the world know, in the United States a jury must be convinced 'beyond reasonable doubt' before it can legitimately pronounce a 'guilty' verdict; it is not sufficient that it is considered 'more likely than not' that the defendant committed the crime.[29] Parallel to this assumption of innocence in criminal law runs the assumption of harmfulness in the precautionary model described above. Activities with a potential environmental impact are considered harmful until proven otherwise, for the plain reason that severe and/or permanent damage to ecosystems is considered a much worse outcome than, for instance, a foregone business opportunity.

The comparison with criminal law highlights an additional argument that has been forwarded in favour of a precautionary allocation of the burden of proof in environmental decision-making. The more substantive resources and expertise that are generally available to the state as compared with the defendant constitute an added reason why prosecution and defense are not equal in the courtroom. Likewise, it has been submitted that with regard to plans with possible environmental implications the onus of proof should be on the party which is in the best position to produce relevant evidence.[30] This is almost invariably the proposing party, which has been planning and preparing for the activity, product or technology in question.

---

[27] See Saunders, 2000; Wan Ho & Saunders, 2000.

[28] Saunders, *ibid.*

[29] *Ibid.*; Wan Ho & Saunders, 2000.

[30] Weintraub, 1992/1996, pp. 22-23; Lemons *et al.*, 1997, p. 230; Tickner *et al.*, 2000, p. 4.

From this perspective it would indeed appear reasonable that a chemical plant, project developer or logging company should bear the evidentiary burden regarding the possible environmental impacts of their plans. For they are normally in a better position and have greater resources to acquire information concerning these impacts than local residents, NGOs, or indigenous peoples that are critical of the planned activities.[31] Moreover, the argument that it is the proponents which ought to be expected to yield evidence showing that a planned activity is environmentally benign because they generally stand more to gain from the activity than society at large, undeniably has a logical appeal.[32] It should be noted that it is possible for public authorities to be in the proposing as much as in the opposing camp. In interstate relations this dual possibility is even more apparent. One time it may be State A which is planning an activity with potentially adverse consequences for the environment of State B, while the next time it may perfectly well be State A which is objecting to a similar activity undertaken by State B. This does not change the fact that in each instance it is routinely the proposing party which is best equipped to produce pertinent data. France, for instance, was naturally in possession of most of the available information concerning the environmental impact of the nuclear tests it carried out in the Pacific, tests which were complained of by New Zealand and brought under the scrutiny of the International Court of Justice in the 1995 *Nuclear Tests* case.[33] As Judge Weeramantry submitted in this regard:

> Where a party complains to the Court of possible environmental damage of an irreversible nature which another party is committing or threatening to commit, the proof or disproof of the matter alleged may present difficulty to the claimant as the necessary information may largely be in the hands of the party causing or threatening the damage. The law cannot function in protection of the environment unless a legal principle is evolved to meet this evidentiary difficulty, and environmental law has responded with what has come to be described as the precautionary principle [..].[34]

Surely it is difficult to deny that requiring proponents of potentially harmful activities to prove that their plans are environmentally innocent as a

---

31 Hattis & Anderson, 1999, p. 99. As Lemons *et al.*, *ibid.*, phrase the argument: "natural resources typically need more risk protection than do promoters of development or human activities because the advocates for protection usually have fewer financial and scientific resources than developers or promoters of activities that potentially can harm the resources."

32 Lemons *et al.*, *ibid.*

33 Order of the ICJ of 22 September 1995 concerning the *Request for an Examination of the Situation in Accordance with Paragraph 63 of the Court's Judgment of 20 December 1974 in the* Nuclear Tests (New Zealand v France) *Case*, in: *ICJ Rep.*, 1995, p. 288.

34 Dissenting Opinion of Judge Weeramantry, appended to the ICJ's Order, *ibid.*, pp. 317-362, at p. 342.

necessary condition for approval, is quite a precautionary way to go about environmental regulation. It comes down to a ban of possibly harmful activities until proof of environmental safety is delivered. This precautionary model with its assumption of 'harmful until proven harmless' has been open to frequent criticism. It is noteworthy, however, that almost without exception this criticism is directed at the strictest version of the model, under which *absolute* proof of *absolute* harmlessness is demanded. The unworkability of such a demand, alluded to earlier on in this study,[35] has been drawn attention to by many writers.[36] According to one author, requiring conclusive proof of no harm from activity proponents would be to treat them like gods in that omniscience, omnipotence, omnipresence and transcendence are expected on their part:

> Omniscience is required to be able to map reality completely unto some simulation device, creating in essence a parallel, twin world. Omnipotence is necessary to create this twin world and to perform an infinite number of experiments on it. Omnipresence is mandatory to be able to assess all aspects of the experiment. Finally, transcendence appears crucial to ensure that entrepreneurs have the ability to extract themselves and their actions from the world upon which they perform the experiments. Clearly, the demands exceed the capacities of mere mortals. It is also logically impossible to satisfy all demands at once.[37]

'No evidence of harm' is about as far as any type of human scrutiny, including empirical science, can go; 'evidence of no harm' cannot realistically be achieved.[38] 'Trial without error' is a utopian perspective.[39] No new technology, including the most innocent, could ever be established if absolute proof of absolute harmlessness would be required up front.[40] Had this requirement always been persistently applied, then humanity would still be in the Stone Age,[41] whereas its implementation today would mean the end of current civilizations.[42] If applied to new activities only this strictest of precautionary models would bring the economy to a standstill by blocking the road to innovation and growth;[43] if consistently applied to all activities,

---

[35] See *supra* paragraphs 4.2 and 4.3.

[36] Iltis, 1988, p. 103; Martin, 1997, p. 277; Wildavsky, 2000, p. 24; Morris, 2000(a); Morris, 2000(b), p. 13; Foster *et al.*, 2000; Cooney, 2000; Blanchfield, 2000; Pieterman & Hanekamp, 2002, pp. vi, 7, 11-13, 16 and 21; Hanekamp, 2002, pp. 10-11; De Sadeleer, 2002, pp. 206-207.

[37] Martin, *ibid.*; see also Hanekamp, *ibid.*, p. 10; Pieterman & Hanekamp, *ibid.*, p. 16.

[38] Pieterman & Hanekamp, *ibid.*, p. 11.

[39] *Ibid.*, p. 13.

[40] Foster *et al.*, 2000; Wildavsky, 2000, p. 24.

[41] Blanchfield, 2000.

[42] Morris, 2000(a).

[43] Pieterman & Hanekamp, 2002, p. 7.

both new and existing, it would shut down the economy as a whole by banning each and every activity. Indeed, it has been submitted that when applied fully and logically, such a rigid precautionary model would cannibalize itself and obliterate all environmental regulation.[44] After all, it cannot be proven to a certainty that the outcome of environmental measures will not be counterproductive itself.[45]

Having studied the precautionary model with its assumption of harmfulness and associated designation of the burden of proof, as well as its rationale and its criticism, it is time to find out how this *model* relates to the precautionary *principle* in public international law. It is time to ask whether the precautionary allocation of the burden of proof, whereby it is for proponents to deliver evidence of the (relative) harmlessness of the activities they wish to carry out, is in fact part of the precautionary principle as a matter of law, as claimed by Judge Weeramantry in the opinion quoted above and as held by many legal scholars. The questions to be addressed to this end are as follows. First, do states in practice apply precautionary burden of proof constructions as just described? Second, if so, do they consider this to be a necessary corollary of the precautionary principle. Third, what level of proof is required from proponents? To find the answer(s), the following paragraph will examine relevant state practice.

8.2. The Burden of Proof in Practice

The Precautionary Burden of Proof in State Practice and Jurisprudence at the International Level

The 1982 *World Charter for Nature* is an example of an instrument of worldwide scope and covering nature in its entirety, in which a precautionary allocation of the burden of proof is called for. After stipulating that activities likely to cause irreversible harm shall be avoided altogether, the Charter details that activities which are likely to pose a significant risk to nature shall be preceded by a thorough investigation of their potential impact; that "their proponents shall demonstrate that expected benefits outweigh potential damage to nature;" and that "where potential adverse effects are *not fully understood*, the activities should not proceed."[46] This provision, besides bringing the benefits of activities into the equation, comes close to the rigid construction discussed above under which the approval of

---

[44] F.B. Cross, "Paradoxical Perils of the Precautionary Principle", in: 53 *Washington and Lee Law Review*, 1996, pp. 851-925, quoted in Pieterman & Hanekamp, *ibid.*, at p. 12. Also Hanekamp, 2002, p. 11.

[45] *Ibid.*

[46] Principle 11(b); emphasis added.

an activity hinges on the availability of *conclusive* information regarding its possible effects on the natural environment. It is different from that construction in that it applies only to "activities which are likely to pose a significant risk", and not to all activities.

Apart from this general postulation, a precautionary approach to the burden of proof has been repeatedly adopted by states in specific contexts. The Antarctic environment is one of these. The 1988 *Convention on the Regulation of Antarctic Mineral Resource Activities* (*CRAMRA*), to begin with, imposed a heavy burden upon entities intending to engage in mining operations in the Antarctic.[47] Under the regime envisaged in the Convention such activities are outlawed until it can be judged, according to the results of an obligatory EIA, that they will not cause harm to the Antarctic environment or dependent and associated ecosystems and not cause significant adverse effects on global or regional climate or weather patterns, *and* only insofar as safe technologies and procedures and environmental monitoring capacity are available.[48] An obviously precautionary approach, that is.[49] With the adoption of the 1991 *Antarctic Protocol*,[50] which effectively superseded the *CRAMRA*, an unconditional, fifty-year moratorium on mineral resource activities was secured,[51] amounting to an even stricter application of the precautionary assumption of harmfulness.[52] For activities not related to mining the Protocol prescribes the performance of an "Initial" or "Comprehensive Environmental Evaluation", depending on the gravity of potential impacts.[53] Only if a certain (non-mineral resource) activity is "determined as having less than a minor or transitory impact, the activity may proceed forthwith."[54] The onus is thus placed on the initiator of the activity to prove that its environmental impact would be less than minor or transitory.[55]

As for Antarctic fisheries, within the framework of the *CCAMLR* a regulatory system has taken shape in the course of the 1990s to restrain harvesting as much as is necessary to guarantee that the development of fisheries does not outpace the development of the information needed to ensure that harvesting is conducted in conformity with the ecosystem conservation

---

[47] Gray, 2000, p. 115.
[48] Article 4(1)-(4).
[49] The same conclusion was drawn by Philippe Sands, 1995(a), at p. 525; and by Birnie & Boyle, 1992, p. 98.
[50] *Protocol on Environmental Protection* to the 1959 *Antarctic Treaty*.
[51] Articles 7 and 25.
[52] Bosselmann, 1995, p. 431.
[53] See Article 8 and Annex I of the Protocol.
[54] Article 1(2) of Annex I.
[55] Gray, 2000, pp. 116-117.

principles of the Convention.[56] The system occasions that the *CCAMLR* area is closed to new fisheries save when a particular procedure is observed aimed at the development of suitable conservation and management measures in advance, so as not to allow any harvesting before it is reasonably clear that this harvesting can and will be ecologically responsible.[57] This precautionary allocation of the burden of proof presently applies not only to new fisheries but also to existing fisheries for which there are insufficient data to estimate potential sustainable yield and the impacts on the wider ecosystem.[58]

The similarly conservation-biased system of the presently inoperative *International Convention for High Seas Fisheries of the North Pacific Ocean*, concluded by Canada, Japan and the US in 1952, was underpinned by the so-called 'abstention principle'.[59] It was the crux of this principle that one or two of the parties would abstain from exploiting stocks of designated species whenever and for as long as the Convention's fisheries commission was unable to determine, on the basis of scientific evidence, that fishing would be sustainable. The burden of proof thus weighed upon the party wishing to enter the fishery.[60] Under a more recent high seas fisheries treaty, the 1994 *Bering Sea Pollock Convention*, fishing for Aleutian Basin pollock is expressly forbidden unless it has been ascertained that the total biomass of the stock exceeds a fixed threshold level.[61]

The UN General Assembly, to stay within the domain of marine living resources, adopted a global moratorium on large-scale pelagic driftnet fishing by consensus in 1989.[62] It was agreed that this moratorium would apply universally, except where states can demonstrate that measures have been taken, based on "statistically sound analysis", which effectively guarantee that driftnet fishing under the jurisdiction of these states does not cause an "unacceptable impact" and ensure the conservation of marine

---

[56] E.g., 1991 *Conservation Measure 31/X* and 1993 *Conservation Measure 65/XII*. See Parkes, 2000, pp. 86-90; Orrega Vicuña, 1999, p. 159; Kimball, 2001, p. 29; Trouwborst, 2002, p. 92.

[57] Orrega Vicuña, *ibid.* According to the first operative paragraph of *Conservation Measure 65/XII on Exploratory Fisheries* of 1993, restraints for exploratory fisheries apply "until sufficient information is available: (a) to evaluate the distribution, abundance, and demography of the target species, leading to an estimate of the fishery's potential yield, (b) to review the fishery's potential impacts on dependent and related species, and (c) to allow the Scientific Committee to formulate and provide advice to the Commission on appropriate harvest catch levels, as well as effort levels and fishing gear, where appropriate."

[58] Kimball, 2001, p. 29; Orrega Vicuña, *ibid.*

[59] The Convention was dissolved when the *Convention for the Conservation of Anadromous Stocks in the North Pacific* entered into force on 16 February 1993. On the abstention principle generally see Van der Molen, 1959.

[60] See further Koers, 1973, pp. 97-100; Freestone, 1999, pp. 149-150; Tsuru, 2004, *passim.*

[61] See Freestone, *ibid.*, pp. 151-153; Birnie & Boyle, 2002, p. 676.

[62] *Resolution 44/225 on Large-Scale Pelagic Driftnet Fishing and its Impact on the Living Marine Resources of the World's Oceans and Seas* of 22 December 1989.

ecosystems.[63] The burden of proof was thus placed on states wishing not to comply with the moratorium, the assumption being that driftnet fishing is environmentally unacceptable so long as sound evidence indicating otherwise is absent.[64] Several members of the international community subsequently reviewed the available scientific information and failed to conclude that large-scale pelagic driftnet fishing had no detrimental impact on marine life, instead confirming initial grounds for concern and leading the General Assembly to note in 1991 that "evidence has not demonstrated that the impact can be fully prevented."[65] The worldwide moratorium was reaffirmed accordingly.[66]

Another characteristic case of a precautionary moratorium and associated burden of proof is the regime that is presently in force under the 1946 *International Convention for the Regulation of Whaling*. The rules that ban commercial whaling, adopted by the International Whaling Commission in 1982, and the much debated 1994 *Revised Management Procedure* exact that extreme caution must be applied when the ban is ever to be lifted and that the onus of proof in this regard lies with the states advocating a resumption of the commercial exploitation of whales.[67] Before 1982 whaling nations demanded sound evidence that whales were in danger, whereas after 1982 sound evidence is required from them to prove that whaling is safe again.[68] At the opening of the 44th Meeting of the IWC in Glasgow in 1992 the representative of the United Kingdom stressed this point by stating that "the burden of proof for lifting the moratorium [..] must rest with those who say they want to continue to exploit [whale stocks]."[69]

During the negotiations for the 1995 *Straddling Stocks Agreement* the sixteen member states of the Forum Fisheries Agency[70] had proposed placing

---

[63] Paragraph 4(a) reads: "Moratoria should be imposed on all large-scale pelagic driftnet fishing by 30 June 1992, with the understanding that such a measure will not be imposed in a region or, if implemented, can be lifted, should effective conservation and management measures be taken based upon statistically sound analysis to be jointly made by concerned parties of the international community with an interest in the fishery resources of the region, to prevent unacceptable impact of such fishing practices on that region and to ensure the conservation of the living marine resources of that region."

[64] Burke, 1990, p. 276; Freestone & Hey, 1996(b), p. 261; Freestone & Makuch, 1996, pp. 17-18; Nollkaemper, 1996, p. 86; Birnie & Boyle, 2002, p. 676; Trouwborst, 2002, pp. 153-154.

[65] Preambular paragraphs 13 and 14 of *Resolution 46/215 on Large-Scale Pelagic Driftnet Fishing and its Impact on the Living Marine Resources of the World's Oceans and Seas* of 20 December 1991.

[66] See preambular paragraph 15 and operative paragraphs 1, 3 and 4.

[67] Lyster, 1985, p. 19; Bosselmann, 1995, p. 431; Rose & Paleokrassis, 1996, p. 159; Nollkaemper, 1996, p. 86, note 64; McIntyre & Mosedale, 1997, pp. 227 and 239; Birnie & Boyle, 2002, pp. 118 and 676.

[68] Nollkaemper, *ibid.*

[69] UK opening statement by John Gumner, as quoted in Rose & Paleokrassis, 1996, p. 159.

[70] Australia, New Zealand, Papua New Guinea and thirteen other South Pacific nations.

the burden of proving the ecological soundness of any fishing effort on the state(s) fishing for the stock in question, as a precautionary measure.[71] In the final result this was not done explicitly, although it has been argued that the Agreement is an example where "the precautionary principle has been applied so as to oblige those wishing to utilise a resource to provide evidence of the sustainability of that use."[72] After all, catch levels are to vary along with the reliability of available information and therefore states wishing to harvest a stock must, in order to sustain or amplify the volume of their quotas, conduct monitoring and scientific research.[73] A comparably subtle position has been taken in the *Technical Guidelines for Responsible Fisheries* issued by the FAO in 1996.[74] According to these Guidelines, implementation of Principle 15 of the *Rio Declaration* requires an "appropriate placement of the burden of proof."[75] In the fisheries context this is taken to mean, among other things, that all fishing activities must be made subject to prior authorization;[76] that all possible undesirable effects must be identified in advance;[77] and that priority must be given to resource conservation when the impacts of fishing are uncertain.[78] With regard to the onus of proof the Guidelines furthermore consider, on the one hand, that all fishing activities have environmental effects and that "it is not appropriate to assume that these are negligible until proved otherwise;"[79] whereas on the other hand they expound that:

> although the precautionary approach to fisheries may require cessation of fishing activities that have potentially serious adverse impacts, it does not imply that no fishing can take place until all potential impacts have been assessed and found to be negligible.[80]

States proposing to ease the level of protection of animal and plant species under *CITES* meet with a more straightforward burden. As a result of the application of the precautionary principle to the procedure for amendment of the Convention's appendices, it is for a state proposing the down-listing of a species to provide evidence that it is safe to do so.[81] Many

---

[71] See Orrega Vicuña, 1999, p. 161.
[72] McIntyre & Mosedale, 1997, p. 239.
[73] *Ibid.*, in note 109.
[74] *FAO Technical Guidelines for Responsible Fisheries*, No. 2, Rome 1996.
[75] *Ibid.*, paragraphs 5 and 6; especially 6(h).
[76] Paragraphs 6(f) and 7(c).
[77] Paragraph 6(b).
[78] Paragraph 6(d).
[79] Paragraph 7(a).
[80] Paragraph 7(b).
[81] See paragraph 2 and Annex 4 of the 1994 *Resolution Conf. 9.24 on Criteria for Amendment of Appendices I and II.*; McIntyre & Mosedale, 1997, p. 239.

states claim, for instance, that the precautionary principle requires that trade in elephant products must be curtailed for as long as the impact of trade on elephant populations is not known to a sufficient degree.[82] The 2002 *Guiding Principles on Invasive Alien Species* present another relevant instance. The instrument provides that decisions concerning intentional introductions within a country of potentially invasive alien species are to be based on the precautionary principle.[83] In particular, no such introduction is to take place without prior authorization from the competent authorities, based on an appropriate assessment of the environmental risks presented by the introduction, whereby only those species may be admitted that are unlikely to threaten biological diversity.[84] The burden of proving that this is the case must, in principle, be allotted to the proponent of the introduction.[85]

More examples can be found in the context of marine pollution. A majority of the contracting parties to the *London Dumping Convention* supported a resolution in 1983 to voluntarily suspend the dumping of all radioactive wastes, complementing the ban on the dumping of high-level radioactive wastes that had been in force since 1975, until the results of an independent study of the impact of such disposal on the marine environment would be available.[86] Although according to the outcome of this study any effects were likely to be insignificant, the 9th meeting of the parties in 1985 decided to prolong the precautionary moratorium so as to allow for yet more research.[87] The provisional ban was kept in place during the years that followed and, after the precautionary principle had been explicitly endorsed by the *LDC* parties in 1991,[88] was converted into a definitive and binding prohibition on the disposal of all radioactive wastes at sea in 1993.[89] Guidelines on the dumping of wastes generally that were adopted under the Convention in 1997 set out that "if a waste is so poorly characterized that proper assessment cannot be made of its potential impacts on human health and the environment, that waste shall not be dumped."[90]

Returning to nuclear wastes, a general rule to govern the introduction of radioactive substances into the oceans has been incorporated

---

[82] Mohamed-Katerere, 2001, p. 8.
[83] Guiding Principle 10(2).
[84] Guiding Principle 10(1).
[85] *Ibid.*
[86] *Resolution LDC 14/7*, adopted at the 7th meeting of the parties.
[87] *Resolution LDC 21/9.*
[88] *Resolution LDC 44/14.*
[89] *Resolution LDC 51/16.* On the links between the development of this moratorium, the burden of proof and the precautionary principle, see also Bosselmann, 1995, p. 431; Birnie & Boyle, 2002, p. 118.
[90] Annex 2 of the 1997 *Guidelines for the Assessment of Wastes and Other Matter that may be Considered for Dumping*, LC 19/10, IMO, as reproduced in Santillo *et al.*, 1999, p. 43.

in two influential, albeit non-legally binding, global programs of action, namely *Agenda 21* and the 1995 *Land-Based Activities Action Programme*. In obedience to this rule, states should:

> Not promote or allow the storage or disposal of high-level, intermediate-level and low-level radioactive wastes near the marine [and coastal] environment unless they determine that scientific evidence, consistent with the [applicable] internationally agreed principles and guidelines, shows that such storage or disposal poses no unacceptable risk to people and the marine [and coastal] environment or does not interfere with other legitimate uses of the sea, making, in the process of consideration, appropriate use of the concept of the precautionary approach.[91]

The 1992 *OSPAR Convention* ordains that states parties wanting to preserve the possibility of disposing of certain (non-high-level) nuclear wastes at sea must present the OSPAR Commission with, *inter alia*, "the results of scientific studies which show that any potential dumping operations would not result in hazards to human health, harm to living resources or marine ecosystems."[92] This provision has been viewed as a typical instance of a burden of proof structure inspired by the precautionary principle.[93] The same is true of the so-called Prior Justification Procedure that was put in place by the Oslo Commission (OSCOM), one of the OSPAR Commission's predecessors, in 1989.[94] Under this procedure it is for any state wishing to dump industrial waste to prove to the Commission "both that there are no practical alternatives on land and that the materials cause no harm in the marine environment."[95]

Successive reports by the Canada-US International Joint Commission (IJC) on the environment of the Great Lakes also advocate employing a precautionary onus of proof as an essential ingredient of a policy to virtually eliminate persistent, toxic substances. Concretely, so the *Fifth Biennial Report on Great Lakes Water Quality* of 1990 states, when approval is sought for the production, use or discharge of a substance that may enter the Great Lakes ecosystem, "the applicant must prove, as a general rule, that

---

[91] Paragraph 22.5(c) of *Agenda 21* and paragraph 111(a) of the *Land-Based Activities Action Programme*. The bracketed words are contained only in the latter.

[92] Annex II, Article 3(3)(c), at 17; see Sands, 1994; Sands, 1995(b), p. 212; Birnie & Boyle, 2002, p. 118.

[93] Sands, *ibid.*; Birnie & Boyle, *ibid.*

[94] *Decision 89/1 on the Reduction and Cessation of Dumping Industrial Wastes at Sea* of 14 June 1989, adopted within the framework of the now defunct 1972 *Convention for the Prevention of Marine Pollution by Dumping from Ships and Aircraft (Oslo Convention)*.

[95] *Ibid.*; see Bosselmann, 1995, p. 431; Freestone has labelled this a "most rigorous application of the precautionary principle": Freestone, D., "The Precautionary Principle", in: Churchill, R. & Freestone, D. (eds.), *International Law and Global Climate Change*, London 1991, 21, p. 25, quoted in McIntyre & Mosedale, 1997, at p. 225.

the substance is not harmful to the environment."[96] The 1992 *Sixth Biennial Report* emphasizes that when "taking a precautionary approach, there can be no defensible alternative" to halting the input of suspicious chemicals and shifting the burden of proof to the proponent of the substance "to show that it does not or will not cause the suspected harm, nor meet the definition of a persistent toxic substance."[97] The parameters of the desired approach are portrayed in more detail in the 1994 *Seventh Biennial Report*, where it is explained that as part of a precautionary strategy it is:

> generally agreed, in principle, that the burden of proof concerning the 'safety' of chemicals should lie with the proponent for the manufacture, import or use of at least substances new to commerce in Canada and the United States, rather than with society as a whole to provide absolute proof of adverse impacts. [..] This principle should in the Commission's view, be adopted for all human-made chemicals shown or reasonably suspected to be persistent and toxic, including those already manufactured or otherwise in commerce. The onus should be on the producers and users of any suspected persistent toxic substance to prove that it is, in fact, both 'safe' and necessary, even if it is already in commerce."[98]

A similar assumption of harmfulness is inherent in the way persistent, toxic and bioaccumulative substances are treated in the various *North Sea Declarations*.[99] Emissions of *all* such substances are to be restricted or avoided, without any need for proof of harmfulness of individual substances.[100]

Already in the applications submitted to the International Court of Justice by Australia and New Zealand in the 1973-74 *Nuclear Tests Cases* versus France, which at that time did not mention the precautionary principle, it had been insisted that under public international law states planning to carry out activities with possibly adverse effects on the environment bear the burden of proving the harmlessness of those activities.[101] When a new series of French tests prompted attempts to reopen proceedings more than twenty years later, the proof issue surfaced once again.[102] In this 1995 *Nuclear Tests* case New Zealand argued before the ICJ

---

[96] International Joint Commission, *Fifth Biennial Report on Great Lakes Water Quality*, 1990; as reproduced in Durnil, 1999, at p. 269.

[97] International Joint Commission, *Sixth Biennial Report on Great Lakes Water Quality*, 1992; as reproduced in Tickner, 1999, at pp. 179-180.

[98] International Joint Commission, *Seventh Biennial Report on Great Lakes Water Quality*, 1994; as cited in Durnil, 1999, pp. 273-274.

[99] Bodansky, 1991(a), p. 416.

[100] See, e.g., paragraph XVI of the 1987 *Second North Sea Declaration* and the preamble of the 1990 *Third North Sea Declaration*.

[101] *ICJ Pleadings, Oral Arguments, Documents: Nuclear Tests Cases*, Vol. I (Australia v France), p. 43; see also Juste Ruiz, 1999, p. 93; Trouwborst, 2002, p. 158.

[102] See Trouwborst, *ibid.*, pp. 158-200.

that the precautionary principle occasioned that "the burden is placed upon the party seeking to carry out the conduct that could give rise to environmental damage to prove that conduct will not lead to such a result."[103] In the circumstances of the case, this meant that:

> France's conduct is illegal in that it causes, or is likely to cause, the introduction into the marine environment of radioactive material, France being under an obligation, before carrying out its new underground nuclear tests, to provide evidence that they will not result in the introduction of such material to the environment, in accordance with the 'precautionary principle' very widely accepted in contemporary international law.[104]

France rejected this argument.[105] As it did not deal with the merits of the case, the Court did not address it.

In the 1996 *NIREX* case Ireland alleged that the precautionary principle had shifted the onus of proof, so that it was for the proponents of the projected British nuclear waste storage plant to prove the absence of risk, rather than for its opponents to demonstrate risk.[106] On this view of the matter, it had been sufficient for the Irish government to point out the "mere possibility of adverse consequences to Ireland."[107] Since this requirement had been complied with, it had been for the applicant company, and ultimately the UK Government, to show that no contamination of the marine environment would result from the project; something which, Ireland argued, both had failed to do.[108] Authorization of the project was eventually withheld because of the potential risk of harm to the Irish Sea by accidental discharges and inadequacies in the performed EIA. In reaching its decision the British Government had been "accutely aware", according to the Secretary of State for the Environment, of its "obligations to other States which are set out in international obligations in respect of the sea and the environment more generally."[109]

Ireland's reasoning has been similar in the MOX plant proceedings before various international tribunals in recent years. When arguing for provisional measures at the ITLOS in 2001 it held that the precautionary principle "places the burden on the United Kingdom to demonstrate that no

---

[103] Paragraph 105 of the ICJ's Order.

[104] Paragraph 5 of the Order.

[105] CR/95/20, p. 78.

[106] Paragraphs 96-100 of the *Irish Statement*; see McIntyre & Mosedale, 1997, pp. 233-234.

[107] *Ibid.*

[108] Paragraph 6 of the Conclusions of the *Irish Statement*; see McIntyre & Mosedale, *ibid.*, p. 234.

[109] Decision of March 1997. John Gumner MP, as quoted in the *Verbatim Record* of the ITLOS *Mox Plant* sitting on 19 November 2001, p. 11 (O'Hagan for Ireland).

harm will arise from discharges and other consequences of the operation of the MOX plant, should it proceed," while serious doubt was expressed whether the UK could indeed so demonstrate.[110] As discussed before, the UK was of a different view, submitting that the burden was on Ireland and that "nothing" had been adduced by way of evidence.[111] In the 2003 *Mox Plant OSPAR Arbitration* a majority of two arbitrators was unwilling to apply the precautionary principle and allotted the onus of proof to Ireland,[112] much to the dismay of third arbitrator Griffith.[113] The proceedings in the *MOX Plant 'Annex VII' Arbitration* are still pending.[114]

Malaysia, finally, in the 2003 *Land Reclamation* proceedings before the ITLOS, submitted that with regard to the precautionary principle:

> the Tribunal should not reject the widely-held view that it is for the State that proposes action that may detrimentally affect the environment to show, not to itself, but to those that may be affected by it, that there is no real likelihood of harm to the environment. And by Singapore's own admission, it has not done this.[115]

This interpretation was contested by Singapore.[116] The Tribunal considered that it could "not be excluded that, in the particular circumstances of this case, the land reclamation works may have adverse effects on the marine environment" and directed Singapore "not to conduct its land reclamation in ways that might cause [..] serious harm."[117] The latter injunction is being implemented through a set of mitigation measures agreed on by the parties in 2005.[118]

The practice of the European Union offers ample instances of precautionary evidentiary designs. One of these is a 1967 Directive prohibiting the introduction of new substances, such as pesticides, on the market unless they have been proven 'safe'.[119] This means, as the European Commission puts it, that "it is up to the business community to carry out the scientific work

---

[110] *Verbatim Record* of the sitting on 19 November 2001, p. 13 (O'Hagan for Ireland).

[111] *Verbatim Record* of the sitting on 20 November 2001, p. 17 (Bethlehem for UK); see also *supra* paragraph 4.3.

[112] Reisman and Mustill; see the Final Award of 2 July 2003 in the *Dispute Concerning Access to Information under Article 9 of the OSPAR Convention*, at http://www.pca-cpa.org.

[113] See the discussion of his Dissenting Opinion below.

[114] See http://www.pca-pca.org.

[115] *Verbatim Record* of 27 September 2003, p. 22 (Lauterpacht for Malaysia).

[116] *Ibid.*, pp. 31-32 (Reisman for Singapore).

[117] Paragraphs 96 and 106(2) of the Order of 8 October 2003.

[118] *Settlement Agreement* of 26 April 2005, endorsed by the 'Annex VII' Arbitral Tribunal in its *Award on Agreed Terms* of 1 September 2005; see http://www.pca-cpa.org.

[119] See Article 7 of *Directive 67/548 on the Approximation of the Laws, Regulations, and Administrative Provisions of the Member States Relating to the Classification, Packaging, and Labelling of Dangerous Substances*, *OJ*, 1967, L 196, p. 1, which has been amended repeatedly afterwards.

needed to evaluate the risk."[120] A proposal for a new regulatory framework filed by the Commission in 2003, known under the name *REACH*, allots the burden of proving safety to industry not only with regard to new chemicals, as is the case at present, but with regard to existing chemicals as well – which latter account for 99 percent of the quantity of substances on the market.[121] In the view of the Commission legislation such as this, enshrining a system of prior approval – or positive or reverse listing – *de facto* applies the precautionary principle by shifting evidentiary requirements in favour of environmental caution.[122] The 1985 decision of the European Commission to ban hormones used for animal growth promotion, taken under EC *Directive 81/602*, was motivated by the circumstance that the safety of these hormones had, in the words of the Commission, "not been conclusively proven."[123] Under the 1991 EC *Urban Waste Water Directive* particular discharges may be subjected to less stringent treatment than the one described in the Directive, but only if and when "comprehensive studies indicate that such discharges will not adversely affect the environment."[124] Furthermore, the 1992 *Habitats Directive* on nature protection indicates that in the case of plans or projects that may bring about significant effects on designated special areas of conservation "competent national authorities shall agree to the plan or project only after having ascertained that it will not adversely affect the integrity of the site concerned."[125] According to *Regulation 345/92*, derogations from the ban this instrument imposes on the use and having on board of driftnets longer than two and a half kilometers, applicable to ships of all nationalities within the territorial seas of member states as well as to EC ships wherever they are located, can only be permitted if scientific evidence proves the absence of ecological risk.[126] Finally, under the terms of *Directive 98/81* on the contained use of genetically modified microorganisms states that where there is doubt as to the appropriate classification of such organisms, the more stringent protective measures shall be executed unless satisfactory evidence justifies the application of less stringent measures.[127] *Directive 2001/18* on the deliberate

---

[120] *Communication COM(2000)1*, p. 21.

[121] European Commission, *Proposal for a Regulation Concerning the Registration, Evaluation, Authorisation and Restriction of Chemicals (REACH)*, 29 October 2003.

[122] *Ibid.*; also Nollkaemper, 1996, p. 85; VanderZwaag, 1994, p. 9.

[123] See Morris, 2000(b), p. 2.

[124] Article 6(2) of *Directive 91/271*; on the precautionary caliber of this provision see also Sands, 1994; Sands, 1995(b), p. 212.

[125] Article 6(3) of the *Directive 92/43 Concerning the Conservation of Natural Habitats and of Wild Fauna and Flora*; see Backes, 1997, pp. 9-12; Douma, 2000, p. 134.

[126] Article 1 of *Regulation 345/92* of 27 January 1992; see Leroy & Ciliento, 1999, pp. 6-7; Orrega Vicuña, 1999, p. 159; Hancher, 1996, p. 203; Douma, *ibid.*, p. 135.

[127] Article 5(4) of 1998 *Directive 98/81*; also Jans, 2000, p. 116 (calling this an "excellent example of the precautionary principle in secondary Community law).

release of GMOs into the environment places the burden of proof on those seeking to introduce such organisms onto the market.[128]

The precautionary burden of proof has also found its way into the jurisprudence of the EU Court of Justice. For instance, in a 1994 prejudicial ruling concerning the interpretation of a provision on hunting in the *Birds Directive*[129] the ECJ determined that the instrument does not empower the national authorities of a member state to fix closing dates for the hunting season which vary according to the bird species, "unless the Member State concerned can adduce evidence, based on scientific and technical data relevant to each individual case, that staggering the closing dates for hunting does not impede the complete protection of the species of bird liable to be affected by such staggering."[130] Ten years afterwards the influence of the precautionary principle on the burden of proof as employed in the *Habitats Directive* just mentioned, was a central element of another prejudicial ruling by the ECJ in a case concerning the alleged adverse effects of mechanical cockle fisheries on the ecosystem of the protected Dutch Wadden Sea area.[131] In light of the precautionary principle, the Court determined, a risk of significant effects on the area and the consequent duty to perform an appropriate assessment of all implications of the fishery, must be deemed to exist "if it cannot be excluded, on the basis of objective information, that it will have a significant effect on that site, either individually or in combination with other plans or projects."[132] The authorization criterion from the *Habitats Directive*, which according to the Court clearly "integrates the precautionary principle,"[133] was then interpreted:

> The competent national authorities, taking account of the appropriate assessment of the implications of mechanical cockle fishing for the site concerned in the light of the site's conservation objectives, are to authorise such an activity only if they have made certain that it will not adversely affect the integrity of that site. That is the case where no reasonable scientific doubt remains as to the absence of such effects.[134]

The mechanical cockle fisheries in the Wadden Sea could not stand this test and was discontinued.

---

[128] See mainly Article 4(3); also Marr, 2003, p. 110.

[129] Article 7(4) of the 1979 *Directive 79/409 Relative to the Conservation of Wild Birds*.

[130] Case C-435/92, ruling of 19 January 1994, paragraph 22. On the precautionary nature of this ruling, see Backes *et al.*, 1997, p. 64. See also Case C-157/89 of 17 January 1991.

[131] Case C-127/02, Judgment of 7 September 2004 (*Cockle Fisheries Case*). The Wadden Sea is a specially protected area under the *Birds Directive*. However, the provisions of the *Habitats Directive* regarding the procedure to be followed in respect of potentially harmful activities and plans apply for areas designated under both Directives: *Habitats Directive*, Article 7.

[132] Paragraphs 44-45.

[133] Paragraph 58.

[134] Paragraph 61.

The Precautionary Burden of Proof in State Practice at the National Level

It is natural that this brief review should end with a peek at the national practice of states. Domestic laws allocating the burden of proof in favour of environmental protection occur, as Freestone and Hey contend, "more often than might be expected."[135] When discussing model legislation for the control of toxic chemicals in 1993, Caribbean Commonwealth states agreed that "the precautionary approach may call for 'reverse listing', that is, chemicals would be prohibited from manufacture or import unless industry has satisfied a government agency of a level of safety or acceptability."[136] In fact, in many countries such a precautionary onus of proof, placed on the manufacturer, is an essential part of legislation dealing with potentially hazardous chemicals such as pesticides.[137] Examples where pesticide approval hinges on the rendering by registration applicants of evidence that no undue environmental impact will occur, include the Canadian *Pest Control Products Act*[138] and the US *Federal Insecticide, Fungicide and Rodenticide Act.*[139] Under Dutch legislation a new pesticide may only be admitted if scientific and technical data render the "reasonable certainty" that the substance is not environmentally harmful.[140] Swedish chemicals law incorporates a similar suspicion of harmfulness.[141] It requires the producer of a substance to transmit scientific information demonstrating, "beyond reasonable doubt," that for their product this suspicion is unfounded. If the producer is unable to do so, authorities will treat the substance as hazardous.[142] Likewise, in the absence of evidence to the contrary a Danish scheme treats a chemical as the most toxic one in its class.[143] The latter three examples of domestic legislation should be viewed in connection with the EU Directive on chemicals treated above. They are included to illustrate the fact that the EU legislation described above is implemented by twenty-five member-states.

To carry on with United States law, a precautionary onus of proof has been integrated in various statutes besides the Act just mentioned, *inter*

[135] Freestone & Hey, 1996(b), pp. 267-268.

[136] As reported by Vanderzwaag, 1994, p. 8.

[137] Wahlström, 1999, p. 60; Tickner, 1999, p. 168.

[138] Vanderzwaag, 1994, p. 9.

[139] In *Environmental Defense Fund v Ruckelshaus*, 439 F.2d, DC Cir. 1971, it was expressly affirmed that under this Act the onus of proving that a pesticide in question will not produce adverse environmental effects is upon the registration applicant; see Bodansky, 1994, pp. 210-211; Weintraub, 1992/1996, p. 23.

[140] Article 3 of the *Bestrijdingsmiddelenwet*; an evident application of the precautionary principle, according to Backes *et al.*, 1997, p. 75.

[141] Wahlström, 1999, p. 53.

[142] *Ibid.*

[143] Tickner, 1999, p. 174, referring to Bro-Rasmussen *et al.*, 1996.

alia in the field of nature conservation.[144] The *Marine Mammal Protection Act* demands that applicants for a permit to capture or kill marine mammals supply proof of the harmlessness of such action.[145] The US judiciary determined in 1976 that this Act was "deliberately designed to permit takings of marine mammals only when it was known that the taking would not be to the disadvantage of the species."[146] Furthermore, in the absence of adequate knowledge enabling the assessment of potential impacts, activities that may be harmful to endangered flora or fauna are not allowed to proceed under the *Endangered Species Act*.[147] The law of the Commonwealth of Massachusetts obliges those wanting to build within a river buffer zone to show the absence of alternative options, whereas proponents of construction near wetlands must demonstrate that no damage to wetland integrity will result from prospective projects.[148] In 2000 Governor Todd Whitman of New Jersey, later to become EPA Administrator, submitted that as part of a precautionary approach to environmental protection policymakers need to "shift the burden of proof away from those advocating protection toward those proposing an action that may be harmful."[149]

One of three essential elements of the precautionary principle identified by the Supreme Court of India in the 1996 *Vellore Citizens* case reads as follows: "The 'Onus of proof' is on the actor or developer/industrialist to show that his action is environmentally benign."[150] In its 1994 *Shehla Zia v WAPDA* judgment the Supreme Court of neighboring Pakistan had also disallowed the potentially harmful activity it was ruling on until such time as additional scientific evidence would repudiate the likelihood of unacceptable effects, basing its argumentation on the precautionary principle as articulated in Principle 15 of the *Rio Declaration*.[151]

Ties between the precautionary principle and the burden of proof are equally strong in Germany.[152] Under German biotechnology legislation the operation and establishment of a biotechnology installation may not be

---

[144] Bodansky, 1994, at p. 209 holds that "a few" US environmental acts include a precautionary burden of proof; Vanderzwaag, 1994, p. 8 speaks of "numerous statutes" doing so.

[145] 16 *USC*; see Bodansky, *ibid.*, p. 210.

[146] *Comm. For Human Legislation v Richardson*, 540 F.2d 1141, DC Cir. 1976, at p. 1145; as quoted in Bodansky, *ibid.*

[147] Paragraph 7(a)(2) of the Act, 16 *USC*, paragraph 1536; see Bodansky, *ibid.*

[148] *Rivers Act* and *Wetlands Statute* of the Commonwealth of Massachusetts; see Raffensperger & Tickner, 1999, p. 7.

[149] Speech of October 2000 at the National Academy of Sciences in Washington, D.C.; quoted in Appell, 2001.

[150] Paragraph 11 of the judgment, as reproduced in Shanmuganathan & Warren, 1997.

[151] *Shehla Zia v WAPDA*, PLD, 1994 Supreme Court 693; see Lyster, 1997, at p. 396.

[152] Boehmer-Christiansen, 1994, pp. 38 and 48.

permitted until it is guaranteed that "the measures required have been taken at all necessary levels of protection, in conformity with the current level of science and technology;"[153] whereas the *Atomic Energy Law* has it that authorizations for nuclear operations may not be granted "unless, based on the current level of scientific and technical knowledge, the occurrence of damage may be practically excluded."[154]

Practically excluding harm was also the purpose of a motion adopted by the Dutch Parliament on the polemic issue, referred to previously in this study,[155] of natural gas exploration in the Wadden Sea:

> The House, having heard the debates, noting that absolute certainty and conclusive guarantees can never be given in advance that subsidence [of the ocean floor, ed.] resulting from gas extraction will not result in permanent harm to the essential qualities of the Waddenzee as a wetland; is of the opinion that no more drilling may take place for testing or extraction purposes; requests that the government incorporate this opinion into the Key National Planning Decision (PKB).[156]

The government, having taken the decision, informed by the precautionary principle, to give permission only if conclusive scientific evidence were to prove that no harm to the vulnerable Wadden Sea ecosystem would occur as a consequence of any drilling activities,[157] adopted this motion, as reflected in the following policy statement issued in 2001:

> As long as any uncertainties and doubt regarding possibly permanent degradation of the Wadden Sea as a result of mineral resource extraction [..] have not been removed to a sufficient extent, the cabinet will not issue any new permits for test drilling for and extraction of such resources. The coming years will be used to gain insight into the question whether remaining uncertainties as to the possibility of meeting watertight conditions can be removed.[158]

During judicial proceedings in 1999 proponents of the manual harvest of mussels in, again, the Wadden Sea were asked to prove the absence of considerable harmful effects on the ecosystem, failed to do so and were

---

153 Article 13 of the *Gentechnikgesetz* of 16 December 1993; translation from De Sadeleer, 2000, p. 147.
154 Quoted from a judgment by the Federal Constitutional Court (*Bundesverfassungsgericht*) on the interpretation of Articles 1 and 7 of the *Atomgesetz*. Judgment of 17 February 1978, 55 *BverGE*, 1978, p. 250; translation from De Sadeleer, *ibid.*, p. 145.
155 See *supra* paragraph 4.2.
156 Translation borrowed from Pieterman & Hanekamp, 2002, p. 21.
157 See Trouwborst, 2002, pp. 210-211; Pieterman & Hanekamp, *ibid.*, pp. 20-21.
158 *Derde Nota Waddenzee, Deel 1: Ontwerp Planologische Kernbeslissing*, 2001, p. 12; author's translation.

consequently not allowed to carry out the harvest.[159] In an earlier ruling by a Dutch court the use of phosphorus slags in maintenance works for a sea-wall had been disallowed on account of the fact that no satisfactory guarantees existed that this would have no more than modest environmental effects.[160]

In Belgian jurisprudence it has been established that in the area of industrial pollution a serious risk of environmental harm must be presumed to exist in all cases where an environmental impact assessment has not been performed.[161] In other words, industrial activities are assumed harmful as long as information to adequately assess their environmental impact is not available.[162] Two judgments of the highest French administrative court, the Council of State, are also of relevance in the present context. In a 1995 ruling concerning water abstraction works the court determined that it was for the authorities advancing the project to deliver positive proof that the narrow safety perimeter established around the bore hole offered adequate guarantees that the environment would not be adversely affected.[163] *In casu* the Council found that the scientific research that had been carried out did not constitute such proof.[164] Along the same lines, the Council adjudged in 1997 that the proponents of a temporary deposition site of dredging spoil on agricultural lands carried the burden of satisfactorily ruling out the possibility of harmful, toxicological effects resulting from such deposition.[165] The evidence provided was not deemed sufficient in this case either.[166]

The voluntary agreement reached between the British government and industry in 1999 to withhold from the commercial growth of genetically modified crops until the results of a three-year program of field trials would have been evaluated serves as another illustration. On this topic Prime Minister Tony Blair declared that "no GM crops will be grown commercially in this country until we are satisfied there will be no unacceptable impact on

---

159 Order by the President of the Department of Administrative Law of the Council of State of 21 December 1999; see Lambers, 2000, p. 179.

160 Order by the President of the Department of Administrative Law of the Council of State, 19 March 1996; see Backes *et al.*, 1997, at p. 97.

161 *Conseil d'État*, No. 45.755, Judgment of 26 January 1994; see De Sadeleer, 2000, p. 149.

162 *Ibid.*

163 Judgment of the *Conseil d'État* in the case of *Ministre de l'Intérieur c/M. Rossi*, 4 January 1995; see De Sadeleer, *ibid.*, p. 147.

164 According to the Council, "the facts that a fluorescine infiltration test may not have confirmed such risks and that the hydrogeological report [..] may not have considered that the narrow safety perimeter is insufficient do not in themselves demonstrate that there is no need to enlarge the said safety perimeter in order to guarantee the quality of the waters in question." Translation from De Sadeleer, *ibid.*

165 *Conseil d'État, Commune de Quévillon*, Judgment of 30 April 1997; see De Sadeleer, *ibid.*, p. 148.

166 *Ibid.*

the environment."[167] In a UK government policy instrument, also of 1999, a refined position is taken on the relationship between the precautionary principle and the burden of proof. According to this position, the principle does not, as a general rule, entail "that we only permit activities if we are sure that serious harm will not arise, or there is proof that the benefits outweigh all possible risks."[168] This would, it is argued in continuation, severely hinder "progress towards improvements in the quality of life."[169]

Peruvian law prohibits the discharge of pollutants likely to cause ecosystem degradation or harm the quality of the environment "unless precautionary measures are taken to ensure purification."[170] Yet another instance is provided by the catch restrictions for orange roughy imposed by the Minister of Agriculture and Fisheries of New Zealand in the mid-1990s.[171] The Minister announced that severe reductions of catch levels for this fish species would be implemented *unless* compelling evidence in the form of dramatic improvements in stock assessments would discard the need to do so – thus placing the evidentiary burden on those opposing the constraints.[172]

The Big Picture

One could continue and continue; the list of examples is practically boundless. The many instances of state practice that have been cited would appear to warrant the preliminary observation that in the fields of pollution control and nature conservation the precautionary burden of proof is a rather commonly occurring feature. This observation stands in need of being complemented by two additional remarks, however, if an even-handed assessment of state practice in the current context is to be arrived at.

First, of the international legal instruments containing general formulations of the precautionary principle, covering the environment as a whole, the *World Charter for Nature* seems to be the only one to *explicitly* call for a precautionary placement of the burden of proof. The *Bergen Declaration* and the *Rio Declaration*, to name a few influential instruments of general scope, do not. It has been held, among others by the authors of the *FAO Technical Guidelines for Responsible Fisheries* and the Supreme Court of Pakistan, that the latter declarations nevertheless *implicitly* call for such a precautionary

---

167 Tony Blair, "The key to GM is its potential both for harm and good", in *The Independent on Sunday* of 27 February 2000; quoted in Gilland, 2000, p. 60.

168 UK Government, *A Better Quality of Life: A Strategy for Sustainable Development for the United Kingdom*, 1999, paragraph 4.2.

169 *Ibid.*

170 Section 14(18) of Chapter IV of the 1990 *Environment and Natural Resources Code (Legislative Decree No. 611)*.

171 See Mascher, 1997, pp. 73-74; Trouwborst, 2002, pp. 238-239.

172 *Ibid.*

allocation of the evidentiary burden.[173] It is open to question, however, whether this outcome is necessarily the only legitimate one when interpreting, for instance, Principle 15 of the *Rio Declaration*: the provision simply does not mention the burden of proof.[174]

The same is true of many formulations of the precautionary principle contained in more specific instruments, such as the *Biodiversity Convention*[175] or the *Climate Change Convention*.[176] Neither did the Forum Fisheries Agency's proposal to incorporate an *expressly* precautionary burden of proof into the *Straddling Stocks Agreement*, spoken of above, make it into the final text of the Agreement.[177] Indeed, it appears that the greater part of the material sources of state practice which concern the precautionary principle do not explicitly assign the onus of proof to the initiator or proponent of potentially harmful activities.[178] In short, while the above-cited instances of adoption by states of a straightforward precautionary burden of proof are many, they do not seem to constitute a convincing majority.

Second, it is important to note that when looking at those cases where a precautionary burden of proof *is* employed, a direct and unambiguous link with the precautionary *principle* can be detected in many of them but is absent in others. When coming across instances such as the ones reviewed above, where states have allocated the burden of proof to the initiators of possibly harmful activities, then it cannot automatically be concluded that they have employed this burden of proof because they felt compelled to on account of the precautionary principle if they did not *indicate* so one way or another. This is the case even when assuming that it would be correct to say that a burden of proof as just described is, as such, *consistent* with the precautionary principle. Subject A acting in accordance with rule Z does not in itself allow for the conclusion that A's behaviour was motivated by rule Z. Different motivations may have played a part and subject A need in fact not even have been aware of rule Z. Indeed, returning to the present subject matter, a number of the described instances pre-date the emergence

---

173 See the 1996 *FAO Technical Guidelines for Responsible Fisheries* and the 1994 *Shehla Zia v WAPDA* case, quoted from above.

174 Bodansky, 1991, p. 416, argues: "To say that definitive scientific evidence is not required [..] does not represent a true shift in the burden of proof." In the opinion of Birnie & Boyle, 2002, p. 117, Principle 15 "does not allow states to proceed with proposed activities on the basis that a risk of harm has not been proved conclusively, but neither does it require proof that there is no risk of harm."

175 Ninth preambular paragraph.

176 Article 3(3).

177 Orrega Vicuña, 1999, p. 161.

178 This is the case, at a minimum, for the sources catalogued in Trouwborst, 2002. There are no indications that this is any different for subsequent practice.

of the precautionary principle in international law, thus conclusively ruling out the principle as a causal agent in these cases.

Summing up, the present paragraph yields the following. The precautionary burden of proof, with its assumption of harmfulness, occurs rather frequently in environmental state practice. On a majority of occasions, however, states have embraced formulations of the precautionary principle which do not specifically call for such a burden. Moreover, it is clear in many, but not every instance that a precautionary burden of proof was adopted because of the precautionary principle and not for a different reason.

8.3. The Burden of Proof under the Precautionary Principle

Doctrine

Before drawing any final conclusions, it is considered appropriate to have recourse to the opinions of scholars on the current theme. Judge Weeramantry, in his Dissenting Opinion on the 1995 *Nuclear Test* case, argued that there was a sufficiently well established principle of international law for the ICJ to act upon "under which, where environmental damage of any sort is threatened, the burden of proving that it will not produce the damaging consequences complained of is placed upon the author of that design."[179] In this view of the matter, he continued, the Court should have considered the environmental damage New Zealand complained of as *prima facie* established in the absence of proof by France of the environmental safety of its proposed atomic tests.[180] In the Dissenting Opinion he appended to the Advisory Opinion on the *Legality of the Threat or Use of Nuclear Weapons* delivered by the World Court in 1996, Judge Weeramantry mentioned the precautionary principle and the, curiously separate, "principle that the burden of proving safety lies upon the author of the act complained of" as two general principles of international environmental law that would be violated by the employment of nuclear weapons.[181] ITLOS Judge Laing, at the occasion of the 1999 *Southern Bluefin Tuna* cases, expressed his view that the thrust of the precautionary approach is, *inter alia*, "shifting the burden of proof to the State in control of the territory from which the harm might emanate or to the responsible actor."[182] His colleague Judge Wolfrum, in his Separate Opinion on the 2001 *MOX Plant* case, also noted that there is

---

179 Dissenting Opinion of Judge Weeramantry, *ICJ Rep.*, 1995, at p. 348.

180 *Ibid.*

181 Dissenting Opinion of Judge Weeramantry concerning the Advisory Opinion on the *Legality of the Threat or Use of Nuclear Weapons*, *ICJ Rep.*, 1996, pp. 429-555, at pp. 502-503.

182 Paragraph 14 of the Separate Opinion of Judge Laing, appended to the Tribunal's Order.

"general agreement" that the burden of proof concerning the environmental impacts of potentially harmful activities is reversed as a consequence of the principle.[183] "A state interested in undertaking or continuing a particular activity has to prove that it will result in no harm, rather than the other side having to prove that it will result in harm."[184] Judge *Ad Hoc* Székely was of a similar opinion.[185] Arbitrator Gavan Griffith strongly disagreed with the majority decision in the 2003 *Mox Plant OSPAR* case to place the onus of proof on Ireland, holding that "the obvious application of the precautionary principle (not considered by the majority) must shift the burden to the United Kingdom."[186] The UK, he continued, had "not established the fact of no adverse effect (as required by the application of the precautionary principle)."[187]

As noted at the outset of this chapter, a large number of authors similarly regard a burden of proof placed on the proponents of potentially harmful activities as inherent in, or as the automatic result of, the precautionary principle.[188] They maintain that the principle imposes a strategy of "no trials without prior guarantees against error", taking the place of the classic trial-and-error strategy.[189] To quote one of the more radical interpretations:

> An underlying mandate of the precautionary principle is that, in the face of scientific uncertainty, a party should refrain from actions that might harm the environment, and that those who oppose this prohibition have the burden of proof for ensuring the safety of the proposed action.[190]

Although some do indeed allege, as is suggested here, that the precautionary principle implies a requirement of *conclusive* proof of safety which must be met by proponents of an activity for it to be permissible,[191] most of those who

---

183 Separate Opinion of Judge Wolfrum, appended to the ITLOS *Mox Plant* Order of 3 December 2001.

184 *Ibid.*

185 Separate Opinion of Judge *Ad Hoc* Székely on the ITLOS *Mox Plant* Order, paragraph 22.

186 Paragraph 72 of his Dissenting Opinion, appended to the Final Award of 2 July 2003. Paragraph 76: "As the majority did not consider the precautionary principle and misdirected itself on the question of onus, I conclude that its finding that Ireland 'has failed to demonstrate' adverse effect within the second category of information must be vitiated as predicated upon the wrong approach to the burden of proof."

187 *Ibid.*, paragraph 90.

188 See the sources quoted in the fifth footnote of *supra* paragraph 8.1.

189 Wildavsky, 2000, p. 22-23.

190 Jones, 2000.

191 See, e.g., Hanekamp, 2002, pp. 9-10; Pieterman & Hanekamp, 2002, p. 6; Annex I of the 1994 European NGO "Seas at Risk" Conference; reproduced in Backes *et al.*, 1997,

argue that the *burden* of proof is on activity proponents specify a *standard* of proof which is more lenient than this. These writers submit, for example, that under the precautionary principle evidence is demanded from project initiators showing that planned activities will not "seriously damage"[192] or cause "undue harm"[193] to the environment; that no "unacceptable environmental impacts"[194] will occur; or that the activities are safe "beyond reasonable doubt".[195]

Claims have been framed in yet more conservative terms by scholars who are not so sure whether a burden of proof on the proponents of possibly harmful activities is actually a necessary or automatic component of the precautionary principle. A number of these writers merely view a burden of proof thus allocated as embodying one possible interpretation of the principle, for instance as its strictest or "strongest" version.[196] It is then added[197] or implied[198] that this interpretation is not perforce the most common one in legal practice. Others have taken a *lege ferenda* position by proposing that it would be desirable to adopt this interpretation and put it into effect.[199] The *Wingspread Statement* is a case in point, upholding that "it is necessary to implement the Precautionary Principle" and that in this context "the proponent of an activity, rather than the public, should bear the burden of proof."[200] Still others regard a precautionary onus of proof as one among several means that are available to states to *implement* the precautionary principle, a means which may be more or less fitting depending on the circumstances of each case.[201] The latter position squares with the point of

---

pp. 69-70. Morris, 2000(b), p. 1, has dubbed this interpretation the "strong precautionary principle".

192 Christie, 1993, pp. 481-482.

193 Tickner *et al.*, 2000, p. 4.

194 Van Dyke, 1996, p. 380.

195 Wan Ho & Saunders, 2000; Saunders, 2000.

196 Freestone & Makuch, 1996, pp. 12-13; Freestone, 1999, p. 140; Sands, 1994; Sands, 1995(b), p. 212; Tinker, 1995, pp. 793-794; Dzidzornu, 1998, pp. 100-101; Morris, 2000(b), p. 1; Rubin, 2000, p. 106.

197 Freestone & Makuch, *ibid.*; Freestone, *ibid.*; Sands, *ibid.*

198 Tinker, 1995, pp. 793-794; Dzidzornu, 1998, pp. 100-101; Morris, 2000(b), p. 1; Rubin, 2000, p. 106.

199 E.g., Hey, 1992, p. 310; DeFur, 1999, pp. 345-346.

200 1998 *Wingspread Statement on the Precautionary Principle.* Another example is Article 2(1)(c) of the model for a *Convention for the Conservation and Wise Use of Forests* that was advanced by the Global Legislators Organization for a Balanced Environment (GLOBE) in 1992, which proposes that the onus of proving that activities will not cause serious or irreversible environmental harm be put on the state in whose territory the activities are planned.

201 As Gullett, 1997, p. 60, puts it: "Where a proposed activity is identified as requiring application of the principle, there is essentially a choice of four operational approaches to implement precaution, [one of which is to] completely reverse the burden of proof to require the proponent to meet a high evidentiary standard pointing to harmlessness before the activity

view defended by the European Commission, namely that allotting the burden of proof to activity initiators is "one way of applying the precautionary principle."[202]

Writers may thus roughly be grouped into two categories. Those belonging to the first, large group consider a burden of proof placed on the activity proponent as part and parcel of the precautionary principle. Those belonging to the second group nurture hesitations in this respect. They either view such a burden of proof as a possible, or desirable, but not predominant interpretation of the principle, or as one way of implementing it. This second group also harbours various guarded opinions as to the status of the assumption of harmfulness and the precautionary burden of proof in international law.[203] It has been maintained in this respect that it is "doubtful" whether the precautionary principle, perceived as embodying these elements, at present constitutes a general requirement of international law;[204] or, similarly, that this interpretation is "beginning to be supported by state practice, even if it still falls short of having sufficient support to allow it to be considered a rule of general application."[205]

The Burden of Proof under the Precautionary Principle in General International Law

Having looked at the reasons for a precautionary allocation of the burden of proof, at relevant state practice and at doctrine, the question is what can be inferred from these in respect of the precautionary principle in its capacity of a norm of customary international law. It is understood in this regard that the issue of the *burden* of proof cannot be treated satisfactorily in isolation from the issue of the *standard* of proof. In other words, the composite question to be addressed is: *who* must prove and *what* must be proven?

As discussed above, in the most precautionary theoretical model, whereby it is for the initiators of possibly harmful activities to demonstrate

– or modified activity – may proceed." Birnie & Boyle, 2002, p. 118, contend as follows: "Who bears the burden of proving that a risk exists cannot be answered by reference to Principle 15 alone, but will depend on the context in which the question arises." See also Backes *et al.*, 1997, p. 49.

202 *Communication COM(2000)1*, p. 21.

203 Freestone & Makuch, 1996, pp. 12-13, state that the "more common understanding of the principle" does not include these ingredients; see also Freestone, 1999, p. 140. O'Riordan & Cameron, 1994, p. 17 consider "the onus of proof on those who propose change" as one of the basic concepts enshrined in the precautionary principle, but explain on p. 18 that "[b]y no means all of these interpretations are formally approved in international law and common practice." Bosselmann, 1995, p. 431 simply submits that "no uniform view exists as to whether the precautionary principle carries a reversal of the burden of proof." Also Molenaar, 1998, p. 34.

204 Birnie & Boyle, 2002, p. 118.

205 Sands, 2003, p. 273.

the relative environmental harmlessness of their plans before they are allowed to proceed, effects are considered harmful until proven otherwise.[206] Analysis of pertinent practice shows that in environmental law and policy states frequently apply this model. The analysis does not, however, allow for the conclusion that the instances considered amount to a sufficiently general and uniform practice for the model to qualify as a candidate feature of the precautionary principle under customary international law. In point of fact, as will be recalled, states have most often embraced formulations of the precautionary principle which do not specifically call for a precautionary onus of proof. In can thus *not* be said that in general international law the burden of proof is placed on activity proponents – be they states, companies or actors – as an automatic result of the precautionary principle. This assessment supports the position taken by the European Commission[207] and by some of the writers from the 'second group' quoted before. It *is* clear, nevertheless, that in many cases where states have actually employed such a burden they did so because under the circumstances involved this was considered an appropriate *implementation* of the precautionary principle.

This outcome, with its distinction between various levels, would seem to fit previous findings on the definition of the precautionary principle[208] and precautionary measures.[209] It is probably useful to briefly reproduce some of these here. The right of states to take precautionary action was defined as follows:

> Wherever, on the basis of the best information available, there are reasonable grounds for concern that significant harm to the environment may occur, effective and proportional action to prevent and/or abate this harm may be taken, including in situations of scientific uncertainty regarding the cause, extent and/or probability of the potential harm.[210]

At the level of legal interstate relations, one can imagine the following dispute scenario: State P exercises its customary right by taking certain precautionary measures and State Q challenges these measures, arguing that the right is not applicable in the situation at hand. When push comes to shove, the question arises as to who is to prove what. Under the traditional model described earlier, it would be for the party wishing to protect the environment to render proof concerning the risk in question. As concluded just now, the precautionary principle does not adjust this initial allotment of

[206] See *supra* paragraph 8.1.
[207] According to *Communication COM(2000)1*, p. 21, a precautionary onus of proof "cannot be systematically entertained as a general principle."
[208] See *supra* Chapters 2 through 6.
[209] See *supra* paragraph 7.4.
[210] See *supra* Chapter 6.

the *burden* of proof.[211] When compared to the traditional model it does, nevertheless, lower the *standard* of proof.[212] Applied to the scenario under consideration, it is for State P to deliver proof justifying its precautionary action. However, instead of being required to produce 'clear and convincing evidence', it suffices for State P to demonstrate that 'on the basis of the best information available, there are reasonable grounds for concern that significant harm to the environment may be caused.' When it appears that State P actually manages to demonstrate the presence of such grounds, it is up to State Q to refute the evidence involved. (Obviously, knowing where the initial burden of proof lies does not negate the reality that in the course of fact-finding, burdens of persuasion may shift.)[213] How it should be judged in individual circumstances whether reasonable grounds for concern indeed exist has already been discussed.[214]

To proceed to the duty of states to take precautionary action, this was defined in the following terms:

> Wherever, on the basis of the best information available, there are reasonable grounds for concern that serious and/or irreversible harm to the environment may occur, effective and proportional action to prevent and/or abate this harm must be taken, including in situations of scientific uncertainty regarding the cause, extent and/or probability of the potential harm.[215]

A scenario can now be envisaged in which State Q fails to take precautionary action in a situation in which, in the opinion of State P, it ought to. Again, it would be for State P – once more being the party aiming to counter environmental harm – to solidify its claims by proving the existence, this time, of 'reasonable grounds for concern that serious and/or irreversible harm to the environment may be caused.' If State P succeeds to deliver evidence meeting this standard, this would trigger the obligation of State Q to take 'effective and proportional action' to prevent or abate the harm threatened – unless and until, of course, State Q in turn manages to disprove that one or more of the thresholds of reasonable grounds, seriousness or irreversibility are crossed.

---

211 Compare the reasoning of the EU Court of First Instance in the Joined Cases T-74/00, T-76/00, T-83/00 to T-85/00, T-132/00, T-137/00 and T-141/00 of 26 November 2002, paragraph 191: "acceptance that in cases of scientific uncertainty reasonable doubts as to the efficacy or safety of a medicinal product are capable of justifying a precautionary measure cannot be treated as equivalent to a reversal of the burden of proof."

212 Also Tinker, 1995, p. 779; Birnie & Boyle, 2002, p. 117.

213 Ashford, 1999, p. 205.

214 See *supra* paragraphs 5.3 and 5.5.

215 See *supra* Chapter 6.

The implementation of the precautionary principle represents the other level at which the burden of proof plays a part in the current context, in line with the views expressed by some of the authors cited *supra*. Banning or restricting an activity until its proponents prove its acceptability can, depending on the circumstances, constitute (part of) the effective and proportional action that may or must be taken by a state or states to comply with the principle.[216] The European Commission has affirmed in this regard that:

> Action taken under the head of the precautionary principle must in certain cases include a clause reversing the burden of proof and placing it on the producer, manufacturer or importer [..]. This possibility should be examined on a case-by-case basis when a measure is adopted under the precautionary principle.[217]

In the implementation of the precautionary principle precautionary burdens of proof can be employed either by individual states or by way of concerted action in the multilateral sphere. Examples of both possibilities abound in the above review of state practice.[218]

A final note is in place concerning the criticism, dealt with in the beginning of this chapter, that a precautionary burden of proof would be an unworkable concept.[219] It will be clear by now that in public international law the precautionary principle does not give rise to any general rule prohibiting potentially harmful activities until their proponents have delivered conclusive proof of absolute harmlessness. Not by a long shot. This state of affairs cheerfully conforms to the opinion of two critics who have, quite sensibly, contended that a principle imposing the inconceivable requirement to prove that some activity will not lead to any harm on any time scale and under any circumstance, can have no place in any sound legal system.[220] As another author has affirmed in respect of such a burden and standard of proof:

> The principle does not, as some critics claim, require industry to provide absolute proof that something new is safe. That would be an impossible demand and would indeed stop technology dead in its tracks, but I do not know of anyone who is actually demanding it.[221]

---

216 On the choice of those measures, see *supra* paragraph 5.4.
217 *Communication COM(2000)1*, p. 21.
218 See *supra* paragraph 8.2.
219 See the end of *supra* paragraph 8.1.
220 Pieterman & Hanekamp, 2002, p. 11.
221 Saunders, 2000.

This does not negate the fact that, for various reasons debated before,[222] precautionary burdens of proof are commonly applied by states to *implement* the precautionary principle in particular situations or issue areas. Depending on the circumstances, demanding proof from the agents of potential harm that unacceptable environmental impacts are not likely to result from their planned activities before permitting these, can obviously be an appropriate way to comply with the principle. The strictness of the standard of proof imposed by states in such cases tends to vary along with the nature of the activity and the vulnerability of the environmental assets in question, in conformity with the requirements of effectiveness and proportionality, and is not usually of the altogether impossible kind.[223]

8.4. Conclusions

In 1919 a Californian fisheries regulator demanded that "proof that seeks to change the ways of commerce and sport must be overwhelming."[224] It is evident that the precautionary principle represents a different outlook on evidence. That outlook has been the focus of this chapter, which started out by comparing traditional and precautionary models of proof. Put *in extremis*, the former operates on an assumption of environmental harm*less*ness and requires opponents of potentially harmful activities to prove their harmfulness before forbidding them; the latter operates on an assumption of harm*ful*ness and requires proponents of activities to prove their harmlessness before permitting them. The main rationale of the precautionary model is that ecologically speaking, the costs of an erroneous lack of precautionary action are inclined to exceed the costs of an erroneous surplus of precautionary action.

Analysis of pertinent state practice shows that precautionary burdens of proof, with their related assumption of harmfulness, are applied frequently by states in order to prevent environmental harm, both internationally and nationally. In many cases there is an apparent link between the use of such burdens of proof and the precautionary principle. This link is not always there, however, and on most occasions the precautionary principle has been formulated in terms which do not include specific reference to a precautionary onus of proof. It can therefore not be concluded that in general international law the precautionary principle causes the burden of proof to be placed automatically on activity proponents.

---

[222] See *supra* paragraph 8.1.
[223] See *supra* paragraph 8.2; also Nollkaemper, 1996, pp. 81-84; Martin, 1997, pp. 277-278.
[224] Cited in MacGarvin, 2001(b), p. 25.

Linking back to the definitions of the precautionary principle distilled earlier in this study, this means that the initial burden of proof rests on the state looking to prevent environmentally harmful activities, whereby the standard of proof that must be met coincides with the thresholds outlined in previous chapters. In other words, in principle it is for the state exercising the right to take precautionary action, respectively the state challenging a lack of precautionary action on the part of another state, to demonstrate the presence of reasonable grounds for concern that significant, respectively serious and/or irreversible harm, may be caused. The precautionary principle has lowered the standard of proof, but not reversed the burden.

That the precautionary onus of proof does not represent the general rule does not rescind the significant role it plays in the *implementation* of the precautionary principle. The effective and proportional action that may or must be taken by states when relevant thresholds are crossed can, and often does, take the form of a ban or restriction which is not lifted until the proponents of the activity in question deliver evidence that it would be responsible to do so. Whether this measure is appropriate and what standard of proof should accompany the burden both depend on the circumstances.

The real question is not whether machines think, but whether men do.
– Burrhus Frederic Skinner (1904-1990)

9. THE PRECAUTIONARY PRINCIPLE AND SOCIO-ECONOMIC INTERESTS

9.1. Precaution, People and Progress

As related in the previous chapter, one reason the precautionary principle has been criticized is for fear that its application may paralyze human societies by requiring comprehensive proof of harmlessness before permitting any activity.[1] It was also related previously that this fear can be considered groundless as far as the allocation of the burden of proof under public international law is concerned.[2] Conclusions reached on the matter of evidence do not, however, by themselves settle the larger issue of the relationship between the precautionary principle and socio-economic interests. Just as inevitable as the topic of proof is the subject of the role of societal and economic considerations in precautionary decision-making.

Several rather fundamental questions are at stake here. It is obviously not permitted to use uncertainty as a reason for postponing or failing to take action, but can the socio-economic costs of such action perhaps be a valid reason to do so? Or is the nature of the precautionary principle absolutist in the sense that environmental protection should by definition outweigh all other interests? But how about people's living standard then, how about employment and the economy, how about the interests of agriculture and fisheries, of industry and transport, of cultural traditions and recreation? And how about the aspirations of developing countries? Should the objective of nature conservation not be balanced against such socio-economic interests when deciding on precautionary action? Is environmental protection always worth any price or should precautionary measures be fashioned so that they are cost-effective? A related concern is raised by the prominent role of uncertainty in environmental management. As recalled at the outset of the previous chapter, mistakes in environmental decision-making are inevitable, which raises the question who should pay for those mistakes, the human economy or the environment? As noted before, advocates of traditional approaches have tended to stress the costs of erroneously taken preventive action, while

---

[1] See *supra* paragraph 8.1.

[2] See the last part of *supra* paragraph 8.3.

proponents of a precautionary approach have been inclined to stress the costs of erroneous lack of such action.[3]

The structure of this chapter is roughly similar to the structure of the preceding one. The remainder of the current paragraph is devoted to sketching the dimensions and intricacies of the subject matter at hand. In the second paragraph relevant state practice is investigated against this background. The third is concerned with putting the combined findings of the first two in perspective by relating them to previous conclusions. Final conclusions are concisely summed up in the last and fourth paragraph.

Much of the above revolves around the big question whether in determinations regarding precautionary action account should be taken only of the proportions of the environmental *risk* at issue, or also of the *costs* of preventive or abatement measures.[4] From whichever angle, the stakes in this matter are high and range from the fate of species and ecosystems to the fate of industries and human lifestyles.[5] Some activities are directly (and all human activities ultimately) dependent on a healthy environment, whereas some activities (and there is overlap here) can only take place at the detriment of that same environment.[6] The interplay of environment, society and economy is intricate and characterized by difficult choices that frequently go between immediate and more enduring results.[7] "The costs of preventive action are usually tangible, clearly allocated and often short term," as the director of the European Environment Agency observes, "whereas the costs of failing to act are less tangible, less clearly distributed and usually longer term."[8] The outcomes of choices, in turn, are influenced by values which differ from society to society and from time to time,[9] and by the bare fact that governments can spend the same euro, dollar, dinar or bolivar only once.[10]

---

[3] See *supra* paragraph 8.1.

[4] Bodansky, 1991(a), p. 416.

[5] Kiss & Shelton, 1991, p. 240; Harding & Fisher, 1994, p. 253; Foster *et al.*, 2000; Thomas & Grader, 2000.

[6] Nollkaemper, 1996, p. 74; Dzidzornu, 1998, p. 99.

[7] O'Riordan & Cameron, 1994(a), p. 15; Nollkaemper, 1996, p. 74; Kaiser, 1997(a), p. 204; Dzidzornu, *ibid.*; Thomas & Grader, 2000; European Environment Agency, 2001, p. 13. E.g., choosing between employment and environment is not something people like to do – although arguably, when forced to, most are likely to favour the former: Wirth, 1999, p. 226.

[8] Jiménez Beltrán, 2001, pp. 3-4.

[9] Kaiser, 1997(a), p. 204; Cooney, 2000.

[10] Von Moltke, 1999. As a report on the economic and social dimensions of climate change by the Intergovernmental Panel on Climate Change (IPCC) notes with respect to the concerns of developing states: "If we take aggressive action to limit climate change they may regret that we did not use the funds instead to push ahead development in Africa, to better protect the [human] species against the next retrovirus, or to dispose of nuclear materials safely. [..] Alternatively, if the developed countries choose to embark on an aggressive control regime

Apart from the concept of sustainable development, which is of self-evident importance in the present context, key terms in the debate on the precautionary principle and socio-economic considerations include 'cost-effectiveness' and 'cost-benefit analysis'. Often quoted in this context is the reference to "cost-effective measures" in Principle 15 of the *Rio Declaration*. Pinning down the exact meaning of this reference with respect to the precautionary principle is quite an abstruse affair, however. According to one explanation a prerequisite of cost-effectiveness connotes that precautionary measures should "make economic sense".[11] As for the general meaning of the term, the dictionary simply states that something is cost-effective when it is effective in relation to its cost.[12] In the words of the 1994 *Energy Charter Treaty*, to take a definition from a legal instrument, cost-effectiveness purports "to achieve a defined objective at the lowest cost or to achieve the greatest benefit at a given cost."[13] Ostensibly, in connection with the precautionary principle the relationship is involved between (1) the expected costs in case a given threat materializes and (2) the costs of precautionary measures to prevent this from happening.[14] A bare reference to cost-effectiveness leaves various questions unsettled, however. For one, given that costs can take many shapes – ecological, social, economic, monetary, and so on – should the term 'cost' be read generally so as to include all of these, or restrictively as denoting only one type, for instance financial costs? For another, according to the definition of the *Energy Charter Treaty*, to achieve cost-effectiveness one can either take an *objective* as benchmark and look for the lowest cost to achieve it, or take a given *sum* as benchmark and look for the best way to spend it. Applied to the precautionary principle, the question is thus for the appropriate starting-point: the objective of harm prevention or the budget.

One common tool in the search for cost-effectiveness in public spending has been cost-benefit analysis. According to its dictionary entry, such analysis entails assessing the relation of the cost of an operation to the

---

now, and if this cuts into their growth rates, the result will shrink export markets for developing countries and thus reduce growth there. In addition, if developed countries view their greenhouse efforts as, in effect, aid to developing countries, they may cut back on other programs (sanitation, education for women, etc.) that have a more immediate impact on life expectancy, health and well-being." Intergovernmental Panel on Climate Change, *Climate Change 1995: Economic and Social Dimensions of Climate Change*, Contribution of Working Group III to the Second Assessment Report of the Intergovernmental Panel on Climate Change, Cambridge 1996, p. 33, as cited in Beckerman, 2000, p. 53.

[11] Soria Jiménez, 1996, p. 394.

[12] Sykes, 1976, p. 230.

[13] Article 19(3)(d).

[14] Douma, 1997(b).

value of resulting benefits.[15] The United States is a country where cost-benefit analysis has become a dominant method to guide environmental decision-making.[16] It involves enumerating all possible consequences, positive and negative, of a policy option; estimating the likelihood of each; estimating the benefit or loss to society should each occur, expressed in monetary terms; calculating the expected social benefit or loss from each consequence by multiplying the amounts of the associated benefit or loss by their probabilities of occurrence; and calculating the net expected social benefit or loss associated with the policy option by summing over the various possible consequences.[17] Consequences are initially represented in their 'natural units', i.e., economic effects in monetary units, health and safety effects in mortality and morbidity figures, and environmental effects in appropriate descriptive terms. In the end, however, all consequences are translated into their current monetary equivalent and a net benefit or cost is computed.[18] The advantages of this method are evident. It is systematic, transparent and allows for straightforward comparison of different policy options by expressing the total impact of each in a single financial figure.[19] Once a dollar or euro value is put on a species threatened by human development, then this sum can be compared, for instance, to the value of the kilowatt-hours produced by a scheduled hydroelectric plant or to the value of prospected real estate.[20]

Opinions on the socio-economic implications of the precautionary principle are wideranging, reflecting the intricacy of the subject matter. Their thorough discussion here is considered imperative for a good grasp of the legal issues proper which will be dealt with in the following paragraphs. To further a clear understanding it is thought convenient to group opinions in two categories, just like the division between the traditional and the precautionary model used when discussing the burden of proof.[21] As in the previous chapter, a distinction can presently be made between those who stress the dangers of too much and those who stress the dangers of too little environmental precaution.[22] This partition is to some extent a simplification of reality but, it is hoped, a helpful one at that.

---

[15] Sykes, 1976, p. 230.
[16] Ashford, 1999, p. 200.
[17] *Ibid.*
[18] *Ibid.*; Hattis & Anderson, 1999, p. 100.
[19] Ashford, *ibid.*, p. 201.
[20] Norton, 1988, p. 204.
[21] See *supra* paragraph 8.1.
[22] This distinction does not coincide with a division between anthropocentric and ecocentric positions since, as will become clear below, anthropocentric considerations play a major part in the second group as well. See also Trouwborst, 2002, pp. 5 and 12-14.

Cost-Benefit Analysis as a Check on the Costs of Precautionary Action

The first group contains the positions of those who hold that in the application of the precautionary principle the environmental interest must be balanced with socio-economic interests; that precautionary measures must be cost-effective in the strictly financial sense; or that the precautionary principle is an outright threat to social and economic progress and had better be abolished altogether. Calling to mind one of the open questions posed above, the starting-point here is the budget. Concern has been expressed that precautionary measures will decrease economic efficiency – e.g., by requiring industries to go the notoriously expensive 'last mile' in pollution reduction[23] – and lower living standards;[24] that excessive precautions will impose unnecessary costs on society;[25] that important benefits offered by biotechnology will be foregone;[26] that the principle will hamper the development of poorer countries and restrict their access to markets;[27] and that application of the precautionary principle will result in the shutdown of forestry or fishery operations.[28] These fears are fuelled by statements such as the 1997 opinion of a *Biodiversity Convention* body that a precautionary approach to forest use is "likely to imply harvesting operations more conservative of ecosystem structure than those to which large-scale industrial forestry has become accustomed."[29] In his Separate Opinion to the 1999 *Southern Bluefin Tuna* cases Judge Laing argued that a decision, inspired by the precautionary principle, to place the evidentiary burden on proponents of fisheries to prove that fishing is acceptable before permitting it "should be made with great care, because of its possible impact on fishermen which, *prima facie*, could be unfair and unrealistic."[30] Likewise, in connection with developing states it has been submitted that these should be exempted from the strictest precautionary obligations and permitted to apply the principle "according to their capabilities,"[31] in accord with the doctrine of common but differentiated responsibilities.[32]

---

[23] Bodansky, 1994, p. 290, describes how marginal costs tend to increase sharply as the zero emission point is approached, in return for relatively modest improvements of environmental quality.

[24] As noted by Bell, 2000, p. 1.

[25] Marchant, 2000.

[26] *Ibid.*

[27] As reported by Cooney, 2001, p. 10.

[28] See Thomas & Grader, 2000.

[29] Working document by the Secretariat, *Forests and Biodiversity*, UNEP/CBD/SBSTTA/3/Inf.22, 11 August 1997, paragraph 72.

[30] See paragraph 21, note 8 of the Separate Opinion.

[31] Principle 15 of the *Rio Declaration*.

[32] E.g., Attfield, 1994, p. 158; see paragraph 9.2 below.

Another worry is that the precautionary principle will stifle innovation. In a 2000 full page newspaper advert the company Pfizer argued that if granted a dominant role in decision-making the principle could "suppress the very forces of economic and technical innovation that make the current world possible" as well as deprive society of necessary investment and jobs, adding that "excessive caution may be the biggest risk of all."[33] Already in 1991 Handl detected "no-growth strands" in the fabric of the precautionary principle.[34] The anxiety that the principle may run counter to economic growth is shared by many of the principle's critics. One commentator, for instance, has drawn attention to the "collision course" of the precautionary *Kyoto Protocol* and the global economy:

> The global economy is moving toward dramatically expanded energy use and substantial increases of energy-related carbon emissions. The Kyoto Protocol aims to restrict energy emissions by restricting energy use. The Kyoto Protocol is at loggerheads with one of the broadest and deepest trends in the global marketplace. How, then, could Kyoto possibly be cheap or painless?[35]

Complementing this fear of economic disruption is the impression of Björn Lomborg and others, that the economic value of parts of nature threatened by human activities, and the size of environmental risks generally, tend to be exaggerated by those in favour of stringent precautions.[36] A befitting example of such alleged exaggeration is the argument used by environmentalists that encroaching upon biological diversity by removing even a single species could mean the end of the biosphere in its entirety.[37] As it is, one expert critical of this view has held that the rarest, most narrowly distributed species – i.e., the ones most likely to become extinct – are precisely the ones least likely to be missed.[38] By no stretch of the imagination can these, he contends, be made out to be vital cogs in the ecological machinery and thus necessary for human survival.[39]

> If the California condor disappears forever from the California hills, this will be a tragedy: but don't expect the chaparral to die, the redwoods to wither, the San Andreas fault to open up, or even the California tourist industry to suffer – they won't.[40]

---

[33] Advert in *European Voice* of 17-23 February 2000, p. 9, entitled "The Dangers of Precaution"; as quoted in Jordan, 2001, p. 154.
[34] Handl, 1991, p. 80.
[35] Lewis, 2000.
[36] Lomborg, 2001, *passim*.
[37] See *supra* paragraph 4.1.
[38] Ehrenfeld, 1988, p. 215.
[39] *Ibid.*
[40] *Ibid.*

As regards the economic price tag of environmental harm, it has been acknowledged even by avowed conservationists that the *direct* economic value of most animal and plant species and of some complete ecosystems is modest or non-existent.[41]

Cost-benefit analysis, coupled with the possibility to weigh the potential benefits of an activity against its potential adverse impact on the environment, has been proposed as a remedy for the claimed adverse effects of the precautionary principle on human society.[42] The European Chemical Industry Council (CEFIC) considers a cost-benefit analysis to be an integral part of the principle's application.[43] According to a CEFIC position statement, all consequences of precautionary action – "economic and social as well as environmental" – should be weighed in the light of existing scientific information so as to make sure that "the economic impact is proportionate to the environmental benefit."[44]

As related above, traditional cost-benefit analysis translates economic, social and ecological impacts into pecuniary equivalents in order to allow for meaningful comparison of the advantages and disadvantages of different courses of action. To limit the discussion to species diversity and to abide by one common division, flora and fauna are capable of having (a) commodity, (b) amenity and (c) moral value.[45] An animal or plant has commodity value when it constitutes, or can be made into, a marketable item.[46] Amenity value is present if a species improves human lives in some non-material way, e.g., when joy is experienced at the sight of a pair of ravens in flight. Wildlife species contribute as amenities to pursuits such as hiking, fishing, hunting and bird-watching, which in turn have market values of their own.[47] Moral value refers to the intrinsic value of species but also to the importance people attach to, for instance, the bare knowledge that snow leopards exist.[48] Economists have invented the notion of (d) option value, applicable to each of the three former categories, to represent the possibility that some day currently unknown uses of a species will be discovered or some other added worth will be assigned to its existence. Option value, in other

---

[41] Leopold, 1970, pp. 246-249.

[42] Pieterman & Hanekamp, 2002, pp. vii and 12.

[43] European Chemical Industry Council, 1995.

[44] *Ibid.*

[45] Norton, 1988, pp. 201-202; Beeckman, 1996, pp. 457-461.

[46] A species may have such value directly, such as the potential value of alligators for the manufacture of leather shoes, or indirectly, e.g. if vinyl shoes stamped in an alligator pattern turn out to sell for more than ordinary vinyl shoes. As many medicines are synthetic copies of biologically produced chemicals, indirect commodity value is of particular significance in the pharmaceutical industry. Norton, *ibid.*, p. 201.

[47] Norton, *ibid.*

[48] *Ibid.*, pp. 201-202.

words, is the benefit obtained by not eradicating a seemingly expendable species with a view to its potential future uses.[49] Several methods have been developed to facilitate the assessment of the full worth of individual species in monetary terms, such as market price methodology, travel cost analysis, hedonistic price valuation and contingent valuation.[50] The latter has been designed to enable putting a financial figure on species in the tricky categories of moral and option value. It employs 'shadow markets' in which people declare how much they would be willing to disburse to conserve a given plant or animal species, independent of any presently known direct uses. Option value is calculated by guessing the possible future uses of a species, assessing the probability of their discovery, attributing a monetary value to each use, and converting these into one present-day amount of money. Given that species are apt to rely on other species for their continued existence,[51] ecological information on such interdependencies needs to be factored in, so that by adding the individual values of any dependent species the final, aggregate value of a species can be obtained.[52] This end product can then be fed into a cost-benefit analysis in order to verify whether the total benefit of a proposed precautionary measure will outweigh its total cost. A matter of informed decision-making.

The Socio-Economic Rationale of Precautionary Action

Switching now to the second, contrasting group of opinions, this harbours those maintaining that long-term environmental preservation should prevail over short-term economic gains; that part of the rationale of the precautionary principle is precisely of a socio-economic nature; and that for various reasons the principle does not combine well with traditional cost-benefit analysis. Point of departure here is the goal of the precautionary principle. The *principal* purpose of the principle is quoted as being the protection, not of socio-economic interests but of the environment, including in its own right. It is felt that in past environmental decision-making natural values have too often been outweighed by social and economic ones, to the detriment of nature, and that the precautionary principle is intended to rectify this by adjusting the balance in favour of the environment.[53] The assertion by several NGOs involved with the marine environment that under the precautionary principle "the environmental implications of each and

---

[49] *Ibid.*, p. 202.

[50] See Norton, *ibid.*, *passim*; Ehrenfeld, 1988; Leakey & Lewin, 1996, pp. 124-144; Beeckman, 1996, pp. 457-466; Backes *et al.*, 1997, pp. 57-61; Alba Alonso & Rivas Infante, 1998, pp. 133-142; Delibes de Castro, 2001, pp. 285-306.

[51] On the interdependendies within ecological communities, see also *supra* paragraph 4.1.

[52] Norton, 1988, p. 203.

[53] Lemons *et al.*, 1997, p. 230; this point is also noted by Nollkaemper, 1996, p. 74.

every activity are considered first"[54] clearly reflects this hierarchy of priorities. In the same statement the conditioning of precautionary measures such as the application of cleaner production processes upon their economic availability is rejected accordingly.[55] In brief, the starting-point here is not the budget but the need to conserve the environment. The environmental risk in question determines whether precautionary action is necessary. And when such action is on balance necessary, the associated costs can by definition not be "excessive".[56] In this regard the point has been made that caution is not something which can generally be balanced:

> Being cautious when deciding whether to cross a busy road cannot mean balancing caution with other matters, such as the urgent need to reach persons on the other side. Certainly a decision can be made to take chances to facilitate crossing the road with greater speed, with keen attention paid to dodging oncoming traffic but, in that instance, caution has been abandoned, not balanced in the decision-making process.[57]

The primacy of environmental considerations aside, it has been contended that the rationale of the precautionary principle is in fact partly socio-economic. This argument is multifaceted and evidently merits closer study in the current context. The main thrust of the argument is that, especially in the long term, it is advantageous and even imperative *from a socio-economic point of view* to treat the environment in a precautionary fashion. It was already briefly discussed at the outset of this study that human health is one of the beneficiaries of sound environmental management.[58] According to the synthesis report on the implications for human health of the outcome of the comprehensive 2001-2005 Millennium Ecosystem Assessment, this outcome "indicates strongly that a precautionary approach to environmental protection is the most effective way to protect and enhance health."[59] On a broader scale, it is open to little dispute that human societies and economies at large are ultimately dependent on a healthy and functioning natural environment.[60] Their very basis is formed by the natural constitution of the planet, that is, the soil, the oceans, the atmosphere, the life forms inhabiting them, the ecosystems connecting all of these. The various Millennium Ecosystem Assessment reports leave no room for doubt regarding the

---

[54] Annex I of the *Final Declaration of the First 'Seas at Risk' Conference* held in Copenhagen, 1994, as cited in Backes et al., 1997, p. 69.
[55] *Ibid.*
[56] Attfield, 1994, p. 158.
[57] Mascher, 1997, p. 77; Lyster, 1997, p. 396 also quoted this passage.
[58] See *supra* paragraph 1.2.
[59] Corvalan *et al.*, 2005, p. 10.
[60] McGarvin, 2001(a), p. 39.

existence of a number of direct and indirect links between ecosystem functioning and human well-being, and between ecosystem health and human health.[61] In this light any strategy impairing these natural systems is deemed short-sighted and imprudent: if the foundation falters there is little future for the house.[62] Timothy Wirth,[63] Mikhaïl Gorbachev,[64] Geoffrey Palmer,[65] Gro Harlem Brundtland,[66] they have all voiced this worry in their own words. This is where the socio-economic rationale of the precautionary principle comes in. In the case of piloting, caution is employed to protect the vessel and the safety of the crew alike. Just so, it has been held, by aiming for the avoidance of environmental harm and erring on the side of caution the focus of the precautionary principle is on the safety of the fish stock *and* the fishery, the forest *and* the logging community, nature *and* society.[67] The inseverable ties between the precautionary principle, sustainable development and intergenerational equity are palpable here.[68] The claim that without conventional economic growth and the associated ecological impairment society as we know it cannot survive, is met by the claim that without a check on such growth no society at all can survive.[69] The

[61] Watson *et al.*, 2005 (Statement of the Board); Reid *et al.*, 2005 (Synthesis Report); Kumar Duralappah *et al.*, 2005 (Biodiversity Synthesis); Finlayson *et al.*, 2005 (Wetlands and Water Synthesis); Adeel *et al.*, 2005 (Desertification Synthesis); Corvalan *et al.*, 2005 (Health Synthesis).

[62] Norton, 1988, p. 205.

[63] "Now how many of the people that we all know – our neighbors, colleagues at work, friends – will tell us that they, too, are concerned about the destruction of the natural world and that they, too, are environmentalists, but we need a little balance? 'I am for the environment,' they say, 'as long as it does not cost jobs.' The truth is that over the long term, living off our ecological capital is a bankrupt economic strategy. The bulk of our economy is rooted in these biological systems. They are the foundation for most economic activity and most jobs. Stated in the jargon of the business world, the economy is a wholly-owned subsidiary of the environment. When the environment is finally forced to file for bankruptcy under Chapter 11 because its resource base has been polluted, degraded, dissipated, irretrievably compromised, then the economy goes bankrupt with it, and so does everything else." Wirth, 1999, p. 226.

[64] "Any growth at the expense of these precious [natural] resources will be short-lived and ultimately detrimental to the economy, the ecosystem and the people concerned." Gorbachev, 2000, p. 3.

[65] "If we are not careful we will be doing scientific research which amounts to a post mortem of our planet." Palmer, 1995, p. 189.

[66] "If we err in our decisions affecting the future of our children and our planet, let us err on the side of caution." As cited in Gullett, 1997, p. 55.

[67] Thomas & Grader, 2000.

[68] Kiss, 1996, p. 27; Trouwborst, 2002, pp. 12-13; see also *supra* paragraph 2.3.

[69] Without economic growth there will not be money for environmental protection, so it goes, muses Tennekes, and without scientific progress society's problems cannot be coped with. But growth refers to the initial stages of a life cycle, he continues, to infancy and puberty. The finite nature of our planet, however, requires adult behaviour. The time has come to stop

protection of nature cannot be seen as "an optional extra, to be considered once more pressing concerns such as wealth creation or national security have been dealt with," as the Board of the Millennium Ecosystem Assessment stated when evaluating the outcome of the project.[70] Instead, the statement continues, the assessment shows that "healthy ecosystems are central to the aspirations of humankind."[71]

Thus, it is argued, the procurement of long-term socio-economic sustainability may justify and even necessitate particular short-term socio-economic sacrifices.[72] The socio-economic costs of restricting a fisheries today are much smaller than the costs incurred when the whole fishery crumples tomorrow. It is the delay of preventive action which will ultimately prove most costly, to society as much as to nature.[73] Better safe than sorry.[74] Applied to the supposed collision course of the *Kyoto Protocol* and the global economy, precautionary action to combat climate change may indeed not be "cheap or painless", but it is necessary and beneficial in the medium and long run – and not only for tiny low-lying island states.[75] Applying the precautionary principle, on this view of the matter, is not (merely) about the selfless protection of nature and its intrinsic value. It is in the very own interest of states and citizens to do so.[76] As the US Congress put it: "Sheer self-interest impels us to be cautious."[77]

In this connection attention has been drawn to the socio-economic implications of the 'false negatives' that have been so abundant in the past record of environmental decision-making. In the field of living marine

---

growing. Tennekes, 2001, p. 108 (present author's approximation of this Dutch text). Also Bateson, 2004, p. 48.

[70] Watson *et al.*, 2005, p. 5.

[71] *Ibid.*

[72] *Ibid.*; Hey, 1992, p. 310; Tinker, 1995, p. 780; O'Riordan & Cameron, 1994(a), p. 17; Borgers, 1999, p. 438.

[73] O'Riordan & Cameron, *ibid.*; McGarvin, 2001(a), p. 39. As Christie, 1993, p. 480, wraps up: "One element of the rationale for the principle is that after taking into account the possible costs of being wrong, it will be better to find out to have been roughly right in due time – rather than precisely right too late."

[74] In the emphatic words of a 19th century North American Cree: "Only when the last tree has died, and the last river has been poisoned, and the last fish has been caught, will we realize that we cannot eat money." Cited in Cameron & Abouchar, 1996, pp. 29.

[75] The predicament of these nations, threatened by physical disappearance as a result of sea-level rise, is captured in the well-known statement: "The proof, we fear, will kill us." Ambassador Robert van Lierop, Permanent Representative of Vanuatu to the UN and co-chair of Working Group 1 of the Intergovernmental Negotiating Committee for a Framework Convention on Climate Change, *Statement to the Plenary Session of the INC/FCCC*, 5 February 1991, as quoted in Sands, 1995(a), at p. 209.

[76] Tinker, 1995, pp. 820-821.

[77] *HR Rep.*, No. 93-412, 1973, cited in Bodansky, 1994, p. 218.

resource management examples of precautionary approaches being applied, successfully, exist but are few and far between.[78] Books can and have been filled with examples, however, of entire fisheries, whether for fish, mollusks or marine mammals, that collapsed on account of overexploitation resulting from a lack of caution.[79] The socio-economic consequences in terms of the disappearance of income, jobs and whole coastal communities along with their traditions, have been tremendous.[80] The Californian sardine fishery discussed earlier comes to mind,[81] and so does the whaling industry.[82] For the North Sea too, "safe" quotas proved unsafe time and again and several species have come close to extinction.[83] Another instance is the Newfoundland Atlantic cod, mentioned before when treating the theme of uncertainty.[84] Cod fishing effort took on tremendous proportions in the second half of the twentieth century, in spite of the absence of reliable stock assessments.[85] As one report recounts: "We acted in substantial ignorance of the animals in which we were principally interested and in almost total ignorance of the dynamics of the ecosystems in which they existed."[86] Historically the largest in the world, the cod stock was driven to commercial extinction in a matter of decades.[87] The formal closure of the fishery in 1992 put 44,000 people out of work.[88] The financial price paid during the 1990s, in the form of lost sales, unemployment benefit and financial assistance of fishermen, amounted to several billion Canadian dollars.[89] Abalone[90] and Pacific groundfish[91] are just two more instances on a long list of similar stories, "all because a little common sense, a little caution, was never exercised up front."[92]

---

[78] Thomas & Grader, 2000.
[79] One recent book is Clover, 2005; see also MacGarvin, 2001(b), *passim*; Restrepo, 1998, pp. 2-3; Restrepo *et al.*, 1998, p. 2; and Thomas & Grader, *ibid.*
[80] Clover, *ibid.*, *passim.*
[81] See *supra* paragraph 8.1.
[82] Lyster, 1985, p. 19.
[83] Kaiser, 1997(a), p. 202.
[84] See *supra* paragraph 4.1.
[85] MacGarvin, 2001(b), pp. 20-22; Clover, 2005, pp. 103-115.
[86] Harris, L., *Independent Review of the State of the Northern Cod Stock*, Department of Fisheries and Oceans, Ontario 1990; quoted in MacGarvin, *ibid.*, p. 21.
[87] MacGarvin, *ibid.*, pp. 20-23.
[88] Clover, 2005, p. 153.
[89] MacGarvin, 2001(b), p. 22.
[90] This historic mollusk fishery along the Californian coast was destroyed by lack of research, lack of monitoring, failure to heed apparent warning signs, failure to adequately deal with diseases and an apparently misplaced trust in aquaculture. Thomas & Grader, 2000.
[91] See Thomas & Grader, *ibid.*
[92] *Ibid.*

Another instance is the dramatic environmental harm inflicted by the not-so-cautious approach taken by governments in the past towards PCBs, always postponing presumably costly precautionary measures pending the generation of yet more substantial scientific proof of noxiousness.[93] The total effects and costs comprising the legacy of this approach can only be guessed at.[94] Examples from the late 1960s and early 1970s include the closure of the striped bass fisheries in the Hudson River due to PCB pollution, and the fish populations of Lake Erie which died below dense mats of algae following excessive contamination.[95] Further examples of the economic and/or social costs of a lack of precautionary action include the heavy financial losses incurred in the oyster (*Crassostrea gigas*) aquaculture of Arcachon Bay in France due to the adverse impact of TBT ship paints on the reproduction of the shellfish;[96] the damage caused by the introduction of destructive species into ecosystems where they do not belong, like the Nile perch in Lake Victoria, rabbits in Australia, Gypsy moths in the eastern United States, or zebra mussels in the Great Lakes;[97] the huge sums of money spent within the framework of the *Montreal Protocol on Substances that Deplete the Ozone Layer* on the replacement of CFCs by hydrochlorofluorocarbons (HCFCs) and, subsequently, on the phasing out of the latter;[98] the enormous costs arising from acid rain;[99] and the socio-economic losses resulting from wetland degradation and unsustainable forest use in many areas of the world. To illustrate the latter, conservative estimates put the damage of the 1997/1998 Indonesian forest fires plus the resulting haze at over 4.4 billion US dollars, the equivalent of 2.5 percent of Indonesia's GDP at the time.[100] This figure is based on losses in timber revenue, agricultural production, water values and non-timber forest products; loss of life, damage to health, malnutrition due to crop destruction and biodiversity depletion are not included.[101] As for wetlands, several studies indicate that the majority of the frequently occurring Mississippi inundations would have been prevented if even half of the wetlands of the watershed had

---

[93] See Koppe & Keys, 2001, *passim*.
[94] *Ibid.*, p. 72.
[95] DeFur, 1999, p. 339.
[96] See Santillo *et al.*, 2001, pp. 136-137.
[97] Bell, 2002, p. 1.
[98] Farman, 2001, p. 81.
[99] Boehmer-Christiansen, 1994, p. 54.
[100] Greenpeace International, "Press backgrounder: Logging as a cause of rainforest fires", October 1999, quoting Down To Earth/International Campaign for Ecological Justice in Indonesia (UK), "Foreign Debt Fuels Forest Fires in Indonesia", 2 August 1999.
[101] *Ibid.*

been conserved instead of drained.[102] One single flooding in 1993 caused economic damages between 12 and 16 billion US dollars.[103] These are dwarfed, in turn, by the damages caused by hurricane Katrina, the most harmful in the record-breaking series of the 2005 Atlantic hurricane season, a series viewed by many scientists as a symptoms of human-induced climate change.[104] According to the US Congressional Budget Office, apart from the heavy toll in terms of human lives, Katrina alone could be responsible for a loss of 400,000 jobs and shaving one percent off US economic growth.[105] Reconstruction costs are estimated as exceeding 200 billion dollars.[106]

Time after time – whether concerning deforestation, desertification, overfishing, acid rain, climate change, TBT, PCBs or CFCs – early warnings, and even "loud and late" warnings, have been effectively ignored by decision-makers because of short-term socio-economic and political considerations.[107] As the European Environment Agency submits, even though 'shooting the messenger' has in the longer run rarely, if ever, promoted societal welfare, it has been a typical response to disturbing news ever since Galileo.[108] Apparently long-term precaution, along with its ensuing long-term socio-economic benefits, does not come naturally.[109] Which is precisely, so the argument goes, why a normative precautionary principle has been developed.

Plentiful analyses confirm that the anthropocentric worth of nature, ignoring ecocentrism, is by itself colossal.[110] This utilitarian value takes multiple shapes, ranging from market to moral values, as set out above. One study assessed the economic value of a Malaysian protected mangrove forest area of 8,700 hectares, the Sawara Mangrove Forest Reserve.[111] It calculated that the area sustained up to 3,000 jobs; marine fisheries worth over 21

---

[102] Various studies published in the magazine *Restoration Ecology*, 1995, referred to in Pascual Trillo, 2000, p. 153.

[103] *Ibid.*

[104] See, e.g., two recent studies in *Nature*, Nr. 436, 2005, pp. 686-688; and *Science*, Nr. 309, 2005, pp. 1844-1846.

[105] CNN/Money, 7 September 2005.

[106] *Ibid*; CNN/Weather, 30 December 2005; Associated Press, 10 September 2005.

[107] European Environment Agency, 2001, p. 168.

[108] *Ibid.*, p. 179.

[109] As the European Environment Agency, *ibid.*, p. 177, explains, "once a technological commitment is made, a host of institutional and market processes act to reinforce its position, even if markedly inferior to potential alternatives." A pre-eminent instance is the continued reliance of modern economies on fossil fuels, despite the availability of alternative sources such as solar energy which would seem to be preferable from nearly every point of view.

[110] See, e.g., Hanemann, 1988; Norton, 1988; Leakey & Lewin, 1996, pp. 124-144; Delibes de Castro, 2001, pp. 257-306.

[111] See *UN Doc.* E/CN.17/IFF/1999/10, Third Session of the UN Intergovernmental Forum on Forests, 24 February 1999, paragraph 25.

million US dollars annually; a tourist industry worth over 3.5 million dollars; and timber products worth about 23,000 dollars yearly. These economic revenues would largely be lost were the forest to be damaged, whereas this would also generate a need for costly engineering works to prevent coastal erosion and flooding[112] – although, as will be seen below, such works might bring in revenues and jobs in their own right. Another study indicates that around 3,000 plants have been identified as active agents against cancers, 70 percent of which occur in rainforests.[113] The value of the world market for prescriptions containing active ingredients from plants has been estimated to exceed 50 billion US dollars per year. Besides, many properties and as many species remain to be discovered.[114] US Congress justified the strict protection a species can be endowed with under the *Endangered Species Act*, *inter alia*, by reference to their option value: "Who knows, or can say, what potential cures for cancer or other scourges, present or future, may lie locked up in the structures of plants which may yet be undiscovered, much less analyzed?"[115] When an animal, plant or ecosystem goes extinct, the potential benefits it had in store for mankind are gone forever.[116] The constantly increasing amounts of species disappearing, irretrievably, on account of insufficient precaution have led Kiss and Shelton to submit that if ever there existed a field where remedial legal techniques have clearly failed, it is the one of nature conservation.[117] "The impoverishment this represents for humanity and the universe in general," they reflect, "is not only biological, but also scientific, cultural and undoubtedly economic."[118]

To comprehend the manifold anthropocentric value of nature it suffices to consider one class of ecosystems, forests. Forest ecosystems regulate the quantity and timing of water flow and control soil erosion, thus *inter alia* preventing floods, mudslides and desertification, they purify water and air, supply oxygen, enrich soils, stabilize local climates, play a key role as carbon stores and sinks in global climate regulation,[119] and are the habitat of an incredible diversity of life forms.[120] For people living in or near them they

---

[112] *Ibid.*

[113] *Ibid.*, paragraph 26.

[114] *Ibid.*; see also Farnsworth, 1988, *passim*.

[115] *HR Rep.*, No. 93-412, 1973, cited in Bodansky, 1994, p. 218.

[116] Norton, 1988, p. 202; Douma, 1997(a), pp. 1-2.

[117] Kiss & Shelton, 1991, p. 240.

[118] *Ibid.*

[119] The total quanitity of carbon stored in the trees and soils of the world's forests is reportedly larger than all the fossil fuels burnt in the last century. Greenpeace International, "Press backgrounder: Logging as a cause of rainforest fires", October 1999.

[120] On the several ecological functions of forests, see Smith & Smith, 2000, pp. 430-450; Pascual Trillo, 1998(a); López-Vera, 1998; Rodríguez Álvarez & Cruz León, 1994, pp. 53-54; Hughes, 1996, pp. 80-83. As for a tiny illustration of forest biodiversity, Australia has reported

fulfill basic needs for food, water, shelter materials and fuel.[121] They supply timber, pulp and a long list of other products traded in the world market. They supply jobs in the logging, pulp and paper industries but also, e.g., in tourism.[122] They are a source of drugs and medicines. They are, besides, of great scientific, cultural,[123] recreational, aesthetic, artistic,[124] spiritual, and religious value.[125] Finally, for the remaining indigenous peoples that never changed the woods for another place to live, the importance of the forests in which they dwell is not adequately conveyed by any listing of ecological, economic or other functions. To them the forest is all of the above and more. In sum, the commodity, amenity, moral and option values of forests are huge. Taking a strictly economic outlook, it could be alleged that not all of these forest products and services can be readily expressed in monetary terms, in spite of the various valuation methods described earlier – an issue which will receive more attention below – but that is not the point here. The dual point is that, whether directly or indirectly, humans profit from all of these products and services and that they are, no economist will fail to notice, provided gratis. When this exercise is done in respect of other ecosystems the outcome is similar: nature works free of charge.[126] To encroach upon this freely multiplying capital is an unsustainable course of action and overtly not an advisable economic strategy.[127] Besides, as stated above, the performance

1168 native tree species alone in its forests; Japan also over one thousand: http://www.unece.org/press/00tim5e.htm.

[121] Hughes, *ibid.*, p. 83-85.

[122] On the directly economic values of forest ecosystems, see Alba Alonso & Rivas Infante, 1998.

[123] Many legends and fairy tales, such as the one of Little Red Riding-Hood, are inextricably linked to the woods.

[124] Robert Frost, Francois Chateaubriand, Ivan Gontsjarov, Henry David Thoreau, Rudyard Kipling, Hermann Löns, Adalbert Stifter, W. Fernández Flórez, Trygve Gulbranssen, Richard Adams, J.R.R. Tolkien, Marten Toonder, Peter Matthiessen, David Guterson, Edward Abbey, Joaquín Araújo, Isabel Allende, Barbara Kingsolver, Kerstin Ekman – what would their work have been like if there had been no forests?

[125] On the various non-material values listed here, see Hughes, 1996, p. 83-85. As for the religious value of forests, the simple advice of Bernard of Clairveaux for those who doubted the existence of God was to "go to the woods." See Messori & Brambilla, 2000, p. 261.

[126] On the side, not everyone is equally pleased with this. Amos W. Steinhacker, one of the wealthiest tycoons of the twentieth century, regularly lost his temper over this issue. As he once angrily exclaimed: "Nature is the enemy of capital. Nature works for free! And for free is a curse! An abomination! Not nature ought to produce! We ought to produce! We! Ourselves!" Citation from Toonder, 2002, p. 394 (author's translation from Dutch).

[127] As the Board of the Millennium Ecosystem Assessment warns, "the benefits reaped from our engineering of the planet have been achieved by running down natural capital assets. In many cases, it is literally a matter of living on borrowed time." Watson *et al.*, 2005, p. 5.

of many of the ecological functions of forests and other natural systems is a *conditio sine qua non* for the reaping of any economic benefits in the long term.[128]

The examination of the 'second group' of arguments, where harm prevention and not the budget is the point of departure, has centred so far on the socio-economic price of environmental false negatives or Type II errors. The down side of acting out a precautionary strategy aiming to avoid false *negatives* is that the prospect of false *positives* occurring becomes patently more than hypothetical.[129] As pointed out by commentators from the 'first group' referred to above, under such a strategy environmental risks may be overstated, resulting in unwarranted costly measures. Various points have, in turn, been raised in reply to this concern. One of them takes the mould of an insurance analogy.[130] In order to ward off future threats to highly valued assets such as health or house, people are prepared to pay for costly insurance policies. That in many cases disaster will never strike does little to alter this. The fact that people *do* take on health and fire insurances obviously signifies that they do not consider the premiums ill-spent. When it comes to health or home most people simply prefer to err on the safe side. Just so, the argument goes, where the natural environment is at stake it is better to run the risk of overstatement than understatement.[131] Precautionary environmental standards have value, it is held, "not just because of actual damage averted, but because of their direct insurance value."[132] That value is unaffected by the subsequent course of events.[133]

Besides, actual examples of false positives, whereby expensive precautionary action turns out to have been misplaced later on, appear fairly hard to come by. Indeed, although the European Environment Agency names the ban on dumping sewage sludge in the North Sea as a tentative candidate, the Agency could not come up with any examples of false positives that were robust enough for inclusion in its 2001 report on "late lessons from early warnings", despite an invitation to industry representatives to submit such examples.[134] In the area of chemicals regulation, it has likewise been suggested that early suspicions about a substance are generally

[128] As David Suzuki put it: "Humanity really won the lottery with this planet. It provides everything we need to survive and to thrive. But right now, like some lotto winners, we are spending as if there is no tomorrow. We are eating away at our natural capital rather than living off the interest." Suzuki, 2005.

[129] Cameron *et al.*,1998, p. 104; Gullett, 1997, pp. 58-59.

[130] *Ibid.*, pp. 103-104; see also Cameron, 2001, p. 118; Jordan & O'Riordan, 1999, p. 29.

[131] "The essence of precautionary philosophy entails that some 'unnecessary' caution (with its associated costs) must be accepted." Gullett, 1997, pp. 58-59.

[132] Cameron *et al.*, *ibid.*

[133] *Ibid.*

[134] European Environment Agency, 2001, pp. 12-13.

confirmed or strengthened by later evidence.[135] Finally, commenting in hindsight on precaution in the United States, another writer found that with few exceptions early warnings warranted heeding and initial predictions were in the right direction, if not understated. "In retrospect, not only were all precautionary actions justified, we waited far too long to take those actions."[136] To all appearances, then, in environmental law and policy Type I errors are a rarity.

Other expostulations within the ambit of the second category of opinions center exclusively on the discipline of economics, claiming that the precautionary principle respects and builds on the basic laws of economics. Not only, as debated *supra*, is safeguarding the capital to enjoy the interest on a sustained basis part of the principle's fabric – besides forestry this economic motive plays a conspicuous role in discussions of, e.g., the precautionary regulation of whaling[137] and fisheries[138] – the principle also, several writers allege, assumes that financial resources may be allocated inefficiently if measures are taken only after proof of environmentally detrimental effects has been acquired.[139] This applies particularly when the aggregate risk in question is great and/or when alternatives for the risky activity, technology or product are available.[140] This argument of cost-efficiency is intimately linked to the broadly accepted contention that in environmental affairs prevention of harm is commonly cheaper than restoration – when this is at all possible – after damage is done.[141] To be precise, reportedly the weight of 28.35 grams of prevention is worth 454 grams of cure.[142] And the greater the value of the natural features in question, the stronger the argument becomes.[143] This rationale is apparent in the following joint position on fisheries of Unilever and Greenpeace:

> Our poor understanding of the marine environment demands that the emphasis be on prevention of damage, rather than attempts to repair mistakes through mitigation or restoration measures. The precautionary approach, therefore, should apply at all times, even when stocks are abundant. To apply the precautionary

---

[135] Wahlström, 1999, p. 68.
[136] Ashford, 1999, p. 205.
[137] Gillespie, 1997, p. 46.
[138] Freestone, 1999, p. 164.
[139] Hey, 1992, p. 309; Freestone & Hey, 1996(a), p. 12; Ashford, 1999, p. 199.
[140] Freestone & Hey, *ibid.*; Tinker, 1995, p. 795.
[141] Kiss & Shelton, 1991, p. 240; Weintraub, 1992/1996, p. 24; Tinker, *ibid.*; Martin, 1997, p. 269; Pascual Trillo, 2000, p. 165; Tickner *et al.*, 2000, p. 15; Tennekes, 2001, p. 64; Verstegen, "Milieumaatregelen Zijn Nooit te Duur" [i.e., "Environmental Measures are Never Too Expensive"], in Dutch newspaper *Trouw*, 15 October 2002.
[142] Appell, 2001.
[143] It has been submitted in this regard that under the precautionary principle damage to the most valuable natural assets should be avoided at *any* cost. Backes, 1997, pp. 5 and 7.

approach only when fish stocks are low is a reactive response and the very opposite of precaution.[144]

One way of looking at irreversible harm is the consideration that practically all costs of measures to prevent it are 'reasonable' and never 'excessive'.[145] After all, the costs of restoring irreversible harm are infinite by definition.

As regards actual instances of how the precautionary principle can save money, the professional trade literature seems to be replete with publications documenting the environmental *and* financial savings resulting from pollution prevention and clean production projects within industrial facilities.[146] An analysis by the Commonwealth of Massachusetts of the results of its precautionary *Toxics Use Reduction Act* shows that between 1990 and 1995 the Act not only made companies in the state reduce their toxic chemical emissions by more than two thirds and their total chemical waste by thirty percent, but also saved Massachusetts industry some fifteen million dollars.[147] In the 1980s in Germany large investments in a precautionary retrofitting program to combat acid rain paid off several ways in that it not only radically reduced emissions from combustion plants of SO2, NOx and particulates, but also reduced unemployment during a period of economic recession and recycled money in the national economy.[148] In answer to the criticism that precaution kills innovation it has been maintained that the precautionary curtailment of some development which is considered too risky actually serves to foster innovation in other areas – as exemplified by the cases, *inter alia*, of PCBs and halocarbons – providing competitive edges to the economies leading environmentally benign innovations in the process.[149] Rather than ending innovation, it is channeled into alternative routes and, as the case may be, even spurred, for instance by duties to apply

---

[144] Unilever, 1996, p. 5, paragraph 21.

[145] Kiss & Shelton, 1991, p. 240; Wildavsky, 2000, pp. 32-33, citing Norton, B., "On the inherent dangers of undervaluing species", Working Paper PS-3, Center for Philosophy and Public Policy, University of Maryland, p. 22. According to Norton's argumentation, incremental choices affecting biodiversity can be likened to the alcoholic's choice of whether to take a single drink - the one drink in this context being no small matter but, rather, a prelude to catastrophe.

[146] See the 1993 UNEP Industry and Environment Activity Center's compendium *Cleaner Production Worldwide*; and Geiser, 1999, pp. 325-326, for a selection of examples.

[147] Massachusetts Toxics Use Reduction Institute, *Massachusetts is Cleaner and Safer: Report on the Toxics Use Reduction Program*, Lowell 1997, cited in Tickner, 1999, p. 178.

[148] Boehmer-Christiansen, 1994, p. 54.

[149] European Environment Agency, 2001, p. 182; Tickner *et al.*, 2000, p. 16; Bell, 2002, p. 1. Attention has been drawn to the German experience with "green" innovation: Boehmer-Christiansen, *ibid.*; Jordan, 2001, p. 145.

clean production methods.[150] Besides, so it is claimed, the economic costs of precautionary measures are sometimes exaggerated.[151] (This point does not concern false negatives, but precautionary measures which, from an ecological point of view, were rightly taken.) The case of Sweden, a front-runner in the regulation of chemical pollution, has been cited in support of this statement. Substantiated evidence that the Swedish industry or its economy in general have suffered as a result of Sweden regulating ahead of or different from other states is reportedly lacking.[152]

The foregoing deliberations can be summarized in the proposition that according to many in the 'second group' of opinions, rather than causing economic bankruptcy, the precautionary principle is in fact a boost for the economy and increases prosperity.[153] It provides "an opportunity for, rather than a constraint upon" economic growth.[154] Pfizer's submission that the principle threatens to "suppress the very forces of economic and technical innovation that make the current world possible" is pitted against the contention that "[f]ar from damaging the economy [..] a precautionary approach can actually enhance economic efficiency, raise living standards, and lead to environmentally benign technological innovation."[155] The linkage between ecological precaution and economic progress has been dubbed a marriage for life.[156] A 'win-win' situation for environment and economy, so to speak.

The *Declaration on the Environment* of the 1990 Liberal International Congress is instructive in that it combines various elements of the alleged socio-economic rationale of the precautionary principle. It indicates that on the global level several environmental problems are emerging as a "threat to our survival" and that hence "action in such areas as global warming or the destruction of the ozone layer must not be further delayed with the argument

---

150 Raffensperger *et al.*, 1999; Tickner & Raffensperger, 2001, p. 200; European Environment Agency, *ibid.*; Bell, *ibid.*, pp. 1 and 4.

151 Wahlström, 1999, pp. 54 and 59-60.

152 *Ibid.*, pp. 59-60. As Bo Wahlström recalls the decision to phase out DDT use in Sweden in the 1970s: "Opponents pointed to the great economic importance of DDT in forestry and the great costs that would entail from a ban on its use. Since forestry based industries (e.g., the timber, pulp, and paper) contribute to a major share of Sweden's export income, this was an important argument. Years later, when the use of aerial spraying of herbicides in forestry was first restricted and then finally banned, the same catastrophic scenario of major export industries going bankrupt was raised by industry, as well as by some diehard herbicides fans in the scientific community. In neither case was there any measurable impact on the economy of individual companies, let alone the national economy." *Ibid.*, p. 54.

153 Tickner *et al.*, 2000, p. 16.

154 Jordan, 2001, p. 145.

155 Bell, 2002, p. 1.

156 Borgers, 1999, p. 441.

that scientific data is incomplete."[157] Moreover, the Declaration continues, in environmental protection "prevention is generally several times cheaper than cleaning up pollution afterwards."[158]

Cost-Benefit Analysis as Incompatible with Precautionary Action

Leaving behind the purported socio-economic rationale of the precautionary principle, the final argument to be addressed here concerns the (in)compatibility of the principle with cost-benefit analysis. In stark contrast with previously quoted opinions it has been suggested by some that subjecting candidate precautionary measures to such analyses would "undermine the anticipatory and visionary nature of precautionary action,"[159] and by others that attempts to do so "must be strongly resisted."[160] Opponents of the performance of cost-benefit analysis under the precautionary principle advocate against this because they consider such performance both *undesirable* and *impossible*, the two reasons being interlinked.

Undesirable, because the economic accounting methods involved in cost-benefit analysis submittedly do not do justice to the true costs of resource depletion and environmental degradation. These methods are biased in that they discount the long-term losses inherent in such impairment and therewith the future benefits of precautionary action taken today to prevent it, while overemphasizing the short-term economic costs of such action.[161] Especially in the area of nature conservation it is often easier said than done to express the advantages of protective measures in monetary units, whereas the sacrifices that follow from those measures often bare an economic character and are easily converted in a euro or dollar value. Undesirable, furthermore, because, as Aldo Leopold termed it in the first half of the previous century, environmental policies based wholly on economic figures are "hopelessly lopsided."[162] To cite some famous examples of the grotesqueness of relying solely on economic figures, in Alaska the GDP and employment figures boomed as a result of the massive clean-up operation after the Exxon Valdez oil spill in 1989, and from a traditional economic cost-benefit perspective even the introduction of Nile perch in Lake Victoria could be termed a success story.[163] The propensity, inherent in

157 Section III, paragraph 5.

158 *Ibid.*

159 Tickner & Raffensperger, 2001, p. 203.

160 Santillo *et al.*, 1999, p. 48.

161 Freestone & Hey, 1996(b), p. 258; Backes *et al.*, 1997, p. 57; Ashford, 1999, pp. 199-201; Jiménez Beltrán, 2001, pp. 3-4; Tickner & Raffensperger, 2001, p. 200.

162 Leopold, 1970, p. 251.

163 Hubert Sauper's 2004 documentary *Darwin's Nightmare* is illustrative, as is Goldschmidt, 1998.

traditional cost-benefit analysis, to value things which can be expressed in numbers higher than things which cannot, has been heavily criticized.[164] It will do to quote one prominent opponent of attempts to express the value of ecosystems, species, biological diversity or a healthy environment in a financial figure:

> It does not occur to us that by assigning value to diversity we merely legitimize the process that is wiping it out, the process that says, 'The first thing that matters in any important decision is the tangible magnitude of the dollar costs and benefits.' People are afraid that if they do not express their fears and concerns in this language they will be laughed at, they will not be listened to. This may be true [..]. But true or not, it is certain that if we persist in this crusade to determine value where value ought to be evident, we will be left with nothing but our greed when the dust finally settles. [..] Value is an intrinsic part of diversity; it does not depend on the properties of the species in question, the use to which particular species may or may not be put, or their alleged role in the balance of global ecosystems. For biological diversity, value *is*. Nothing more and nothing less.[165]

Here, undesirability meets impossibility. Representing the value of any part of the environment in a credible and comprehensive single figure, economic or otherwise, is considered by many commentators as a plain impracticality; and any such figure as arbitrary by nature.[166] The result of this impossibility to adequately quantify the value of species and ecosystems is the criticized misrepresentation of the future environmental costs of proposed activities, i.e., of the future benefits of precautionary measures, in cost-benefit analysis with its logic of "what cannot be counted does not count".[167]

The main obstacles standing in the way of a reliable monetary valuation of nature, which is the same as saying the main causes of the asserted incompatibility of the precautionary principle and cost-benefit analysis, are (1) uncertainty, (2) irreversibility and (3) the intrinsic value of nature. Reasoning regarding the first obstacle coincides to a large extent with previous observations made in the present study on the complexity and variability of nature, the many sorts of, often irresolvable, uncertainty which mar environmental decision-making, and the ensuing frequent impossibility to predict environmental impacts and to quantify risks.[168] The corresponding

---

164 Leopold, 1970, pp. 246-251; Ehrenfeld, 1988, pp. 213-214; Norton, 1988, p. 204; Tennekes, 2001, p. 106.

165 Ehrenfeld, *ibid.*; emphasis in original.

166 Leopold, 1970, pp. 246-251; Ehrenfeld, *ibid.*, p. 214; Iltis, 1988, p. 99; Norton, 1988, pp. 203-205; Tinker, 1995, p. 810; Hansson, 1997, p. 295; Schuppert, 1997, pp. 248-249 and 256; Ashford, 1999, p. 201; Wahlström, 1999, p. 60; European Environment Agency, 2001, p. 168.

167 Tennekes, 2001, p. 107; Jordan & O'Riordan, 1999, p. 17.

168 See *supra* paragraph 4.1.

challenges are rather impressive. Given the fundamental limitations on scientific knowledge and understanding of the functions and relations of species, ecosystems and natural processes, how is one to figure out the true value of any piece of the natural world?[169]

> We do not know enough about any gene, species, or ecosystem to be able to calculate its ecological and economic worth in the larger scheme of things. Even in relatively closed systems (or in systems that they pretend are closed), economists are poor at describing what is happening and terrible at making even short-term predictions based on available data. How then should ecologists and economists, dealing with huge, open systems, decide on the net present or future worth of any part of diversity?[170]

And when the relatively tangible commodity and amenity values of species and ecosystems are hard to determine,[171] how about their option value? How is one to imagine, let alone value a use which has not yet been imagined?[172] Computing the cost of erasing even a square meter of old-growth forest appears unfeasible in this light. And how to calculate the monetary damage of a species disappearing whose very existence had not even been detected?[173] As described before, not even by a long shot are all species known to science.[174] Given all these open questions, one natural scientist has portrayed contemporary efforts to put a number on the value of species and ecosystems as "clumsy rewrites of 'The Emperor's New Clothes'."[175]

The second weak spot in the mechanism of cost-benefit analysis pointed out by critics is that it has trouble comparing options when one or more of them are irreversible.[176] How to factor in the value of irretrievable loss? "If we decide to have a dam and give up a species, blowing up the dam won't bring the species back."[177] In other words, the costs and benefits of decisions of this kind cannot be juggled with at will. The intrinsic value of nature is the third and last obstacle to a credible monetary valuation to be

---

169 Norton, 1988, p. 203; De Sadeleer, 2002, p. 299.

170 Ehrenfeld, 1988, p. 214.

171 Norton, 1988, p. 202.

172 Ehrenfeld, 1988, p. 214, provides an instance: "Before we fully appreciated the vital role that mycorrhizal symbiosis plays in the lives of many plants, what kind of value would we have assigned to the tiny, threadlike fungi in the soil that make those relationships possible?" See also Norton, *ibid.*; Iltis, 1988, p. 99.

173 Iltis, *ibid.*; Ehrenfeld, *ibid.*

174 See *supra* paragraph 4.1.

175 Ehrenfeld, 1998, p. 214. He added: "I cannot help thinking that when we finish assigning values to biological diversity, we will find that we don't have very much biological diversity left." *Ibid.*, p. 216.

176 Norton, 1988, pp. 202-203; Jordan & O'Riordan, 1999, p. 17.

177 Norton, *ibid.*, p. 203.

treated here. Expressing the dimensions of a value which is defined as non-anthropomorphic in anthropomorphic terms – not to speak of the pinnacle of utilitarian language: monetary terms – is a logical impossibility.[178] It does not take much to comprehend that this poses a particularly hardy challenge for cost-benefit analysis in the context of the precautionary principle.

In a nutshell, uncertainty, irreversibility and intrinsic value are fundamental *ingredients* of the precautionary principle and fundamental *problems* for cost-benefit analysis. The impossibility and undesirability of submitting precautionary action to such analysis were the focus of a speech by Bryan Norton to a major conference on biological diversity held in 1988, in which he addressed the recurrent demand for quantification:

> If we are not taken seriously unless we quantify our answer, I would like to suggest some new units of measurement. An *oops* is the smallest unit of chagrin that we would feel if we willfully extinguish a species we need later on. A *boggle* is the amount of ignorance encountered when an economist asks a biologist a question about species and ecosystems, and the biologist answers: 'I don't know, and I'm so far from knowing, it boggles the mind.' If I understand what the economists are saying, irreversible oopses and boggles of uncertainty are the main factors in decisions affecting biodiversity. In the passion to express the values of species in dollar figures, it will be unfortunate if we forget to count oopses and boggles as well.[179]

Instead of economic valuation methods Norton suggests adopting the "big picture method", in a statement clearly incorporating the socio-economic rationale of the precautionary principle:

> Now, the question is easier. The value of biodiversity is the value of everything there is. It is the summed value of all the GNPs of all countries from now until the end of the world. We know that, because our very lives and our economies are dependent upon biodiversity. If biodiversity is reduced sufficiently, and we do not know the disaster point, there will no longer be any conscious beings. With them will go all value - economic and otherwise. I am afraid this answer will not be useful to those who want to know the value lost when they extinguish a species, but it seems a better answer than a guess, even a guess that counts oopses and boggles as well as dollars. One thing we know, if we lose enough species, we will be sorry.[180]

Much of the above culminates in the simple acknowledgement that proposing to submit precautionary measures to cost-benefit analysis is to fundamentally misunderstand the precautionary principle. After all, was it

---

[178] See also Ehrenfeld, 1988, pp. 213-214; Norton, *ibid.*, p. 201; Tinker, 1995, p. 810; De Sadeleer, 2002, p. 300.
[179] Norton, *ibid.*, pp. 204-205.
[180] *Ibid.*, p. 205.

not precisely the crux of the principle that limiting the basis of environmental decision-making to quantifiable data has proved to be a very bad idea?[181]

A Middle Way
With this paragraph drawing to a close, many aspects of the controversy surrounding the relationship between the precautionary principle and socio-economic interests have been reviewed in the course of a discussion of contrary opinions. As said before, the debate is not as black-and-white as sketched so far. Some commentators take an intermediate stance. As regards the opposing portrayals of the precautionary principle as, on the one hand, a barrier to the forces of economic progress and, on the other hand, a positive enabler of sustainable development, one author observes that "truth lies somewhere between these two extremes."[182] Various writers, while duly stressing the primacy of environmental harm avoidance or the impossibility of traditional cost-benefit analysis, nevertheless consider *some* consideration of socio-economic aspects or *some* form of cost-benefit comparison inevitable in decision-making under the precautionary principle, arguing that the prevention of environmental risks may not always be worth *any* price.[183] Accordingly, costs and benefits of precautionary action, whether economic, social or environmental, should be considered, but in a truly comprehensive way, meaning that effects on *all* values of the environment, including in the long term, are accorded their genuine weight and any uncertainties are accounted for.[184] So-called trade-off analysis has been proposed as an alternative to traditional cost-benefit analysis in the context of the precautionary principle.[185] Trade-off analysis sets out in the same way as the traditional method but stops short of assigning monetary values to non-monetary effects. All consequences are put in their natural units, the time period in which each effect is experienced is wholly revealed, future effects are not discounted to present value, and uncertainties are acknowledged and entirely described.[186]

The focus must now shift from the multitude of positions on how the law should be, and from the logic and philosophy behind these, to the law itself, and therefore to the practice of states. It will be interesting to see how

---

181 See *supra* paragraphs 3.1 and 4.1; Schuppert, 1997, pp. 248-249, 256; Tickner & Raffensperger, 2001, p. 200.
182 Jordan, 2001, p. 154.
183 Von Moltke, 1999; Cameron *et al.* ,1998, p. 104; Gullett, 1997, pp. 58-59; Nollkaemper, 1996, p. 73; Freestone & Hey, 1996(a), p. 12; Bodansky, 1994, p. 219.
184 Backes *et al.*, 1997, p. 61; Freestone & Hey, *ibid.*; Howard & Saunders, 1999.
185 Ashford, 1999, p. 201.
186 *Ibid.*

the opinions treated above correspond to the positions of states – who necessarily make up their minds after individuals do.

9.2. *Socio-Economic Interests in Practice*

The route to be taken in the subsequent examination of state practice is plotted by a number of questions. How do socio-economic considerations relate to the goal and rationale of the precautionary principle? Is there a general requirement for precautionary measures to be cost-effective? If so, what is meant by cost-effectiveness and how is it to be achieved? If not, what then is the place, if any, of socio-economic considerations in the application of the principle? In particular, is there any room for a balancing of environmental and socio-economic benefits and costs when deciding on precautionary measures?

State Practice and the Rationale of the Precautionary Principle

Setting off with the first question, deliberations in previous chapters have already revealed that the *primary aim* of the precautionary principle as it has been adopted by states is undeniably to *protect the environment* as a whole, including in its own right.[187] In this sense, environmental stakes clearly seem to assume superiority over economic stakes under the principle. The EU Court of Justice has stated unequivocally in this regard that the precautionary principle obliges competent authorities "to take appropriate measures to prevent specific potential risks to public health, safety and the environment, by giving precedence to the requirements related to the protection of those interests over economic interests."[188]

This is not to say that considerations of an economic or social nature have not been of any consequence in the motivations of governments to accept and abide by the principle. The strong ties between the precautionary principle and the notion of sustainable development is testimony to the fact that in the larger scheme of things such considerations evidently do play a part.[189] The *Biosafety Protocol*, for instance, recognizes that precautionary action with regard to living modified organisms may be called for to protect not only biological diversity but also, in the process, the indigenous and local communities dependent on such diversity, expressly allowing contracting parties to take account of such socio-economic factors when deciding on

---

[187] See, especially, *supra* paragraph 3.1.

[188] Paragraph 184 of Joined Cases T-74/00, T-76/00, T-83/00 to T-85/00, T-132/00, T-137/00 and T-141/00, Judgment of the Court of First Instance of 26 November 2002.

[189] See *supra* paragraph 2.3.

precautionary measures.[190] It is important to note in this regard that socio-economic factors may, depending on the circumstances, constitute arguments against as much as in favour of precautionary action.[191]

It is abundantly clear from the history of international environmental law that the past and present motives of states to protect the environment and to conserve natural resources are multiple, and include ecocentric as much as anthropocentric ones. Not only the intrinsic, but also the huge and multifaceted values for mankind of nature and a healthy environment have been emphasized time and again. As far as the human health benefits of a precautionary approach to environmental protection are concerned it suffices to quote a 2000 statement by the Environment Ministers of the G-8 countries:

> The protection of human health from the effects of pollution and other forms of environmental degradation is an issue on the forefront of citizens' concerns. Our policies should be based on the precautionary approach, as set forth in Principle 15 of the Rio Declaration.[192]

Many relevant statements concerning the multiple values of nature can be found in the preambles of legal instruments.[193] The very first words of the *Biodiversity Convention* confirm that its contracting parties are conscious of "the intrinsic value of biological diversity and of the ecological, genetic, social, economic, scientific, educational, cultural, recreational and aesthetic values of biological diversity and its components," besides the importance of such diversity "for evolution and for maintaining life sustaining systems of the biosphere."[194] Parties also recognize the "close and traditional dependence of many indigenous and local communities embodying traditional lifestyles on biological resources."[195] It is instructive to consider a selection of similar statements:

> Recognizing the interest of the nations of the world in safeguarding for future generations the great natural resources represented by the whale stocks;
>
> Having decided to conclude a convention to provide for the proper conservation of whale stocks and thus make possible the orderly development of the whaling industry;[196]

---

[190] Article 26(1).

[191] Marr, 2003, pp. 39 and 105.

[192] Communiqué by the G8 Environment Ministers' Meeting in Otsu, Japan, 7-9 April 2000, paragraph 23.

[193] See also *supra* paragraph 5.3.

[194] First and second preambular paragraphs.

[195] Preambular paragraph 12.

[196] 1946 *International Convention for the Regulation of Whaling*, first and seventh preambular paragraphs.

> Fully conscious that soil, water, flora and fauna resources constitute a capital of vital importance to mankind;[197]
>
> Considering the fundamental ecological functions of wetlands as regulators of water regimes and as habitats supporting a characteristic flora and fauna, especially waterfowl;
> Being convinced that wetlands constitute a resource of great economic, cultural, scientific and recreational value;[198]
>
> Conscious of the ever-growing value of wild animals from environmental, ecological, genetic, scientific, aesthetic, recreational, cultural, educational, social and economic points of view;[199]
>
> Recognizing that wild flora and fauna constitute a natural heritage of aesthetic, scientific, cultural, recreational, economic and intrinsic value;
> Recognizing the essential role played by wild flora and fauna in maintaining biological balances;[200]
>
> Civilization is rooted in nature, which has shaped human culture and influenced all artistic and scientific achievement, and living in harmony with nature gives man the best opportunities for the development of his creativity, and for rest and recreation;[201]
>
> Recognizes that climate change is a common concern of mankind, since climate is an essential condition which sustains life on earth;[202]
>
> Concerned over the existence and threats of adverse effects, in the short or long term, of changes in the conditions of transboundary watercourses and international lakes on the environment, economies and well-being of the member countries of the Economic Commission for Europe.[203]

In these statements, all of which are taken from instruments widely adhered to by states, one will recognize many ingredients of the alleged socio-economic rationale of the precautionary principle discussed in the preceding paragraph. Sustainable economies, safeguarding the capital, reserving potential future gains, life-support systems, the utter survival of human societies, values ranging from commodity to moral values: the arguments are all there. It is the unequivocal intention of the international community not to jeopardize this priceless environment with its multiple functions and values. A matter of "sheer self-interest".[204] The precautionary principle, as

---

197 1968 *African Convention*, first preambular paragraph.

198 1971 *Ramsar Convention*, second and third preambular paragraphs.

199 1979 *Bonn Convention*, third preambular paragraph. The second preambular paragraph of the 1973 *CITES* is similarly phrased, although it lists only the "ever-growing" aesthetic, scientific, cultural, recreational and economic values of wild flora and fauna.

200 1979 *Berne Convention*, third and fourth preambular paragraphs.

201 1982 *World Charter for Nature*, preambular paragraph 2(b).

202 1988 UNGA *Resolution 43/53*, first paragraph.

203 1992 *Helsinki Watercourses Convention*, second preambular paragraph.

204 See the US Congress pronouncement quoted in the previous paragraph.

the most developed form of prevention,[205] has been adopted by states to this end. As the British administration has phrased its reasons for accepting the principle: "Just as we believe that it is irresponsible for Government to be extravagant with taxpayers money, so we see even stronger arguments against wasting the world's or this country's natural resources and bequeathing a burden of environmental debt tomorrow."[206]

To further exemplify this point it is worthwhile to recall the functions and values of forest ecosystems enumerated above. The massive and multiple worth described there does not just exist in the overstated opinions of a few scientists and environmentalists: it has been formally recognized by the worldwide community of states, foremostly in the *Forest Principles* adopted at the 1992 Earth Summit.[207] There it is stated that all types of forests embody "complex and unique ecological processes which are the basis for their present and potential capacity to provide resources to satisfy human needs;" are besides of value "to local communities and to the environment as a whole;"[208] and if sustainable managed offer "potential for development."[209] The protection and sustainable management of forest ecosystems is called for to meet the "social, economic, ecological, cultural and spiritual human needs of present and future generations," which needs are for "wood and wood products, water, food, fodder, medicine, fuel, shelter, employment, recreation, habitats for wildlife, landscape diversity, carbon sinks and reservoirs, and for other forest products."[210] The instrument moreover stresses the "vital role" of forests in the maintenance of ecological processes at various levels through, among other things, "protecting fragile ecosystems, watersheds and freshwater resources and as rich storehouses of biodiversity and biological resources and sources of genetic material for biotechnology products, as well as photosynthesis."[211]

It becomes apparent from all these formal assertions that even arguments of a purely economic character are part and parcel of the motivations of states for taking precautionary action. As the World Commission on Environment and Development put it, "the economic values inherent in the genetic materials of species are alone enough to justify species

---

[205] See *supra* paragraph 4.2.

[206] *White Paper: "This Common Inheritance: Britain's Environmental Strategy"*, September 1990, paragraph 1.88, as cited in O'Riordan & Cameron, 1994(a), p. 24.

[207] *Non-Legally Binding Authoritative Statement of Principles for a Global Consensus on the Management, Conservation and Sustainable Development of All Types of Forests.*

[208] Preamble, under (f).

[209] *Ibid.*, under (c).

[210] Principle 2(b).

[211] Principle 4.

preservation."[212] As for another economic argument, from the outset states have repeatedly indicated that one of the reasons for adopting the precautionary principle is the idea that preventing environmental harm is liable to be more efficient and cost-effective than undoing it after the act.[213] Indeed, this argument has been a major factor in the application of *Vorsorge* in the cradle of the principle, Germany.[214] Hungarian legislation stipulates that "the use of the environment shall be subject to the precautionary principle, *meaning* that the components of the environment are treated carefully and *economically*."[215] Baltic coastal states have expressed the conviction that damage to the marine environment "can be irreversible or remediable only in a long term perspective and *at considerable expense* and that, *therefore*, Contracting Parties to the Convention must adopt a precautionary approach."[216] North Sea governments have issued a similar statement.[217] The same notion has been expressed, *inter alia*, in the contexts of international watercourses, where states have professed that preventive action "addresses the harm more efficiently and can be more cost-effective than remedial action,"[218] and of invasive alien species, in respect of which it has been stated that prevention is generally "far more cost-effective" than measures taken following introduction and establishment of a species.[219] Furthermore, it has been noted in the *Climate Change Convention* that various precautionary measures can be "justified economically in their own right."[220] An instance of the latter in the context of marine pollution is represented by a 1990 OSCOM Decision prohibiting incineration at sea:[221]

> This Decision takes into account concerns expressed about potential implications of incineration at sea, but is not based on evidence that harmful effects have been observed. The decision is based on the fact that Contracting Parties are in the process of developing methods for the reduction of wastes which result from production processes and that Contracting Parties have developed, or intend to develop, land-based alternatives for recycling and destruction. In most cases of

---

[212] World Commission on Environment and Development, 1987, p. 155.
[213] See also Douma, 1997(a), p. 5.
[214] Boehmer-Christiansen, 1994, p. 39.
[215] Chapter I, Section 6(2) of the 1995 *Law No. 53 Promulgating General Rules on the Protection of the Environment*, as quoted in Marr, 2003, p. 93 (emphasis added).
[216] Paragraph 8 of the preamble to the 1988 *Baltic Sea Declaration* (emphasis added).
[217] Paragraph A7 of the 1984 *First North Sea Declaration*.
[218] Article 5(c) of the 1999 *Protocol on Water and Health* to the 1992 *Helsinki Watercourses Convention*.
[219] 2002 *Guiding Principles on Invasive Alien Species*, Guiding principle 2.
[220] 17th preambular paragraph.
[221] OSCOM *Decision 90/2* of 23 June 1990, discussed in Freestone & Hey, 1996, p. 12.

avoidance and recycling, land-based treatment may be cheaper than incineration at sea.[222]

The link between precaution and innovation, discussed previously, has also been stressed, for instance by the Government of Germany when it submitted in a report under the *Biodiversity Convention* that "the principle of precautionary action obliges us to reduce the risks to humankind, nature and the environment using the advances made in science and technology."[223] As for another clue, it is probably fair to say that it is doubtful whether states would ever have embraced the precautionary principle in the first place had they not believed that doing so was, on balance, economically sound.

Summing up, social and economic considerations, although not its principal focus, have plainly been an indispensable feature of the precautionary principle from the beginning of its evolution in public international law. They are innate.

State Practice and Cost-Effectiveness

The second question posed above concerns the condition of cost-effectiveness. A literal reading of Principle 15 of the *Rio Declaration* would appear to suggest that precautionary measures which *are* allowed to be postponed on account of uncertainty are those which are not "cost-effective".[224] Before embarking on a closer examination of the meaning of the term, however, it must be corroborated whether indeed the criterion of cost-effectiveness embodies a standard of general application within the framework of the precautionary principle.

The *Rio Declaration* does not stand alone with its reference to "cost-effective measures". Besides the considerable number of instruments alluding to Principle 15,[225] of the intergovernmental instruments that define the precautionary principle (rather than merely name it) at least seven contain an allusion to cost-effectiveness, including the *Climate Change Convention*[226] and the *Waigani Convention*.[227] Other provisions lack such reference, however. Out of

---

[222] As cited by Freestone & Hey, *ibid.*, in note 41. According to these authors, the Decision illustrates the assumption inherent in the precautionary principle that finances may be spent inefficiently if action is taken only after proof of harm has become available. *Ibid.*, p. 12.

[223] *Federal Government Report under the Convention on Biological Diversity* of March 1998; Marr, 2003, p. 112.

[224] González Campos, 1998, p. 799.

[225] See *supra* paragraph 2.3.

[226] Article 3(3) states that "policies and measures to deal with climate change should be cost-effective so as to ensure global benefits at the lowest possible cost."

[227] Article 1 contains the phrase "cost-effective measures", identical to Principle 15 of the *Rio Declaration*. The same reference is included in Principle 7 of the 1990 *Ministerial Declaration of the Second World Climate Conference*; Article 4(3)(a) of the *Barcelona Convention* as amended in 1995;

the international instruments containing some definition of the principle some fourty, including the *Bergen Declaration*,[228] the *Biodiversity Convention*,[229] the *OSPAR Convention*[230] and the *Straddling Stocks Agreement*,[231] speak only of "action", "measures" and the like, without the slightest hint at the cost-effectiveness of this action or these measures.[232] Two curious cases are the *Biosafety Protocol* and the *Albatross Agreement*. Whereas both agreements

---

and paragraph 24 of the 1995 *Land-Based Activities Action Programme*. Article 19(1) of the 1994 *Energy Charter Treaty* lists an obligation to "act in a Cost-Effective manner" alongside the duty to take precautionary measures. According to the fourth preambular paragraph of the 1994 *Second Sulphur Protocol* to the *LRTAP Convention*, it must be taken into account that "precautionary measures to deal with emissions of air pollutants should be cost-effective."

[228] Paragraph 7: "measures".

[229] Ninth preambular paragraph: "measures".

[230] Article 2(2)(a): "preventive measures". Marr, 2003, p. 61 also notes the absence of a cost-effectiveness criterion here.

[231] Article 6(2): "conservation and management measures".

[232] 1984 *First North Sea Declaration*, paragraph A7: "action"; 1987 *Second North Sea Declaration*, preambular paragraph VII: "action to control inputs"; *ibid.*, paragraph XVI: "reducing polluting emissions"; 1988 *Baltic Sea Declaration*, eighth preambular paragraph: "action"; 1989 PARCOM *Recommendation 89/1*: "appropriate measures"; 1989 *Declaration of the Nordic Council's International Conference on Pollution of the Seas*: "eliminating and preventing polluting emissions"; 1990 *Third North Sea Declaration*, preamble: "action"; 1991 HELCOM *Recommendation 12/3*, paragraph 1: "action"; 1991 OECD *Council Resolution C(90)164 on Integrated Pollution Prevention and Control*, section "Guidance": "precautionary action"; 1991 *Action Plan for the Conservation of Cetaceans in the Mediterranean Sea*, paragraph 4: "action"; 1991 *Trilateral Wadden Sea Declaration*, paragraph 3: "action"; 1991 *Bamako Convention*, Article 3(f): "preventing the release into the environment of substances" and "appropriate measures to implement the precautionary principle"; 1992 HELCOM *Recommendation 13/6*, paragraph 1(3): "preventive measures"; 1992 *Helsinki Watercourses Convention*, Article 2(5): "action"; 1992 Agenda 21, paragraph 17.21: "precautionary measures"; 1992 *Central American Hazardous Wastes Agreement*, Article 3(3): "medidas apropiadas" (i.e., appropriate measures); 1992 *Baltic Sea Convention*, Article 3(2): "preventive measures"; 1993 *General Guidelines for the Conservation of the Biodiversity of European Forests*, preambular paragraph F: "measures"; 1994 *SPS Agreement*, Article 5(7): "sanitary or phytosanitary measures"; 1994 *Convention on the Protection of the Meuse*, Article 3(2)(a): "action"; 1994 *Convention on the Protection of the Scheldt*, Article 3(2)(a): "action"; 1994 CITES *Resolution Conf. 9.24*, fourteenth preambular paragraph, second operative paragraph and Annex 4, paragraph A: "act in the best interest of the conservation of the species"; 1995 *IUCN Draft Covenant*, Article 7: "action"; 1995 *Mediterranean SPA and Biodiversity Protocol*, fifth preambular paragraph: "measures"; 1995 *Pan-European Biological and Landscape Diversity Strategy*, Section 2.4, paragraph 3: "action"; 1995 *FAO Code of Conduct for Responsible Fisheries*, Principle 6.5: "measures"; *ibid.*, Principle 7.5.1: "conservation and management measures"; 1996 *Mediterranean Hazardous Wastes Protocol*, Article 8(3): "appropriate measures"; 1996 *LDC Protocol*, Article 3(1): "appropriate preventive measures"; 1996 *ACCOBAMS*, Article II(1): "all necessary measures"; 1997 *Trilateral Wadden Sea Plan*, paragraph 8: "action"; 1999 *Protocol on Water and Health* to the *Helsinki Watercourses Convention*, Article 5(a): "action"; 2000 *Galapagos Agreement*, Article 5(1)(b): "precautionary measures"; 2000 *Honolulu Convention*, Article 6(2): "conservation and management measures"; 2001 *Convention on the Conservation and Management of Fishery Resources in the South-East Atlantic Ocean*, Article 7(2): "conservation and management measures".

mention Principle 15 of the *Rio Declaration*, in their substantive provisions actually spelling out the precautionary principle no allusion whatsoever to cost-effectiveness can be found.[233] Domestic practice matches the intergovernmental picture, as most formulations of the principle in national laws and policy documents do not incorporate a reference to cost-effectiveness while some, sometimes within the same country, do.[234] Simon Marr analyzed legislation and policy instruments incorporating the precautionary principle of 34 states.[235] He detected requirements to carry out some form of cost-benefit analysis in six cases,[236] whereas such requirements were found to be absent in the domestic precautionary practice of the other 28 countries.[237]

Obviously, numbers do not always say everything.[238] At present, however, the odds appear to persuasively rule out the possibility that a separate requirement of cost-effectiveness is part of the precautionary

---

233 The fourth preambular paragraph and Article 1 of the 2000 *Biosafety Protocol* refer to Principle 15 of the *Rio Declaration*, whereas the substantive Articles 10(6) and 11(8) do not incorporate the criterion of cost-effectiveness; see also Fukudu-Parr *et al.*, 2001, p. 70. The 16th preambular paragraph of the 2001 *Albatross Agreement* refers to the *Rio Declaration*, "Principle 15, that, in order to protect the environment, the precautionary approach should be widely applied;" whereas Article II(3) sets out the application of the precautionary principle as an actual obligation of the contracting parties in wording closely following Principle 15 but lacking reference to cost-effectiveness: "the Parties shall widely apply the precautionary approach. In particular, where there are threats of serious or irreversible adverse impacts or damage, lack of full scientific certainty shall not be used as a reason for postponing measures to enhance the conservation status of albatrosses and petrels."

234 An example is given of each of these three possibilities: (1) In the Czech and Slovak *Federal Act on the Environment* of 5 December 1991 reference is made simply to "measures intended to prevent" damage, with no reference to cost-effectiveness. (2) The 1997 *Massachusetts Precautionary Principle Act* does speak of "cost-effective measures to prevent costly environmental degradation." (3) Canadian law wavers between the two. The English version of the *Canadian Environmental Protection Act* as amended in 1999 refers to "cost-effective measures", whereas the French version refers to "mesures effectives". The Nova Scotia *Environment Act* (*An Act to Reform the Environmental Laws of the Province and to Encourage and Promote the Protection, Enhancements and Prudent Use of the Environment*, SNS 1994-1995 c.1); and the New Brunswick *Clean Air Act* (Chapter C-5.2 SNB 1997) refer simply to "measures". See Abouchar, 2001, pp. 238 and 241-244; Friends of the Earth Canada, 2000.

235 Marr, 2003, *passim*.

236 Australia, Cameroon, Canada, Germany, France and Sweden. *Ibid.*, p. 39.

237 Austria, the Bahamas, Belgium, Bulgaria, Chile, China, Czech Republic, Denmark, Egypt, Eritrea, Estonia, Guyana, Hungary, Iceland, Indonesia, Ireland, Ivory Coast, Mozambique, the Netherlands, New Zealand, Norway, Oman, Peru, Romania, Slovenia, South Africa, Switzerland and Uganda.

238 Especially bearing in mind the discussion in the previous paragraph of the (im)possibility of quantifying the value of nature.

principle as it stands in customary international law.[239] There is evidently no general and uniform state practice to that effect. It is too soon, however, to conclude that the precautionary principle is cost-oblivious or does not allow for a balancing of interests at the moment of deciding on precautionary action. The absence of a requirement of cost-effectiveness does not by itself warrant such inferences. Moreover, as uncovered above, considerations of cost-effectiveness form part of the very rationale of the precautionary principle.

While cost-effectiveness may not constitute a mandatory requirement of general international law in respect of the precautionary principle, the treaties and declarations employing the criterion nevertheless form such a significant minority that it generates curiosity as to why the element of cost-effectiveness was expressly encompassed in those instruments and how it should be interpreted. The two open questions put forward in the introduction to this chapter come to mind. First, what kinds of costs and benefits should be regarded when determining whether action is cost-effective? Second, recalling the definition from the *Energy Charter Treaty*, which is the proper way to go about it in the current context, "to achieve a defined objective at the lowest cost" or "to achieve the greatest benefit at a given cost"?[240]

The *Climate Change Convention* contains a pointer, at least in respect of the second question. Reportedly, the direct link in the Convention between precaution and cost-effectiveness was inserted on the insistence of the United States and Saudi Arabia, two countries which also ensured that no mandatory greenhouse gas reductions were incorporated in the treaty, in order to avoid wasteful expenses under the precautionary principle.[241] The text of the provision involved expresses a clear choice for one of the two options from the *Energy Charter Treaty* definition by stating that "policies and

---

[239] This finding squares with the assessments of other authors who have drawn attention to the relative scarcity of the cost-effectiveness criterion in state practice. Marr, 2003, whose findings were just discussed, observes at p. 39 that "only a few national laws require a cost-benefit analysis to be applied" when implementing the precautionary principle. According to Abouchar, 2001, p. 238, "the majority of international conventions do not refer to cost-effective." In support of this statement she cites definitions from six treaties and three declarations which do not contain the clause, and one treaty and two declarations which do. Douma, 2003, p. 125, draws a similar conclusion. Backes *et al.*, 1997, p. 65, hold that the element of cost-effectiveness is typical for the formulation of the *Rio Declaration* and is lacking in the precautionary principle as found in other documents. Epiney & Scheyli, 1998, p. 122, speak of "Vereinzelte Formulierungen des Vorsorgeprinzips" that refer to cost-effectiveness. Cooney, 2001, p. 10, notes that the *Rio Declaration*'s reference to cost-effectiveness is "absent from many other formulations."

[240] Article 19(3)(d) of the *Energy Charter Treaty*.

[241] Palmer, 1995, pp. 135-136; Bernstein, 1999, pp. 157-158; Schuppert, 1997, pp. 183-184.

measures to deal with climate change should be cost-effective so as to ensure global benefits at the lowest possible cost."[242] The starting-point is not a limited amount of money with which to achieve the 'greatest possible benefits'. Instead, the benefits inherent in the abatement of climate change are the benchmark and cost-effectiveness entails that this objective should be met at "the lowest possible cost" – if there is a cheap way and an expensive way to arrive at those *same* benefits, the cheap way is to be preferred. It should be noted that this qualification says nothing about the final height of the cost, as the lowest *possible* cost may still be very high. Neither does the provision clarify what sort of costs must be considered, nor whether cost-effectiveness presumes the performance of cost-benefit analysis prior to the taking of precautionary action, nor, in case it does, of what version.

The wording of Principle 15 of the *Rio Declaration* leaves even more questions unanswered, since it lacks any explicit inklings as to what must be understood by "cost-effective" measures – the clause again having been included largely on the initiative of the US delegation at UNCED.[243] In consequence, there is no alternative but to fall back on the ordinary meaning of the term in its context, this ordinary meaning being that action taken should be effective in relation to its cost. According to different interpretations, in order to comply with Principle 15 precautionary measures must "make economic sense,"[244] be "economically feasible,"[245] not entail "excessive"[246] or "disproportionate"[247] costs, or, similarly, be "proportionate" with a view to their costs and the environmental interests served.[248]

Although without a doubt the ordinary meaning of cost-effectiveness allows for a variety of interpretations, the *context* of the term in Principle 15 limits the scope for interpretation to a significant degree. In particular, in the context of the precautionary principle cost-effectiveness can plainly *not* be understood in the strict economic sense and *not* be taken to imply the submission of candidate precautionary measures to traditional cost-benefit analysis. The obstacles posed by uncertainty, irreversibility and intrinsic value, as discussed above, would seem to rather fundamentally prevent this.[249] That discussion has made clear that, to all appearances, determining the monetary

---

[242] Article 3(3).
[243] Bernstein, 1999, p. 153.
[244] Soria Jiménez, 1996, p. 394.
[245] *Ibid.*
[246] *Ibid.*; González Campos, 1998, p. 799.
[247] González Campos, *ibid.*
[248] Backes *et al.*, 1997, pp. 65 and 71. According to Backes, 1997, pp. 5 and 7, this nevertheless entails that harm to the most valuable natural features ought to be prevented at all cost. Also Epiney & Scheyli, 1998, p. 123.
[249] See *supra* paragraph 9.1.

equivalent of the value of most components of the environment, and therewith the extent of any damage to them, is no enviable affair. By way of a tiny illustration, a 1999 report by the UN Intergovernmental Forum on Forests (IFF) names 22 benefits deriving from the protection of forest areas, grouped in the categories of biological diversity (4),[250] ecological processes (5),[251] watershed protection (3),[252] education and research (1),[253] economic benefits (4),[254] non-consumptive benefits (4)[255] and future values (1),[256] while explicitly recognizing that most of these are difficult to value in monetary terms.[257]

And when determining the anthropocentric value of species, ecosystems and other parts of the environment is difficult if not – recalling, among other things, previous remarks on option value – unrealistic, their intrinsic value, recognized under the precautionary principle,[258] can *by definition* not be expressed in numbers. As the US Supreme Court stressed in 1978, the value represented by the existence of each species is, "quite literally, incalculable."[259] To this may be added the several sorts of uncertainty that *by definition* render the accurate prediction of environmental impacts infeasible.[260] And if one or more elements of an environmental risk are uncertain, then the costs and benefits of precautionary measures can *by definition* not be adequately identified, let alone compared. Various commentators, along the entire spectrum from critical to supportive of the precautionary principle, have observed with regard to Principle 15 that dropping the demand for proof of causality has *by definition* entailed the elimination of the possibility of guaranteeing up front the cost-effectiveness, in the traditional economic sense, of precautionary measures.[261] Noting the difficulties and complexities involved, the Great Lakes International Joint Commission specifically rejected cost-benefit analysis when devising its

---

[250] Gene resources; species protection; ecosystem diversity; evolutionary processes.

[251] Fixing and cycling of nutrients; soil formation and conservation; circulation and cleansing of air; conservation and regulation of water flow; global life support.

[252] Erosion control; flood reduction; regulation of streamflows.

[253] Knowledge base.

[254] Recreation/tourism; herbs; medicines; food etc.

[255] Aesthetic; spiritual; cultural/historical; existence value.

[256] Ethical.

[257] *UN Doc.* E/CN.17/IFF/1999/10, Third Session of the IFF, 24 February 1999, paragraph 24.

[258] See *supra* paragraphs 3.1, 3.4 and 5.3.

[259] *Tennessee Valley Authority v. Hill* et al., 437 US 153, 180, 1978; as quoted in De Sadeleer, 2002, at p. 145.

[260] See *supra* paragraph 4.1.

[261] No causal evidence equals no reliable damage assessment equals no cost-effectiveness, according to Hanekamp, 2002, p. 11; also Pieterman & Hanekamp, 2002, p. 6; Douma, 1997(a), pp. 5 and 7.

precautionary policy.[262] For its part, the European Commission, which has proposed that when comparing the pros and cons of various precautionary measures an "economic cost-benefit analysis" should be performed "where this is appropriate and possible,"[263] may find this to be the case on precious few occasions.

One possible interpretation of Principle 15 and akin formulations is that, when push comes to shove, the express mention of "cost-effective" does not truly add much, if anything.[264] As established above, considerations of cost-effectiveness are an inherent part of the rationale of the precautionary principle. Prevention being cheaper than cure, when relevant thresholds are crossed "measures to prevent environmental degradation" are supposedly cost-effective, whether the notion is mentioned or not. This point merits a brief excursion into the practice of Scottish Natural Heritage (SNH), a British government agency charged with safeguarding the flora, fauna and other natural features of Scotland. A policy guidance note on the application of the precautionary principle developed by the agency in 1996 shows an intimate linkage between cost-effectiveness in the wider sense, proportionality and the thresholds of the principle.[265] The note explains that it is official SNH policy that the precautionary principle should only be applied "if the balance of likely costs and benefits justifies it (the so-called 'proportionality' principle). This balance is not measured but is rather a matter of judgment."[266] After describing a number of selection criteria that have been developed to aid the agency in the determination of whether the possible harm associated with a particular activity qualifies as 'significant', focussing, among other things, on the legal designations of areas and species potentially affected, the document observes that if the risk in question "does fall within one of these categories, then an initial cost-benefit test is met, in that there may well be a significant cost of not taking precautionary action."[267] In other words, if anticipated harm meets the threshold of significance then action to prevent this harm is *assumed* to be cost-effective and proportional.

This presumption that, as soon as threshold conditions are met, an *effective* precautionary measure is also a *cost-effective* measure may well exhaust much of the relevance of cost-effectiveness, given that traditional cost-benefit analysis has not much of a role to play under the umbrella of the precautionary principle. On this view of the matter, formulations which speak of "cost-effective" precautionary measures do little more than state the

---

[262] Tickner, 1999, p. 179.
[263] *Communication COM(2000)1*, p. 19.
[264] Douma, *ibid.*, p. 5, seems to lean in this direction.
[265] See Scottish Natural Heritage, 1999.
[266] *Ibid.*, p. 191.
[267] *Ibid.*, p. 192.

obvious – besides reminding states, probably needlessly, of the wisdom of choosing the cheapest of several equally effectual courses of action. Naming Principle 15 of the *Rio Declaration* while not mentioning cost-effectiveness in their substantive definitions of the precautionary principle, instruments such as the *Albatross Agreement* and the *Biosafety Protocol*, just considered, confirm this impression by implying that versions of the principle with and without explicit reference to cost-effectiveness are perfectly compatible. Incidentally, the French version of Principle 15 refers not to "cost-effective measures" but to "mesures effectives",[268] that is, *effective* measures...

State Practice and the Balancing of Interests

The last pair of questions guiding the current tour of state practice are for the role of socio-economic considerations besides the issue of cost-effectiveness and, particularly, for the appropriateness of weighing environmental, social and economic interests when determining what precautionary action to take. The following part of this paragraph will straightforwardly focus on what it is that sources of state practice have to say on these issues. A number of formulations featuring the precautionary principle, while not naming cost-effectiveness as such, contain some allusion or other to socio-economic factors. The first of the 2002 *Guiding Principles on Invasive Alien Species* has it that decisions relating to such species should be based on the precautionary approach as laid down in the *Rio Declaration* and the *Biodiversity Convention* – one of which, by the way, does and one of which does not mention cost-effectiveness – while adding the fairly peculiar phrase, "in particular with reference to risk analysis."[269] In a footnote the term 'risk analysis' is denoted as entailing the assessment of the risks involved in alien species introductions and the identification of appropriate measures to deal with these risks, "taking into account socio-economic and cultural considerations."[270] It should be noted that the objections against some of the Guiding Principles tabled by Australia at the *Biodiversity Convention*'s sixth COP were aimed, *inter alia*, at the latter phrase, for fear that such considerations might be used to justify unwarranted precautionary action interfering with international trade.[271] After all, the introduction of alien species can entail socio-economic losses as much as socio-economic benefits. Another guiding principle specifies that any "examination of benefits and costs (environmental, economic and social) should be done on a long-term basis."[272]

---

[268] The two different versions have subsequently found their way into the English and French versions of the *Canadian Environmental Protection Act*; Abouchar, 2001, pp. 238 and 241-242.
[269] Guiding principle 1.
[270] Footnote 57.
[271] 2002 *Report of the Sixth Conference of the Parties to the Convention on Biological Diversity*.
[272] Guiding principle 2.

The long run is also stressed in a 1991 LDC resolution, which names the evaluation of the "environmental and economic consequences of alternative methods of waste management, including long-term consequences" and socio-economic research as some of the "necessary steps to ensure the effective implementation of the precautionary approach."[273] Under the *Montreal Protocol* as amended in 1990 a role is reserved for "technical and economic considerations" in the adoption of precautionary measures to protect the ozone layer.[274] Likewise, a 1990 UNEP Governing Council decision on hazardous waste appeals to governments, "taking economic costs into consideration," to consider clean production methods as a means of implementing the precautionary principle.[275]

The *Climate Change Convention* which, unlike most of the instruments just listed, expressly calls for cost-effectiveness, moreover stipulates that precautionary policies and measures to deal with climate change should "comprise all economic sectors" and "take into account different socio-economic contexts."[276] Account has certainly been taken of such different contexts under the *POPs Convention*, which continues to allow the use of DDT for the control of the malaria mosquito pending the absence of environmentally friendly and affordable alternatives.[277] It also appears that socio-economic considerations may play a part in decisions on control measures for chemicals that are considered for inclusion in the Convention.[278] In the *Straddling Stocks Agreement* it is provided that in implementing the precautionary approach states shall take into account, *inter alia*, "existing and predicted oceanic, environmental and socioeconomic conditions."[279] The 1992 *EEA Agreement* sets out the determination of its parties to "ensure a prudent and rational utilization of natural resources on the basis, in particular, of the principle of sustainable development, as well as the principle that precautionary and preventive action should be taken."[280] Correspondingly, the fisheries commissions established under the 1997 *GFCM Agreement* and the 1999 *RECOFI Agreement*, respectively, are to "apply the precautionary approach to conservation and management decisions" and take into account also "the need to promote the development and proper

---

[273] *Resolution LDC 44/14 on the Application of the Precautionary Approach to Environmental Protection within the Framework of the London Dumping Convention.*
[274] Sixth preambular paragraph.
[275] *Decision SS II/4 B on a Comprehensive Approach to Hazardous Waste.*
[276] Article 3(3). The latter clause is also included in Principle 7 of the 1990 *Ministerial Declaration of the Second World Climate Conference.*
[277] Article 3(2) and Annex B.
[278] This seems to be implied in Annex F.
[279] Article 6(3)(c).
[280] Sixth preambular paragraph.

utilization of the marine living resources."[281] In a similar spirit, the definition from the *World Charter for Nature* clearly incorporates a balancing of interests. While unconditionally forbidding activities likely to cause irreversible harm and activities whose potential adverse effects are not fully understood, proponents of activities "likely to pose a significant risk to nature" are required to demonstrate "that expected benefits outweigh potential damage to nature." For activities which "may disturb nature" the Charter determines that "if they are to be undertaken" – implying that there may be compelling reasons of a socio-economic nature for doing so – they shall be planned and carried out so as to minimize potential harm.[282] Under the 2004 *Precautionary Approach Framework* of the NAFO Fisheries Commission limits on fishing effort may be set by managers "based on criteria of their choosing (e.g. stable TACs; socio-economic considerations)" as long as the fish stock in question is in the 'safe zone'.[283] When a fishery enters the 'overfishing', 'cautionary', 'danger' or 'collapse' zone, however, particular precautionary management strategies are prescribed to safeguard the stock, and socio-economic considerations cease to be a determining factor.[284]

The European legislator too appears to have left some strictly defined room for a balancing of interests in the application of the precautionary principle under the *Habitats Directive*.[285] Subject to a number of conditions, an activity encroaching upon the natural features of a protected area may be permitted after all if there are imperative reasons of great public importance for doing so. In such cases any natural features lost are to be compensated for in an integral manner – if such compensation is not possible the activity cannot be permitted.[286] Generally speaking, it is the view of the European Commission that socio-economic factors, in the broad sense, should be considered when determining the appropriate way to implement the precautionary principle in individual cases:

> A comparison must be made between the most likely positive or negative consequences of the envisaged action and those of inaction in terms of the overall cost to the Community, both in the long- and short-term. The measures envisaged must produce an overall advantage as regards reducing risks to an acceptable level. Examination of the pros and cons cannot be reduced to an economic cost-benefit analysis. It is wider in scope and includes non-economic considerations. However,

---

281 Article III(2) of either.
282 Principle 11.
283 *NAFO/FC Doc. 4/18* of September 2004, p. 3; see also *supra* paragraph 7.2.
284 *Ibid.*, pp. 2-4.
285 See also Heukers, 1997, p. 28.
286 Article 6(4).

> examination of the pros and cons should include an economic cost-benefit analysis where this is appropriate and possible.[287]

Again, here as on other occasions, the Commission is adamant in underlining the importance in precautionary decision-making of contemplating the long run.[288]

The French *Code Rural* requires that the precautionary principle be put into practice through "effective and proportional measures [..] at an economically acceptable cost,"[289] whereas a similar formulation can be found in the law of Cameroon.[290] In a case concerning global warming an Australian judge ruled that the application of the principle dictates that a cautious approach should be adopted in evaluating relevant factors, but "does not require that the greenhouse issue should outweigh all other issues."[291] In Germany the application of the precautionary principle is subject to principles of administrative law such as the principle of the proportionality of administrative action to the achievement of a prescribed goal and the principle of prohibiting "excessive actions", both of which are said to require at least some consideration of the costs and benefits of precautionary measures.[292] The German judiciary has held in this regard that economic considerations in the may play a part only in atypical cases, i.e., when precautionary action is likely to entail extreme economic costs.[293] The UK Government has submitted that "precautionary action must be based on objective assessments of the costs and benefits of action. The Government is committed to acting proportionately."[294] Precautionary action is deemed appropriate "particularly where there are good grounds for judging either that action taken promptly at comparatively low cost may avoid more costly

---

287 *Communication COM(2000)1*, p. 19; see also p. 4.

288 See also *ibid.*, p. 8.

289 Article 200(1); translation from De Sadeleer, 2000, p. 148.

290 Article 9 of Chapter III of *Law No. 96/12 Relating to Environmental Management* of 5 August 1996, refers to "effective and commensurate measures [..] at an economically acceptable cost." See Marr, 2003, p. 168.

291 NSW Land and Environment Court (Pearlman J), *Greenpeace Australia Ltd v Redbank Power Co Pty Ltd*, judgment of 10 November 1994, 81 *LGERA*, p. 143, at p. 154; see Sperling, 1999, p. 430, in note 36; Gullett, 1997, pp. 62-63.

292 Haigh, 1994, p. 231.

293 Bundesverwaltungsgericht, 10 January 1995, 14 *NVwZ*, p. 996; and Bundesverwaltungsgericht, 30 August 1996, 16 *NVwZ*, p. 500; see Marr, 2003, pp. 74-75.

294 Paragraph 76 of UK Department of the Environment, Transport and the Regions, *The Government's Response to the Royal Commission on Environmental Pollution's 21st Report*, 21 November 2000; an identical statement can be found in UK Government, *A Better Quality of Life: A Strategy for Sustainable Development for the United Kingdom*, 1999, paragraph 4.2.

damage later, or that irreversible effects may follow if damage is delayed."[295] The latter statement conforms to the submission dealt with earlier that when there is a threat of irreversible harm precautionary measures are always appropriate, whatever the costs. In addition, the Scottish Natural Heritage document discussed before makes clear that in the context of the precautionary principle harm that is reversible but only *at high cost* and over a long time period is regarded as 'irreversible damage', reinforcing the need for precautionary action.[296] Finally, the administration holds, when deciding on precautionary action "it is always necessary to account for the possible social and economic implications of any such action, in line with the requirements of sustainable development."[297]

Application of the best available technology, as discussed previously, is one of the tools states have agreed to employ in the implementation of the precautionary principle in particular contexts.[298] It has been submitted that where BAT is required, the scope for a balancing of interests is reduced but not wholly eliminated.[299] On the one hand, the economic feasibility, i.e., the costs, of a technology are used to determine whether it qualifies as best *available* technology.[300] On the other hand, when the best technology from an environmental perspective is readily available in technological and economic terms, it simply has to be applied, rendering a full balance of interests impermissible.[301] On balance, the "marginal test of proportionality" between costs and, e.g., emission reductions implied in BAT requirements submittedly leave some limited room for exceptions to be made "in the case of high costs and little risk reduction."[302] The question remains where the threshold lies between an unlawful balancing of interests and a legitimate exception in instances of high disproportionality, an obviously fine distinction.[303] Arguably, commitments to apply 'clean technology', also

---

[295] *White Paper: "This Common Inheritance: Britain's Environmental Strategy"*, September 1990, paragraph 1.88, as cited in Haigh, 1994, at pp. 249-250.
[296] Scottish Natural Heritage, 1999, p. 193.
[297] See paragraph 1.6 of UK Department of the Environment, Transport and the Regions, *Guidelines for Environmental Risk Assessment and Management: Revised Departmental Guidance*, 2 August 2000, at: http://www.environment.detr.gov.uk/eramguide/02.htm.
[298] See *supra* paragraph 7.2.
[299] See, especially, Nollkaemper, 1996, pp. 89-92.
[300] *Ibid.*, p. 89; see Annex I, paragraph 1 of the *Helsinki Watercourses Convention*; Appendix I to the *OSPAR Convention*; and Annex II to the 1992 *Baltic Sea Convention*. According to the *Heavy Metals Protocol* to the *LRTAP Convention*, Annex III, paragraph I(2); the *POPs Protocol* to the *LRTAP Convention*, Annex V, paragraph I(2); and the *POPs Convention*, Annex C, Part V(B), in the determination of what is the BAT weight should be accorded not only to considerations of precaution and prevention but also to "the likely costs and benefits of a measure."
[301] Nollkaemper, *ibid.*, pp. 89-90 and 92.
[302] *Ibid.*, p. 90.
[303] *Ibid.*

discussed above, remove much of the room for balancing left by obligations to apply BAT, given that by themselves they leave no room for consideration of costs.[304] Where clean technology does not yet exist, such commitments can force innovation.[305] In this respect, the 2000 *Malmö Declaration* advocates pursuing a greater commitment by the private sector to "a precautionary approach in investment and technology decisions," which in turn is linked to the "development of cleaner and more resource efficient technologies for a life-cycle economy."[306]

According to the doctrine of common but differentiated responsibilities the weight of obligations to tackle, especially global, environmental problems should vary according to the developmental situation of individual states, with a view to those states' (1) different degrees of contribution to the problems and their (2) different capacities to deal with them; responsibilities and capabilities being two components which are hardly divisible in this connection.[307] While Principle 6 of the *Rio Declaration* expresses the latter component,[308] the former is especially prominent in Principle 7:

> States shall cooperate in a spirit of global partnership to conserve, protect and restore the health and integrity of the Earth's ecosystem. In view of the different contributions to global environmental degradation, States have common but differentiated responsibilities. The developed countries acknowledge the responsibility that they bear in the international pursuit of sustainable development in view of the pressures their societies place on the global environment and of the technologies and financial resources they command.[309]

The same notion is incorporated in Principle 11, which addresses the national level.[310] In its report the WTO body deciding the 2001 *Shrimp-*

---

[304] *Ibid.*, pp. 90-91; see *supra* paragraph 7.2.
[305] Nollkaemper, *ibid.*, p. 90.
[306] Paragraph 11.
[307] As Birnie & Boyle, 2002, p. 101 define the notion: "Although responsibility is common to all states, developed and developing alike, higher standards of conduct are explicitly set for developed states on the grounds that they have both contributed most to causing problems such as ozone depletion and climate change and that they also possess greater capacity to respond than is generally available to developing states." On the doctrine and its two components see also paragraphs 3.2 and 3.3 of the *ILA Declaration on Sustainable Development*; Schrijver, 2003, pp. 68-71; Sands, 2003, pp. 285-289.
[308] "The special situation and needs of developing countries, particularly the least developed and those most environmentally vulnerable, shall be given special priority."
[309] Principle 7.
[310] "States shall enact effective environmental legislation. Environmental standards, management objectives and priorities should reflect the environmental and developmental context to which they apply. Standards applied by some countries may be inappropriate and

Turtles dispute also underlined "the principle that States have common but differentiated responsibilities to conserve and protect the environment."[311] In sum, the doctrine sets lesser standards for developing states.[312]

Generally, the extent to which legally binding environmental instruments in fact incorporate the doctrine, varies substantially.[313] Several agreements, such as the *Biodiversity Convention* and the *Biosafety Protocol*, feature general statements in their preambles alluding to the notion without translating these in explicitly differentiated material obligations.[314] The clearest examples in which higher standards of conduct are actually imposed on developed states can be found in multilateral agreements dealing with ozone layer depletion[315] and climate change.[316] Arguably, differentiated duties also result from the obligation of any coastal state party to the 1982 *UN Convention on the Law of the Sea* (*LOS Convention*) to protect the living resources in its exclusive economic zone from over-exploitation through conservation and management measures taking into account "the best scientific evidence available *to it*." [317] In the greater number of legal instruments, however, obligations are uniformly phrased for developing and developed states alike, for instance in the fields of trade in endangered species, nuclear safety, vessel-sourced marine pollution or dumping at sea.[318]

With particular regard to the precautionary principle, the position of developing countries has been addressed in some definitions. The *Montreal Protocol* as amended in 1990 speaks of protecting the ozone layer by taking precautionary measures "bearing in mind the developmental needs of developing countries."[319] Principle 15 of the *Rio Declaration* requires states to apply the precautionary approach "according to their capabilities,"[320] a

---

of unwarranted economic and social cost to other countries, in particular developing countries."

[311] *United States Import Prohibition of Certain Shrimp and Shrimp Products: Recourse to Art. 21.5 by Malaysia*, 22 October 2001, *WTO Doc.* WT/DS58/AB/RW.

[312] Birnie & Boyle, 2002, p. 101.

[313] See Birnie & Boyle, *ibid.*, pp. 101-103.

[314] The nineteenth preambular paragraph of the *Biodiversity Convention* acknowledges that "economic and social development are the first and overriding priorities of developing countries;" whereas the eighth preambular paragraph of the *Biosafety Protocol* takes note of the "limited capabilities of many countries, particularly developing countries, to cope with the nature and scale of known and potential risks associated with living modified organisms."

[315] See Article 5 of the 1985 *Convention for the Protection of the Ozone Layer.*

[316] See Article 4 of the *Climate Change Convention* and the differentiated obligations regarding the reduction of greenhouse gas emissions in the *Kyoto Protocol*; see also Article 3(1) of the *Climate Change Convention.*

[317] Article 61(2); emphasis added.

[318] For these and other examples see Birnie & Boyle, 2002, p. 103.

[319] Sixth preambular paragraph.

[320] See Dzidzornu, 1998, p. 98; Jordan & O'Riordan, 1999, p. 29.

stipulation which is echoed, *inter alia*, in the 1995 version of the *Barcelona Convention*.[321] Precautionary measures taken under the *Land-Based Activities Action Programme* are supposed to correspond, among other things, to "resources and capacities at the national level."[322] Already mentioned were two legal instruments dealing with climate change which detail that precautionary action should take account of "different socio-economic contexts."[323] Nonetheless, in the host of formulations of the principle adopted by states any reference to the limited capacities or responsibilities of developing states is absent.

The sources of state conduct pondered on these last pages might on the whole give the impression that the socio-economic costs of measures may to some extent be taken into account by states when deciding on precautionary action. In contrast, however, most of the great cluster of instruments cited before that as lacking reference to cost-effectiveness, also lack any other reference to socio-economic considerations.[324] And if they are not mentioned, a logical conclusion would be that such considerations have no part to play.[325] *These* instruments would thus seem to indicate that the precautionary principle is cost-oblivious in the sense that the prevention of (significant, serious and/or irreversible) environmental degradation is automatically regarded as worth any price, no matter the social and economic implications.[326] As Nollkaemper describes this feature of the principle which, he finds, has "a solid basis in treaty-law":

> Costs or technological (in-)feasibility of control measures cannot be invoked to eschew the obligation to prevent risks. As soon as risk-thresholds are crossed, the

---

321 Article 4(3)(a) contains the duty of contracting parties to "apply, in accordance with their capabilities, the precautionary principle." Parties to the 2002 *Antigua Convention* must apply the principle "in accordance with their capacity" (Article 5(6)(a)).

322 Paragraph 24.

323 Paragraph 7 of the 1990 *Ministerial Declaration of the Second World Climate Conference* and Article 3(3) of the *Climate Change Convention*.

324 As Marr, 2003, p. 39 summarizes, in state practice with regard to the precautionary principle "socio-economic considerations have seldomly been specified in a precise form."

325 An analogy may be drawn with Article 192 of the *LOS Convention*: "States have the obligation to protect and preserve the marine environment." As Lauterpacht argued on behalf of Malaysia in the *Land Reclamation* case, 'equity' and 'balancing of interests' "may have their place where they are specified" in the Convention. "They are specific to particular situations. They do not appear in Part XII where [..] the obligation to protect and preserve the marine environment is mandatory and unqualified. There was no intention that the rights of the Parties should be exposed to so subjective or variable an element of interpretation." *Verbatim Record* of 27 September, p. 22.

326 According to Nollkaemper, 1996, p. 76, "in most treaties the precautionary principle is cost-oblivious."

> activities concerned should not be undertaken, whatever devastating impacts a decision to that effect may have on profits of agricultural or industrial activities.[327]

The same goes for the resolutions adopted by the UN General Assembly on the driftnet issue, which lack any consideration of costs and benefits and turn a deaf ear to repeated complaints concerning the allegedly hefty social and economic consequences of the abrupt termination of driftnet fisheries.[328] Precautionary regimes such as this, obliging those wanting to exploit a natural resource to submit proof of the sustainability of that exploitation, further examples of which have been discussed in the previous chapter, entail that the best interest of the species in question must predominate, "rather than the short term economic interests of those dependent upon their utilisation."[329] Likewise, in the 1996 *Vellore Citizens* case the Supreme Court of India, applying the precautionary principle in association with the concept of sustainable development, severely restricted some environmentally destructive activities despite high socio-economic costs:

> It is no doubt correct that the leather industry in India has become a major foreign exchange earner and at present Tamil Nadu is the leading exporter of finished leather accounting for approximately 80% of the country's export. Though the leather industry is of vital importance to the country as it generates foreign exchange and provides employment avenues it has no right to destroy the ecology, degrade the environment and pose [..] a health hazard. It cannot be permitted to expand or even to continue with the present production unless it tackles by itself the problem of pollution created by the said industry.[330]

As two commentators summarized this approach: "The short-term economic advantage of export funds derived from the leather industry does not justify long-term environmental degradation if sustainable development is the yardstick."[331]

The review of state practice ends here.

9.3. *Socio-Economic Interests under the Precautionary Principle*

By applying its own version of Norton's 'big picture method', this paragraph is intended to finally provide answers to the several questions posed above. There will be no last stop on the journey towards that final destination in the

---

[327] *Ibid.*

[328] *Ibid.*, p. 86. These resolutions were treated in *supra* paragraph 8.2.

[329] McIntyre & Mosedale, 1997, p. 239, referring to the IWC *Revised Management Procedure*, the *Straddling Stocks Agreement*, and CITES *Resolution Conf. 9.24*.

[330] Paragraph 9 of the judgment.

[331] Shanmuganathan & Warren, 1997, p. 400.

form of a separate review of legally relevant scholarly opinions, given that such opinions have been dealt with to a large extent throughout the above paragraphs, and that some others will be treated as an integral part of the remaining text. It is time, in other words, for the current writer's analysis of the subject matter – a subject matter the convolution of which is reflected in the length of this chapter.

Socio-Economic Interests under the Precautionary Principle in General International Law

First in this final analysis comes the acknowledgement that the interplay between socio-economic considerations and the precautionary principle in international law is a nuanced affair. Social and economic considerations, to begin with, are an integral part of the rationale of the precautionary principle. As has been explained sufficiently above, despite the fact that under international law it is undoubtedly the primary purpose of the principle to protect the environment, including for the sake of it, reasons of a socio-economic nature have influenced the choice of governments to adopt the precautionary principle. In accordance with the concept of sustainable development, precautionary action is deemed necessary not only to protect the intrinsic worth of the environment but also its great and multiple value for humanity. With an eye on this value and the fragility of the environment to harm inflicted by human activities, states have in adopting the precautionary principle judged it better to run the risk of overstating risks than understating them. Cost-effectiveness is an important element of this rationale, as precautionary measures to prevent harm are assumed to be more cost-effective than restoration after environmental damage has occurred – and even more so when restoration is not possible. Cost-effectiveness in the strict economic sense, however, does not constitute a separate legal requirement to be met by precautionary measures.[332] Evidence in state practice for the existence of such a requirement is just too scant and inconsistent. This lack of support is in accordance with common sense, since for various reasons exhaustively discussed above, submitting candidate precautionary measures to a traditional cost-benefit analysis is an incongruity. The mandatory performance of such analysis and the taking of precautionary action are mutually exclusive.

Conversely, the precautionary principle is not "absolutist"[333] either; its application is not wholly cost-oblivious. This should be clear, if only from

[332] See Epiney & Scheyli, 1998, p. 123, and the sources quoted earlier. The same conclusion was drawn, furthermore, by the drafters of the 2002 *ILA Declaration on Sustainable Development* (see paragraphs 4(1) through 4(4)) and the 2004 *ILA Berlin Rules on Water Resources* (see Article 23(2) and Commentary), who consciously omitted criteria of cost-effectiveness from their definitions of the precautionary principle.

[333] Nollkaemper, 1996, *passim*.

the fact that the principle does not incorporate any general rule which permits potentially harmful activities only upon delivery by their opponents of proof of harmlessness.[334] *That* would be absolutist. Instead, the search for a pattern in the totality of state practice examined in the previous paragraph, combined with findings from previous chapters, reveals that socio-economic factors not only form part of the rationale but also of the very make-up of the precautionary principle as it has developed in international law. As in the previous chapter, it is helpful here to reproduce the definitions of the right and the duty of states to take precautionary action that were assembled in the first part of this study:[335]

> Wherever, on the basis of the best information available, there are reasonable grounds for concern that significant harm to the environment may occur, effective and proportional action to prevent and/or abate this harm may be taken, including in situations of scientific uncertainty regarding the cause, extent and/or probability of the potential harm.

> Wherever, on the basis of the best information available, there are reasonable grounds for concern that serious and/or irreversible harm to the environment may occur, effective and proportional action to prevent and/or abate this harm must be taken, including in situations of scientific uncertainty regarding the cause, extent and/or probability of the potential harm.

The magic word at this point, recurrent in the state practice reviewed, is proportionality, which is all about matching costs and benefits.[336] Without repeating too much from previous deliberations, in the context of environmental law and policy this notion is understood as: the greater the risk, the more rigorous the measures to counter it, and *vice versa*.[337] In concrete decision-making this implies that when an environmental risk is negligible, social and economic interests are likely to predominate the outcome. Alternatively, when an environmental risk is great, social and economic considerations tend to take a back seat. This purely describes what sensible governments have always done.[338] Within the framework of the precautionary principle this common conduct has been effectuated at different levels.[339] For one, proportionality is incorporated in the various thresholds set out in the

---

[334] See the preceding chapter.

[335] See *supra* Chapter 6.

[336] See Epiney & Scheyli, 1998, p. 123; González Campos, 1998, p. 799; O'Riordan *et al.*, 2001(a), p. 20; Backes *et al.*, 1997, pp. 65 and 71; Haigh, 1994, p. 238. Juste Ruiz, 1999, p. 440, has dubbed the proportionality notion to be the *legal* counterpart of *economic* concepts such as cost-benefit analysis.

[337] See *supra* paragraph 5.4.

[338] Birnie & Boyle, 2002, p. 120.

[339] See *supra* paragraph 5.4.

definitions *supra*. From a socio-economic perspective, these threshold levels are, to borrow the words of one commentator, "of decisive significance in relation to the degree to which balancing is permitted in the implementation of the precautionary principle."[340] When there are no 'reasonable grounds for concern' or threatened harm is not 'significant', the precautionary principle allows for an unlimited balancing of environmental, social and economic interests; for contemplation of costs and benefits of any given kind. When there are reasonable grounds for concern that significant harm may be caused, states have a right to take 'effective and proportional action to prevent and/or abate this harm.' Naturally, states are free to decide whether to make use of this right, a decision which itself may well be influenced by socio-economic considerations. In terms of cost-effectiveness, when the threshold of significance is crossed, then action to prevent the harm in question is presumed cost-effective. Finally, when anticipated harm is also serious and/or irreversible, the right is joined by a duty. In those circumstances there is no more free balancing;[341] states are simply expected to take 'effective and proportional' precautionary measures.[342] The latter qualification, of course, represents the second level at which the proportionality concept is integrated in the precautionary principle.

Before addressing this second level, a word is in place on the determination of whether thresholds are crossed, a topic treated before.[343] In particular, it is worthwhile to consider an analogy with Principle 21's duty to refrain from causing significant transboundary harm. Notably, this duty does not incorporate a threshold determined by an equitable balancing of interests.[344] Neither international case law nor treaty definitions of environmental harm suggest the existence of such a threshold.[345] This was a controversial issue in the work of the ILC that preceded the adoption of the 1997 *Watercourses Convention*.[346] As finally agreed, the Convention requires states to "take all appropriate measures to prevent the causing of significant harm to other watercourse states," apparently without subordinating this duty to any

---

340 Nollkaemper, 1996, p. 81.

341 See also the definition of the precautionary principle in paragraphs 4(1) through 4(4) of the *ILA Declaration on Sustainable Development*.

342 Article 5(6)(a) of the 2002 Antigua Convention is interesting in that it states that when confronted with "serious or irreversible threats to the environment," scientific uncertainty should "not serve as a pretext for delaying the adoption of effective measures to prevent environmental degradation, because of the costs involved."

343 See *supra* paragraph 5.3.

344 Birnie & Boyle, 2002, p. 123-124; Jurgielewicz, 1996, p. 58.

345 Birnie & Boyle, *ibid.*

346 *Convention on the Law of the Non-Navigational Uses of International Watercourses*; see Birnie & Boyle, *ibid.*, p. 124.

threshold of equitable balancing.[347] As Birnie and Boyle contend, "the case for making the customary threshold of harm dependent on an equitable balance of interests is not a strong one. The notion that states must act with due diligence to prevent significant harm is a formula which already allows for flexibility in individual cases, including taking account of the more limited technical and economic capacity of developing states, while excluding *de minimis* pollution."[348] The thresholds involved in the application of the precautionary principle are of a similarly objective nature. They are either crossed or not. In principle, costs play no part in that determination and no balancing is involved. As discussed above, however, there may be some room available for discretionary judgments by governments, room which is defined by various factors and varies from case to case as it depends on factual circumstances.[349] As one jurist observes:

> It is important to note that in principle the threshold determination excludes consideration of costs. However, although there is no doubt that this is the correct legal conclusion, the discretion left by the thresholds is so great that as a practical matter it may be difficult to assess whether a state's determination that a threshold is or is not crossed is a purely scientific affair or involves some consideration of costs.[350]

So, from a socio-economic angle, here is yet another mitigation of the potential "absolutist" effects of the precautionary principle.

Only when the combined threshold of 'reasonable grounds for concern that serious or (significant) irreversible harm may be caused' is crossed, does the precautionary principle become, in a way, cost-oblivious.[351] In such a case effective action must be taken to prevent or abate the threatened harm; even if the socio-economic costs of such action are high, this can not be used as an argument for taking less-than-effective action – the more so if anticipated harm is serious *and* irreversible.[352] In the current context, proportionality means that the more serious or probable the possible damages might be, "the more is to

---

[347] Article 7. "Apparently", because there is no uniform agreement of the relationship of this provision with the obligation to utilize watercourses in an equitable and reasonable manner, laid down in Article 5.

[348] Birnie & Boyle, 2002, p. 124 (footnotes omitted). As they further reflect on the background of this circumstance: "To add yet more variables would be subversive of efforts to establish minimum standards of environmental protection and prove much too favorable to the polluter. Only if the obligation to prevent harm is an absolute one, rather than an obligation of diligence, might it be justifiable to resort to equitable manipulation of the threshold of harm to mitigate the rigours of what would then be an extreme rule." *Ibid.*

[349] See *supra* paragraph 5.3.

[350] Nollkaemper, 1996, p. 82.

[351] Also Epiney & Scheyli, 1998, p. 123; Backes, 1997, pp. 5 and 7; Van Wijmen, 1997, p. 15.

[352] Epiney & Scheyli, *ibid.*

be spent on precautionary measures."[353] Proportionality at this second level also means that if the same effect of harm prevention can be arrived at by different pathways, the least rigorous of these should be chosen.[354] Determining which is the 'least rigorous', i.e., the most proportional, course of action in this respect will entail some consideration, whether rudimentary or elaborate, of the costs and benefits associated with the available alternative measures. The precautionary principle leaves discretion as to the method by which this consideration is performed, as long as the method chosen does not interfere with the effectiveness of the precautionary action taken, for instance by thwarting its timeliness.[355] After all, as discussed before, in case of doubt effectiveness takes precedence over proportionality.[356] Yet another dimension of proportionality from the point of view of social and economic interests is embodied in the rule that measures to implement the precautionary principle are provisional and are not maintained in force longer than necessary.[357]

Finally, the role of the notion of common but differentiated responsibilities in the present context remains to be assessed. As established above, the concept has been incorporated in several legal regimes alongside the precautionary principle, whereas it is lacking in others. With regard to the precautionary principle as such, the definition of Principle 15 of the *Rio Declaration* and some other formulations suggest that in the implementation of the principle account should be taken of the limited economic and technical capabilities of developing countries. In most (inter)governmental formulations of the principle the notion of differentiated responsibilities is absent, however. State practice in this respect is, in other words, far from unequivocal[358] – whereas the same can be said of legal doctrine.[359] In sum, on the one hand the conclusion appears to be warranted that the concept of differentiated responsibilities is an important one *in its own right*, which may influence the implementation of the precautionary principle – as of other legal norms – in the particular contexts where it has been fleshed out; while on the other hand it is not possible to conclude that the notion has been positively established as a standard feature of the *precautionary principle* itself under general international law.

---

[353] Douma, 1997(a), p. 5.
[354] See *supra* paragraph 5.4.
[355] See *supra* paragraph 7.3; also Tickner, 1999, p. 164.
[356] See *supra* paragraph 5.4; also Epiney & Scheyli, 1998, p. 123.
[357] See *supra* paragraph 7.3; also Gullett, 1997, p. 59.
[358] Birnie & Boyle, 2002, p. 120.
[359] The 2004 *ILA Berlin Rules on Water Resources* are just one instance where the notion is (purposefully) lacking in the context of the precautionary principle; see Article 23(2) plus Commentary.

9.4. Conclusions

The main purpose of the precautionary principle under general international law is to protect the environment, including for its own sake. This does not mean, however, that in the demands it places on states to achieve this purpose the precautionary principle is cost-oblivious or disregards social and economic interests. In fact, socio-economic factors and considerations of cost-effectiveness are part both of the rationale of the precautionary principle and of its make-up, in line with the overarching concept of sustainable development. The great and multifaceted utilitarian value of nature, a capital which should not be encroached upon if its interest is to be enjoyed on a sustained basis by present and future generations and, indeed, if the very existence of human societies and economies in the long run is to be advanced, has clearly played a part in the motives of states to adopt the precautionary principle. Moreover, erring on the safe side is regarded important in terms of cost-effectiveness, as the prevention of environmental harm is considered more economic than undoing it, not to mention the impossibility of repairing irreparable damage.

Just like in the previous chapter it was concluded that the burden of proof does not, as a rule, rest on activity proponents, so in this chapter it has become clear that in the application of the precautionary principle there is no separate requirement for precautionary measures to be cost-effective – rather, as described above, precautionary measures to deal with significant harm are *assumed* to be so. It has become equally clear that traditional cost-benefit analysis has no role to play in the implementation of the principle, a conclusion warranted by state practice as much as common sense.

Under the precautionary principle there *is* room for states to balance environmental, social and economic interests, but this room is conditioned in various ways by the criterion of proportionality.[360] In general, this criterion implies that the greater the risk, the more should be done (and spent) to counter it. *Only* when there are reasonable grounds for concern that serious and/or significant irreversible harm may be caused are states under a duty to take effective precautionary measures even if the socio-economic costs of such measures are high. In line with the notion of proportionality, the least rigorous way to effectively deal with a given risk is to be preferred. In certain regimes the concept of common but differentiated responsibilities plays a role alongside the precautionary principle, resulting in more lenient duties for developing countries, although generally speaking it does not appear to be a standard component of the principle itself.

---

[360] Also Epiney & Scheyli, 1998, p. 123.

"The precautionary concept does not insist that all risk of harm be avoided at any cost," Ellen Hey concluded in 1992.[361] It appears this conclusion still holds true today.

---

[361] Hey, 1992, pp. 309-310.

PART FOUR

CONCLUSIONS

Everything is vague to a degree you do not realize
till you have tried to make it precise.
– Bertrand Russell (1872-1970)

10. THE PYTHIA REPLACED: CONCLUSIONS

10.1. Bird's-Eye View of Outcomes

The first sentence of this study indicated that humans are among the apparently scarce beings that are uncomfortable with uncertainty. The raven (*Corvus corax*) is another. Ravens, like humans, fear what they do not understand.[1] Ravens are also, like humans, among the most intelligent beings around. New things fascinate and scare them at the same time. They are, in truth, helplessly neophobic. Again and again a raven will approach a newly detected carcass with extreme care, repeatedly jumping back nervously and approaching anew before finally making up its mind as to the acceptability of the risks involved.[2] This does not mean that in the end the raven will usually abstain from exploiting the object of its interest. Indeed, it would starve if it did, carrion being the species' main food source. All ravens do is take precautions. Some proof of the effectiveness of this approach is formed by the bird's longevity and its continued presence in most of the Northern hemisphere, from the Californian deserts to the tundras of Greenland.[3] Besides the inescapable parallels with the human species portrayed here, ravens have something in common with the precautionary principle too: throughout their existence they have been adored by some and despised by others.[4] To complete the circle that was begun to be drawn in the introductory chapter of this study, it should be added that ravens are also among the most fabled of birds. In tales of old they have been depicted, *inter alia*, as oracle birds and as companions of Odin, Noah and – how could it be otherwise – Apollo. Despite their cautious behaviour as just described, the legendary birds are not precisely given to *preaching* precaution, that is, assuming that Augustine of Hippo understood correctly when he heard them cry: "Cras, cras, semper cras / Et sic elabitur aetas..."[5] Adding to this the

---

[1] Heinrich, 1999, p. 225.
[2] *Ibid.*, pp. 216-225.
[3] Glandt, 2003, pp. 50-54.
[4] *Ibid.*, pp. 117-122; Ratcliffe, 1997, pp. 7-26.
[5] Approximate interpretation: "Tomorrow, tomorrow, always tomorrow / And so time passes [without sorrow]..." According to Augustine the devil himself spoke through the raven's voice, trying to persuade people to postpone an important preventive measure, their conversion to the Christian faith, always one more day.

playful nature of many ravens,[6] it would seem that the birds manage to combine the cautious and the carefree rather successfully. Whichever way, it is appropriate at this point to take a bird's-eye view at the main results of the present study.

Definition

The task set at the beginning was to clarify the legal implications of the precautionary principle by learning, mainly, what rights and/or duties of states derive from the principle under general, or customary, international law.[7] Building on the conclusion reached in a former study that the principle has attained the status of customary international law,[8] the question addressed in the present study is what that means precisely.

Part Two of this study focussed on definition. Amidst the diversity of definitions that have been employed by states in different contexts, three core elements of the principle were found to recur on all occasions: (1) a threat of harm, (2) uncertainty, and (3) action.[9] *"In dubio pro natura"* and erring on the side of environmental protection were identified as fitting general descriptions of the gist of the precautionary principle under general international law.[10] In addition, it was ascertained that the principle should always be viewed with the overarching concept of sustainable development in mind.[11]

An elaborate search for patterns and common denominators in the practice of states concerning the principle resulted in the following definitions of a right and a duty to take precautionary action, definitions which are deemed to be representative of contemporary customary international law.[12]

> THE *RIGHT* OF STATES TO TAKE PRECAUTIONARY ACTION
>
> Wherever, on the basis of the best information available, there are reasonable grounds for concern that significant harm to the environment may occur, effective and proportional action to prevent and/or abate this harm may be taken, including in situations of

---

[6] Ratcliffe, 1997, pp. 108, 115-117; Heinrich, 1999, *passim*; Glandt, 2003, p. 115; and field observations by the present author in Finland, Poland, the Netherlands, France and Spain over the past eight years.
[7] See *supra* paragraph 1.2.
[8] Trouwborst, 2002.
[9] See *supra* paragraph 2.3.
[10] *Ibid*; see also *supra* paragraph 7.3.
[11] See *supra* paragraph 2.3.
[12] See *supra* Chapter 6.

scientific uncertainty regarding the cause, extent and/or probability of the potential harm.

THE *DUTY* OF STATES TO TAKE PRECAUTIONARY ACTION

Wherever, on the basis of the best information available, there are reasonable grounds for concern that serious and/or irreversible harm to the environment may occur, effective and proportional action to prevent and/or abate this harm must be taken, including in situations of scientific uncertainty regarding the cause, extent and/or probability of the potential harm.

The precautionary principle mirrors the framework of the risk concept, its basic structure being formed by two interacting scales representing, respectively, the gravity and likelihood of anticipated harm.[13] Both sliding scales are marked by thresholds which to a large extent determine the legal effect of the precautionary principle in individual cases, as depicted graphically in Figure 10.[14] The two scales and the three thresholds are combined in one diagram in Figure 11.[15]

When anticipated environmental impacts are either not *adverse* or not *significant*, the principle does not apply at all. State practice and common sense coincide in this respect.[16] The precautionary principle finds no application either in situations where there are no *reasonable grounds for concern*. This threshold is located in between the possibility and the probability of a given effect materializing, although it does not correspond to a particular percentage of probability (in Figures 10 and 11 no numerical value is assigned to the point where the threshold intersects the scale of likelihood). At a minimum, however, the requirement of 'reasonable grounds' excludes purely hypothetical threats from the ambit of the precautionary principle.[17]

---

[13] See *supra* paragraph 2.2.
[14] This is a combination of *supra* Figures 2 and 5.
[15] This is *supra* Figure 8 in a slightly different form.
[16] See *supra* paragraphs 3.1 and 3.2, and Figure 1.
[17] See *supra* paragraph 4.3 and Figure 5.

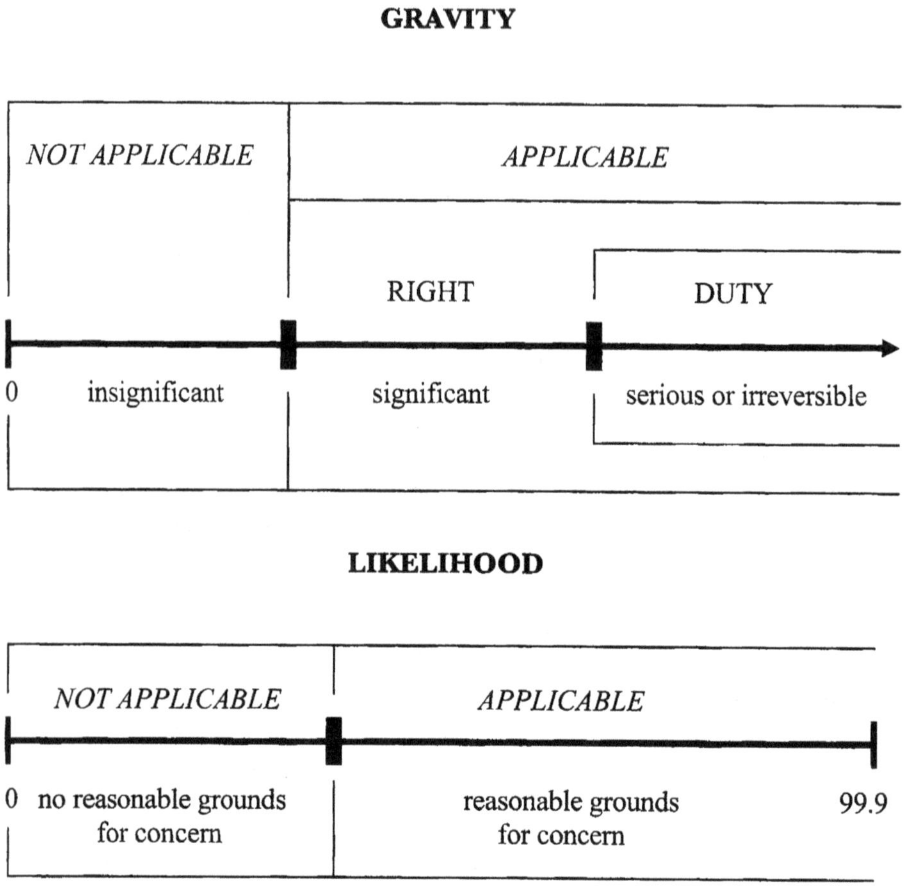

Figure 10. Scales and thresholds (I). The upper, arrowheaded axis represents the scale of gravity. The two boldest printed bars are the thresholds of 'significant' and 'serious or irreversible' harm. Relevant qualifications of harm are indicated below the axis, and corresponding legal effects above it. The lower axis represents the scale of likelihood (%). The boldest printed bar is the minimum threshold of 'reasonable grounds for concern'. Relevant qualifications of evidence are indicated below the axis, and corresponding legal effects above it.

When there are such grounds to believe that *significant*, i.e., appreciable and tangible, harm may come about, customary international law *entitles* states to take precautionary action to prevent or abate it.[18] When the anticipated harm is not only significant but also *serious* and/or (practically) *irreversible*, this right is complemented with a *duty* to take

[18] See *supra* paragraph 3.2.

precautionary action.[19] In the context of the precautionary principle, 'irreversible' harm includes damage which is virtually irreversible in the sense that it cannot be undone during several human generations.[20] In sum, under modern general international law a right and a duty of states to take precautionary action exist. 'Reasonable grounds for concern that significant environmental harm may be caused' give rise to the right. 'Reasonable grounds for concern that serious and/or significant irreversible environmental harm may be caused' give rise to the duty. When these threshold requirements are met, uncertainty is not a bar to the right or obligation of states to take precautionary action. The outcome of the analysis of pertinent material sources of customary international law performed in this study firmly evinces the reality of the respective thresholds and their respective legal effects as set out here.

Whether an anticipated impact is in fact to be qualified as adverse, significant, serious and/or irreversible is determined by a mixture of objective and subjective factors.[21] When such an impact, if it came about, would transgress a substantive norm of international environmental law, it would certainly qualify as significant and raise a suspicion of seriousness besides. Former statements by states, for instance in preambles of legal instruments, also provide clues as to what should be regarded as constituting significant or serious environmental harm. The respective weight of these and other factors, and consequently the room available for discretionary judgments by the authorities involved, varies along with the circumstances of each case.[22] Whether 'reasonable grounds for concern' exist is determined on the basis of the *best information available.* In practice such information will often be the result of scientific research, although this is not a prerequisite for the precautionary principle to be triggered. Neither need the risk in question be quantifiable in order to give rise to reasonable grounds for concern.[23]

---

[19] See *supra* paragraph 3.3 and Figure 2.
[20] See *supra* paragraph 5.3.
[21] *Ibid.*
[22] *Ibid.*
[23] *Ibid.*

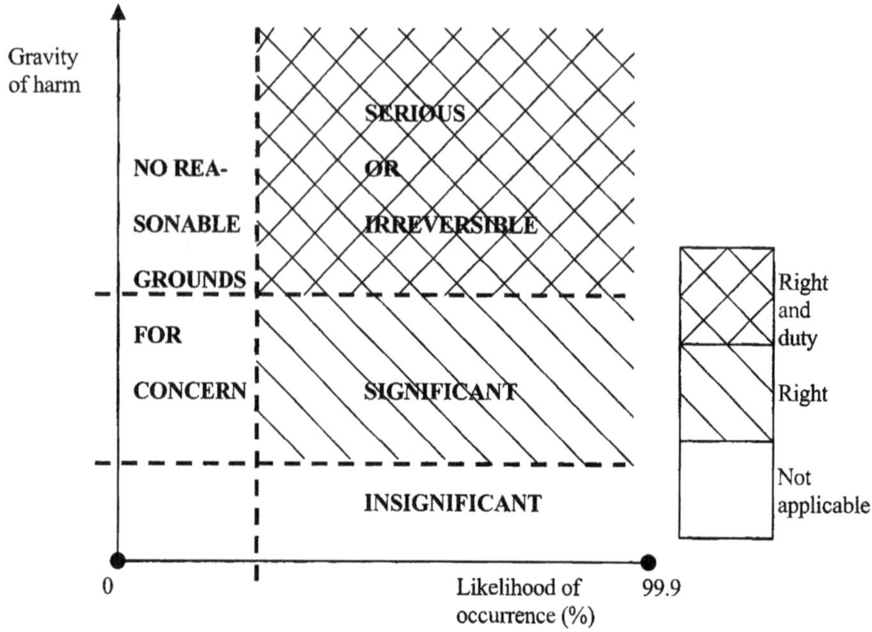

Figure 11. Scales and thresholds (II). Diagram made up of the scales of gravity and likelihood and incorporating the legally relevant threshold lines of 'reasonable grounds for concern', 'significant harm' and 'serious or irreversible harm'. These thresholds are depicted by dotted lines. Coordinates located outside the hatched parts of the diagram represent situations in which precautionary action is not called for. The hatched part with 'significant' corresponds to a right to take precautionary action; 'serious or irreversible' corresponds to (a right and) a duty to take such action.

Although the scope of the precautionary principle under general international law does not include all *levels* of uncertainty – in the absence of reasonable grounds for concern the principle finds no application – it does span all *types* of uncertainty, including situations of quantifiable risk, uncertainty proper and ignorance. Reasonable grounds for concern may arise in all of these.[24] It is in line with the above definitions and, indeed, with any classical statement on the precautionary principle, that the presence of uncertainty as such is not a valid excuse for failing to take preventive action. As indicated by the word 'including' in the above definitions, it is nevertheless *not* correct to say that the presence of uncertainty is a *prerequisite*

---

[24] See *supra* paragraphs 4.1 and 5.2, and Figure 4.

for the precautionary principle to apply.[25] On the contrary, the criterion of proportionality dictates that the strictness of precautionary measures should match the probability of harm. When there is certainty – assuming such a thing exists – that a given threat will materialize then this is all the more reason to take action. In this sense the precautionary principle has absorbed, or may be considered the most developed form of, the so-called preventive principle. Under the precautionary principle action is taken in spite of uncertainty, not because of it. The right and the duty just defined apply *whether there is uncertainty or not.*[26]

As with uncertainty, even though particular *levels* of harm are excluded from the reach of the precautionary principle, it does encompass all *types* of environmental harm.[27] Under customary international law the principle covers the environment as a whole. That is to say, on the condition that threats are sufficiently qualified so as to pass the relevant threshold tests specified above, the principle applies to (a) the environment in all geographic areas, both within and beyond the limits of national jurisdiction; (b) all environmental issue areas; and (c) all human activities with environmental implications, whether existing or new.[28] As a beneficiary of environmental protection human health is covered by the precautionary principle under general international law as well, although health issues proper such as food safety probably are not.[29]

In order to comply with the precautionary principle, the preventive and abatement action performed by states must be *effective* and *proportional.*[30] The requirement of effectiveness entails that measures are to be adopted which effectively safeguard the part of the environment in jeopardy. Observation of the proportionality requirement results in a course of action which corresponds to the dimensions – gravity and likelihood – of the risk involved, thus ensuring that excessively rigorous measures are avoided. The greater the aggregate risk, i.e. the more to the top and/or right of the diagram of Figure 11, the more rigorous the precautionary action to match it and *vice versa.*[31] This is where definition touches on implementation and Part Three of this study comes within sight. Before proceeding, it is probably expedient to contemplate the substance of the findings reviewed hitherto schematically. (See Figure 12.[32])

---

[25] See *supra* paragraph 4.2.
[26] *Ibid.*
[27] See *supra* paragraph 3.1.
[28] See *supra* paragraph 5.2.
[29] See *supra* paragraph 1.2.
[30] See *supra* paragraph 5.4.
[31] *Ibid.*
[32] This is *supra* Figure 9, duplicated here for convenience.

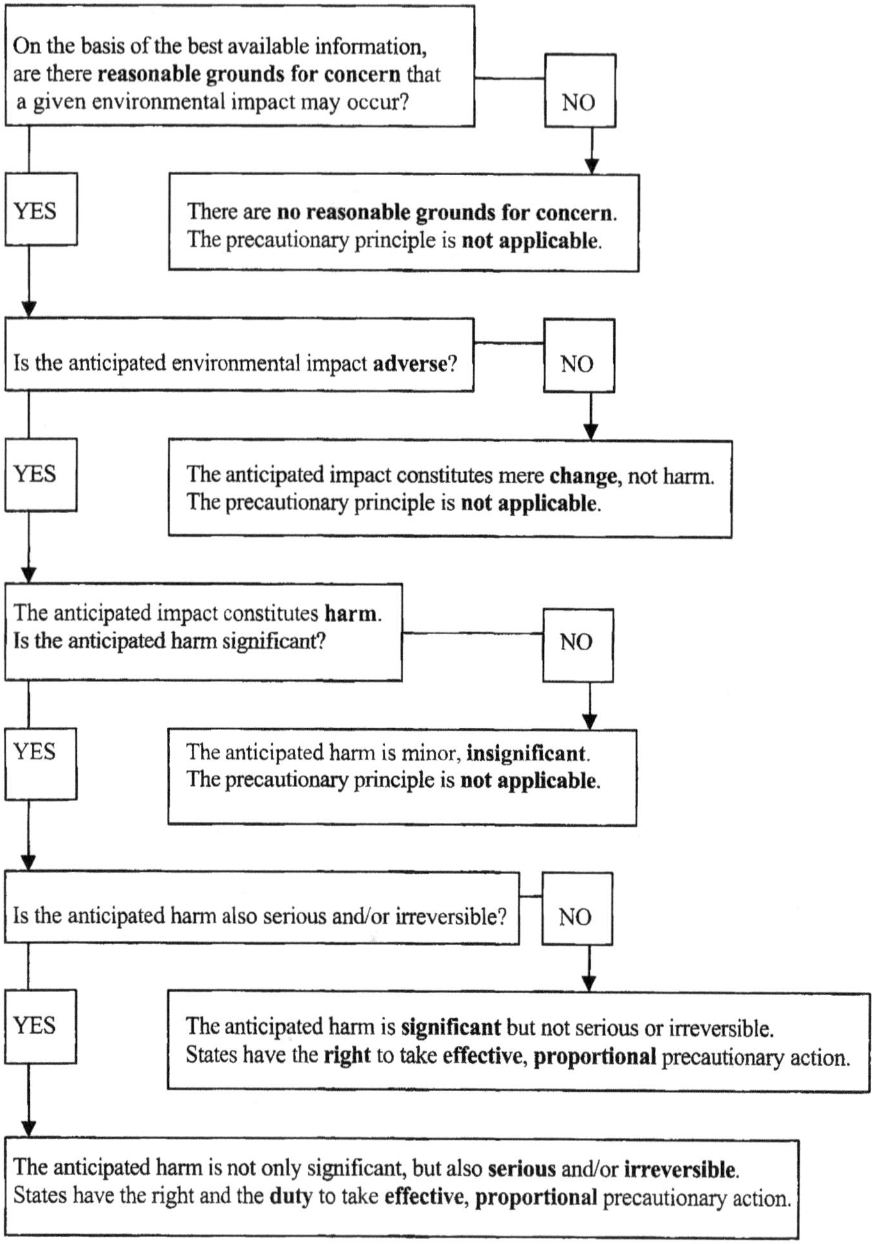

Figure 12. Precautionary rights and duties step by step. The various qualifications of impacts and the accompanying legal effects are printed boldly.

Implementation

Part Three was devoted to a number of aspects regarding the *implementation* of the right and the duty that were defined in Part Two. Scrutiny of the choice of precautionary measures by states, with the associated interplay of effectiveness and proportionality, enabled the deduction of several guidelines which appear to govern the implementation of the precautionary principle within the limits already imposed by the criteria of effectiveness and proportionality or which, alternatively, help determine what is effective and proportional action in individual instances. According to these guidelines states ought to settle upon a course of action which (a) is timely; (b) is tailored to the circumstances of the case at hand; (c) does not replace one risk with another of equal or greater size; (d) is regularly reviewed and maintained as long as necessary to prevent the harm in question, but not longer; and (e) in case of doubt regarding the aptness of different measures, errs on the side of environmental protection.[33] An assortment of measures is readily associated with the precautionary principle, including research, EIA, safety margins, clean production methods, the allocation of the burden of proof on activity proponents and the moratorium, the latter being the precautionary measure *par excellence*.[34] Apparently, however, *any* other measure will constitute an appropriate implementation of the precautionary principle if it fits the criteria of effectiveness and proportionality and respects the added guidelines outlined above. Application of these criteria and guidelines will in some cases result in the suitability of only one specific measure or set of measures, whereas in others it will leave the authorities involved an ample margin of discretion.[35]

The inevitable issue of *proof* proved to be versatile. Significantly, the analysis of state practice carried out in this regard showed that, contrary to popular belief, under customary international law the precautionary principle does not automatically place the onus of proving the acceptability of potentially harmful activities on their proponents.[36] Instead, on the intergovernmental level the initial burden of proof rests on the state wishing to prevent such activities, whereby the standard of proof to be met coincides with the thresholds outlined earlier. It is thus for states invoking their right to take precautionary action, respectively states challenging a lack of precautionary action on the part of other states, to demonstrate the presence of reasonable grounds for concern that significant, respectively serious and/or irreversible harm, may be caused. The precautionary principle has

[33] See *supra* paragraphs 5.4 and 7.3.

[34] See *supra* paragraph 7.2.

[35] See *supra* paragraph 7.3.

[36] See *supra* paragraphs 8.2 and 8.3.

lowered the standard of proof, but not reversed the traditional burden.[37] This does not take away the fact that the 'reversed onus' or 'precautionary burden of proof' plays a legitimate and important part in the implementation of the principle, in that the exercise by states of the right or duty to take effective and proportional precautionary action often takes the form of a prohibition which is only lifted upon delivery by the proponents of the prohibited activities or products of evidence proving the latter's relative harmlessness.[38]

The final issue studied in Part Three concerned the role of *socio-economic interests*. Even though the primary aim of the precautionary principle under general international law is obviously to protect the environment, including for its own sake, socio-economic factors and considerations of cost-effectiveness turn out to be part of the rationale and make-up of the precautionary principle as well, in accordance with the concept of sustainable development.[39] As a matter of customary international law there is, however, no separate requirement for precautionary action to be cost-effective. Rather, precautionary measures meeting the conditions set out previously are generally assumed to be so. In any case, cost-benefit analysis in the traditional sense has, for various reasons, no role to play in the implementation of the precautionary principle.[40] It has also become clear that there *is* room for states to balance environmental, social and economic interests when implementing the principle, although not unconditionally so. Generally, the proportionality criterion occasions that the greater a risk is, the more should be done and therefore spent to counter it, and the other way around. Only in cases where reasonable grounds for concern indicate that serious or significant irreversible harm may occur are states under a duty to take effective precautionary measures even if socio-economic costs are very high.[41] The notion of common but differentiated responsibilities, lastly, is a potential factor of significance in that it may, depending on the particular context, allow developing nations to take their limited capabilities into account when implementing obligations to protect the environment, including the precautionary principle – although the notion's establishment as a set feature of the principle itself cannot be inferred from state practice.[42]

Here ends this raven's-eye view of results.

---

[37] See *supra* paragraph 8.3.

[38] See *supra* paragraphs 8.2 and 8.3.

[39] See *supra* paragraphs 9.2 and 9.3.

[40] See *supra* paragraph 9.3.

[41] *Ibid.*

[42] See *supra* paragraphs 9.2 and 9.3.

10.2. Putting the Outcomes in Perspective

Since the prognostications of the oracular priestesses in ancient Delphi the ability of mankind to foresee future effects has undoubtedly improved. Still, even the predictive capacity of modern science is confined by inherent boundaries.[43] To cope with the fact that uncertainty will always be there to hinder decision-making, in particular with respect to the natural environment, the international community has replaced the Pythia with the precautionary principle. Evidently, of the two the latter is deemed to indicate the more reliable course to steer by.

A way of viewing the current study is as one large account of the way in which the precautionary principle, a general principle of international environmental law, is guiding the actions of states in a wide variety of concrete circumstances. The main purpose of this study as set out in the first chapter was to clarify the implications of the precautionary principle under general international law. By addressing some of the recurrent misunderstandings surrounding this topic, an attempt has been made to facilitate the fascinating debate on risk, uncertainty and precaution in international environmental law. To this end, the many available material sources of customary international law – sources of state practice proper and *opinio juris* – with bearing on the precautionary principle have been duly charted in all their diversity *and* regularity, analyzed from various perspectives, and lighted up by the occasional shimmer of common sense. On some counts this examination permitted for the inference of straightforward standards governing the application of the precautionary principle; on other counts no clear-cut conclusions were warranted. The outcomes have just passed in review and in this final paragraph there is just the space for some brief remarks to reflect on them.

To the extent possible, a customary right and a customary duty of states to take precautionary action, each conditioned by their own set of parameters, have been delineated. As universal custom, this right and this duty apply to every state, except to any states which have persistently objected to their application from the outset.[44] The precautionary principle has fundamentally altered the rules of customary international law in the area of the exploitation and protection of the environment. Before its establishment, this customary law regime was dominated by the right of states to exploit their natural resources pursuant to their own policies and the duty to ensure that activities within their jurisdiction or control do not cause significant damage to the environment of other states or of areas beyond the limits of national

---

[43] See *supra* paragraph 4.1.

[44] See Trouwborst, 2002, pp. 278-282 and *supra* paragraph 1.2.

jurisdiction, known as 'Principle 21'.[45] When the precautionary principle attained customary law status, the regime changed in at least two ways. First, when at present the standard of reasonable grounds for concern is met, then not only certain, probable or foreseeable harm but also *uncertain* threats may or must, depending on the gravity of anticipated harm, be prevented or abated. Second, the obligation to prevent environmental harm has, in the case of serious or irreversible harm, been extended to cover not only transboundary damage but also harm to states' own *domestic environment*. This extended scope might explain the fact that the duty to take action under the precautionary principle is not so readily triggered – there must be a prospect of serious or irreversible harm – as the traditional duty to prevent transboundary harm of Principle 21, for which a prospect of significant harm suffices.[46]

Like the consultation of the oracle of Delphi in its time, the application of the precautionary principle does not always yield a plain yes or no. Although at first sight the principle appears rather more straightforward than the oracular utterances of the Pythia, some of its elements as defined above may in concrete instances be open to interpretation by the authorities involved or by the international legal 'clergy'.[47] To some extent, this condition would seem to be innate to any general principle of international law with a broad scope of application. As Brierly phrased it:

> It is a natural consequence of the absence of authoritative law-declaring machinery that many of the principles of international law, and even more the detailed application of accepted principles, are uncertain. But on the whole the layman tends to exaggerate this defect. It is not in the nature of any law to provide mathematically certain solutions of problems which may be presented to it; for uncertainty cannot be eliminated from law so long as the possible conjunctions of facts remain infinitely various.[48]

Despite these intrinsic limitations, the precautionary principle has frequently proved to be sufficiently specific to direct the actions of states in concrete cases[49] and to be applied by national and international legal tribunals.[50]

Plenty of scenarios are imaginable which are sufficiently unambiguous to determine, through application of the definitions and guidelines laid bare in this study, whether the precautionary principle is

---

[45] See also *supra* paragraph 4.2.
[46] See also *supra* paragraph 5.3.
[47] See also *supra* Chapter 6 and paragraphs 5.3, 7.3, 9.3.
[48] Brierly, *The Law of Nations*, 6th ed., 1963, as quoted in Harris, 1998, p. 4.
[49] The present study and Trouwborst, 2002, bear ample witness to this.
[50] It suffices to consider the following jurisprudence: Supreme Court of India, *Vellore Citizens*, 1996; Supreme Court of Canada, *Spray-Tech v. Hudson*, 2001; ITLOS, *Southern Bluefin Tuna Cases*, 1999; ECJ, *Cockle Fisheries Case*, 2004; see also Marr, 2003, p. 225.

either complied with or violated as a matter of general international law. By way of a few extreme but not necessarily unrealistic examples, it is illustrative to imagine a North-American or European developed state knowingly allowing the clear-cutting of the last remaining primary forests on its territory, or permitting road and dam construction in the habitat of the last hundred specimens of the world's most threatened big cat species, with scientific reports in both cases warning against the potentially grave and irreparable consequences of such activities for the ecosystems and species involved. Certainly it would in either situation be difficult to argue that this imaginary state were acting in conformity with its obligation to take effective and proportional precautionary action when there are reasonable grounds for concern that serious or irreversible harm may be caused to the environment. The relevant thresholds seem to have been crossed, the gravity of the anticipated harm should evidently prevail over the socio-economic costs of halting the projects in question, and the state in the example is not a developing one which might legitimately opt for less effective action due to its limited capabilities. The fact that, as indicated above, these scenarios are not unrealistic ones fits the dire level of compliance with international environmental law generally, with legal commitments not always matching the action taken. This study heeds the approach taken by the ICJ and most commentators, who do not consider the frequently occurring practice of states running counter to, e.g., the 'paper' obligation of Principle 21 as a reason for denying its customary law status.[51] The passing of a red traffic light, even if repeated a million times, does not by itself remove the illegality of such action. Rather, it raises the question how the level of compliance can be improved.[52]

Besides its direct legal effect as a customary right or duty, the precautionary principle may also have indirect effect. In particular, it would seem concrete enough to serve as an interpretative tool in the application of other legal norms. As the 1969 *Vienna Convention on the Law of Treaties* stipulates, "any relevant rules of international law applicable in the relations between the parties" can be used in the interpretation of treaty obligations.[53] The principle provides, as it were, "a new lens with which to view existing obligations."[54] The dual role thus reserved for the precautionary principle under general international law can be exemplified by reference to Ireland's submission to the ITLOS in the 2001 *MOX Plant* case that "the precautionary principle is now recognised as a rule of customary

[51] See *supra* paragraph 4.2.
[52] See also *supra* paragraph 1.2.
[53] Article 31(3)(c).
[54] Freestone, 1999, p. 141; see also Marr, 2003, p. 43.

international law"[55] and as such "binding upon Ireland and the United Kingdom" both as a "free-standing obligation" and as a "principle applicable to the interpretation of each and every provision of LOSC upon which Ireland relies, including the interpretation and application of 'urgency' under Article 290(5) LOSC."[56] Similar considerations apply to Australia and New Zealand in the 1999 *Southern Bluefin Tuna* cases,[57] whereas in the 2003 *Land Reclamation* case Malaysia also relied on a number of provisions from the *LOS Convention* in conjunction with "the precautionary principle, which, under international law, must direct any State party in the application and implementation of those obligations."[58] One will also recall the regular recourse to the principle by the ECJ to inform the interpretation of particular rules of EU environmental law.[59] The precautionary principle, to name one more example of its potential indirect effect, may arguably be of use as well in the interpretation of some of the terms qualifying obligations in the *Biodiversity Convention*, e.g., when determining in concrete circumstances whether *in-situ* conservation measures are "appropriate".[60] In practice the two capacities of the principle, the direct and the indirect one, may not always be readily separable.

Nova et vetera. Many things have changed since the glory days of the oracle of Delphi. For one, the Pythia has been replaced by the precautionary principle. Other things remain unchanged. One of them is the fact that for human beings, as one Hugo Baskerville reportedly put it in 1742, "that which is clearly known hath less terror than that which is but hinted at and guessed."[61] It is hoped that this study has gone some way in reducing such terror by making the implications of the precautionary principle under general international law more clearly known, so that these need no longer be but hinted at and guessed.

---

[55] This was not challenged by the UK; see, e.g., the *Verbatim Records* of the sittings on 19 (p. 13, O'Hagan for Ireland) and 20 (p. 25, Plender for UK) November 2001.
[56] Paragraph 97 of the *Request for Provisional Measures and Statement of Case of Ireland* of 9 November 2001 (LOSC stands for the 1982 *UN Convention on the Law of the Sea*). As for the second role, in paragraph 112 Ireland argued that discharges into the Irish Sea would be "incompatible with the United Kingdom's obligations under Part XII of the LOSC, particularly when read in the light of the precautionary principle."
[57] See paragraphs 63-66 of the *Statements of Claim* of Australia and New Zealand, 15 July 1999.
[58] Paragraph 18 of the *Request for Provisional Measures* by Malaysia.
[59] See, e.g., the discussion of the 2004 *Cockle Fisheries Case* in *supra* paragraph 8.2.
[60] See Article 8 of the Convention.
[61] Conan Doyle, 1996, p.18.

BIBLIOGRAPHY

Abbreviations Used in the Bibliography

AA	Ars Acqui
AADI	Anuario Argentino de Derecho Internacional
ADI	Anuario de Derecho Internacional
AE/EY	Annuaire Européen/European Yearbook
AFDI	Annuaire Français de Droit International
AIDI	Annuaire de l'Institut de Droit International
AJE	African Journal of Ecology
AJIL	American Journal of International Law
AM	Agricoltura Mediterranea
ANZJS	Australian and New Zealand Journal of Statistics
APJEL	Asia Pacific Journal of Environmental Law
ASIL Proc.	Proceedings of the American Society of International Law
AV	Archiv des Völkerrechts
BC	Biodiversity and Conservation
BCICLR	Boston College International and Comparative Law Review
BYIL	British Yearbook of International Law
CESP	Cahiers Européens de Sciences Po
CJEL	Columbia Journal of European Law
CJIELP	Colorado Journal of International Environmental Law and Policy
CYIL	Canadian Yearbook of International Law
EA	Ecological Applications
EE	Ethics and the Environment
EELR	European Environmental Law Review
EJIL	European Journal of International Law
IUCN-ELPN	IUCN Environmental Law Programme Newsletter
ELR	European Law Review
EnvLR	Environmental Law Review
EMA	Environmental Monitoring and Assessment
EO	Ecologie en Ontwikkeling
EP	Environmental Pollution
EPLJ	Environmental and Planning Law Journal
ETFRN-News	European Tropical Forest Research Network News
FLR	Fordham Law Review
FS	Foundations of Science
GB	Global Biodiversity
GIELR	Georgetown International Environmental Law Review
GLJ	Georgetown Law Journal
GYIL	German Yearbook of International Law
HILJ	Harvard International Law Journal
HJIL	Heidelberg Journal of International Law
ICLQ	International and Comparative Law Quarterly
IEA	International Environmental Agreements: Politics, Law and Economics
IJECL	International Journal of Estuarine and Coastal Law
IJMCL	International Journal of Marine and Coastal Law
IJGLS	Indiana Journal of Global Legal Studies

ILF	International Law FORUM
JAEE	Journal of Agricultural and Environmental Ethics
JASA	Journal of the Acoustical Society of America
JEL	Journal of Environmental Law
JIEL	Journal of International Economic Law
JIWLP	Journal of International Wildlife Law and Policy
JRR	Journal of Risk Research
LC	Law and Critique
LF	Label France
LIEI	Legal Issues of Economic Integration
LO	Limnology and Oceanography
MEHD	Microbial Ecology in Health and Disease
MLR	Melbourne Law Review
MP	Marine Policy
MPB	Marine Pollution Bulletin
MR	Milieu en Recht
NILR	Netherlands International Law Review
NJB	Nederlands Juristenblad
NLR	NEPTUNUS Law Review
NSS	Natures, Sciences, Sociétés
NYIL	Netherlands Yearbook of International Law
NYUELR	New York University Environmental Law Review
OCM	Ocean and Coastal Management
ODIL	Ocean Development and International Law
PE	Plant Ecology
PR	Polar Record
RA	Risk Analysis
RBDI	Revue Belge de Droit International
RECIEL	Review of European Community and International Environmental Law
RGDA	Revista Giuridica Dell' Ambiente
RGDIP	Revue Générale de Droit International Public
RIWC	Report of the International Whaling Commission
SJIL	Stanford Journal of International Law
STE	The Science of the Total Environment
TIBG	Transactions of the Institute of British Geographers
TM	Tijdschrift voor Milieurecht
UNGAOR	Official Records of the United Nations General Assembly
VF	Voice for the Forest
VJTL	Vanderbilt Journal of Transnational Law
WASP	Water, Air, and Soil Pollution
WLR	Willamette Law Review
YEL	Yearbook of European Law
YIEL	Yearbook of International Environmental Law
ZaöRV	Zeitschrift für Ausländisches Öffentliches Recht und Völkerrecht

Bibliography

- Abouchar, J., "Implementation of the Precautionary Principle in Canada", in: O'Riordan, T. *et al.* (eds.), *Reinterpreting the Precautionary Principle*, London 2001, pp. 235-267
- Abouchar, J., "Case Notes: Spray-Tech v. Hudson (Ville)", in: 11 *RECIEL*, 2002, pp. 104-106
- Adams, J., "A Richter Scale for Risk?", in: Morris, J. (ed.), *Rethinking Risk and the Precautionary Principle*, Oxford 2000, pp. 229-246
- Adeel, Z. *et al.*, *Ecosystems and Human Well-Being: Desertification Synthesis: A Millennium Ecosystem Assessment Report*, Washington, D.C. 2005
- Alba Alonso, J. & Rivas Infante, D., "El Valor Económico del Bosque", in: Alba Alonso, J. *et al.*, *Nuestros Bosques*, Madrid 1998, pp. 131-150
- Alexandrowicz, G.W., "International Legal Instruments and Institutional Arrangements: A Discussion Paper", in: Canadian Council on International Law (ed.), *Global Forests and International Environmental Law*, London 1996, pp. 315-351
- Araújo, J., *Ecos... Lógicos: Para Entender la Ecología*, Madrid 2000
- Altieri, M.A., "Riesgos Ambientales de los Cultivos Transgénicos", in: 20 *Ecologista*, 2000, pp. 24-29
- Apel, A., "'Substantial Equivalence' and the Precautionary Principle: A Challenge to Risk Assessment", 2000, http://www.biotech-info.net/risk_assessment_challenge.html
- Appell, D., "The New Uncertainty Principle", 2001, http://www.biotech-info.net/uncertainty.html
- Ashford, N.A. *et al.*, *Wingspread Statement on the Precautionary Principle*, Racine, Wisconsin, 25 January 1998, reproduced in: Raffensperger, C. & Tickner, J. (eds.), *Protecting Public Health and the Environment: Implementing the Precautionary Principle*, Washington 1999, pp. 353-355
- Ashford, N.A., "A Conceptual Framework for the Use of the Precautionary Principle in Law", in: Raffensperger, C. & Tickner, J. (eds.), *Protecting Public Health and the Environment: Implementing the Precautionary Principle*, Washington 1999, pp.198-206
- Assmann, T., "The Ground Beetle Fauna of Ancient and Recent Woodlands in the Lowlands of North-West Germany (Coleoptera, Carabidae)", in: 8 *BC*, 1999, pp. 1499-1517
- Attfield, R., "The Precautionary Principle and Moral Values", in: O'Riordan, T. & Cameron, J. (eds.), *Interpreting the Precautionary Principle*, London 1994, pp. 152-164
- Backes, C., "Het Voorzorgbeginsel in het Natuurbeschermingsrecht, Verslag van een Onderzoek", in: Backes, C., Gilhuis, P.C. & Verschuuren, J.M. (eds.), *Het Voorzorgbeginsel in het Natuurbeschermingsrecht*, Deventer 1997, pp. 1-12
- Backes, C. *et al.*, "Onderzoeksrapport: 'Het Voorzorgbeginsel in het Natuurbeschermingsrecht'", in: Backes, C., Gilhuis, P.C. & Verschuuren, J.M. (eds.), *Het Voorzorgbeginsel in het Natuurbeschermingsrecht*, Deventer 1997, pp. 49-111
- Backes, C. *et al.*, "Reacties: De Ongerijmde Angst van Pieterman voor het Voorzorgbeginsel", in: *NJB*, No. 36, 2001, pp. 1760-1761
- Backes, C. *et al.*, *Codificatie van Milieurechtelijke Beginselen in de Wet Milieubeheer*, Den Haag 2002
- Baird, R.J., "Ocean Dumping – an Overview of the International and Domestic Regulatory System", in: 15 *EPLJ*, 1998, pp. 174-189
- Barrett, K. & Raffensperger, C., "Precautionary Science", in: Raffensperger, C. & Tickner, J. (eds.), *Protecting Public Health and the Environment: Implementing the Precautionary Principle*, Washington 1999, pp. 106-122
- Bateson, M.C., "Wat is Natuurlijk en Wat Niet?", in: Brockman, J. & Matson, K. (eds.), *Simpele Feiten*, Amsterdam 2004, pp. 39-48
- Beckerman, W., "The Precautionary Principle and Our Obligations to Future Generations", in: Morris, J. (ed.), *Rethinking Risk and the Precautionary Principle*, Oxford 2000, pp. 46-59

- Beeckman, K., "Transboundary Damage to the Environment *Per Se*: Remedial Measures and Standing", in: 29 *RBDI*, 1996, pp. 453-492
- Bell, A.M., "Taking Externalities Seriously: An Economic Perspective on the Precautionary Principle", Accurate Prices Issue Brief, February 2002, http://www.rprogress.org/publications/precaution0202.pdf
- Bereano, P.L., "Politics, Sound Science and the Precautionary Principle", 2000, http://www.cid.harvard.edu/cidbiotech/comments/comments92.htm
- Bernstein, A., "Precaution and Respect", in: Raffensperger, C. & Tickner, J. (eds.), *Protecting Public Health and the Environment: Implementing the Precautionary Principle*, Washington 1999, pp. 148-158
- Besné Mañero, R., *El Crimen Internacional*, Bilbao 1999
- Bilder, R.B. *et al.*, "International Land-Use Law", in: *ASIL Proc.*, 1993, pp. 488-507
- Birnie, P.W. & Boyle, A.E., *International Law and the Environment*, Oxford 1992
- Birnie, P.W. & Boyle, A.E. (eds.), *Basic Documents on International Environmental Law*, Oxford 1995
- Bishop, K.H., "Liming of Acid Surface Waters in Northern Sweden: Questions of Geographical Variation and the Precautionary Principle", in: 22 *TIBG*, 1997, pp. 49-60
- Blanchfield, R., "Commentary on the Precautionary Principle", 2000, http://www.biotech-info.net/PP_commentary.html
- Bodansky, D., "New Developments in International Environmental Law: Remarks by Daniel Bodansky", in: *ASIL Proc.*, 1991, pp. 413-417
- Bodansky, D., "Scientific Uncertainty and the Precautionary Principle", in: 33 *Environment*, 1991, pp. 4-
- Bodansky, D., "The Precautionary Principle in US Environmental Law", in: O'Riordan, T. & Cameron, J. (eds.), *Interpreting the Precautionary Principle*, London 1994, pp. 203-228
- Bodansky, D., "Customary (and Not So Customary) International Environmental Law", in: 3 *IJGLS*, 1995, pp. 105-120
- Bodansky, D., "Legal Issues Related to Geo-Engineering", *Elements of Change*, Aspen Global Change Institute 1996, http://www.agci.org/publications/eoc95/sessionII/Bodansky.html
- Boehmer-Christiansen, S., "Precautionary Principle", in: 35 *Environment*, 1993, pp. 42-
- Boehmer-Christiansen, S., "The Precautionary Principle in Germany – Enabling Government", in: O'Riordan, T. & Cameron, J. (eds.), *Interpreting the Precautionary Principle*, London 1994, pp. 34-60
- Boer, B., "Commentary: Developments in International Environmental Law Relating to Forests", in: 14 *ELPJ*, 1997, pp. 378-385
- Bohnsack, J.A., "Incorporating No-Take Marine Reserves into Precautionary Management and Stock Assessment", in: Restrepo, V.R. (ed.), *Proceedings of the Fifth National NMFS Stock Assessment Workshop: Providing Scientific Advice to Implement the Precautionary Approach Under the Magnuson-Stevens Fishery Conservation and Management Act*, NOAA Technical Memorandum NMFS-F/SPO-40, 1999, pp. 8-16
- Boisson de Chazournes, L., "La Gestion de l'Intérêt Commun à l'Épreuve des Enjeux Économiques – le Protocole de Kyoto sur les Changements Climatiques", in: 43 *AFDI*, 1997, pp. 700-715
- Boisson de Chazournes, L., "The Precautionary Principle", in: *Precaution from Rio to Johannesburg: Proceedings of a Geneva Environment Network Roundtable*, International Environment House, Geneva, 16 May 2002, pp. 10-12
- Borgers, H.C., "*In Dubio Pro Natura:* Het Functionele Perspectief van het Voorzorgbeginsel", in: 48 *AA*, 1999, pp. 431-441
- Bosselmann, K., "Power, Plants and Power Plants: New Zealand's Implementation of the Climate Change Convention", in: 12 *EPLJ*, 1995, pp. 423-439

- Bou Franch, V. & Badenes Casino, M., "La Protección Internacional de Zonas y Especies en la Región Mediterránea", in: 13 *ADI*, 1997, pp. 33-129
- Bou Franch, V., "La Protección de los Mamíferos Marinos en el Mar Mediterráneo", in: 14 *ADI*, 1998, pp. 3-51
- Bouma, J., Den Butter, F. & Wissink, B., "Algemene Inleiding", in: Wissink, B. & Bouma, J. (eds.), *Perspectieven op Milieurisico's*, Wetenschappelijke Raad voor het Regeringsbeleid Werkdocument W128, The Hague 2002, pp. 7-24
- Boy, L., "La Nature Juridique du Principe de Précaution", in: 7 *NSS*, 1999, pp. 5-11
- Boyle, A.E., "The Rio Convention on Biological Diversity", in: Bowman, M. & Redgwell, C. (eds.), *International Law and the Conservation of Biological Diversity*, London/The Hague/Boston 1996, pp. 33-49
- Bragdon, S.H., "National Sovereignty and Global Environmental Responsibility: Can the Tension be Reconciled for the Conservation of Biological Diversity?", in: 33 *HILJ*, 1992, pp. 381-392
- Brans, E.P.H., *Liability for Damage to Public Natural Resources: Standing, Damage and Damage Assessment*, The Hague/London/New York 2001
- Bridges, E.M. & Van Baren, J.H.V., "Soil: an Overlooked, Undervalued and Vital Part of the Human Environment", in: 17 *The Environmentalist*, 1997, pp. 15-20
- Brilmont, J., "Science of Chaos or Chaos of Science?", 1996, http://cdfinfo.in2p3.fr/~bouquet/Bricmont/node2.html (accessed 21 November 2002)
- Brown, L.R. *et al.*, *State of the World 1997* (Worldwatch Institute Report), New York 1997
- Brownlie, I., *Principles of Public International Law*, 5th ed., Oxford 1998
- Brown Weiss, E. *et al.*, "New Developments in International Environmental Law", in: *ASIL Proc.*, 1991, pp. 401-427
- Bruce, D., "Finding a Balance over Precaution", in: 15 *JAEE*, 2002, pp. 7-16
- Brunnée, J., "A Conceptual Framework for an International Forests Convention: Customary Law and Emerging Principles", in: Canadian Council on International Law (ed.), *Global Forests and International Environmental Law*, London 1996, pp. 41-77
- Brunnée, J., "The United States and International Environmental Law: Living with and Elephant", in: 15 *EJIL*, 2004, pp. 617-649
- Bryant, D. *et al.*, *The Last Frontier Forests: Ecosystems & Economies on the Edge* (World Resources Institute report), Washington 1997
- Bryde, B.-O., "Umweltschutz Durch Allgemeines Völkerrecht?", in: 31 *AV*, 1993, pp. 1-12
- Burke, W.T., "Regulation of Driftnet Fishing on the High Seas and the New International Law of the Sea", in: 3 *GIELR*, 1990, pp. 265-310
- Bustamante, R.O. & Castor, C., "The Decline of an Endangered Temperate Ecosystem: the Ruil (*Nothofagus Alessandrii*) Forest in Central Chile", in: 7 *BC*, 1998, pp. 1607-1626
- Byrne, D., "Address by David Byrne on the Precautionary Principle in the Domain of Human Health and Food Safety", 2000, http://europa.eu.int/comm/dgs/health_consumer/library/speeches/speech66_en.html
- Cameron, J., "The Status of the Precautionary Principle in International Law", in: O'Riordan, T. & Cameron, J. (eds.), *Interpreting the Precautionary Principle*, London 1994, pp. 263-289
- Cameron, J., "The Precautionary Principle in International Law", in: O'Riordan, T. *et al.* (eds.), *Reinterpreting the Precautionary Principle*, London 2001, pp. 113-142
- Cameron, J. & Abouchar, J., "The Status of the Precautionary Principle in International Law", in: Freestone, D. & Hey, E. (eds.), *The Precautionary Principle and International Law*, The Hague 1996, pp. 29-52

- Cameron, J., Wade-Gery, W. & Abouchar, J., "Precautionary Principle and Future Generations", in: Agius, E. *et al.* (eds.), *Future Generations & International Law*, London 1998, pp. 93-113
- Campins Eritja, M., "La Acción Internacional para Reducir los Efectos del Cambio Climatico: El Convenio Marco y el Protocolo de Kyoto", in: 15 *ADI*, 1999, pp. 71-113
- Canelas de Castro, P., "The Judgment in the *Case Concerning the Gabcikovo-Nagymaros Project*: Positive Signs for the Evolution of International Water Law", in: 8 *YIEL*, 1997, pp. 21-31
- Canelas de Castro, P., "The Future of International Water Law", in: Vlachos, E. & Nunes Correia, F. (ed.), *Shared Water Systems and Transboundary Issues; With Special Emphasis on the Iberian Peninsula*, Proceedings of the Conference held at FLAD in Lisbon, Portugal, 11-12 March 1999, pp. 149-216
- Cannizzaro, E., *Il Principio della Proporzionalità nell'Ordinamento Internazionale*, Milan 2000
- Carr, S., "Ethical and Value-Based Aspects of the European Commission's Precautionary Principle", in: 15 *JAEE*, 2002, pp. 31-38
- Castells, N. & Ravetz, J., "Science and Policy in International Environmental Agreements: Lessons from the European Experience on Transboundary Air Pollution", in: 1 *IEA*, 2001, pp. 405-425
- Castillo Daudi, M., "La Protección y Preservación de los Cursos de Agua Internacionales: El Convenio sobre el Derecho de los Usos de Agua Internacionales para Fines Distintos de la Navegación de 21 Mayo 1997", in: 15 *ADI*, 1999, pp. 115-158
- Centre for Resource Solutions, "Meadowlark Economics: Erring on the Side of Caution", 1997, http://www.safe2use.com/data/precaut2.htm
- Chalmers, D., "Environmental Law", in: *YEL*, 1996, pp. 571-599
- Chalmers, D., "Environmental Law", in: *YEL*, 1997, pp. 491-513
- Christensen, M., "The Precautionary Principle and GMOs: An Australian Perspective", in: *IUCN-ELPN*, No. 1, 2001, pp. 5-6, 21
- Christie, E., "The Eternal Triangle: The Biodiversity Convention, Endangered Species Legislation and the Precautionary Principle", in: 10 *EPLJ*, 1993, pp. 470-485
- Citizens for Healthy Growth, "The Precautionary Principle", http://www.citizens4healthygrowth.org/precaution.html
- Clover, *The End of the Line: How Overfishing is Changing the World and What We Eat*, London 2005
- Cohen, J., "Waarom Zijn We Wie We Zijn?", in: Brockman, J. & Matson, K. (eds.), *Simpele Feiten*, Amsterdam 2004, pp. 75-86
- Conan Doyle, A., *The Hound of the Baskervilles*, London 1996
- Cooney, R., "Summary of the Workshop on 'The Precautionary Principle in Wildlife Conservation'", 2000, http://www.traffic.org/briefings/precautionary.html
- Cooney, R., "The Precautionary Principle in Development Context: Natural Resource Management, Conservation, Liveliho y, R., *The Precautionary Principle in Biodiversity Conservation and Natural Resource Management*, IUCN Policy ods and Trade", in: *IUCN-ELPN*, No. 1, 2001, pp. 10-11
- Coone and Global Change Series No. 2, Gland/Cambridge 2004
- Cordonier Segger, M.-C. & Gehring, M.G., "The WTO and Precaution: Sustainable Development Implications of the WTO Asbestos Dispute", in: 15 *JEL*, 2003, pp. 289-321
- Cornwell, L. & Costanza, R., "Environmental Bonds: Implementing the Precautionary Principle in Environmental Policy", in: Raffensperger, C. & Tickner, J. (eds.), *Protecting Public Health and the Environment: Implementing the Precautionary Principle*, Washington 1999, pp. 220-240
- Cors, T.A., "Biosafety and International Trade: Conflict or Convergence?", 1999, http://www.biotech-info.net/conflict_convergence.html

- Corvalan, C., Hales, S. & McMichael, A., *Ecosystems and Human Well-Being: Health Synthesis: A Report of the Millennium Ecosystem Assessment*, World Health Organization, Geneva 2005
- Cotter, J., Johnston, P. & Santillo, D., "The Precautionary Principle and Forest Exploitation: Implications for the Implementation of the FSC Principle 9", Greenpeace Research Laboratories Technical Note No. 08/00, 3 November 2000
- Cranor, C.F., "Asymmetric Information, the Precautionary Principle, and Burdens of Proof", in: Raffensperger, C. & Tickner, J. (eds.), *Protecting Public Health and the Environment: Implementing the Precautionary Principle*, Washington 1999, pp. 74-99
- Danilenko, G.M., "International *Jus Cogens*: Issues of Law-Making", in: 2 *EJIL*, 1991, pp. 42-65
- Darwin, C., *The Origin of Species*, Ware (Wordsworth) 1998
- Davies, P.G.G. & Redgwell, C., "The International Legal Regime of Straddling Fish Stocks", in: 68 *BYIL*, 1997, pp. 199-274
- DeFur, P.L., "The Precautionary Principle: Application to Policies Regarding Endocrine-Disrupting Chemicals", in: Raffensperger, C. & Tickner, J. (eds.), *Protecting Public Health and the Environment: Implementing the Precautionary Principle*, Washington 1999, pp. 337-348
- DeFur, P.L. & Kaszuba, M., "Implementing the Precautionary Principle", in: 288 *STE*, 2002, pp. 155-165
- Delibes, M. & Delibes de Castro, M., *La Tierra Herida*, Barcelona 2005
- Delibes de Castro, M., "Lobos y Bosques en el Anticiclón", in: *Biológica*, No. 47, 2000, pp. 68-69
- Delibes de Castro, M., *Vida: La Naturaleza en Peligro*, Madrid 2001
- Denman Forestry Initiative, "Hancock Sold, but Not to Us", in: 1 *VF*, No. 2, 1997, pp. 1-4
- De Sadeleer, N., "The Enforcement of the Precautionary Principle by German, French and Belgian Courts", in: 9 *RECIEL*, 2000, pp. 144-151
- De Sadeleer, N., *Environmental Principles: From Political Slogans to Legal Rules*, Oxford 2002
- De Sadeleer, N., "Book Review of Arie Trouwborst, *Evolution and Status of the Precautionary Principle in International Law*", in: 13 *RECIEL*, 2004, pp. 116-117
- Diez de Velasco, M., *Instituciones de Derecho Internacional Público*, 10th ed., Vol. I, Madrid 1994
- Dixon, M., *Textbook on International Law*, 5th ed., Oxford 2005
- Douma, W.T., "The Precautionary Principle", 1997, http://www.eel.nl/virtue/precprin.htm
- Douma, W.T., "Principles of European Environmental Law", 1997, in: Virtual University for Europe video lecture series *European Environmental Law: The Challenges for the 21st Century*
- Douma, W.T., "The Precautionary Principle in the European Union", in: 9 *RECIEL*, 2000, pp. 132-143
- Douma, W.T., "The Precautionary Principle in the Netherlands", in: O'Riordan, T. *et al.* (eds.), *Reinterpreting the Precautionary Principle*, London 2001, pp. 163-181
- Douma, W.T., *The Precautionary Principle: Its Application in International, European and Dutch Law*, dissertation, Groningen 2003
- Drnas de Clément, Z., "Concepto y Elementos Jurídicos del Desarrollo Sostenible", in: 8 *AADI*, 1998, pp. 163-173
- Dudley, N., *Forests in Trouble: A Review of the Status of Temperate Forests Worldwide* (World Wide Fund for Nature report), Gland 1992
- Dudley, N. *et al.*, *Bad Harvest?: The Timber Trade and the Degradation of the World's Forests* (World Wide Fund for Nature report), Gland 1995
- Dupuy, P.-M., "Où en est le Droit International de l'Environnement à la Fin du Siècle?", in: 101 *RGDIP*, 1997, pp. 873-903
- Durnil, G.K., "How Much Information Do We Need Before Exercising Precaution?", in: Raffensperger, C. & Tickner, J. (eds.), *Protecting Public Health and the Environment: Implementing the Precautionary Principle*, Washington 1999, pp. 266-276

- Dzidzornu, D.M., "Four Principles in Marine Environment Protection: A Comparative Analysis", in: 29 *ODIL*, 1998, pp. 91-123
- Earll, R.C., "Common-Sense and the Precautionary Principle - an Environmentalist's Perspective", in: 24 *MPB*, 1992, pp. 182-186
- Ebbesson, J., *Compatibility of International and National Environmental Law*, Dordrecht 1996
- Edeson, W., "Towards Long-Term Sustainable Use: Some Recent Developments in the Legal Regime of Fisheries", in: Boyle, A. & Freestone, D. (eds.), *International Law and Sustainable Development*, Oxford 1999, pp. 165-203
- Ehrenfeld, D., "Why Put Value on Biodiversity?", in: Wilson, E.O. (ed.), *Biodiversity*, Washington, D.C. 1988, pp. 212-216
- Ellis, J., "The Precautionary Principle: From Paradigm to Rule of Law", in: 2 *ILF*, 2000, pp. 127-129
- Emerson, R.W. & Thoreau, H.D., *Nature – Walking*, Boston 1991
- Environmental Investigation Agency, *The Case for a New Global Forests Agreement*, London 1997
- Epiney, A. & Scheyli, M., *Strukturprinzipien des Umweltvölkerrechts*, Baden-Baden 1998
- European Chemical Industry Council, "Precautionary Principle: The Precautionary Principle, Industry and Law-Making (Position Paper)", 1995, http://www.cefic.org/position/sec/pp_sec05.htm (accessed 12 March 2000)
- European Environment Agency, *Late Lessons from Early Warnings: The Precautionary Principle 1896-2000*, Environmental Issue Report No. 22, Copenhagen 2001
- Ezeonu, I.C. & Ezeonu, F.C., "The Environment and Global Security", in: 20 *The Environmentalist*, 2000, pp. 41-48
- Farman, J., "Halocarbons, the Ozone Layer and the Precautionary Principle", in: European Environment Agency, *Late Lessons from Early Warnings: The Precautionary Principle 1896-2000*, Environmental Issue Report No. 22, Copenhagen 2001, pp. 76-83
- Farnsworth, N.R., "Screening Plants for New Medicines", in: Wilson, E.O. (ed.), *Biodiversity*, Washington, D.C. 1988, pp. 83-97
- Faure, M.G., "Het Voorzorgsbeginsel in het Belgisch en Vlaams Recht", in: Faure, M.G. & Vos, E. (eds.), *Juridische Afbakening van het Voorzorgsbeginsel: Mogelijkheden en Grenzen*, Gezondheidsraad Publication Nr. A03/03, The Hague 2003, pp. 235-258
- Faure, M.G. & Vos, E., "Conclusies and Slotbeschouwingen", in: Faure, M.G. & Vos, E. (eds.), *Juridische Afbakening van het Voorzorgsbeginsel: Mogelijkheden en Grenzen*, Gezondheidsraad Publication Nr. A03/03, The Hague 2003, pp. 259-272
- Federale Raad voor Duurzame Ontwikkeling, "Advies over de Mededeling van de Europese Commissie over de Toepassing van het Voorzorgsbeginsel (COM(2000)1)", in: 10 *TM*, 2001, pp. 11-19
- Finlayson, C.M. *et al.*, *Ecosystems and Human Well-Being: Wetlands and Water Synthesis: A Millennium Ecosystem Assessment Report*, Washington, D.C. 2005
- Fisher, E. & Harding, R., "The Precautionary Principle in Australia: From Aspiration to Practice?", in: O'Riordan, T. *et al.* (eds.), *Reinterpreting the Precautionary Principle*, London 2001, pp. 215-233
- Fisk, D., "Environmental Science and Environmental Law", in: 10 *JEL*, 1998, pp. 3-8
- Fitzmaurice, M.A., "International Environmental Law as a Special Field", in: 25 *NYIL*, 1994, pp. 181-226
- Fleming, D., "The Economics of Taking Care: An Evaluation of the Precautionary Principle", in: Freestone, D. & Hey, E. (eds.), *The Precautionary Principle and International Law*, The Hague 1996, pp. 147-167
- Fombad, C.M., "The Effectiveness of Environmental Protection Measures in Cameroon's 1994 Law Laying Down Forestry, Wildlife and Fisheries Regulations", in: 9 *JEL*, 1997, pp. 43-58

- Food and Agriculture Organization of the United Nations, *State of the World's Forests 1997*, Oxford 1997
- Foster, K.R. *et al.*, "Science and the Precautionary Principle", 2000, http://www.biotech-info.net/science_and_PP.html
- Foster, C.E., "The 'Real Dispute' in the Southern Bluefin Tuna Case: A Scientific Dispute?", in: 16 *IJMCL*, 2001, pp. 571-601
- Fowler, C.W., "Nature's Monte Carlo Experiments in Sustainability", in: Restrepo, V.R. (ed.), *Proceedings of the Fifth National NMFS Stock Assessment Workshop: Providing Scientific Advice to Implement the Precautionary Approach Under the Magnuson-Stevens Fishery Conservation and Management Act*, NOAA Technical Memorandum NMFS-F/SPO-40, 1999, pp. 25-32
- Francescon, S., "The Precautionary Principle in the European Union", in: *IUCN-ELPN*, No. 1, 2001, pp. 14-15, 19
- Freestone, D., "International Fisheries Law Since Rio: The Continued Rise of the Precautionary Principle", in: Boyle, A. & Freestone, D. (eds.), *International Law and Sustainable Development*, Oxford 1999, pp. 135-164
- Freestone, D. & Hey, E., "Origins and Development of the Precautionary Principle", in: Freestone, D. & Hey, E. (eds.), *The Precautionary Principle and International Law*, The Hague 1996, pp. 3-15
- Freestone, D. & Hey, E., "Implementing the Precautionary Principle: Challenges and Opportunities", in: Freestone, D. & Hey, E. (eds.), *The Precautionary Principle and International Law*, The Hague 1996, pp. 249-268
- Friedberg, J.J., "Views of Doñana: Fragmentation and Environmental Policy in Spain", in: 3 *CJEL*, 1996/1997, pp. 1-48
- Fuentes, X., "Sustainable Development and the Equitable Utilization of International Watercourses", in: 69 *BYIL*, 1998, pp. 119-200
- Fukudu-Parr, S. *et al.*, *Human Development Report 2001* (UNDP report), New York 2001
- Galán Cela, P., "La Vegetación Forestal", in: Alba Alonso *et al.*, *Nuestros Bosques*, Madrid 1998, pp. 89-116
- Gallacher, H., *Waarom Jagen: 12 Argumenten Tegen het Licht Gehouden*, Voorhout 1990
- Geiser, K., "Establishing a General Duty of Precaution in Environmental Protection Policies in the United States", in: Raffensperger, C. & Tickner, J. (eds.), *Protecting Public Health and the Environment: Implementing the Precautionary Principle*, Washington 1999, pp. xxi-xxvi
- Geiser, K., "Cleaner Production and the Precautionary Principle", in: Raffensperger, C. & Tickner, J. (eds.), *Protecting Public Health and the Environment: Implementing the Precautionary Principle*, Washington 1999, pp. 323-336
- Gilbertson, M., "The Precautionary Principle and Early Warnings of Chemical Contamination of the Great Lakes", in: European Environment Agency, *Late Lessons from Early Warnings: The Precautionary Principle 1896-2000*, Environmental Issue Report No. 22, Copenhagen 2001, pp. 126-134
- Gilland, T., "Precaution, GM Crops and Farmland Birds", in: Morris, J. (ed.), *Rethinking Risk and the Precautionary Principle*, Oxford 2000, pp. 60-83
- Gillespie, A., *International Environmental Law, Policy and Ethics*, Oxford 1997
- Glandt, D., *Der Kolkrabe*, Wiebelsheim 2003
- Gleick, J., *Chaos: The Amazing Science of the Unpredictable*, London 1998
- Glenning, M.J., "Has International Law Failed the Elephant?", in: 84 *AJIL*, 1990, pp. 1-43
- Godard, O., "Vers une Prévention des Risques", in: *LF*, No. 38, 2000, http://www.france.diplomatie.fr/label_france/FRANCE/DOSSIER/2000/16risques.html (accessed 21 May 2002)

- Goklany, I.M., "Applying the Precautionary Principle in a Broader Context", in: Morris, J. (ed.), *Rethinking Risk and the Precautionary Principle*, Oxford 2000, pp. 189-228
- Goldschmidt, T., *Darwin's Dreampond*, Cambridge 1998
- González Campos, J.D. *et al*, *Curso de Derecho Internacional Público*, 6th ed., Madrid 1998
- González-Laxe, F., "The Precautionary Principle in Fisheries Management", in: 29 *MP*, 2005, pp. 495-505
- Gorbachev, M., "Editorial", in: *Naturopa*, No. 92, 2000, p. 3
- Government of Canada, "A Canadian Perspective on the Precautionary Approach/Principle: Discussion Document", 2001, http://www.ncr.dfo.ca/cppa/menu.htm (accessed 12 June 2002)
- Government of Canada, "A Canadian Perspective on the Precautionary Approach/Principle: Proposed Guiding Principles", 2001, http://www.ncr.dfo.ca/cppa/menu.htm (accessed 12 June 2002)
- Gray, J.S., "Integrating Precautionary Scientific Methods into Decision-Making", in: Freestone, D. & Hey, E. (eds.), *The Precautionary Principle and International Law*, The Hague 1996, pp. 133-146
- Gray, K.R., "International Environmental Impact Assessment", in: 11 *CJIELP*, 2000, pp. 83-128
- Greenpeace International, *Implementing the Precautionary Approach in the Mediterranean Action Plan* (discussion paper), Amsterdam 1994
- Greenpeace International, *Principles and Guidelines for Ecologically Responsible Forest Use*, Amsterdam 1994
- Greenpeace International, *Analysis of the United Nations Treaty for the Conservation and Management of Straddling Fish Stocks and Highly Migratory Fish Stocks*, Amsterdam 1995
- Greenpeace International, *Full of Holes: The Montreal Protocol and the Continuing Destruction of the Ozone Layer*, Amsterdam 1995
- Greenpeace International, *Greenpeace Principles for Ecologically Responsible Fisheries (Preliminary Document)*, Amsterdam 1996
- Greenpeace Melanesia, *Working Together: Sustaining Forests and Communities in Melanesia*, 1996
- Griffin, P., "Endangered Species Diversity 'Hot Spots' in Russia and Centers of Endemism", in: 8 *BC*, 1999, pp. 497-511
- Grimeaud, D., "The Precautionary Principle in International Environmental and Trade Law", in: Faure, M.G. & Vos, E. (eds.), *Juridische Afbakening van het Voorzorgsbeginsel: Mogelijkheden en Grenzen*, Gezondheidsraad Publication Nr. A03/03, The Hague 2003, pp. 47-118
- Guix, J. *et al.*, "Ciudades y Pueblos Exportan Semillas de Plantas Exóticas", in: *Quercus*, No. 172, 2000, pp. 6-7
- Gullett, W., "Environmental Protection and the 'Precautionary Principle': A Response to Scientific Uncertainty in Environmental Management", in: 14 *EPLJ*, 1997, pp. 52-69
- Gündling, L., "Our Responsibility to Future Generations", in: 84 *AJIL*, 1990, pp. 207-212
- Gupta, A., "Precaution and the Survival Threshold", 2000, http://www.cid.harvard.edu/cidbiotech/comments/comments98.htm
- Gupta, J., "Glocalization: the Precautionary Principle and Public Participation, with special reference to the UN Framework Convention on Climate Change", in: Freestone, D. & Hey, E. (eds.), *The Precautionary Principle and International Law*, The Hague 1996, pp. 231-246
- Guttiérrez Espada, C., "La Contribución del Derecho Internacional del Medio Ambiente al Desarrollo del Derecho Internacional Contemporáneo", in: 14 *ADI*, 1998, pp. 113-200
- Hagenah, E., "A Regulatory View on Science and Predictive Models", in: 100 *EP*, 1999, pp. 13-18
- Haigh, N., "The Introduction of the Precautionary Principle into the UK", in: O'Riordan, T. & Cameron, J. (eds.), *Interpreting the Precautionary Principle*, London 1994, pp. 229-251
- Hammond, H., *Seeing the Forest Among the Trees*, Vancouver 1991

- Hammond, H., "What is Ecoforestry?", in: 2 *GB* 7, 1997, pp. 3-7
- Hancher, L., "EC Environmental Policy - a Pre-cautionary Tale?", in: Freestone, D. & Hey, E. (eds.), *The Precautionary Principle and International Law*, The Hague 1996, pp. 187-208
- Handl, G., "Environmental Security and Global Change: The Challenge to International Law", in: Lang, W. *et al.* (eds.), *Environmental Protection and International Law*, Dordrecht 1991, pp. 59-87; partly reprinted in: D'Amato, A. & Engel, K. (eds.), *International Environmental Law Anthology*, Cincinnati 1996, p. 28
- Handl, G., "International Efforts to Protect the Global Atmosphere: A Case of Too Little, Too Late?", in: 1 *EJIL*, 1990, pp. 250-257
- Hanekamp, J.C., "Het Morele Falen van het Voorzorgprincipe", in: *Spil*, No. 181-182, 2002, pp. 8-12
- Hanemann, W.M., "Economics and the Preservation of Biodiversity", in: Wilson, E.O. (ed.), *Biodiversity*, Washington, D.C. 1988, pp. 193-199
- Hansson, S.O., "The Limits of Precaution", in: 2 *FS*, 1997, pp. 293-306
- Hardaway, R. & Dacres, K.D., "Tropical Forest Conservation Legislation and Policy: Focus on South-East Asia", in: 11 *EPLJ*, 1994, pp. 419-431
- Harding, R. & Fisher, L., "The Precautionary Principle in Australia", in: O'Riordan, T. & Cameron, J. (eds.), *Interpreting the Precautionary Principle*, London 1994, pp. 252-261
- Harris, D.J., *Cases and Materials on International Law*, 5th ed., London 1998
- Hattis, D. & Anderson, E.L., "What Should be the Implications of Uncertainty, Variability, and Inherent 'Biases'/'Conservatism' for Risk Management Decision-Making?", in: 19 *RA*, 1999, pp. 95-107
- Hayashi, M., "The 1995 UN Fish Stocks Agreement and the Law of the Sea", in: Vidas, D. & Østreng, W. (eds.), *Order for the Oceans at the Turn of the Century*, The Hague 1999, pp. 37-53
- Heinrich, B., *Mind of the Raven: Investigations and Adventures with Wolf-Birds*, New York 1999
- Henriksen, T., Hønneland, G. & Sydnes, A., *Law and Politics in Ocean Governance: The UN Fish Stocks Agreement and Regional Fisheries Management Regimes*, Leiden 2006
- Herrero de la Fuente, A.A., "Medio Ambiente y Seguridad. Algunas Reflexiones a Raíz de la Segunda Cumbre de la Tierra", in: 13 *ADI*, 1997, pp. 561-581
- Heukers, J.L.D., "Het Voorzorgbeginsel in de Natuurbeschermingswetgeving", in: Backes, C., Gilhuis, P.C. & Verschuuren, J.M. (eds.), *Het Voorzorgbeginsel in het Natuurbeschermingsrecht*, Deventer 1997, pp. 23-33
- Hey, E., "The Precautionary Concept in Environmental Policy and Law: Institutionalizing Caution", in: 4 *GIELR*, 1992, pp. 303-318
- Hey, E., "The International Regime for the Protection of the North Sea: From Functional Approaches to a More Integrated Approach", in: 17 *IJMCL*, 2002, pp. 325-350
- Hey, E., "Duurzame Ontwikkeling en Normatieve Ontwikkeling en Legitimiteit van Besluitvorming", in: *Preadviezen, Mededelingen van de Nederlandse Vereniging voor Internationaal Recht*, Nr. 127, November 2003, pp. 93-155
- Higgins, R., *Problems and Process: International Law and How We Use It*, Oxford 1994
- Hohmann, H., *Precautionary Legal Duties and Principles of Modern International Environmental Law*, Dordrecht 1994
- Holm, S. & Harris, J., "Commentary: Precautionary Principle Stifles Discovery", 1999, http://www.biotech-info.net/PP_stifles.html
- Hønneland, G., "Towards a Precautionary Fisheries Management in Russia?", in: 48 *OCM*, 2005, pp. 619-631
- Howard, C.V. & Saunders, P.T., "Commentary: Sensible Precautions Make Good Science...", 1999, http://www.biotech-info.net/sensible_precautions.html

- Hughes, E.L., "Forests, Forestry Practices and the Living Environment" (with an Appendix by Kevin Moore), in: Canadian Council on International Law (ed.), *Global Forests and International Environmental Law*, London 1996, pp. 79-125
- Iltis, H.H., "Serendipity in the Exploration of Biodiversity: What Good Are Weedy Tomatoes?", in: Wilson, E.O. (ed.), *Biodiversity*, Washington, D.C. 1988, pp. 98-105
- International Alliance of Indigenous Tribal Peoples of the Tropical Forest, *Indigenous Peoples, Forest and Biodiversity*, London 1997
- International Law Commission, *Report of the International Law Commission on the Work of its Forty-sixth Session*, 1994, in: *UNGAOR* A/49/10
- International Law Commission, *Report of the International Law Commission on the Work of its Fifty-second Session*, 2000, in: *UNGAOR* A/55/10
- International Law Commission, *Report of the International Law Commission on the Work of its Fifty-third Session*, 2001, in: *UNGAOR* A/56/10
- Iremonger, S., Ravilious, C. & Quinton, T., "Statistical Analysis of Global Forest Conservation", in: Iremonger *et al.* (eds.), *A Global Overview of Forest Conservation (including GIS files of forests and protected areas, version 2)*, CD-ROM, (Centre for International Forestry Research and World Conservation Monitoring Centre report), Cambridge 1997
- Jackson, W., "Foreword", in: Raffensperger, C. & Tickner, J. (eds.), *Protecting Public Health and the Environment: Implementing the Precautionary Principle*, Washington 1999, pp. xv-xix
- Jans, J.H., "Communication on the Precautionary Principle: Is It Really Necessary?", in: 27 *LIEI*, 2000, pp. 115-117
- Jiménez Beltrán, D., "Preface: To Know and Not to Know. To Act or Not to Act?", in: European Environment Agency, *Late Lessons from Early Warnings: The Precautionary Principle 1896-2000*, Environmental Issue Report No. 22, Copenhagen 2001, pp. 3-5
- Jones, P.B.C., "Implementing the Precautionary Principle", 2000, http://www.biotech-info.net/BPCJ_viewpoint.html
- Jordan, A., "The Precautionary Principle in the European Union", in: O'Riordan, T. *et al.* (eds.), *Reinterpreting the Precautionary Principle*, London 2001, pp. 143-161
- Jordan, A. & O'Riordan, T., "The Precautionary Principle in Contemporary Environmental Policy and Politics", in: Raffensperger, C. & Tickner, J. (eds.), *Protecting Public Health and the Environment: Implementing the Precautionary Principle*, Washington 1999, pp. 15-35
- Jurgielewicz, L.M., *Global Environmental Change and International Law*, Lanham 1996
- Juste Ruiz, J., *Derecho Internacional del Medio Ambiente*, Madrid 1999
- Kaiser, M., "'The Precautionary Principle and its Implications for Science' - Introduction", in: 2 *FS*, 1997, pp. 201-205
- Kaiser, M., "Fish-Farming and the Precautionary Principle: Context and Values in Environmental Science for Policy", in: 2 *FS*, 1997, pp. 307-341
- Kamminga, M.T., "The Precautionary Approach in International Human Rights Law: How It can Benefit the Environment", in: Freestone, D. & Hey, E. (eds.), *The Precautionary Principle and International Law*, The Hague 1996, pp. 171-186
- Kappelle, M. *et al.*, "Effects of Climate Change on Biodiversity: A Review and Identification of Key Research Issues", in: 8 *BC*, 1999, pp. 1383-1397
- Kaye, S.M., *International Fisheries Management*, The Hague/London/Boston 2001
- Kimball, L.A., *International Ocean Governance* (IUCN report), Gland/Cambridge 2001
- Kirgis, F.L., Jr., "Standing to Challenge Human Endeavors That Could Change the Climate", in: 84 *AJIL*, 1990, pp. 525-530
- Kirk, E.A., "Current Developments: The 1996 Protocol to the London Dumping Convention and the *Brent Spar*", in: 46 *ICLQ*, 1997, pp. 957-964

- Kirschenmann, F., "Can We Say 'Yes' to Agriculture Using the Precautionary Principle: A Farmer's Perspective", in: Raffensperger, C. & Tickner, J. (eds.), *Protecting Public Health and the Environment: Implementing the Precautionary Principle*, Washington 1999, pp. 279-293
- Kiss, A.C.H., "The Rights and Interests of Future Generations and the Precautionary Principle", in: Freestone, D. & Hey, E. (eds.), *The Precautionary Principle and International Law*, The Hague 1996, pp. 19-28
- Kiss, A.C.H., "Nature: The Common Heritage of Humankind", 1999, http://www.nature.coe.int/english/main/naturopa/magazine/common1.htm
- Kiss, A.C.H. & Shelton, D., *International Environmental Law*, New York 1991
- Kiss, A.C.H. & Shelton, D., *International Environmental Law*, 2nd ed., New York 2000
- Klinke, A. & Renn, O., *Prometheus Unbound; Challenges of Risk Evaluation, Risk Classification, and Risk Management*, Akademie für Technikfolgenabschätzung Working Paper No. 153, Stuttgart 1999
- Kloeg, D. (ed.), *Natuur & Milieu Encyclopedie*, Ede 1991
- Kock, K-H, "Fishing and Conservation in Southern Waters", in: 30 *PR*, 1994, pp. 3-22
- Koers, A.W., *International Regulation of Marine Fisheries*, London 1973
- König, D., "Abfallentsorgung auf See: Die Londoner Konvention von 1972", in: Gehring, T. & Oberthür, S. (eds.), *Internationale Umweltregime*, Opladen 1997
- Kooijmans, P.H., *Internationaal Publiekrecht in Vogelvlucht*, 9th ed., Deventer 2002
- Koppe, J.G. & Keys, J., "PCBs and the Precautionary Principle", in: European Environment Agency, *Late Lessons from Early Warnings: The Precautionary Principle 1896-2000*, Environmental Issue Report No. 22, Copenhagen 2001, pp. 64-75
- Kosko, B., *Fuzzy Thinking: The New Science of Fuzzy Logic*, London 1994
- Kucinich, D.J., "Comments from Representative Kucinich (OH)" (address delivered at the French Embassy Meeting on the Precautionary Principle, July 2000), http://www.biotech-info.net/Kucinich_comments.html
- Kumar Duralappah, A. *et al.*, *Ecosystems and Human Well-Being: Biodiversity Synthesis: A Millennium Ecosystem Assessment Report*, Washington, D.C. 2005
- Kwiatkowska, B., "Southern Bluefin Tuna (New Zealand v. Japan; Australia v. Japan), Order on Provisional Measures (ITLOS Cases No. 3 and 4)", in: 94 *AJIL*, 2000, pp. 150-155
- Lambers, C., "Het Voorzorgsbeginsel: Vluchten Kan Niet Meer", in: 27 *MR*, 2000, pp. 176-181
- Lammers, J.G. *et al.*, *Environmental Protection and Sustainable Development: Legal Principles and Recommendations* (WCED Experts Group on Environmental Law report), Dordrecht 1986
- Lang, W., "Auf der Suche nach einem Wirksamen Klima-Regime", in: 31 *AV*, 1993, pp. 13-29
- Larmuseau, I., "Het Voorzorgsbeginsel Geïntroduceerd in de Belgische Rechtspraak: Zoveel Hoofden, Zoveel Zinnen?", in: 9 *TM*, 2000, pp. 24-32
- Larmuseau, I., "The Precautionary Principle in Belgian Jurisprudence", in: 9 *EELR*, 2000, pp. 40-47
- Lasén Diaz, C., "Biotechnology and the Cartagena Protocol", in: *Precaution from Rio to Johannesburg: Proceedings of a Geneva Environment Network Roundtable*, International Environment House, Geneva, 16 May 2002, pp. 16-22
- Lastra, C., "Una Mina de Carbón Daña el Hábitat del Oso en el Suroeste de Asturias", in: *Quercus*, No. 172, 2000, pp. 46-47
- Lauck, T. *et al.*, "Implementing the Precautionary Principle in Fisheries Management Through Marine Reserves", in: 8 *EA*, 1998, pp. S72-S78
- Leakey, R. & Lewin, R., *The Sixth Extinction: Patterns of Life and the Future of Humankind*, New York 1996
- Lefeber, R., *Transboundary Environmental Interference and the Origin of State Liability*, Dordrecht 1996

- Lemons, J. *et al.*, "The Precautionary Principle: Scientific Uncertainty and Type I and Type II Errors", in: 2 *FS*, 1997, pp. 207-236
- Lenzi Grillini, C.R. *et al.*, "Structural Analysis of the Chambura Gorge Forest (Queen Elizabeth National Park, Uganda)", in: 38 *AJE*, 2000, pp. 295-302
- Leopold, A., *A Sand County Almanac; With Essays on Conservation from Round River*, New York 1970
- Leroy, A. & Ciliento, F., "Le Principe de Précaution Appliqué à la Politique Commune des Pêches (PCP)", in : *NLR*, 1999, pp. 1-10
- Lewin, R., *Complexity: Life at the Edge of Chaos*, 2nd ed., Chicago 1999
- Lewis, M., "Precautionary Foolishness", 2000, http://www.biotech-info.net/precautionary_foolishness.html
- Lewis, S., "The Precautionary Principle and Corporate Disclosure", in: Raffensperger, C. & Tickner, J. (eds.), *Protecting Public Health and the Environment: Implementing the Precautionary Principle*, Washington 1999, pp. 241-251
- Lierop, R.F. van *et al.*, "Compliance with International Environmental Treaties: The Empirical Evidence", in: *ASIL Proc.*, 1997, pp. 234-258
- List, M., "Das Regime zum Schutz der Ostsee", in: Gehring, T. & Oberthür, S. (eds.), *Internationale Umweltregime*, Opladen 1997, pp. 133-146
- Lomborg, B., *The Skeptical Environmentalist: Measuring the Real State of the World*, Cambridge 2001
- López-Vera, F., "El Sistema Forestal y el Ciclo del Agua", in: Alba Alonso, J. *et al.*, *Nuestros Bosques*, Madrid 1998, pp. 117-129
- Lovelock, J.E., *Gaia: A New Look at Life on Earth*, Oxford 2000
- Lucas, A., "Het Risicobegrip vanuit het Perspectief van de Financiële Economie en Kansrekening", in: Wissink, B. & Bouma, J. (eds.), *Perspectieven op Milieurisico's*, Wetenschappelijke Raad voor het Regeringsbeleid Werkdocument W128, The Hague 2002, pp. 25-66
- Luff, D., "An Overview of International Law of Sustainable Development and a Confrontation Between WTO Rules and Sustainable Development", in: 29 *RBDI*, 1996, pp. 90-144
- Lyster, R., "The Relevance of the Precautionary Principle: Friends of Hinchinbrook Society Inc v Minister for the Environment", in: 14 *EPLJ*, 1997, pp. 390-401
- Lyster, S., *International Wildlife Law*, Cambridge 1985
- MacDonald, J., "Big Beef Up or Consumer Health Threat?: the WTO Food Safety Agreement, Bovine Growth Hormone and the Precautionary Principle", in: 15 *EPLJ*, 1998, pp. 115-126
- Mace, P.M. & Gabriel, W.L., "Evolution, Scope, and Current Applications of the Precautionary Approach in Fisheries", in: Restrepo, V.R. (ed.), *Proceedings of the Fifth National NMFS Stock Assessment Workshop: Providing Scientific Advice to Implement the Precautionary Approach Under the Magnuson-Stevens Fishery Conservation and Management Act*, NOAA Technical Memorandum NMFS-F/SPO-40, 1999, pp. 65-73
- MacGarvin, M., "Science, Precaution, Facts and Values", in: O'Riordan, T. *et al.* (eds.), *Reinterpreting the Precautionary Principle*, London 2001, pp. 35-60
- MacGarvin, M., "Taking Stock: Fisheries", in: European Environment Agency, *Late Lessons from Early Warnings: The Precautionary Principle 1896-2000*, Environmental Issue Report No. 22, Copenhagen 2001, pp. 17-30
- Maguire, S. & Ellis, J., "Uncertainty, Precaution and Global Interdependence: Implications of the Precautionary Principle for State and Non-State Actors", in: Biermann, F., Brohm, R. & Dingwerth, K. (eds.), *Proceedings of the 2001 Berlin Conference on the Human Dimensions of Global Environmental Change "Global Environmental Change and the Nation State"*, Potsdam 2002, pp. 256-265
- Mainguet, M. & Létolle, R., "Pourquoi l'Environnement se Dégrade-t-il? Pourquoi cette Dégradation s'Accélère-t-elle en cette Fin de XXe Siècle?", in: 41 *AE/EY*, 1995, pp. 17-32
- Manabe, T. *et al.*, "Population Structure and Spatial Patterns for Trees in a Temperate Old-Growth Evergreen Broad-Leaved Forest in Japan", in: 151 *PE*, 2000, pp. 181-197

- Mann, H., "Comment on the Paper by Philippe Sands", in: Lang, W. (ed.), *Sustainable Development and International Law*, Dordrecht 1995, pp. 67-72
- Marceau, G., "The Precautionary Principle under WTO Law" in: *Precaution from Rio to Johannesburg: Proceedings of a Geneva Environment Network Roundtable*, International Environment House, Geneva, 16 May 2002, pp. 23-28
- Marchant, G.E., "Two Problems with the Precautionary Principle", 2000, http://www.cid.harvard.edu/cidbiotech/comments/comments90.htm
- Marchant, G.E. & Mossman, K.L., *Arbitrary and Capricious: the Precautionary Principle in the European Union Courts*, London 2005
- Marco, A. & Quilchano, C., "Impacto Sobre los Anfibios de la Contaminación por Fertilizantes Químicos", in: *Quercus*, No. 172, 2000, pp. 14-19
- Marechal, P., *Woordenwijzer Ecologie*, Lisse 1991
- Marr, S., *The Precautionary Principle in the Law of the Sea: Modern Decision Making in International Law*, The Hague 2003
- Martin, P.H., "'If You Don't Know How to Fix it, Please Stop Breaking it!': The Precautionary Principle and Climate Change", in: 2 *FS*, 1997, pp. 263-292
- Mascher, S., "Taking a 'Precautionary Approach': Fisheries Management in New Zealand", in: 14 *EPLJ*, 1997, pp. 70-79
- Matthee, M., "The International Integration of European Precautionary Measures on Biosafety", in: 10 *EELR*, 2001, pp. 183-193
- Matthee, M. & Vermersch, D., "Are the Precautionary Principle and the International Trade of Genetically Modified Organisms Reconcilable?", in: 12 *JAEE*, 2000, pp. 59-70
- Matthews, R.A.J., "Facts Versus Factions: The Use and Abuse of Subjectivity in Scientific Research", in: Morris, J. (ed.), *Rethinking Risk and the Precautionary Principle*, Oxford 2000, pp. 247-282
- Mayer, S. & Stirling, A., "Finding a Precautionary Approach to Technological Developments – Lessons for the Evaluation of GM Crops", in: 15 *JAEE*, 2002, pp. 57-71
- McBride, G.B., "Equivalence Tests Can Enhance Environmental Science and Management", in: 41 *ANZJS*, 1999, pp. 19-29
- McIntyre, O., "Case Law Analysis: Environmental Protection of International Rivers", in: 10 *JEL*, 1998, pp. 79-91
- McIntyre, O., "The Emergence of an 'Ecosystem Approach' to the Protection of International Watercourses under International Law", in: 13 *RECIEL*, 2004, pp. 1-14
- McIntyre, O. & Mosedale, T., "The Precautionary Principle as a Norm of Customary International Law", in: 9 *JEL*, 1997, pp. 221-241
- McKinney, W.J. & Hill, H.H., "Of Sustainability and Precaution: The Logical, Epistemological, and Moral Problems of the Precautionary Principle and Their Implications for Sustainable Development", in: 5 *EE*, 2000, pp. 77-87
- McNelis, N., "EU Communication on the Precautionary Principle", in: 3 *JIEL*, 2000, pp. 545-551
- Medvedev, N., "Levels of Heavy Metals in Karelian Wildlife, 1989-91", in: 56 *EMA*, 1999, pp. 177-193
- Mee, L.D., "Scientific Methods and the Precautionary Principle", in: Freestone, D. & Hey, E. (eds.), *The Precautionary Principle and International Law*, The Hague 1996, pp. 109-132
- Mentens, J., *Hakken in Kameroen : Koopman en Dominee in Afrika*, Breda 2001
- Mercure, P.-F., "Le Rejet du Concept de Patrimoine Commun de l'Humanité afin d'Assurer la Gestion de la Diversité Biologique", in: 33 *CYIL*, 1995, pp. 281-302
- Messori, V. & Michele Brambilla, *Algunas Razones para Creer*, Barcelona 2000

- Meyers, G.D., "Of Woodchips, Wildlife and Wetlands: A New Ecological Ethic for a Planet in Crisis", in: 12 *EPLJ*, 1995, pp. 211-214
- M'Gonigle, R.M., "The Political Economy of Precaution", in: Raffensperger, C. & Tickner, J. (eds.), *Protecting Public Health and the Environment: Implementing the Precautionary Principle*, Washington 1999, pp. 123-147
- Mickelson, K., "Notes and Comments: Rereading *Trail Smelter*", in: 31 *CYIL*, 1993, pp. 219-233
- Miller, H.I. & Conko, G., "Genetically Modified Fear and the International Regulation of Biotechnology", in: Morris, J. (ed.), *Rethinking Risk and the Precautionary Principle*, Oxford 2000, pp. 84-104
- Miner, C., "Recent Developments: The World Bank Global Environment Facility: First Project Approved in Poland", in: 33 *HILJ*, 1992, pp. 642-648
- Mohamed-Katerere, J.C., "The Precautionary Principle: Implications for Development and Poverty Alleviation in Southern Africa", in: *IUCN-ELPN*, No. 1, 2001, pp. 7-9
- Molenaar, E.J., *Coastal State Jurisdiction over Vessel-Source Pollution*, Dordrecht 1998
- Molenaar, E.J., "Some More Equal than Others: Improved Status of Marine Mammals Necessitates Difficult Societal Choices", in: *Samudra*, March 2002, pp. 28-34
- Molenaar, E.J., "Addressing Regulatory Gaps in High Seas Fisheries", in: 20 *IJMCL*, 2005, pp. 533-570
- Montague, P., "Precautionary Action Not Taken: Corporate Structure and the Case Study of Tetraethyl Lead in the United States", in: Raffensperger, C. & Tickner, J. (eds.), *Protecting Public Health and the Environment: Implementing the Precautionary Principle*, Washington 1999, pp. 294-308
- Morey, M., "Bosques y Paisaje", in: Alba Alonso, J. *et al.*, *Nuestros Bosques*, Madrid 1998, pp. 65-87
- Morris, J., "Defining the Precautionary Principle", 2000, http://www.cid.harvard.edu/cidbiotech/comments/comments79.htm
- Morris, J., "Defining the Precautionary Principle", in: Morris, J. (ed.), *Rethinking Risk and the Precautionary Principle*, Oxford 2000, pp. 1-21
- Morris, J., "The Relationship Between Risk Analysis and the Precautionary Principle", in: 181-192 *Toxicology*, 2002, pp. 127-130
- Mucklow, F., "The Integration of Environmental Principles into the World Bank", in: 9 *RECIEL*, 2000, pp. 100-111
- Murase, S. *et al.*, "Compliance with International Standards: Environmental Case Studies", in: *ASIL Proc.*, 1995, pp. 206-224
- Myhr, A.I. & Traavik, T., "The Precautionary Principle Applied to Deliberate Release of Genetically Modified Organisms (GMOs)", in: 11 *MEHD*, 1999, pp. 65-74
- Nettesheim, M., "Die Ökologische Intervention: Gewalt und Druck zum Schutz der Umwelt?", in: 34 *AV*, pp. 168-217
- Nollkaemper, A., "'What You Risk Reveals What You Value', and Other Dilemmas Encountered in Legal Assaults on Risks", in: Freestone, D. & Hey, E. (eds.), *The Precautionary Principle and International Law*, The Hague 1996, pp. 73-94
- Nollkaemper, A., "Habitat Protection in European Community Law: Evolving Conceptions of a Balance of Interests", in: 9 *JEL*, 1997, pp. 271-286
- Norton, B., "Commodity, Amenity, and Morality: The Limits of Quantification in Valuing Biodiversity", in: Wilson, E.O. (ed.), *Biodiversity*, Washington, D.C. 1988, pp. 200-205
- O'Brien, M., "Alternatives Assessment: Part of Operationalizing and Institutionalizing the Precautionary Principle", in: Raffensperger, C. & Tickner, J. (eds.), *Protecting Public Health and the Environment: Implementing the Precautionary Principle*, Washington 1999, pp. 207-219
- Oria de Rueda, J.A., "Choperas: El Bosque Ribereño Fluvial", in: *Biológica*, No. 47, 2000, pp. 30-41

- O'Riordan, T., "The Precautionary Principle and Civic Science", in: O'Riordan, T. *et al.* (eds.), *Reinterpreting the Precautionary Principle*, London 2001, pp. 95-111
- O'Riordan, T. & Cameron, J., "The History and Contemporary Significance of the Precautionary Principle", in: O'Riordan, T. & Cameron, J. (eds.), *Interpreting the Precautionary Principle*, London 1994, pp. 12-30
- O'Riordan, T. & Cameron, J., "Editorial Introduction: Implications for Science", in: O'Riordan, T. & Cameron, J. (eds.), *Interpreting the Precautionary Principle*, London 1994, pp. 62-68
- O'Riordan, T., Jordan, A. & Cameron, J., "The Evolution of the Precautionary Principle", in: O'Riordan, T. *et al.* (eds.), *Reinterpreting the Precautionary Principle*, London 2001, pp. 9-33
- O'Riordan, T., Jordan, A. & Cameron, J., "Reinterpreting the Interpretation", in: O'Riordan, T. *et al.* (eds.), *Reinterpreting the Precautionary Principle*, London 2001, pp. 269-272
- Orrega Vicuña, F., *The Changing International Law of High Seas Fisheries*, Cambridge 1999
- Oudenaarden, T.A., "Verslag van de Discussie", in: Backes, C., Gilhuis, P.C. & Verschuuren, J.M. (eds.), *Het Voorzorgbeginsel in het Natuurbeschermingsrecht*, Deventer 1997, pp. 43-47
- Ozonoff, D., "The Precautionary Principle as a Screening Device", in: Raffensperger, C. & Tickner, J. (eds.), *Protecting Public Health and the Environment: Implementing the Precautionary Principle*, Washington 1999, pp. 100-105
- Pallemaerts, M., "La Conférence de Rio: Grandeur ou Décadence du Droit International de l'Environnement?", in: 28 *RBDI*, 1995, pp. 175-223
- Palmer, G., *Environment: The International Challenge*, Wellington 1995
- Paradell-Trius, L., "Principles of International Environmental Law: An Overview", in: 9 *RECIEL*, 2000, pp. 93-99
- Paris, P. & Paris, Q., "Agriculture in the Twenty-First Century: Agronomic and Economic Perspectives", in: 126 *AM*, 1996, pp. 113-148.
- Parkes, G., "Precautionary Fisheries Management: The CCAMLR Approach", in: 24 *MP*, 2000, pp. 83-91
- Parnell, M., "Southern Bluefin Tuna Feedlotting – ESD, the Precautionary Principle and Burden of Proof", in: 2 *JIWLP*, 1999, pp. 334-337
- Parsons, S., "Ecosystem Considerations in Fisheries Management: Theory and Practice", in: 20 *IJMCL*, 2005, pp. 381-422
- Pascual Trillo, J.A., "Ecología y Cultura de Nuestros Bosques", in: Alba Alonso, J. *et al.*, *Nuestros Bosques*, Madrid 1998, pp. 13-63
- Pascual Trillo, J.A., "Conservación y Gestión Sostenible de los Bosques", in: Alba Alonso, J. *et al.*, *Nuestros Bosques*, Madrid 1998, pp. 151-182
- Pascual Trillo, J.A., *El Teatro de la Ciencia y el Drama Ambiental: Una Aproximación a las Ciencias Ambientales*, Madrid 2000
- Passchier-Vermeer, W. *et al.*, *Milieu en Gezondheid 2001: Overzicht van Risico's, Doelen en Beleid*, Netherlands Organization for Applied Scientific Research (TNO) report PG/VGZ/2001.95, 2001
- Peeters, M., "Het Voorzorgsbeginsel in het Nederlands Milieurecht", in: Faure, M.G. & Vos, E. (eds.), *Juridische Afbakening van het Voorzorgsbeginsel: Mogelijkheden en Grenzen*, Gezondheidsraad Publication Nr. A03/03, The Hague 2003, pp. 187-234
- Perrez, F.X., *Cooperative Sovereignty: From Independence to Interdependence in the Structure of International Environmental Law*, The Hague/London/Boston 2000
- Perrez, F.X., "Precaution from Rio to Johannesburg: An Introduction", in: *Precaution from Rio to Johannesburg: Proceedings of a Geneva Environment Network Roundtable*, International Environment House, Geneva, 16 May 2002, pp. 5-9

- Perry, R.I., Walters, C.J. & Boutillier, J.A., "A Framework for Providing Scientific Advice for the Management of New and Developing Invertebrate Fisheries", in: 9 *RFBF*, 1999, pp. 125-150
- Pieterman, R., "Weg met het Voorzorgbeginsel? Een Rechtssociologische Cultuurkritiek", in: *NJB*, No. 22, 2001, pp. 1023-1029
- Pieterman, R., "Naschrift: Weg met het Voorzorgbeginsel?", in: *NJB*, No. 36, 2001, pp. 1762-1763
- Pieterman, R. & Hanekamp, J.C., *The Cautious Society? An Essay on the Rise of the Precautionary Culture*, Heidelberg Appeal Netherlands report, 2002
- Pieterman, R., Hanekamp, J.C. & Bergkamp, L., "Onzekere Voorzorg Bedreigt Rechtszekerheid", in: 81 *NJB*, 2006, pp. 2-8
- Philippopoulos-Mihalopoulos, A., "The Silence of the Sirens: Environmental Risk and the Precautionary Principle", in: 10 *LC*, 1999, pp. 175-197
- Phillips, O.L., "The Changing Ecology of Tropical Forests", in: 6 *BC*, 1997, pp. 291-311
- Polachek, T., "Experimental Catches and the Precautionary Approach: The Southern Bluefin Tuna Dispute", in: 26 *MP*, 2002, pp. 283-294
- Pollan, M., "Precautionary Principle", in: *New York Times*, 9 December 2001
- Ponce Nava, D., "International Land-Use Law: Remarks by Diana Ponce Nava", in: *ASIL Proc.*, 1993, pp. 494-498
- Quiroga, H., *Cuentos de la Selva y Otros Relatos*, Madrid 2000
- Raad voor de Volkshuisvesting, de Ruimtelijke Ordening en het Milieubeheer, *Waar een Wil is, is een Weg: Advies over het NMP4*, Den Haag 2001
- Radday, M., "News: Criteria and Indicators", in: 19 *ETFRN-News*, 1997, pp. 19-26
- Raffensperger, C., "The Precautionary Principle and Biotechnology", 2000, http://www.cid.harvard.edu/cidbiotech/comments/comments71.htm
- Raffensperger, C. *et al.*, "Commentary: ...And Can Mean Saying 'Yes' to Innovation", 1999, http://www.biotech-info.net/saying_yes.html
- Raffensperger, C. & Tickner, J., "Introduction: To Foresee and to Forestall", in: Raffensperger, C. & Tickner, J. (eds.), *Protecting Public Health and the Environment: Implementing the Precautionary Principle*, Washington 1999, pp. 1-11
- Raffensperger, C. & Tickner, J., "Implementing the Precautionary Principle", 2000, http://www.islandpress.com/ecocompass/prevent/index.html
- Randall, A., "What Mainstream Economists Have to Say About the Value of Biodiversity", in: Wilson, E.O. (ed.), *Biodiversity*, Washington, D.C. 1988, pp. 217-223
- Rashbrooke, G., "The International Tribunal for the Law of the Sea: A Forum for the Development of Principles of International Environmental Law?", in: 19 *IJMCL*, 2004, pp. 515-535
- Ratcliffe, D., *The Raven*, London 1997
- Redgwell, C., "Protection of Ecosystems under International Law: Lessons from Antarctica", in: Boyle, A. & Freestone, D. (eds.), *International Law and Sustainable Development*, Oxford 1999, pp. 205-224
- Rehbinder, E., *Das Vorsorgeprinzip im Internationalen Vergleich*, Düsseldorf 1991
- Reid, C.T., "The Changing Pattern of Environmental Regulation: British Forestry and the Environmental Agenda", in: 9 *JEL*, 1997, pp. 23-42
- Reid, V.R. *et al.*, *Ecosystems and Human Well-Being: Synthesis: A Report of the Millennium Ecosystem Assessment*, Washington, D.C. 2005
- Remiro Brotóns, A. *et al.*, *Derecho Internacional*, Madrid 1997

- Resit Akçakaya, H. & Raphael, M.G., "Assessing Human Impact Despite Uncertainty: Viability of the Northern Spotted Owl Metapopulation in the Northwestern USA", in: 7 *BC*, 1998, pp. 875-894
- Rest, A., "Die Rechtliche Umsetzung der Rio-Vorgaben in der Staatenpraxis", in: 34 *AV*, 1996, pp. 145-167
- Restrepo, V.R., "The Precautionary Approach: A New Paradigm, or Business as Usual?", feature article of *Our Living Oceans*, 1998, at: http://spo.nwr.noaa.gov/fa1.pdf
- Restrepo, V.R. *et al.*, *Technical Guidance on the Use of Precautionary Approaches to Implementing National Standard 1 of the Magnuson-Stevens Fishery Conservation and Management Act*, NOAA Technical Memorandum NMFS-F/SPO-##, 1998, available at: http://www.nmfs.noaa.gov/sfa/NSGtkgd.pdf
- Reynolds, J.R. & Jasny, M.D., "Assessing Ocean Noise: A Conservationist Approach", in: 108 *JASA*, 2000, pp. 2515-
- Rip, A. & Smit, W.A., "Het Risicobegrip vanuit een Wetenschapsfilosofisch en Sociologisch Perspectief", in: Wissink, B. & Bouma, J. (eds.), *Perspectieven op Milieurisico's*, Wetenschappelijke Raad voor het Regeringsbeleid Werkdocument W128, The Hague 2002, pp. 67-102
- Robinson, N.A., "Legal Procedures for Ecosystem Management: Environmental Law's First Challenge of the New Millennium", in: 5 *APJEL*, 2000, pp. 203-206
- Robinson, N.A., "From the Chair: Precaution: Government's Sound Risk Management", in: *IUCN-ELPN*, No. 1, 2001, p. 3
- Rodríguez Álvarez, I. & Cruz León, A., *Ciencias de la Naturaleza: Biología y Geología*, Madrid 1994
- Rodríguez de la Fuente, F., *Cuadernos de Campo: Pajaros Carpinteros*, Barcelona
- Rogers, M.D., "Scientific and Technological Uncertainty, the Precautionary Principle, Scenarios and Risk Management", in: 4 *JRR*, 2001, pp. 1-15
- Rose, G. & Paleokrassis, G., "Compliance with International Environmental Obligations: A Case Study of the International Whaling Commission", in: Cameron, J., Werksman, J. & Roderick, P. (eds.), *Improving Compliance with International Environmental Law*, London 1996, pp. 148-175
- Rubin, C.T., "Asteroid Collisions and Precautionary Thinking", in: Morris, J. (ed.), *Rethinking Risk and the Precautionary Principle*, Oxford 2000, pp. 105-126
- Ruiz, R., "Nutria, la Salud de los Ríos", in: *El Pais Semanal*, No. 1247, 20 August 2000, pp. 26-29
- Rüster, B., Simma, B. & Bock, M. (eds.), *International Protection of the Environment: Treaties and Related Documents*, 29 vols. plus index, New York 1983
- Salmon, N., "A European Perspective on the Precautionary Principle, Food Safety and the Free Trade Imperative of the WTO", in: 27 *ELR*, 2002, pp. 138-155
- Samb, A., "Sulphur Dioxide: From Protection of Human Lungs to Remote Lake Restoration", in: European Environment Agency, *Late Lessons from Early Warnings: The Precautionary Principle 1896-2000*, Environmental Issue Report No. 22, Copenhagen 2001, pp. 101-109
- Sandalow, D.B., "Protecting and Conserving the World's Forests" (address delivered at the National Press Club, Washington, 6 January 2000), http://www.state.gov/www/policy_remarks/2000/000106_sandalow_forests.html
- Sandin, P., *Better Safe than Sorry: Applying Philosophical Methods to the Debate on Risk and the Precautionary Principle*, Stockholm 2004
- Sands, P., "The 'Greening' of International Law: Emerging Principles and Rules", in: 1 *IJGLS*, 1994; partly reprinted in: D'Amato, A. & Engel, K. (eds.), *International Environmental Law Anthology*, Cincinnati 1996, pp. 21-22

- Sands, P., "International Law in the Field of Sustainable Development: Emerging Legal Principles", in: Lang, W. (ed.), *Sustainable Development and International Law*, Dordrecht 1995, pp. 53-66
- Sands, P., *Principles of International Environmental Law I: Frameworks, Standards and Implementation*, Manchester 1995
- Sands, P., "Compliance with International Environmental Obligations: Existing International Legal Arrangements", in: Cameron, J., Werksman, J. & Roderick, P. (eds.), *Improving Compliance with International Environmental Law*, London 1996, pp. 48-83
- Sands, P., "Sustainable Development: Treaty, Custom and the Cross-Fertilization of International Law", in: Boyle, A. & Freestone, D. (eds.), *International Law and Sustainable Development*, Oxford 1999, pp. 39-60
- Sands, P., "International Courts and the Precautionary Principle", in: *Precaution from Rio to Johannesburg: Proceedings of a Geneva Environment Network Roundtable*, International Environment House, Geneva, 16 May 2002, pp. 29-34
- Sands, P., *Principles of International Environmental Law*, 2nd ed., Cambridge 2003
- Saner, M., "An Ethical Analysis of the Precautionary Principle", 2000, http://www.cid.harvard.edu/cidbiotech/comments/comments80.htm
- Santillo, D. *et al.*, "The Precautionary Principle in Practice: A Mandate for Anticipatory Preventive Action", in: Raffensperger, C. & Tickner, J. (eds.), *Protecting Public Health and the Environment: Implementing the Precautionary Principle*, Washington 1999, pp. 36-50
- Santillo, D. *et al.*, "Tributyltin (TBT) Antifoulants: A Tale of Ships, Snails and Imposex", in: European Environment Agency, *Late Lessons from Early Warnings: The Precautionary Principle 1896-2000*, Environmental Issue Report No. 22, Copenhagen 2001, pp. 135-148
- Saunders, P.M., "Notes and Comments: Moving on from Rio: Recent Initiatives on Global Forest Issues", in: 32 *CYIL*, 1994, pp. 143-172
- Saunders, P.M. *et al.*, "Development Cooperation and Compliance with International Environmental Law", in: *ASIL Proc.*, 1996, pp. 359-367
- Saunders, P.T., "Use and Abuse of the Precautionary Principle", 2000, http://www.biotech-info.net/precautionary_use-and-abuse.html
- Savoia, R., "Hungarian Environmental Law and Biodiversity Protection", in: 9 *EELR*, 2000, pp. 182-186
- SCA Skog, *SCA Skog and Biodiversity*, Sundsvall 1994
- Schellnhuber, H.J.,"'Earth System' Analysis and the Second Copernican Revolution", in: 401 *Nature*, 1999, pp. C19-C23
- Schettler, T., "Manganese in Gasoline: A Case Study of the Need for Precautionary Action", in: Raffensperger, C. & Tickner, J. (eds.), *Protecting Public Health and the Environment: Implementing the Precautionary Principle*, Washington 1999, pp. 309-322
- Schmidt-Bleek, F.B., *The Fossil Makers*, Birkhäuser 1993
- Schrijver, N.J., "De Verankering en Betekenis van Duurzame Ontwikkeling in het Internationale Recht", in: *Preadviezen, Mededelingen van de Nederlandse Vereniging voor Internationaal Recht*, Nr. 127, November 2003, pp. 1-92
- Schröder, M., "Sustainable Development: Ausgleich Zwischen Umwelt und Entwicklung aus Gestaltungsaufgabe der Staaten", in: 34 *AV*, 1996, pp. 251-275
- Schuppert, S., *Neue Steuerungsinstrumente in Umweltvölkerrecht am Beispiel des Montrealer Protokoles und des Klimaschutzrahmenübereinkommens*, Berlin 1997
- Sclove, R.B. & Scammell, M.L., "Practicing the Principle", in: Raffensperger, C. & Tickner, J. (eds.), *Protecting Public Health and the Environment: Implementing the Precautionary Principle*, Washington 1999, pp. 252-265

- Scott, A. *et al.*, "Precautionary Approach to Risk Assessment", 1999, http://www.biotech-info.net/precautionary_approach.html
- Scottish Natural Heritage, "Applying the Precautionary Principle in Practice: Natural Heritage Conservation in Scotland", in: Raffensperger, C. & Tickner, J. (eds.), *Protecting Public Health and the Environment: Implementing the Precautionary Principle*, Washington 1999, pp. 187-197
- Semb, A., "Sulphur Dioxide: From Protection of Human Lungs to Remote Lake Restoration", in: European Environment Agency, *Late Lessons from Early Warnings: The Precautionary Principle 1896-2000*, Environmental Issue Report No. 22, Copenhagen 2001, pp. 101-107
- Shanmuganathan, D. & Warren, L.M., "Case Law Analysis: Status of Sustainable Development as a Principle of National and International Law: The Indian Approach", in: 9 *JEL*, 1997, pp. 387-402
- Shaw, M.N., *International Law*, 4th ed., Cambridge 1997
- Shelton, D., "The Impact of Scientific Uncertainty on Environmental Law and Policy in the United States", in: Freestone, D. & Hey, E., *The Precautionary Principle and International Law*, The Hague 1996, pp. 209-230
- Smith, R.L. & Smith, T.M., *Elements of Ecology*, 4th ed. update, 2000
- Solbrig, O.T., "The Origin and Function of Biodiversity", in: 33 *Environment*, 1991, pp. 16-20, 34-38
- Soria Jiménez, A., "Ecological Catastrophes in Light of the Rio Agreements", in: 39 *GYIL*, 1996, pp. 388-408
- Soule, E., "Assessing the Precautionary Principle", 2000, http://www.cid.harvard.edu/cidbiotech/comments/comments73.htm
- Sperling, K., "If Caution Really Mattered", in: 16 *EPLJ*, 1999, pp. 425-440
- Stairs, K. & Taylor, P., "Non-Governmental Organizations and the Legal Protection of the Oceans: A Case Study", in: Hurrell, A. & Kingsbury, B. (eds.), *The International Politics of the Environment*, Oxford 1992, pp. 110-141
- Stec, S. & Eckstein, G.E., "Of Solemn Oaths and Obligations: The Environmental Impact of the ICJ's Decision in the *Case Concerning the Gabcikovo-Nagymaros Project*", in: 8 *YIEL*, 1997, pp. 41-50
- Stein, P.L., "Are Decision-makers too Cautious with the Precautionary Principle?", contribution to Land and Environment Court of New South Wales Annual Conference, 1999, http://www.lawlink.nsw.gov.au/sc%5Csc.nsf/pages/Stein_3 (accessed 11 June 2002)
- Stein, P.L., "Opinion: A Cautious Application of the Precautionary Principle", in: 2 *EnvLR*, 2000, pp. 1-10
- Stirling, A., "The Precautionary Principle in Science and Technology", in: O'Riordan, T. *et al.* (eds.), *Reinterpreting the Precautionary Principle*, London 2001, pp. 61-94
- Sunstein, C.R., "Cost-Benefit Analysis and the Environment", in: 115 *Ethics*, 2005, pp. 351-385
- Sunstein, C.R., *Irreversible and Catastrophic*, Joint Center Working Paper 05-04, 2005, available at: http://www.aie-brookings.org
- Susskind, L.E., *Environmental Diplomacy: Negotiating More Effective Global Agreements*, New York 1994
- Suzuki, D., "Ecosystem Assessment Provides Baseline", statement of 14 April 2005, published on: http://www.millenniumassessment.org
- Swanson, T. & Johnston, S., *Global Environmental Problems and International Environmental Agreements*, Northampton 1999
- Sykes, B. (ed.), *The Concise Oxford Dictionary*, 6th ed., Oxford 1976
- Tallacchini, M., "A Legal Framework from Ecology", in: 9 *BC*, 2000, pp. 1085-1098
- Tanaka, Y., "Zonal and Integrated Management Approaches to Ocean Governance: Reflections on a Dual Approach in International Law of the Sea", in: 19 *IJMCL*, 2004, pp. 483-514

- Tanaka, Y., "Obligation to Co-operate in Marine Scientific Research and the Conservation of Marine Living Resources", in: 65 *ZaöRV/HJIL*, 2005, pp. 937-965
- Tarasofsky, R.G. & Weiss, F., "1997: The Year in Review: World Trade Organization", in: 8 *YIEL*, 1997, pp. 582-603
- Taylor, P., *An Ecological Approach to International Law: Responses to Challenges of Climate Change*, London 1998
- Tennekes, H., *Broeikasramp en Weerbericht: Voorspelbare Blunders van Wetenschap en Techniek*, Bloemendaal 2001
- Testart, J., "How to Let Ordinary People in on the Future: Be Careful, Take Precautions", in: *Le Monde Diplomatique*, 2000, reprinted at: http://www.biotech-info.net/ordinary_people.html
- Thomas, C., *The Environment in International Relations*, London 1992
- Thomas, M. & Grader, Z., "The Precautionary Principle: Making it Work for Fish and Fishermen", in: *Fishermen's News*, June 2000, http://www.pond.net/~pcffa/fn-jun00.htm
- Tickner, J., "Precautionary Principle", in: 2 *The Networker*, No. 4, 1997, http://www.safe2use.com/data/precaut1.htm
- Tickner, J., "A Map Toward Precautionary Decision Making", in: Raffensperger, C. & Tickner, J. (eds.), *Protecting Public Health and the Environment: Implementing the Precautionary Principle*, Washington 1999, pp. 162-186
- Tickner, J. *et al.*, *The Precautionary Principle in Action: A Handbook*, Windsor 2000, http://www.biotech-info.net/handbook.pdf
- Tickner, J. & Raffensperger, C., "The American View on the Precautionary Principle", in: O'Riordan, T. *et al.* (eds.), *Reinterpreting the Precautionary Principle*, London 2001, pp. 183-214
- Tinker, C., "Responsibility for Biological Diversity Conservation Under International Law", in: 28 *VJTL*, 1995, pp. 777-821
- Tinker, C., "State Responsibility and the Precautionary Principle", in: Freestone, D. & Hey, E. (eds.), *The Precautionary Principle and International Law*, The Hague 1996, pp. 53-72
- Toonder, M., *De Slijtmijt*, Amsterdam 1994
- Toonder, M., "De Bovenbazen", in: Toonder, M., *Het Beste van Bommel*, Amsterdam 2002, pp. 363-463
- Trouwborst, A., *The Preservation of Primary and Old-Growth Forests & International Law* (student paper, not published), Utrecht 1997
- Trouwborst, A., *Evolution and Status of the Precautionary Principle in International Law*, The Hague 2002
- Trouwborst, R.E. *et al.*, "Lateral Injection of Oxygen with the Bosporus Plume – Fingers of Oxidizing Potential in the Black Sea", in: 48 *LO*, 2003, pp. 2369-2376.
- Trouwborst, R.E. *et al.*, "Iron, Sulfur and Phosphorus Cycling in the Sediments of a Shallow Coastal Bay: Implications for Sediment Nutrient Release and Benthic Macroalgal Blooms", in: 47 *LO*, 2002, pp. 1346-1354
- Trudgill, S. & Richards, K., "Environmental Science and Policy: Generalizations and Context Sensitivity", in: 22 *TIBG*, 1997, pp. 5-12
- Tsuru, Y., "Rethinking the Principle of Abstention: The North Pacific and Beyond", in: 28 *MP*, 2004, pp. 541-552
- Unilever, *Unilever's Response to Greenpeace 'Principles for Ecologically Responsible Fisheries'*, 1996
- Van den Belt, H. & Gremmen, B., "Between Precautionary Principle and 'Sound Science': Distributing the Burdens of Proof", in: 15 *JAEE*, 2002, pp. 103-122
- Van den Eynde, M., *20 Jaar Voorzorgsprincipe in het Milieubeleid: Milieuethische en Sociaalwetenschappelijke Perspectieven*, Master's thesis, Leuven 2004

- Van den Hout, K.D. *et al.*, "The Impact of Atmospheric Deposition of Non-Acidifying Substances on the Quality of European Forest Soils and the North Sea", in: 109 *WASP*, 1999, pp. 357-396
- Van der Molen, G.H.J., "The Principle of Abstention and the Freedom of the Seas", in: 6 *NILR*, Special Issue, 1959, pp. 203-212
- Van der Straaten, J., "De Mogelijke Werking van het Voorzorgbeginsel in de Natuurbeschermingswetgeving vanuit Economisch Perspectief", in: Backes, C., Gilhuis, P.C. & Verschuuren, J.M. (eds.), *Het Voorzorgbeginsel in het Natuurbeschermingsrecht*, Deventer 1997, pp. 35-41
- Vanderzwaag, D., "The Implications of the Precautionary Principle for the Canadian Environmental Protection Act (CEPA)", 1994, http://www2.ec.gc.ca/cepa/ip18_01.html#j26
- Vanderzwaag, D., "Regionalism and Arctic Marine Environmental Protection: Drifting between Blurry Boundaries and Hazy Horizons", in: Vidas, D. & Østreng, W. (eds.), *Order for the Oceans at the Turn of the Century*, The Hague 1999, pp. 231-247
- VanderZwaag, D., "The Precautionary Principle and Marine Environmental Protection: Slippery Shores, Rough Seas and Rising Normative Tides", in: Johnston, D.M. & Sirivivatnanon, A., *Ocean Governance and Sustainable Development in the Pacific Region*, Proceedings of the SEAPOL Inter-Regional Conference held in Bangkok on 21-23 March 2001, Bangkok 2002, pp. 188-210
- Vanderzwaag, D. & MacKinley, D., "Towards a Global Forests Convention: Getting Out of the Woods and Barking Up the Right Tree", in: Canadian Council on International Law (ed.), *Global Forests and International Environmental Law*, London 1996, pp. 1-39
- Van Dunné, J.M., "Het Risicobegrip vanuit het Perspectief van het Milieuaansprakelijkheidsrecht", in: Wissink, B. & Bouma, J. (eds.), *Perspectieven op Milieurisico's*, Wetenschappelijke Raad voor het Regeringsbeleid Werkdocument W128, The Hague 2002, pp. 103-147
- Van Dyke, J.M., "Applying the Precautionary Principle to Ocean Shipments of Radioactive Materials", in: 27 *ODIL*, 1996, pp. 379-397
- Van Hoorick, G., *Internationaal en Europees Natuurbehoudsrecht*, Antwerpen/Groningen 1997
- Van Wijmen, P.C.E., "Natuurwaarden en Voorzorg: Het Anterieuriteitsbeginsel", in: Backes, C., Gilhuis, P.C. & Verschuuren, J.M. (eds.), *Het Voorzorgbeginsel in het Natuurbeschermingsrecht*, Deventer 1997, pp. 13-21
- Vasconcelos, H.L., "Effects of Forest Disturbance on the Structure of Ground-Foraging Ant Communities in Central Amazonia", in: 8 *BC*, 1999, pp. 409-420
- Verschuuren, J., "Naar een Codificatie van Beginselen van het Milieurecht", 1995, http://infolab.kub.nl/till/data/topic/envartkrit.html
- Verschuuren, J., *Principles of Environmental Law*, Baden-Baden 2003
- Victor, D.G., "The Use and Effectiveness of Nonbinding Instruments in the Management of Complex International Environmental Problems", in: *ASIL Proc.*, 1997, pp. 241-250
- Von Moltke, K., "The Relationship between Policy, Science, Technology, Economics and Law in the Implementation of the Precautionary Principle", in: Freestone, D. & Hey, E. (eds.), *The Precautionary Principle and International Law*, The Hague 1996, pp. 97-108
- Von Moltke, K., "The Dilemma of the Precautionary Principle in International Trade", in: 3 *Bridges*, No. 6, 1999
- Von Moltke, "The Institutions of Precaution", 2000, http://www.cid.harvard.edu/cidbiotech/comments/comments74.htm
- Vos, E., "Globalisation des Marchés et Précaution: Le Principe de Précaution et le Droit Alimentaire de l'Union Européenne", in: *CESP*, No. 5, 2001

- Vos, E., "Het Voorzorgsbeginsel in EU Recht", in: Faure, M.G. & Vos, E. (eds.), *Juridische Afbakening van het Voorzorgsbeginsel: Mogelijkheden en Grenzen*, Gezondheidsraad Publication Nr. A03/03, The Hague 2003, pp. 119-186
- Wahlström, B., "The Precautionary Approach to Chemicals Management: A Swedish Perspective", in: Raffensperger, C. & Tickner, J. (eds.), *Protecting Public Health and the Environment: Implementing the Precautionary Principle*, Washington 1999, pp. 51-69
- Wahlström, B., "Precaution and the Stockholm Convention", in: *Precaution from Rio to Johannesburg: Proceedings of a Geneva Environment Network Roundtable*, International Environment House, Geneva, 16 May 2002, pp. 13-15
- Wallace, R.M.M., *International Law*, 2nd ed., London 1992
- Wallace, R.M.M., *International Law*, 3rd ed., London 1997
- Wan Ho, M. & Saunders, P., "The Precautionary Principle is Coherent", 2000, http://www.biotech-info.net/PP_coherent.html
- Watson, R.T. *et al.*, *Living Beyond Our Means: Natural Assets and Human Well-Being (Statement from the Millennium Ecosystem Assessment Board of Directors)*, March 2005, available from: http://www.millenniumassessment.org
- Weintraub, B.A., "Science, International Environmental Regulation, and the Precautionary Principle: Setting Standards and Defining Terms", 1992, partly reprinted in: D'Amato, A. & Engel, K. (eds.), *International Environmental Law Anthology*, Cincinnati 1996, pp. 22-24
- Westra, L., "Post-Normal Science, the Precautionary Principle and the Ethics of Integrity", in: 2 *FS*, 1997, pp. 237-262
- White, N.D., *The Law of International Organisations*, Manchester 1996
- Wildavsky, A., "No Risk is the Highest Risk of All", in: Glickman, T.S. & Gough, M. (eds.), *Readings in Risk*, Washington 1990, pp. 120-127
- Wildavsky, A., "Trial and Error Versus Trial Without Error", in: Morris, J. (ed.), *Rethinking Risk and the Precautionary Principle*, Oxford 2000, pp. 22-45
- Wildhaber, L., "Commentary", in: Lang, W. *et al.* (eds.), *Environmental Protection and International Law*, Dordrecht 1991, pp. 88-89
- Wirth, T.E., "Environmental Policy and International Cooperation: A Framework for the 21st Century - Despair or Determination?", in: 35 *SJIL*, 1999, pp. 221-229
- Wolf, A., *Quotas in International Environmental Agreements*, London 1997
- World Commission on Environment and Development, *Our Common Future*, Oxford 1987
- World Wildlife Fund, *Living Planet Report 2002*, Gland 2002, http://www.panda.org/livingplanet/lpr02/Final_LPR_2002_pp_01-36.pdf
- Yamin, F. & Zahid, I., "1997: The Year in Review: Forests", in: 8 *YIEL*, 1997, pp. 296-306
- Yankov, A., "The Law of the Sea Convention and Agenda 21: Marine Environmental Implications", in: Boyle, A. & Freestone, D. (eds.), *International Law and Sustainable Development*, Oxford 1999, pp. 271-295

TABLE OF INSTRUMENTS

Legally Binding International Instruments

---

* I.f. = in force.

1981 *Convention for the Protection of the Marine Environment and Coastal Area of the South-East Pacific* (Lima), i.f. 19 May 1986

1982 *Protocol (to the 1976 Barcelona Convention) Concerning Mediterranean Specially Protected Areas* (Geneva), i.f. 23 March 1986

1982 *United Nations Convention on the Law of the Sea* (Montego Bay), i.f. 16 November 1994: 272, 273, 298

1983 *Convention for the Protection and Development of the Marine Environment of the Wider Caribbean Region* (Cartagena de Indias), i.f. 11 October 1986

1985 *Convention for the Protection of the Ozone Layer* (Vienna), i.f. 22 September 1988: 22

1985 *Convention for the Protection, Management and Development of the Marine and Coastal Environment of the Eastern African Region* (Nairobi), i.f. 30 May 1996

1985 *Protocol (to the 1985 Convention for the Protection, Management and Development of the Marine and Coastal Environment of the Eastern African Region) Concerning Protected Areas and Wild Flora and Fauna in the Eastern African Region* (Nairobi), i.f. 30 May 1996

1985 *Protocol (to the 1979 Convention on Long-Range Transboundary Air Pollution) on the Reduction of Sulphur Emissions or their Transboundary Fluxes* (Helsinki), i.f. 2 September 1987

1985 *ASEAN Agreement on the Conservation of Nature and Natural Resources* (Kuala Lumpur), n.i.f.**: 61

1986 *Convention on Early Notification of a Nuclear Accident* (Vienna), i.f. 27 October 1986

1986 *Convention for the Protection of the Natural Resources and Environment of the South Pacific Region* (Noumea), i.f. 22 August 1990

1987 *Protocol (to the 1985 Convention for the Protection of the Ozone Layer) on Substances that Deplete the Ozone Layer* (Montreal), i.f. 1 January 1989: 22, 166-167, 176, 181, 241, 267, 272

1988 *Convention on the Regulation of Antarctic Mineral Resource Activities* (Wellington), n.i.f.: 202

1988 *Protocol (to the 1979 Convention on Long-Range Transboundary Air Pollution) Concerning the Control of Emissions of Nitrogen Oxides or their Transboundary Fluxes* (Sofia), i.f. 14 February 1991

1989 *Convention on the Control of Transboundary Movements of Hazardous Wastes and their Disposal* (Basel), i.f. 5 May 1992

1989 *Protocol (to the 1981 Convention for the Protection of the Marine Environment and Coastal Area of the South-East Pacific) for the Conservation and Management of Protected Marine and Coastal Areas of the South-East Pacific* (Paipa), n.i.f.

1989 *Convention for the Prohibition of Fishing with Long Driftnets in the South Pacific* (Wellington), i.f. 24 November 1989

1990 *Protocol (to the 1983 Convention for the Protection and Development of the Marine Environment of the Wider Caribbean Region) Concerning Specially Protected Areas and Wildlife in the Wider Caribbean* (Kingston), i.f. 5 May 2002

1990 *Amendments to the 1985 Convention for the Protection of the Ozone Layer and the 1987 Protocol on Substances that Deplete the Ozone Layer* (London), i.f. 10 August 1992: 22, 176, 181, 267, 272

1990 *International Convention on Oil Pollution Preparedness, Response and Cooperation* (London), i.f. 13 May 1995: 22

1991 *Convention on the Ban of Import into Africa and the Control of Transboundary Movement and Management of Hazardous Wastes Within Africa* (Bamako), i.f. 20 March 1996: 45, 84, 90, 100, 111, 171, 186, 260

1991 *Convention on Environmental Impact Assessment in a Transboundary Context* (Espoo), i.f. 10 September 1997

1991 *Protocol (to the 1959 Antarctic Treaty) on Environmental Protection* (Madrid), i.f. 14 January 1998: 41, 202

** N.i.f. = not in force.

1995 *Agreement for the Implementation of the Provisions of the 1982 UNCLOS Relating to the Conservation and Management of Straddling Fish Stocks and Highly Migratory Fish Stocks* (New York), i.f. 11 December 2001: 22-23, 90, 101, 103, 105, 123, 128, 168, 170, 181, 188, 204-205, 218, 260, 267, 274

1995 *Convention to Ban the Importation into Forum Island Countries of Hazardous Wastes and Radioactive Wastes and to Control the Transboundary Movement and Management of Hazardous Wastes Within the South Pacific* (Waigani), i.f. 21 October 2001: 53, 103, 106, 259

1996 *Amendments to the 1980 Protocol for the Protection of the Mediterranean Sea Against Pollution from Land-Based Sources* (Syracuse), n.i.f.: 22

1996 *Protocol (to the 1960 Treaty Between the Netherlands and Germany on Cooperation in the Ems River Mouth) on Cooperation in the Area of Water and Nature Protection in the Ems River Mouth* (MS Warsteiner Admiral): 22, 173

1996 *Protocol (to the 1976 Convention for the Protection of the Mediterranean Sea Against Pollution) on the Prevention of Pollution of the Mediterranean Sea by Transboundary Movements of Hazardous Wastes and their Disposal* (Izmir), n.i.f.: 22, 171, 260

1996 *Protocol (to the 1972 Convention for the Prevention of Marine Pollution by Dumping of Wastes and Other Matter)* (London), i.f. 24 March 2006: 45, 93, 103, 107, 167, 180, 260

1996 *Agreement on the Conservation of Cetaceans of the Black Sea, Mediterranean Sea and Contiguous Atlantic Area* (Monaco), i.f. 1 June 2001: 22, 127, 260

1997 *Convention on the Law of the Non-Navigational Uses of International Watercourses* (New York), n.i.f.: 35, 51, 277-278

1997 *Amendments to the 1949 Agreement for the Establishment of a General Fisheries Council for the Mediterranean*, i.f. 29 April 2004: 22, 105, 267-268

1997 *Protocol to the 1992 Framework Convention on Climate Change* (Kyoto), i.f. 16 February 2005: 234, 239, 272

1998 *Agreement on the International Dolphin Conservation Program* (Washington), i.f. 15 February 1999: 22, 105

1998 *Protocol (to the 1979 Convention on Long-Range Transboundary Air Pollution) on Heavy Metals* (Aarhus), i.f. 29 December 2003: 32, 173, 270

1998 *Protocol (to the 1979 Convention on Long-Range Transboundary Air Pollution) on Persistent Organic Pollutants* (Aarhus), i.f. 23 October 2003: 32, 173, 270

1998 *Convention on the Prior Informed Consent Procedure for Certain Hazardous Chemicals and Pesticides* (Rotterdam), i.f. 24 February 2004

1999 *Convention on the Protection of the Rhine* (Berne), i.f. 1 January 2003: 22, 127

1999 *Agreement Between the Government of Iceland, the Government of Norway and the Government of the Russian Federation Concerning Certain Aspects of Cooperation in the Area of Fisheries* (St. Petersburg): 22

1999 *Protocol (to the 1992 Convention on the Protection and Use of Transboundary Watercourses and International Lakes) on Water and Health* (London), i.f. 4 August 2005: 13, 48, 258, 260

1999 *Protocol (to the 1983 Convention for the Protection and Development of the Marine Environment of the Wider Caribbean Region) Concerning Pollution from Land-Based Sources and Activities* (Oranjestad), n.i.f.

1999 *Agreement for the Establishment of the Regional Commission for Fisheries* (Rome), i.f. 26 February 2001: 22, 105, 267-268

1999 *Agreement Concerning the Creation of a Marine Mammal Sanctuary in the Mediterranean* (Rome)

1999 *Protocol (to the 1979 Convention on Long-Range Transboundary Air Pollution) to Abate Acidification, Eutrophication and Ground-Level Ozone* (Gothenburg), i.f. 17 May 2005: 32

2000 *Protocol (to the 1992 Convention on Biological Diversity) on Biosafety* (Cartagena de Indias), i.f. 11 September 2003: 13, 32, 46, 90-91, 103, 123, 188-189, 254-255, 260-261, 266, 272

2000 *Framework Agreement for the Conservation of Living Marine Resources on the High Seas of the South Pacific* (Santiago), n.i.f.: 100, 260

Non-Legally Binding International Instruments

1990 *Declaration of the Third International Conference on the Protection of the North Sea* (The Hague): 40, 93, 99, 110-111, 172, 208, 260
1990 *Declaration on the Environment of the 1990 Liberal International Congress* (Helsinki): 103, 177, 248-249
1990 *Ministerial Declaration on Sustainable Development in the ECE Region* (Bergen): 24, 34, 41, 53, 95, 103, 106, 149, 157, 217, 260
1990 *ECE Code of Conduct on Accidental Pollution of Transboundary Inland Waters*: 27
1990 *UNEP Governing Council Decision SS II/4 on a Comprehensive Approach to Hazardous Waste*: 171, 267
1990 *Declaration on Environmentally Sound and Sustainable Development in Asia and the Pacific* (Bangkok): 34
1990 *Ministerial Declaration of the Second World Climate Conference* (Geneva): 53, 99, 104, 149, 259, 267, 273
1991 *OECD Council Recommendation C(90)164 on Integrated Pollution Prevention and Control*: 48, 102, 180, 260
1991 *Action Plan for the Conservation of Cetaceans in the Mediterranean Sea* (Cairo): 90, 188, 260
1991 *Ministerial Declaration of the Sixth Trilateral Governmental Conference on the Protection of the Wadden Sea* (Esbjerg): 48, 93, 103, 107, 166, 260
1991 *UNGA Resolution 46/215 on Large-Scale Pelagic Driftnet Fishing and its Impact on the Living Marine Resources of the World's Oceans and Seas*: 204, 274
1992 *GLOBE Model for a Convention for the Conservation and Wise Use of Forests*: 221
1992 *Declaration of the UN Conference on Environment and Development* (Rio de Janeiro): 12, 15, 23, 24, 32-33, 34, 37, 42, 44, 47, 53, 56, 64, 74-75, 90, 92, 102, 104, 106, 122-123, 125-127, 128, 148, 156, 180, 205, 214, 217-218, 222, 231, 255, 259, 261-266, 271, 272, 279
1992 *Agenda 21* (Rio de Janeiro): 175, 179, 206-207, 260
1992 *Non-Legally Binding Authoritative Statement of Principles for a Global Consensus on the Management, Conservation and Sustainable Development of All Types of Forests* (Rio de Janeiro): 257
1993 *Declaration on a Sanctuary for the Protection of Marine Mammals in the Mediterranean* (Brussels)
1993 *Ministerial Declaration on the Protection of the Black Sea* (Odessa)
1993 *General Guidelines for the Conservation of the Biodiversity of European Forests* (Helsinki): 48-49, 140-141, 260
1993 *Resolution H2 of the Ministerial Conference on the Protection of Forests in Europe* (Helsinki): 135
1993 *Declaration on Environment and Development in the Arctic* (Nuuk): 22, 175
1994 *ILC Draft Articles on the Law of the Non-Navigational Uses of International Watercourses*: 51
1995 *Draft International Covenant on Environment and Development (IUCN)*: 41, 49, 58-59, 100, 151, 168, 169, 180, 186, 190, 260
1995 *UNEP Governing Council Decision 18/32 on Persistent Organic Pollutants*: 32, 176
1995 *Declaration of the Fourth Ministerial Conference on the Protection of the North Sea* (Esbjerg): 99-100, 166, 187
1995 *Action Plan for the Protection of the Marine Environment and the Sustainable Development of the Coastal Areas of the Mediterranean (MAP Phase II)* (Barcelona)
1995 *Panama Declaration* (Panama City): 105
1995 *Pan-European Biological and Landscape Diversity Strategy* (Sofia): 41, 46, 99, 103, 111, 180, 260
1995 *Environmental Programme for Europe* (Sofia): 22
1995 *FAO Code of Conduct for Responsible Fisheries*: 22-23, 90, 101, 103, 105, 123, 170, 181, 260
1995 *Global Programme of Action for the Protection of the Marine Environment from Land-Based Activities* (Washington): 11, 33, 47, 53, 104, 106, 131, 146, 173, 175, 178, 180, 206-207, 259-260, 273

European Union Instruments

TABLE OF CASES

International Court of Justice

International Tribunal for the Law of the Sea

WTO Dispute Settlement

Arbitration

European Union Court of Justice

National Cases

COUNTRY INDEX

KEYWORD INDEX